Huntington Library Publications

SHAKESPEARE'S

USE OF LEARNING

 *An Inquiry into the Growth of his Mind & Art*

---

by VIRGIL K. WHITAKER

🦢 THE HUNTINGTON LIBRARY

SAN MARINO, CALIFORNIA : 1964

*The first edition was designed by Joseph Simon and printed by
Anderson & Ritchie, Los Angeles. This second printing is a
photolithographic facsimile by the private press of C F Braun & Co,
Alhambra, California.*

CONTENTS

PREFACE

THE TITLE of the present work has been chosen, it must be acknowledged, for brevity rather than for precision. It designates what is actually an attempt to study Shakespeare's acquisition and use of contemporary learning and the effect of his knowledge upon his development as a dramatist. When Shakespeare set out to dramatize an Italian tale or one of Plutarch's lives, he obviously selected and adapted his material to produce the effects that he wanted. As we watch this process of choice and alteration, we have a unique opportunity to see his mind at work, and the sources are an invaluable clue to his art and his thought that has been strangely neglected. The plays themselves also contain many passages that reveal the extent to which he had mastered contemporary lore. Following these two approaches leads to the discovery that Shakespeare grew in learning while he developed in skill as a playwright, and that his progress as a dramatist depended to a considerable extent upon his increasing mastery of contemporary science and philosophy. In fact, about the time of *Julius Caesar* a new way of looking at man and the universe led him to adopt a new and much better way of building his plays from their sources, and *Macbeth* is a greater play than *Richard III* not so much because Shakespeare knew more about the theater as because he had developed a new understanding of life in terms of traditional Christian thought. Charting the progress of his learning and his thinking should provide those who love his plays with another tool for understanding and enjoying them.

The approach is a new one, and some of the conclusions run counter to prevailing assumptions and even to recent scholarship, particularly with respect to the history plays. An attempt has therefore been made to present evidence in some detail, even at the risk of laboring a point now and then. One does not differ from scholars such as Lily B. Campbell or E. M. W. Tillyard without offering proof. *Hamlet*, as usual, has been a problem. It apparently involved a reworking of the old play in terms of some of the ideas that helped to shape the other tragedies. But the old play, on the other hand, seems likely itself to have furnished several important elements in Hamlet's thought and character and to have stimulated Shakespeare's own thinking, just as *The Trouble-*

some Raigne provided ideas not only for *King John* but also for *Richard II*. Yet attempting to reconstruct the earlier *Hamlet* involves reviewing a tremendous amount of somewhat tedious detail. As a compromise solution, Chapter XI on *Hamlet* merely summarizes the probable characteristics of the play that was Shakespeare's source. But, to avoid offering the reader unsupported conclusions, an Appendix contains a detailed review of the available evidence and an explanation of the reasoning that has led to the conclusions summarized at the beginning of Chapter XI.

The plays have been considered in the order generally accepted as that in which they were written, with one exception: for reasons that I hope the chapter will make apparent to the reader, the so-called "problem" comedies have been treated immediately after the romantic comedies and before the mature tragedies.

Investigating the development of Shakespeare's thinking has inevitably meant considering the work of a good many scholars who have interpreted plays or groups of plays in Elizabethan terms, and students who wish to approach Shakespeare from this point of view may possibly find the present account of some use as a guide. To that end, four policies have been adopted. First, conventional documentation indicates sources of information, and important writers on various subjects have been mentioned in the text rather freely, even at the risk of overworking a few professorial clichés. Second, dissent as well as indebtedness has been indicated. There is danger that the result may seem contentious rather than helpful; but the reader will at least have warning, so that, if interested, he may find contrary interpretations elsewhere. Third, all quotations from Latin writers have been given in an English translation, in recognition of—but not in deference to—the present unfortunate state of affairs. Occasionally a phrase for which no satisfactory English equivalent could be found has been added in square brackets. Fourth, whenever possible the notes refer to editions or texts that are generally available. For classical writers the Loeb Library is, of course, invaluable; and there are a considerable number of modern reprints and published facsimiles of minor Elizabethan works. Whenever a standard modern edition of any English writer exists, it has been cited. References to Shakespeare follow the American "New Cambridge Edition," edited by William Allen Neilson and Charles Jarvis Hill and published by Houghton Mifflin Company. This seems to be the only complete one-volume text readily available which gives a reasonable number of variant readings, and it also conforms to the standard Globe line-numbering.

This policy of citing modern texts has required considerable self-control as I enjoyed the vast riches of the Huntington Library, to the staff of which I must acknowledge my deepest gratitude for their unfailing patience and assistance. Mr. Godfrey Davies, especially, has contributed generously of his time and offered helpful suggestions. I must also express my appreciation to my fellow readers, who listened patiently or argued helpfully over the lunch table or elsewhere. I gratefully acknowledge the permission of the University of Iowa Press to republish material which first appeared in my article "Shakespeare's Use of his Sources," *Philological Quarterly*, XX (July, 1941), and the permission of the Stanford University Press to reprint parts of my "Philosophy and Romance in Shakespeare's 'Problem' Comedies," from *The Seventeenth Century: Studies in the History of English Thought and Literature from Bacon to Pope* (1951). I should have found my task much harder than it was, had I not been able, in revising and trying to improve my work, to draw upon the interest and encouragement of Professor Paul Kocher. To Stanford University I am indebted for help in meeting the cost of preparing my manuscript. My colleague and office-mate Mr. Robert Hoopes has read my chapters. I owe him thanks for detecting a number of oversights and making many valuable suggestions, but even more for discussing with me, day by day, my latest ideas and enthusiasms.

Finally, I should acknowledge my obligation to Professor E. M. W. Tillyard, especially since I have questioned a number of his findings rather vigorously. I was asked to review his *Shakespeare's History Plays* shortly after it appeared. I found the book immensely stimulating; but the more I worked over it, the more I doubted the validity of some of its conclusions. My review was never published, probably because it had ceased to be timely before I finally made up my mind. But the investigations which I then began led ultimately to the present work. My debt is perhaps of an unusual kind, but it is very real.

Stanford, California   VIRGIL K. WHITAKER
March, 1953

SHAKESPEARE'S USE OF LEARNING

Introduction

AN ATTEMPT to survey Shakespeare's use of contemporary learning is indeed presumptuous. It would be hard enough to explore the knowledge of a modern writer, whose intellectual background is somewhat familiar. But we are separated from Shakespeare by three centuries which have brought a revolution involving the very foundations of natural science and philosophy. The difficulties of antiquarian scholarship are therefore added to those of critical interpretation. I have no illusions as to the difficulty of the undertaking or my own inadequacy to perform it. I can only ask the reader's indulgence for what is, I hope, a pioneering effort of some value, however slight. Perhaps the main directions of progress can be charted even though some of the landmarks are overlooked.

Shakespeare's plays reveal a considerable knowledge of contemporary learning and thought, as modern scholars have abundantly demonstrated. It therefore becomes an interesting problem to examine the plays to see what they reveal about his acquisition of this learning. Did he bring it with him to London, or did he acquire it gradually? If gradually, did his developing knowledge affect his art as a dramatist? Such an inquiry is the subject of this book.

The problem to be considered seems all the more important because scholars investigating Shakespeare's ideas have tended to treat the plays as a unified body of material, selecting passages almost at random in building a reconstruction of his mind and world. Tillyard, especially, uses Ulysses' famous speech on order from *Troilus and Cressida* (I, iii, 85-137) as a basis for interpreting lines even in the earliest plays.[1] Perhaps he is right and Shakespeare's thought remained static, at least on this point. But we have all recognized the change of our own ideas from year to year, as knowledge and experience increased; and it is most unlikely that a man whose vigorous imagination and intellectual profundity are revealed by everything that he wrote would fail to grow in mind as we know that he did in art. Only a systematic survey can show whether such growth exists, and, if his learning and philosophic grasp did increase, only such a survey can enable us to place details in the various plays in their proper intellectual perspective as we try to understand them.

An attempt to study the growth of Shakespeare's mind immediately produces a difficult problem of methodology. Drama is one of the more impersonal art forms, and Shakespeare is among the most impersonal dramatists. He must have known what his characters know, but we dare not assume that he thought what they think. Libraries are stored with the follies of writers who have taken what Shakespeare made his characters say for his own interpretation of life. There seem, actually, to be only two ways to get at his intellectual development in so far as it involved a use of contemporary learning, in the form either of allegedly factual information or of philosophic thought.

The first of these is to study those plays which he based upon one or more clearly identified sources. We know that he habitually followed his sources as closely as he could, taking from them everything possible—plot structure, characterization, even whole passages that he merely versified. Stauffer, whose concern with the development of Shakespeare's moral ideas is a notable exception to the habit of regarding his thought as static, has remarked upon the importance of this clue:

That Shakespeare used other men's stories is no more than a trivial literary truism, though it must be remarked that he knew the best that had been thought and said up to his time. But that he *changed* those stories is of overwhelming interest to anyone seeking to know what he thought and felt.[2]

It will be interesting, consequently, to see what Shakespeare took from his sources, for he presumably had a free hand in selecting

[1] *Shakespeare's History Plays*, passim.
[2] *Shakespeare's World of Images*, p. 363.

them and they must have interested him. But it will be doubly revealing to consider what he added to them or why he deviated from them. If he manifestly failed to understand what he found clearly stated in an old play, we can infer either that he was very badly prepared to comprehend that kind of material, or, more probably, that he was not interested in it. If he tried to correct a reference to the Psalms, we can assume both knowledge and interest. If he followed a *novella* closely except for one episode, for which he went to considerable trouble to find a substitute, we can inquire why he found that passage distasteful. If he rearranged Scottish history to provide different motives for the action, presumably he thought such motives interesting or important. Above all, if he added matter almost irrelevant to the development of his plot or characters, matter which he or his fellow actors apparently cut in making an acting version, we can infer that he was himself preoccupied with those ideas, since his company would presumably have retained them had they been intended to appeal to special interests of the audience.

The second possibility is to look out for occurrences in the plays of allusions to the learning of his day, to see in which plays they occur and how important a part they play. If they do not have parallels in the source, if they are greatly developed from the source, or if they occur in other plays in such a way as to suggest that the source itself was chosen because it contained them, then they must have played an important part in Shakespeare's thinking. Isolating this material should make it possible to determine whether it is distributed uniformly throughout the plays or develops in quantity or in kind during his dramatic career. If such development appears, it will be profitable to inquire whether it bears any relationship to the kind of plays that he wrote and the subjects that he selected for dramatic treatment.

This method of investigation obviously cannot produce a complete picture of Shakespeare's reading or of the ideas which he encountered during a busy lifetime, rich in contacts and in intellectual stimuli. Some of what he read must simply have bored him; much more of it must have failed to provide material for his plays and poems. His other experiences must often have been similarly unproductive. We can infer with assurance only what he knew or thought; seldom can we conjecture with any safety what he did not know or did not think, and then only when something is missing which the context obviously demands or which he later used regularly under similar circumstances. When such conjectures are made, the evidence will be presented as candidly as possible, and with reasonable fullness.

In addition to this general and fundamental limitation, a number of problems and dangers involved in this undertaking are immediately obvious. The first, and perhaps the greatest, of these is our almost complete ignorance of the details of his life. Scholars have reconstructed his grammar-school training on the basis of probability only, because his father's social and financial position made it likely that he attended the King's New School at Stratford and because references in his plays show familiarity with the usual grammar-school texts.[3] Of his life in London outside the theater almost as little is known. He lived for a while with a family from whom he could have learned French;[4] he must have been on intimate terms with a group of young nobles and their literary friends. Since his poems circulated in manuscript, we can assume that he had access to works and ideas being discussed in the tight-knit literary circles of London, where almost every writer can be demonstrated to have had some kind of possible connection with other contemporary authors. There is clear evidence that he was a favorite member of the theatrical group. But, for the most part, all that we actually know with certainty about his intellectual life is what appears in his published works. It is therefore impossible to check inferences drawn from the plays by reference to his other activities, as would be standard procedure in studying a modern writer, or even as interpretations of Spenser's early poems can be tested by references in the works of his close friend Gabriel Harvey, about whose personal life we know more than about almost any other Elizabethan literary figure. Details or allusions in Shakespeare's plays and poems must themselves justify any use of contemporary ideas or even of contemporary books, and the only proof that he knew or used a philosophic concept will normally be the pragmatic one that it "works" as a key to his meaning.

Another problem is inherent in the methodology proposed

---

[3]Baldwin, *William Shakspere's Small Latine & Lesse Greeke*, I, 464.
[4]Alexander, *Shakespeare's Life and Art*, pp. 141-42.

because of its reliance upon a comparison of the plays with their sources. Some plays have no known source or have been pieced together from so many sources, including Shakespeare's own earlier work, that detailed comparison is impossible. These, however, are neither numerous nor important, and such a play as *Love's Labour's Lost* can be studied for its allusions to grammar-school texts and contemporary literature even though no major source exists. A more serious problem arises where an old play may have intervened between the known source and Shakespeare. Where the old play exists, it is, of course, an invaluable clue to his ideas and methods. *The Troublesome Raigne of King John,* to mention the most important, is the best possible guide in estimating Shakespeare's knowledge of English history or in contrasting his indifference to historical causes with his concern for lively dramatic characterization. Yet, as we shall see, its implications have sometimes been ignored by modern scholars. For *Hamlet,* on the other hand, we have a prose source and three versions of the Shakespearean play (or at least two versions and part of a third underlying the First Quarto); but the earlier non-Shakespearean play which almost certainly existed, and which has been rather light-heartedly ascribed to Kyd, has disappeared. The First Quarto version is in a few respects closer to the extant source than the later draft; and the differences between the existing play and the source are extremely interesting and thoroughly consistent with Shakespeare's practice in adapting his sources to the great tragedies. But it is very nearly impossible to say how many of these divergences were due to Shakespeare and how many may have been made by the earlier playwright. Peter Alexander has apparently removed a similar problem by demonstrating that *The Contention* and *Richard Duke of York* are merely bad quartos of *2* and *3 Henry VI* and not earlier versions of the play by another hand or hands. *The Merchant of Venice,* on the other hand, is complicated by Stephen Gosson's reference in 1579 to a *Iew,*[5] and Brooke mentioned in the preface to his *Romeus and Juliet* a play based on the story which he had "lately" seen.[6] Other more obscure and hypothetical plays have been proposed by various scholars as sources. But the play to which Gosson alludes would

[5]Chambers, *William Shakespeare,* I, 373.
[6]Ibid., 347.

have been hopelessly out of date before Shakespeare wrote, even if it had survived and been available to him, and Brooke's poem is obviously later than the play he mentions, as well as being Shakespeare's indubitable source. So we shall not run much danger in neglecting these and other hypothetical source plays. If we did not disregard them, such a study as is proposed would be seriously limited in scope, and we should be frightened away by shadows.

A third, although relatively minor, difficulty lies in the Elizabethans' fondness for repeating each other. They certainly took an infinite delight in passing on their favorite ideas and witticisms, and apparently they felt that a good thing improved by repetition. Excerpting and annotating were also favorite occupations. It is often very difficult, consequently, to isolate the source of an idea or a purple passage in Shakespeare. In writing *Venus and Adonis*, for example, he used Ovid and possibly Italian sources, as well as other English poets;[7] but his attention may first have been drawn to the story by Aphthonius' *Progymnasmata*, one of his school books, where he found Ovid's treatment of it analyzed as an example of *narratio*, one of the kinds of deliberative writing. It is significant that Aphthonius' next example is the story of Pyramus and Thisbe, which is quoted from Ovid.[8] According to Baldwin, the famous passage on the seven ages of man in *As You Like It* (II, vii, 139-66) is based primarily upon Palingenius' *Zodiacus Vitae*, another school text, plus Ovid.[9] But during a summer's reading in Elizabethan books on the natural sciences and psychology I collected the following additional discussions of from five to seven ages: Levinus Lemnius, *Touchstone of Complexions* (1565); Pedro Mexia, *The Foreste* (1571); Pierre de la Primaudaye, *The French Academie* (1586); and William Vaughan, *Directions for Health* (1600); not to mention the less specific treatment of the theme in Castiglione.[10] And Baldwin refers to

[7]*Shakespeare's Poems*, ed. C. Knox Pooler (Arden Shakespeare), pp. xxix-xxx; Baldwin, *On the Literary Genetics of Shakspere's Poems & Sonnets*, pp. 1-107.

[8]Fols. 16ᵛ-21.

[9]*W. S. Small Latine*, I, 652-73.

[10]Lemnius (1581), ff. 29ᵛ-30, has seven ages: infancie (1 to 4 or 7), childhood (to 15), pubertie (to 18), adolescencie (to 25), youth (to 35), man's age (to 63 or 65), old age. Mexia, I, xvii (ff. 45-46ᵛ): infancie (1-4) under moon; *pueritia* (5-14) under Mercury; adolescencie (14-22) under Venus; youth (23-42) under sun; *aetas virilis* (42-56) under Mars; *senectus* (56-68) under Jupiter; last (68-88)

still others. It is more important, fortunately, to recognize when Shakespeare shared and reproduced the ideas of his age and to understand what they meant to him than it is to determine exactly where he derived them. It is relatively easy to identify ideas, though impossible to determine the precise sources.

The present study is also subject to limitations imposed by my own time and energy and interest. In the first place, I have not tried to determine independently the chronology of the plays, even though I well recognize that the validity of all conclusions depends upon the validity of the dates assumed. I have accepted as a working basis the approximate order and dating at which E. K. Chambers arrived in his *William Shakespeare*, doing so with the more confidence because whatever independent evidence I did come upon almost invariably supported his findings.

In the second place, no attempt has been made at further research into the nature and extent of Shakespeare's education. Baldwin's conclusions have been accepted and taken as a point of departure for the discussion in the next chapter. But I have examined carefully the books that Shakespeare may have studied, with a view to ascertaining both the probable extent of his knowledge when he came to London and more especially the kind of training that he received. His plays can be shown to reflect to a considerable degree the habits of composition and the literary taste that he learned in grammar school, and an attempt will be made to suggest ways in which this influence operated.

In the same way, no attempt will be made, except incidentally, to propose additional sources for the plays. The zeal of scholars or the frantic ingenuity of doctoral candidates has led to the suggestion of many far-fetched sources recommended neither by proof nor by probability. They will generally be neglected. The

---

under Saturn. "And if any emonge us passe nowe this Laste Age (whiche assuredly happeneth very seldome in these days) the same then returneth to the state, in manner of Infancie, and ones again shall have the Moone for his Ladye and Mistresse." La Primaudaye, ch. lii, pp. 564-73: infancie, childhood (from speech to 7), youth (7-14), adolescencie (14-28), man's estate (29-50), old age (50 on). But he notes that Isidore terms from 50 to 70 "Gravitie" and then begins old age. Vaughan, pp. 53-54: infancie (1-7) under moon; childhood (8-14) under Mercury; stripling (14-22) under Venus; young man (22-34) under sun; man's age (34-50) under Mars; "termed (although improperly) old age" (50-62) under Jupiter; last age (62-80) under Saturn. Hoby's Castiglione (Everyman's Library), p. 110.

following investigation rests on the principle that Shakespeare tended to follow a main source or sources and to deviate from them only for a very good reason. If our purpose can be served by examining the plays in which he obviously did just that, a search for possible sources for the minor details becomes unimportant, since it is the nature of the details themselves that illustrates the extent and directions of Shakespeare's independent thinking. The kind of material involved in such additions will be clear enough. If Shakespeare is drawing heavily upon classical mythology or contemporary psychology, we need not ask, except for a few points that will be fully discussed, whether he got the classical allusions from Ovid or via Palingenius and Aphthonius, and we need not determine which of a number of available treatises on psychology he used. The effect of the idea or image upon his mind is the same, no matter what its immediate source may have been; and our problem, like that of all study of Shakespeare, is to illuminate the meaning and increase the enjoyment of his works.

Finally, there is no need to continue tracing elements in Shakespeare's thought if, once mastered, they remain a part of his intellectual equipment and continue to be used in much the same way. Only their disappearance need be noted. But the reader should be warned that following this principle will inevitably produce a gradual shift of emphasis in the following chapters, as Shakespeare's interests grow from popular learning to philosophic ideas. It will also mean paying relatively little attention to plays later than *Lear* and *Macbeth*. Except for *The Tempest*, they reveal no significant development of learning or thought; in the absence of detailed sources, the method of approach used in this book offers little additional insight into *The Tempest*.

Such is the method and such are the limitations of the following study. Its purpose will be to demonstrate that Shakespeare underwent a steady intellectual development that paralleled his growth in technical skill as a dramatist, so that *Twelfth Night* is a better play than *Two Gentlemen of Verona*, or *Othello* than *Romeo and Juliet*, not merely because Shakespeare knew better how to put a play together and how to make it effective on the stage but even more because he had acquired more experience and more learning. Out of that combination of experience and study he developed a richer understanding of his fellow men, of their immediate personal problems, and of the ultimate questions that face all mankind. In his first plays he drew upon the classical authors of his school days or upon recent English history, and he used grammar-school materials and especially Ovid to season the accounts that he took from his sources. In the next period he drew upon the fashionable literature of his day—the Italian *novella* or the English prose tale—and he worked back into an earlier period of English history, from the Wars of the Roses to Henry IV and Henry V or even John, although in writing about the last-named he merely recast an older play. He now flavored his material with a much wider range of allusions drawn from the Homilies, popular manuals on conduct and on science, and more advanced Latin and Greek writers or translations thereof. Echoes of contemporary literature sometimes outnumbered those of the classics, and the latter became subtler. He showed increased interest in a number of political problems. Finally, about the turn of the century, his interests shifted markedly to the philosophical and theological interpretation of life which Christianity had erected during the Middle Ages upon the basis of Plato, Aristotle, and the Stoics, the Scriptures, and St. Augustine. Most of the tragedies are constructed to study the working out of these principles in human conduct, and even a play like *Measure for Measure* is loaded with theological detail. The popular psychological concepts that appeared in plays of the middle period are now used for the first time with a full understanding of the system of which they are a part, and they often present and explain the making of a moral choice and the consequences of that choice, once it is made. In his last plays there is no fundamental change of thought, but the learning is worn more lightly and less obviously.

This intellectual development apparently led to a fundamental change in Shakespeare's method of building his plays from his sources, and the shift of method serves, in turn, to confirm in a remarkable way the theory just stated. During the first two periods mentioned Shakespeare, in general, followed the sequence of events—the narrative—of his sources as closely as possible, making only such changes as were necessary to produce a dramatic plot or plausible characters. Often he was content with an almost slovenly plot. His best efforts he lavished increasingly upon the construction of his wonderful characters, but those characters, be it noted, were always developed to make acceptable and interesting the original source action, imperfect as that might be. The plot determined the characters. Beginning with *Hamlet* the exact opposite is true. In using Plutarch, who furnished biographies that are really character studies worked out in terms of an elaborate ethical theory, Shakespeare made relatively few changes (which are therefore doubly significant). But he reshaped his other sources drastically in order to make the action reveal characters that illustrate or conform to philosophic concepts, the best examples of this process being *Macbeth* and *Lear*. Like the comedies of this period, the tragedies are also, though from a different point of view, problem plays. Whereas the plot derived from the source had previously determined the characterization, a character problem now determined the plot. The result was a much greater play.

This investigation of the development of Shakespeare's thought has, for me at least, a present-day application. Twentieth-century literature has been a melancholy procession of authors who promised well but never developed into masters, of men whose best works were written before they were forty and who sank into mere eccentricity or sensationalism, but seldom, unfortunately, into silence. The path from *Anna Christie* to *The Iceman Cometh* is little more melancholy than that from *Main Street* to *Cass Timberlane*, and the list could be extended indefinitely. One feels that these writers have great technical virtuosity; they have mastered the tricks of their trade superlatively well. But they have nothing of importance to say. It is in contrast to them that Shakespeare's intellectual growth is so significant. To us the learning of his age, taken by itself, seems hopelessly inadequate, some of it downright foolish. But Shakespeare took that learning and used it to grapple with the problems that he found in life, and as it appears in his plays it seems neither inadequate nor foolish. Perhaps it was because he kept expanding his own intellectual horizons— because he took the learning of his age and tested it by reflection and experience—that he continued to grow as a dramatist. The ideas basic to *Macbeth* were as old as St. Augustine but as contemporary as Richard Hooker, and Shakespeare used them to fashion a timeless tragedy of human temptation, sin, and degradation. Our own age has a far richer store of learning and thought, bewildering because of its very wealth and complexity. But how many modern writers use it effectively in the sense that they have really mastered the implications of a modern discipline as opposed to playing with a few superficial notions? One would not wish to press the contrast too far, but it seems very likely that the learning of Spenser, Shakespeare, and Milton—a learning tested by application to the lives of busy men of affairs—had something to do with their greatness as writers.

CHAPTER II

Shakespeare's Grammar-School Training

N O RECORD of Shakespeare's schooling exists. But if, as seems very likely, he attended the King's New School at Stratford-on-Avon, the absence of information about a student in a provincial town is not at all surprising. Consider how little we know about the record of Edmund Spenser at a famous foundation like the Merchant Taylors' School of London, under the greatest schoolmaster of his generation. Numerous allusions in the plays make it certain that Shakespeare did attend grammar school, and it is very improbable that he left Stratford to do so.

From ancient times a school had been maintained in Stratford by the Guild of the Holy Cross, a philanthropic organization which had accumulated revenues that enabled it to undertake a variety of activities, among them the education of the town's children. Under the terms of the school endowment the same cleric cared for the souls of the dead benefactors and the minds of the living pupils, and the endowment was therefore confiscated by the Crown under the Chantries Act of Edward VI. In 1553 the Common Council of Stratford regained part of this wealth; and part of the recovered income, in turn, was used to reestablish the old school, which was chartered as the King's New School.[1]

A salary of twenty pounds a year and a lodging were provided for the master. During the period of Shakespeare's probable attendance the master was expected to use four pounds of this sum to pay an usher who handled the boys in the lower school,

[1]Alexander gives a good summary of the history and refounding of the school (*Shakespeare's Life and Art*, pp. 15-17).

14

who were still learning their grammar. But sixteen pounds plus lodging was a respectable income according to the standard of the times, and the school apparently attracted good men—too good, perhaps. For a confused education is all too familiar in modern schools where the personnel changes rapidly, and the Stratford masters often moved on to a better position after a short stay. That the income of the master was at least adequate may be inferred from the fact that in 1575 John Shakespeare, William's father, paid forty pounds for the western of the two houses still preserved in Henley Street, the one now shown as the birthplace.[2] Few teachers today earn two-fifths of the cost of a house in a year's time and receive free lodging in addition.

And the masters were well-trained men. Baldwin concludes that Shakespeare probably moved up from the lower school to the upper school about the time that a Thomas Jenkins became master. Simon Hunt, the previous incumbent, had gone abroad to become a Jesuit. Jenkins is described in *Alumni Oxonienses* as "fellow or scholar of ST. JOHN'S COLL., B.A. 6 April, 1566, M.A. 8 April, 1570."[3] Although he may possibly have served as usher under Hunt, it is more likely that he arrived and became master on Lady Day, 1575. He remained until 1579, when he sold the position for six pounds to John Cottom, "late of London." His fellowship or scholarship at St. John's suggests that he was at least competently trained, and his tenure at Stratford implies that the Council approved of his work.

It was easily possible, therefore, to obtain a competent education up to the university level at Stratford; and, though the school was a small one, a boy would have encountered in much larger and more famous schools the same division of duties between usher and master and the same method of instruction, under which one man handled several groups of boys at different levels of preparation. Nor should we overlook the fact that this system has advantages. Granted a very simple curriculum and a competent teacher, and granted, above all, a group of students small enough for the instructor to give them some personal attention, it is possible for a gifted student to progress much more rapidly under this arrange-

---

[2]Ibid., p. 18. But the forty pounds may actually have bought two houses. Cf. Chambers, *William Shakespeare*, II, 33. Statements about the school and masters are summarized from Baldwin, *William Shakspere's Small Latine & Lesse Greeke*, I, 464-81.　　　　　　　　　　[3]Foster, *Alumni Oxonienses*, II, 808.

15

ment than in the rigidly separated grades that American efficiency has imposed upon the school system. As every teacher knows, each class in a typical modern school includes children whose actual comprehension in reading or skill in arithmetic approximates to the theoretical norm for four or more grades; and too often subjecting these various abilities to the same complicated program of instruction, necessarily adapted to the average, merely stultifies the brilliant students and bewilders the retarded. The best modern methods actually involve setting up in each class the same kind of fluid program adapted to the needs of various small sub-groups that regularly characterized the Elizabethan school; and the practice of letting the more advanced youngsters aid and instruct their fellows, which was systematically used by Elizabethan masters, is highly approved today, although the terminology is different and the techniques are less obvious. Few indeed are the modern students in junior and senior high school whose teacher has progressed to the end of the program of instruction in one of the great universities. It should not be forgotten that in terms of modern educational customs Master Jenkins' equivalent would be a Harvard Ph.D., the kind of man found teaching on the secondary level today only in the best private preparatory schools. Such equations are helpful when we start thinking about Shakespeare's "small Latin and less Greek."

Turning to Shakespeare's curriculum enables us to exchange speculation for probability, for we can infer his studies from allusions in his plays even if we cannot surely tell what school he attended. Before commencing the curriculum in Latin, which was the proper business of the grammar school, he learned the rudiments of English. Perhaps he attended a Petty School such as that kept in the first years of the seventeenth century by Thomas Parker and his wife, who taught sewing. Perhaps he even learned his ABC's under the upper students in the grammar school itself, although this practice was contrary to regulations at Stratford.[4] Children were first introduced to their letters through a horn book, which consisted of a piece of paper mounted under a thin sheet of horn on a wood tablet with a projecting horn handle. Shakespeare mentions it in *Love's Labour's Lost* (V, i, 48) and *Richard III* (I, i, 54-57), where it is called a cross-row, from the

[4]Baldwin, *William Shakspere's Petty School*, pp. 137-38.

arrangement of letters. It contained the alphabet in several type faces in capital and small letters, the vowels, the elements of syllabification, an invocation to the Trinity, and probably the Lord's Prayer.[5] In three respects the horn book itself established a pattern of education which continued throughout the grammar school. This pattern differed fundamentally from that with which we are familiar. In the first place, the pupil was expected to learn by intensive drill upon a very small body of material, generally memorizing it verbatim. Second, the inevitable concessions to immature minds were made not in quality but in quantity. The child was not expected to master much, but what he did study was on an adult level of ideas. Modern beginners read simple stories, copiously and colorfully illustrated, about Rover or the little red hen or children of other lands; Shakespeare learned the Lord's Prayer, the Little Catechism, and the Psalms. Third, from the first day of school no effort was spared to make him a moral man and a Christian according to the ideas and ideals of the Church of England, and all other objectives were definitely and firmly subordinated to that primary purpose.

From the horn book the child progressed to *The ABC with the Catechism*. This, too, contained the alphabet in black letter, roman, and italic type, and the invocation to the Trinity. It added simple spelling exercises, a catechism, and graces before and after meals.[6] The catechism was that which still appears in the Book of Common Prayer, except that the questions on the sacraments were not added until 1604.

That the catechism was the part of this book that made an impression upon Shakespeare we can infer from the Bastard's reference to it in *King John*:

> And when my knightly stomach is suffic'd,
> Why then I suck my teeth and catechise
> My picked man of countries. "My dear sir,"
> Thus, leaning on mine elbow, I begin,
> "I shall beseech you"—that is question now;
> And then comes answer like an Absey book.
> "O sir," says answer, "at your best command,
> At your employment, at your service, sir." (I, i, 191-98)[7]

[5]Ibid., pp. 121-23. Anders reproduces a horn book from the reign of Charles II (*Shakespeare's Books*, p. 9).

[6]Baldwin, *William Shakspere's Petty School*, pp. 123-26.

[7]Anders, *Shakespeare's Books*, p. 12.

Shakespeare amply demonstrates his knowledge of the contents of the catechism. He regularly alludes to the Ten Commandments in the version used in the catechism and Communion Service. Berowne's "Not by might mast'red, but by special grace" (*Love's Labour's Lost*, I, i, 153) is an allusion to the catechism, and Hamlet's "by these pickers and stealers" (III, ii, 349) is a reference to "to keep my hands from picking and stealing" in the response interpreting the commandments.[8]

The ABC with the Catechism or Absey Book, as Shakespeare calls it, had formerly been followed by a primer containing selections from the services of the church, especially those prayers in which the congregation participated, the canticles, and selected Psalms.[9] Shakespeare was probably taught this material directly from the Book of Common Prayer. He quotes from Psalms more often than from any other book of the Bible, and he regularly uses the Prayer Book version.[10] His reading in Petty School would subsequently have been reinforced by use of the Psalms in morning and evening prayer and possibly by turning passages into Latin as part of his grammar-school composition. The Act of Uniformity of 1559 prohibited disrespectful use of the Prayer Book, whereas no such prohibition existed for the Bible until 1606.[11] Direct reference to the services of the church were therefore avoided in plays; but Shakespeare has allusions to the General Confession and the Litany, with which he might have become familiar either in Petty School or in church. He has even more references, however, to the orders for matrimony and baptism, which he would hardly have read as a beginner.[12]

By the time he was ready for grammar school, Shakespeare should therefore have acquired some ability to read English and a very much sounder knowledge of the elements of Christianity than most modern church members ever possess. His reading, if limited, had been centered in the finest examples of English prose

[8]Noble, *Shakespeare's Biblical Knowledge*, pp. 86, 143, 204.

[9]Earlier primers in English and Latin are reprinted in *Private Prayers Put Forth by Authority during the Reign of Queen Elizabeth* (Parker Society 37), which is generally available in university libraries.

[10]Noble, *Shakespeare's Biblical Knowledge*, p. 76.

[11]Ibid., p. 82.

[12]Ibid., p. 83.

available and in the great religious poetry of the Psalms. If it was heavy going for a little boy, it was at least better preparation for life and for writing poetry than most beginners get today. I once visited a missionary school for Indians in the Southwest where the children were also being taught to read right out of the Bible. To them English was, moreover, a foreign language, but they seemed to be learning at least as much as their playmates who were using the most modern readers in the Government school across the way, for which I was then responsible. Shakespeare's works afford ample evidence that, once mastered, his early reading stayed with him.

The "grammar" of grammar school was, of course, Latin; and a thorough mastery of that language was the principal—and sometimes one is tempted to think the only—aim of instruction, except, of course, for morality and religion. The student was expected to learn not only to read Latin easily but to write it and to speak it as well. He must be prepared so that he could go on to university studies if such was his lot; and before the introduction of laboratory and field work or even the multiplication of books, university work consisted solely of the mastery of a fairly limited number of authorities, almost all of them in Latin. University lectures were still in Latin, although such surviving examples as Gabriel Harvey's discourses on rhetoric have obviously been revised and adorned for publication; and Latin was the language not merely of international scholarship but even of sermons on formal occasions, for which, as many a published *concio* bears witness, there were not only listeners but also a bookseller's market. But the young student must also be prepared for the text books of the grammar school itself, which, beyond the introductory pages of Lily's grammar, were in Latin—Latin that was some of it far more difficult, because more technical, than the standard school authors. The following enumeration of the books that Shakespeare studied is based upon Baldwin's conclusions, and includes those books in the grammar-school curriculum of which the plays show a knowledge.

Shakespeare was introduced to Latin grammar by means of William Lily's *A Shorte Introduction of Grammar*. An English "Introduction of the Eyght Partes of Latine Speache" and "The Concordes of Latine Speache" listed inflections and summarized elementary rules of syntax. This section concluded, in conformity with the moral bias of Elizabethan schooling, with Latin elegiac verses of Lily's own composition which gave instructions for studying, admonished the students to work hard, and listed a few moral precepts that Polonius may have recalled in parting with Laertes. Then came paraphrases in Latin verse of the Apostles' Creed, the Decalogue, the Scriptural accounts of the institution of baptism and the Lord's Supper, and finally graces before and after meat. Presumably these were used for analysis to illustrate the rules studied. The material on accidence and syntax was repeated and amplified in Latin in Lily's *Brevissima Institutio*. Rules for gender, irregular declensions, and the conjugation of verbs were elaborately summarized in Latin hexameters, obviously to be memorized. After the syntax came figures of speech, though not tropes, and the principles of Latin prosody. Examples from various Latin authors were scattered throughout, and Shakespeare quoted a number of them, at one point (*Titus Andronicus*, IV, ii, 20-23) acknowledging his debt to Lily.[13] The inevitable moral instruction and a Latin-English vocabulary concluded the book.[14]

The study of this grammatical material extended throughout the lower school. It was paralleled almost from the beginning by the construing and translating of Latin writers, contemporary as well as classical. The student's religious instruction was attended to by having him study and memorize in Latin the catechism (which included the Lord's Prayer and Apostles' Creed) and the parts of the Prayer Book which he had encountered in English in the Petty School.[15] If, as is likely, Shakespeare studied the new version of the catechism prepared by Nowell in 1571, it added sections on the duties of subjects, children, parishioners, servants, parents, masters, and married persons, and at the end questions and answers on the sacraments much like those now in the Book of Common Prayer.[16] The detailed description of moral obligations in terms of social categories was, of course, profoundly significant of Elizabethan habits of thought and introduced Shake-

[13]Cf. Anders, *Shakespeare's Books*, pp. 13-16.

[14]I have used the reprint of the edition of 1567 edited by Vincent J. Flynn for Scholars' Facsimiles & Reprints, 1945.

[15]Baldwin, *W. S. Small Latine*, I, 433, 490.

[16]Baldwin, *W. S. Petty School*, pp. 123-26.

speare to the practical applications of the philosophic concept of an ordered, hierarchical universe, in which he later became so much interested.

The regular sequence of secular texts for construing began with the *Sententiae Pueriles* of Leonhardus Culmannus. Shakespeare almost certainly used this, and probably the *Disticha Moralia* of Cato with scholia by Erasmus.[17] The *Sententiae Pueriles* (at least in the collection published in 1723 that I used) consisted of brief maxims of conduct arranged alphabetically in groups of two words, then of three, and so on—that is, according to the amount of construing involved. Parallels to a number of them have been found in Shakespeare;[18] the work was, moreover, a universal textbook, and he must have used it. As educational material the maxims have interesting implications. Despite a moral emphasis, they are both mature and worldly, if not actually cynical, in point of view. Friendship is repeatedly praised; love, women, and wine are constantly stigmatized as dangerous; ambition is a great pestilence in a state; civil war is a most pernicious evil; eyes are to be trusted rather than ears; money wins where nothing else can. A boy who laboriously construed such sentences was not leading an intellectually sheltered life. The imitations of them in the plays are racy in the extreme and suggest that considerable pains was taken in school to achieve the same idiomatic vigor that is a glory of Elizabethan translations. "The end of war's uncertain" (*Coriolanus*, V, iii, 141), sleep is the "ape of death" (*Cymbeline*, II, ii, 31) or "death's counterfeit" (*Macbeth*, II, iii, 81).[19] Such drill in pithy statement was undoubtedly a most valuable counterbalance to the long-windedness encouraged by later rhetorical studies.

Cato's *Disticha Moralia* are similar.[20] "Play with a top; avoid dice." "Avoid harlots; learn letters." The distichs return constantly to the subject of death: whoever fears it loses what life he has; it is either good or at least the end of woes; it follows wherever

[17]Cf. Baldwin, *W. S. Small Latine*, I, 591-606.

[18]Anders, *Shakespeare's Books*, p. 47.

[19]Ibid., pp. 47-48.

[20]I used *Catonis Disticha moralia ex castigatione D. Erasmi Roterdodami vná cum annotationibus & scholijs Richardi Tauerneri Anglico idiomate conscriptis in vsum Anglicae iuuentutis*, sig. A2v.

you walk, as a shadow follows the body. "Lex universi est, quae iubet nasci et mori" suggests Gertrude's "Thou know'st 'tis common, all that lives must die," which Shakespeare then amplifies with "Passing through nature to eternity" (*Hamlet*, I, ii, 72-73).

As the student moved on through the lower school taught by the usher, these collections of phrases or sentences were followed by the easy connected prose of Aesop's fables.[21] After Aesop came Terence, which was good for the development of colloquial Latin; although a play or two of Plautus might also be read, Shakespeare's indebtedness to him, rather than to Terence, is distinctly out of line with the relative emphasis given to the two men by the grammar-school curriculum. Mantuan's *Eclogues*, which belonged to this same period in the student's development, Shakespeare fortunately did not imitate, as Spenser did, and one doubts that he paid real attention very far beyond the first line that Holofernes quotes (*Love's Labour's Lost*, IV, ii, 95-96). The next of the customary texts, Palingenius' *Zodiacus Vitae*, deserves more attention because it is less familiar than Aesop, Terence, or Plautus and much more interesting than Mantuan.[22]

A major effort of Renaissance scholarship was devoted to excerpting from Greek and Roman writers. Such collections (*Adagia, Apothegmata*) constituted a considerable part of Erasmus' published work, and they furnished a good share of the classical quotations that seem so impressive in writers of the period. Palingenius took the same kind of collection, added allegory, psychology, and astronomy, stirred the mixture well, and produced a long poem where favorite Renaissance commonplaces abound and the most contradictory philosophic doctrines combine happily. Most of the poem is devoted to ethical problems, but Book XI, much the clearest and best constructed, summarizes the accepted astronomy; it is said to have been memorized by Thomas Digges.[23] Book XII states the philosophic principle of the plentitude of God[24] and the neo-Platonic concept of light

[21]Baldwin (*W. S. Small Latine*, I, 615) believes that Shakespeare used the version by Ioachimus Camerarius.

[22]Both the original and Googe's translation, ed. Tuve, have been used. See bibliography.

[23]*The Zodiake of Life*, tr. Googe, ed. Tuve, p. v.

[24]Cf. Lovejoy, *The Great Chain of Being*, pp. 115-16, which notes the same ideas in Books VII and XI.

as an emanation of God, and then considers man's proper approach to God.

It is very unlikely that Shakespeare read the whole poem. The copy which I used, printed in England in 1572 and therefore probably used as a textbook at just about Shakespeare's time, had English glosses written between the lines of Book I, marginal line numbers inserted as far as Book III, and a few marginal scribblings in Books VII and VIII. Shakespeare obviously read the last part of Book VI, which describes the world as a stage on which men are wretched in every age. He must also have read Book III, from which he took ideas for the following speech in the *Tempest*:

> These our actors,
> As I foretold you, were all spirits, and
> Are melted into air, into thin air;
> And, like the baseless fabric of this vision,
> The cloud-capp'd towers, the gorgeous palaces,
> The solemn temples, the great globe itself,
> Yea, all which it inherit, shall dissolve
> And, like this insubstantial pageant faded,
> Leave not a rack behind.
>
> (IV, i, 148-56)[25]

From the same context may have come the inspiration for Falstaff's catechism on the futility of honor in the presence of death (*1 Henry IV*, V, i, 128-44).[26] More doubtful parallels exist to Books IV and V,[27] and Baldwin remarks that other possible parallels collected by a student of his were mostly with the first six books.[28] Let us hope that Master Jenkins, or perhaps the Usher, made as intelligent selections from Palingenius in his other assignments as he did in the passages from which Shakespeare borrowed, and it is only fair to assume that he did so.

But a discussion of Shakespeare's possible debt to Palingenius that concentrated upon parallel passages would totally obscure the real significance of the *Zodiacus Vitae*. It was the one work that Shakespeare studied in grammar school that enabled him to

[25]Watson, *The Zodiacus Vitae*, pp. 34-35; Baldwin, *W. S. Small Latine*, I, 673-77.

[26]Baldwin, *W. S. Small Latine*, I, 678-79.

[27]Watson, *The Zodiacus Vitae*, pp. 39-40.

[28]*W. S. Small Latine*, I, 679, n. 108.

see beyond the extremely confining horizons of the curriculum into realms of philosophy, psychology, and especially astronomy that were otherwise restricted to the university student; and this would be true even if he read only selections. An intelligent teacher, looking, as good teachers always have looked, for a chance to make his own knowledge of service to his students and to enliven the routine of the school day, would have explained and dilated upon many passages, impressing them upon the boys' memory. It took a good and intelligent teacher to fix Shakespeare's attention so firmly upon the central point of a passage in Palingenius that he remembered it years later as he wrote *The Tempest*, when philosophy had come to have much more meaning for him. For he must have remembered the drift even if, as is probable, he looked up the poem again to refresh his memory. To a reader looking for organized exposition Palingenius is a frightful ordeal. To a schoolboy with a vigorous imagination open to stimuli, his very diversity, plus his real ability to elevate borrowed ideas into passages of genuine poetry, would be an enthralling experience. Shakespeare's boyhood, except for his rich contact with nature, offered only a fraction of the experiences that beat upon a modern child. His fewer experiences must therefore have operated upon him powerfully, just as, from walking along a country road, one may bring a rich memory of sights and sounds that one would never encounter in racing over hundreds of miles in an automobile.

While he was reading from the books mentioned above, Shakespeare was also learning to write and to speak Latin. Baldwin believes that the sentences which he turned from English into Latin were derived principally from Psalms, Proverbs, and Ecclesiasticus,[29] which abound in the sententious wisdom which delighted Elizabethans, and that these exercises account for the unusual familiarity with these books which led Noble to consider them, along with Genesis and Job, his favorites.[30] Noble argues, however, that Shakespeare probably did not become familiar with these books, except for the Psalms, as early as his boyhood and that he did not study them in school.

[29]Ibid., 707.

[30]*Shakespeare's Biblical Knowledge*, p. 43.

Those who, like Dr. Carter, ascribe to Shakespeare's boyhood a good grounding in Scripture do so under the impression that Biblical phrases and thoughts flowed spontaneously and unconsciously from his pen. As far as the earlier plays are concerned, with the exception of the *Psalms*, it is not my impression that Shakespeare used Biblical phrases and thoughts other than consciously . . . a very large proportion of them are uttered by a comparatively small number of characters. It will also be observed that while some plays, like the Historical Plays, *Love's Labour's Lost* and *The Merchant of Venice*, abound in Scriptural quotation and allusions, others, like *The Two Gentlemen of Verona* and *The Taming of the Shrew*, for no obvious reason, have remarkably few of them.[31]

It seems to me, on the contrary, that Shakespeare's use of these books in the form of *sententiae* for composition explains precisely the phenomena that Noble points out. The quotations occur as units, deliberately inserted, because he had learned to treat them as such; and the uneven distribution among the characters and plays results from a calculating of effects. *Love's Labour's Lost* involves an ostentatious parade of school learning, the *Merchant of Venice* an attempt to establish a Jewish and therefore an Old Testament background for Shylock. The Biblical quotations in the Chronicles are part of an attempt to suggest wisdom and high policy that we shall note in considering Shakespeare's method of composing those plays.[32] We shall also notice that Shakespeare's classical allusions in the early plays have the same self-consciousness, whereas he later came to weave them more easily into his text.

This method of learning to write Latin was of fundamental importance in determining Shakespeare's own style.[33] Shakespeare abounds in quotable sentences simply because he learned to think in *sententiae* as he sweated over translation from Latin to English or from English to Latin, trying in each exercise to achieve maximum brevity and maximum point. Later he would learn to use these same *sententiae* as the basis for elaborate compositions involving the devices of amplification—and no one can be more prolix than he, except most of his contemporaries! But even his rambling structures were built of good hard bricks, and he learned young to make his bricks strong.

[31]Ibid., p. 47.

[32]Cf. Lever, "Proverbs and *Sententiae* in the Plays of Shakspere," p. 181.

[33]Cf. Baldwin, *W. S. Small Latine*, I, 708-709.

When he moved into the upper school, Shakespeare continued his reading of Latin authors. We do not know whether he finished the grammar-school course, and we can only infer how far he advanced from his knowledge of the standard authors. Ovid he clearly knew in great detail. Root has collected evidence that he knew parts, at least, of the *Heroides, Fasti, Amores,* and perhaps the *Ars Amatoria* and the *Tristia.* The bulk of his mythology comes from the *Metamorphoses,* and "with nearly all of the important episodes of the poem, with each of the fifteen books, save perhaps the twelfth and fifteenth, his familiarity is clearly demonstrable."[34] From Ovid he constantly drew material to supplement his sources when he wrote the early histories, and there is ample evidence that he knew the poet in Latin as well as in Golding's translation.[35] Shakespeare also knew Virgil, although he made far less use of him than of Ovid; and even the wonderful picture of Dido wafting "her love to come again to Carthage" (*Merchant of Venice,* V, i, 9-12) he owed to Ovid's Ariadne in the tenth *Heroides.*[36] But Baldwin believes that he studied both the *Bucolics* and the *Georgics* in school,[37] and Root has shown that he consulted the *Aeneid* both in the original and in Phaer's translation.[38] His marked preference for the first six books of the *Aeneid* invites suspicion that little more was read in the Stratford grammar school than is customary in American high schools.

Among other Latin school poets numerous parallels have been cited with Horace, usually with the *Odes, Epistles,* and *Ars Poetica* rather than the *Satires.*[39] Hamlet's satirical rogue who describes old men (II, ii, 193-208) has been identified with Juvenal, and other allusions have been noted.[40] In adding Persius to the list, Baldwin remarks that the three poets were regularly bound together and were used to provide verse forms in teaching the boys versification.[41] The quarrying of phrases by a boy laboriously

[34]Root, *Classical Mythology in Shakespeare,* pp. 3-4.
[35]Baldwin, *W. S. Small Latine,* II, 423-40.
[36]Root, *Classical Mythology in Shakespeare,* pp. 4-5.
[37]*W. S. Small Latine,* II, 464-79.
[38]*Classical Mythology in Shakespeare,* p. 7. Cf. Anders, *Shakespeare's Books,* p. 32.
[39]Baldwin, *W. S. Small Latine,* II, 497.
[40]Anders, *Shakespeare's Books,* p. 38; Baldwin, *W. S. Small Latine,* II, 526-42.
[41]Baldwin, *W. S. Small Latine,* II, 547-48.

writing Latin verses would explain Shakespeare's indebtedness to these poets and even his two borrowings from Lucan. In view of the frequency with which translations or imitations of Catullus and Martial appear among Elizabethan lyrics, it is surprising that Shakespeare apparently did not know either of them, although they were taught to the highest forms in some of the schools.

Of the prose writers ordinarily read in grammar school Shakespeare shows no knowledge of Sallust and only the most general knowledge of Caesar's reputation as an author rather than of what he wrote. Livy he undoubtedly used for *The Rape of Lucrece*;[42] but he may have looked up the passage in connection with some school rhetorical exercise, as Baldwin conjectures,[43] or he may have consulted Livy when he was writing the poem. It was intended, like *Venus and Adonis*, to establish him as a man of letters, and use of all the learning at his command would have been appropriate. Of Cicero's works only the *Tusculan Disputations* seem clearly to have been read by Shakespeare, at least in part.[44] They are the most genuinely philosophical of Cicero's works and would have been a revelation to the boy. Bargulus "the strong Illyrian pirate" (*2 Henry VI*, IV, i, 108) is an obvious reference to the *De Officiis*[45] but need not prove that Shakespeare read it. In short, it was clearly the poets who interested Shakespeare (and perhaps Master Jenkins as well); and as we approach the more advanced levels of grammar-school instructions—the *De Officiis*, for example, being read in the last year—the evidence for Shakespeare's knowledge of the authors, whether in verse or prose, becomes increasingly thin.

As the student moved from the lower into the upper school, writing Latin became an important part of his training; and he progressed from translation of sentences to the writing of extended discourses, from drill in grammar to the study of rhetoric as applied both in prose and in verse composition. The customary order was to begin with epistles in prose or verse and then to go on to themes of set types and finally to orations.[46] That Shakespeare himself mastered the rules governing the various types of composition has been amply demonstrated both by Bald-

[42]*Shakespeare's Poems*, ed. Pooler, p. liv.
[43]Baldwin, *W. S. Small Latine* II, 573.
[44]Ibid., 601-10.   [45]Ibid., 596.   [46]Ibid., 71-72.

win and by Sister Miriam Joseph in her monograph *Shakespeare's Use of the Arts of Language*.[47]

The basic text in rhetoric was the *Rhetorica ad C. Herennium*, which was used throughout the upper school. It was then universally attributed to Cicero and carried the authority of his renown as orator and master of Latin prose style. After distinguishing the three types of causes—demonstrative, deliberative, and judicial—it considers the five skills of the orator: invention, disposition, elocution, memory, and pronunciation. Invention, the finding of matter for the oration, is discussed at length as it applies to the judicial cause, and suggestions are made for adapting the rules given to demonstrative and deliberative causes. Disposition, pronunciation, and memory follow. Elocution, or what we should call style, is discussed in terms of the use of *exempla* and of the three conventional levels of style (*gravis, mediocris, attenuata*). It also involves the proper use of figures of speech and thought, to which the remainder of the work is devoted. Shakespeare very nearly memorized at least the first two books (through the parts of a judicial oration), for they are reflected not only in passages involving formal judicial procedure but also in much clowning.[48]

The same emphasis upon types of evidence and court procedure is to be found in Cicero's *Topics* and in Quintilian's treatment of the oration proper, which Shakespeare also studied. From these works he would not have acquired a knowledge of English law, to be sure; but he might develop an interest in legal problems and a considerable knowledge of legal methods and habits of thought. His grammar-school training was quite adequate for interpreting the law of Verona or Venice and undoubtedly helpful in understanding the English law that he found in the sources of his chronicle plays. In other words, Shakespeare's law and his obvious fondness for judicial or quasi-judicial proceedings came, in large measure, from his grammar-school studies, although he undoubtedly picked up more law in London as he became acquainted with men of affairs.

The treatment of invention proper regularly involved the study not only of the *Ad Herennium* but also of the fuller and logically

---

[47]See pp. 8-13 for an excellent brief summary of Shakespeare's schooling constructed on somewhat different principles than the present one.

[48]Cf. Baldwin, *W. S. Small Latine*, II, 73-101.

superior *Topics* of Cicero, which organized Aristotle's logical predicaments in such a way that they could be used by an orator and misused by clowns and the pedant Holofernes (*Love's Labour's Lost*, IV, ii, 67-74).[49] Shakespeare must also have picked up a knowledge of formal logic at some point in his career, but no probable textbook has been identified.[50] In the hands of a well-trained master, however, the *Topics* itself would surely yield considerable training in formal logic, and one should not dismiss too lightly the possibility that Shakespeare's knowledge of logic may have been imparted by Master Jenkins or his equivalent.[51] Shakespeare's writings do not expound a logical system but reflect it, and so would the instructions of a careful teacher, especially when he habitually taught by dictating his material so that his students could memorize it. Rambling class discussions were not in vogue during the Renaissance.

In the meantime, Shakespeare was learning to write letters, very probably[52] from Erasmus' *De Conscribendis Epistolis*.[53] The first eleven chapters of this work are really addressed to the master rather than to the student, and the method recommended is interesting (Ch. x, p. 355):

But the teacher will not set forth the matter [in making his assignment] completely drawn out, lest he leave nothing to the invention of the boys; nor bare, on the other hand, but with some of the circumstances written in, so that they may become accustomed to aim their arrows, as it were, at a definite target and out of these shafts to contrive sentences, arguments, trials of arguments, amplifications, and other figures.

The resulting assignment, as Erasmus makes clear by example, would actually set up a dramatic context into which the letter was to fit; nor were chances to inculcate sound morals overlooked. A boy might be told, for example, to assume that he had gone to another country and mended his ways. He was then to write a letter (cause, *suasorium*; genus, *dehoratio*) urging an unregener-

---

[49]Ibid., 108-28. For Holofernes see pp. 111-12.

[50]Cf. Craig, "Shakespeare and Formal Logic."

[51]Baldwin (*W. S. Small Latine*, II, 128) doubts this.

[52]Ibid., 271-86.

[53]References are to the text in *Opera Omnia*, I, 346-483.

ate companion of his former sins to repent, abandon his dissipations, and embrace learning. Apparently Erasmus had no fear that the sins specified, which were of no mean order, would put ideas into the boys' heads. Shakespeare must have found some aspects of such assignments a challenge to his imagination.

With Chapter xii the work becomes a manual, giving instructions for conventional sentences of salutation, for what in modern jargon is called the complimentary close, and for indicating the place and date. It provides lists of formulae suitable for different kinds of people, from which Shakespeare drew matter for fun (cf. *Taming of the Shrew*, IV, v, 27-40). In Chapter xxxii Erasmus assigns the various types of letters possible (although most of them are extremely improbable) to a large number of genera listed under the three traditional causes, which he calls suasory, encomiastic, and judicial. The familiar letter may be added to these three types, although Erasmus implies that no well-bred man would do so since it cannot be fitted into the three traditional categories. After giving instruction, Erasmus discusses each genus of letters, stating principles to be observed in writing, giving examples, and citing further examples in the collections of letters by Cicero and others.

These letters may actually have developed Shakespeare's genius as well as his sense of humor, for a series of assignments according to Erasmus' types would have demanded a perfectly fantastic ingenuity in both masters and students. Like the assignment mentioned above, they would have to be a dramatic game if they were to be endurable at all. Erasmus' own treatment of love letters is itself amusing. In Chapter lv he writes: "Of the Love Letter . . . I see that some have made two species of this genus, the honest and the base ["honest," of course, means "chaste"]. We call the honest letter conciliatory, the other amatory" (p. 454). This chapter seems to have caught Shakespeare's attention, for Antipholus of Syracuse puts its precepts to good use in wooing Luciana (*Comedy of Errors*, III, ii, 29-52).[54]

In conjunction with the *De Conscribendis Epistolis* the boy usually studied Erasmus' *Copia*,[55] which was intended to develop variety and elegance of expression. Actually it must often have

[54]Baldwin, *W. S. Small Latine*, II, 283-84.
[55]*Opera Omnia*, I, 3-110.

produced, if taken seriously by the budding writer, the kind of long-windedness and outlandish vocabulary that is parodied by the fantastics in *Love's Labour's Lost* and by Osric. The work reaches its climax in Chapter xxxiii of Book I, where all possible variations (or at least all that Erasmus could think of) are given for the formulae: "Your letter pleased me greatly" and "I shall remember you as long as I live." The variants of the latter are printed in small type, and yet they fill one and one-half pages almost double the size even of a normal folio (pp. 26-30). Since the variants tend to follow patterns, they amount to instruction in the fine art of the cliché. Nor is Shakespeare himself without *copia*. It is parody when Falstaff says:

> For God's sake, lords, convey my tristful queen;
> For tears do stop the flood-gates of her eyes.
> (*1 Henry IV*, II, iv, 434-35)

It is unfortunately not parody when Hamlet says:

> Ere yet the salt of most unrighteous tears
> Had left the flushing of her galled eyes.
> (*Hamlet*, I, ii, 154-55)

But Erasmus was well aware of these dangers. Chapter i is headed: "Affectation of *Copia* is Dangerous."

To make sure that the unfortunate students knew their tropes and schemes, English schools often used Susenbrotus' *Epitome Troporum ac Schematum et Grammaticorum et Rhetoricorum*,[56] and Shakespeare's was evidently no exception.[57] Susenbrotus divides figures into nineteen kinds of tropes, which involve a variation of meaning, and one hundred twenty-one kinds of schemes, the latter being defined with typical clarity as follows: "A form of writing or speaking somehow changed [or "invented" —*novata*]. Or it is a certain plan of writing or speaking invented by art." The term for each kind is followed by the Greek equivalent, a definition, and examples from classical writers. Unless Shakespeare found the definitions much clearer than I did, he must frequently have had to puzzle out the nature of the figures from the examples, to the considerable enrichment of his store of striking phrases as well as his knowledge of rhetoric. Nor should

[56]The edition used was not published until 1621. See bibliography.
[57]Baldwin, *W. S. Small Latine*, II, 141-75.

31

any but the stupidest boys have been unable to write at length after mastering the forty-one figures of amplification.

By this time the student was well prepared to take up the study of themes, and for this Shakespeare, like most of his contemporaries, used Aphthonius' *Progymnasmata* as a basic test.[58] He may have found it one of the most interesting books that he studied, at least for its illustrative material and notes if not for its treatment of theme writing. The *Progymnasmata* is an advanced work; it assumes in the student a knowledge of the three types of causes and the conventional subheads, of the "places" of rhetoric, and of figures, so that it merely instructs him to follow a conventional organization or to use certain places without explaining them. Its role in the educational scheme may be inferred from the history of the copy that I consulted. It was used by Thomas Egerton, later Baron Ellesmere and Viscount Brackley, who was born about 1540 and entered Brasenose College, Oxford, in 1556. Since the book was printed in 1553, Egerton was at least thirteen when he acquired it, and it belonged to the last few years before his entry into college. He has adorned the last blank page and the inside of the back cover with doodlings, mostly sketches of a face, and he has marked various passages of the text. These are generally brief summaries to be memorized (sometimes verse summaries intended to aid the memory), moral sentiments and other *sententiae*, mythological information in the notes, and remarks on the follies of women. One suspects that the master was a confirmed misogynist and that he indicated the passages marked. Egerton contributed the slim, well-manicured, and beautifully drawn hands that mark many of the sentences.

The book divides the three conventional causes into various types of discourse. Each section consists of a definition of the type and an indication of its uses, a schematic organization for a theme based upon it and a list of the "places" to be used, and examples for imitation. The examples that were part of the original text, and others added by Renaissance editors, are furnished with elaborate notes explaining the historical and mythological allusions. Since many of the subjects are drawn from Greek

[58]Ibid., 310-41. Cf. Johnson's discussion of Aphthonius in the introduction to his reprinting of Rainolde's *The Foundacion of Rhetorike*, which is based upon Aphthonius.

history or mythology, the *Progymnasmata* undoubtedly offered
the best introduction to Greek history that Shakespeare received
and supplemented the mythology that he obtained from Ovid.
One encounters a surprising number of references that may well
have been Shakespeare's first introduction to material that he
afterwards used. Baldwin has called attention to many parallels,
including Aphthonius' citation, under the fable, of Menenius
Agrippa, "who is reported to have brought the common people
back into harmony with the fathers. For the fable about the parts
of the human body quarreling with the stomach is well known."[59]
Egerton has marked this sentence. Allusion has already been made
to the analysis of the story of Venus and Adonis as told by Ovid
and the quoting of Ovid's Pyramus and Thisbe under the heading
"narration." Hamlet's reference to his mother's following his
"father's body like Niobe all tears" (I, ii, 149) may well have
been a recollection of an example of *ethopoeia*, an imitation of the
manner of a selected person. Since Baldwin has not noted the
passage, and it is a good example of Aphthonius' method, it is
worth quoting. (Note that the allusion to Hecuba is also paralleled
in *Hamlet*.) "Ethopoeia," says Aphthonius,

is divided. For some is *passive*, which expresses the state of mind to
which it pertains, which directly signifies the emotion of the soul,
such as the words which Hecuba would choose at the fall of Troy.
Moral, which depicts manners alone, such as what an inlander would
say when he first saw the sea. *Mixed*, which equally involves manners
and a state of the mind, such as the words which Achilles would say
over the dead Patroclus, when he determined to fight, for a decision
involves manners and custom, but a dead friend involves a state of
mind.

You will handle Ethopoeia with a plain manner of speaking, short,
embellished, disconnected, with all variation, and without figures.
And for headings you will divide it by the three times: present, past,
and future.

Example of passive ethopoeia. Argument: What Niobe's words would
be when her children lay dead.

From the Present: Wretched am I; what one calamity shall I weep
above the rest, bereft now of the children for whom I was once
preeminent? What wealth has for my wretched self been reduced
to what poverty? In my misery I am no longer the mother of one

[59]Ibid., 321.

33

child, who once walked famous for so many. How much better were it to have been barren rather than fertile in tears and grief. For those who weep their loss of children are far more unhappy than those who have never given birth. Their experience of the love of children causes their bitterest grief in destitution. [Egerton marked the last two sentences.]

From the past: Unhappy am I, who have experienced a fate like his who bore me. For I was born of Tantalus, who was happy in the company of the gods, but in the end was lost from the friendship of the gods. By my disasters I prove that I am his child. For I am related to Latona, and by her I am now oppressed with these evils, and I wail her kinship in the loss of my children. This for me is the end of my relationship with the goddess, that I should live amid calamities. For before I was acquainted with Latona, I was myself the happier mother; but as I became better known to her, I was deprived of my children; before she knew me, I was blessed with a distinguished multitude of them. That happy number of either sex now lies before me to my heavy grief. Where shall I turn in my unhappiness? To what shall I shift? What tomb will suffice for my dead children? Wretched me, in such woes even the honor due my calamities escapes me, and funeral rites are denied unhappy me.

From the future: But why do I complain and bewail these things, when the Gods permit them that they may change me into another nature? I see this one remedy of my miseries: that it should change me into the form of another thing which is without sense or life. But I fear in my misery that, however changed, I may not cease to be among tears.[60]

I shall have to ask the reader to assume on trust that the awkwardness and frigidity of Niobe's lament are not due entirely to the translation. Aphthonius has indeed avoided figures of speech, as he instructed, but the amplification in the second paragraph is both obvious and tedious. Shakespeare could, of course, have got a sufficiently lachrymose impression of Niobe from Ovid or elsewhere; but, if he worked through this lament, more remarkable for its mythological ingenuity than for its genuine emotion, he certainly would have associated her with tears forever after. Moreover—and this is the important point—if he wrote themes of the customary type, he spent his time imagining himself in just such fictitious situations. Modern theory demands that a

---

[60]Fols. 177-78. The Latin *affectus* has been translated "state of mind."

student's compositions be based upon his own experience. Not so Shakespeare's. They were based upon a maximum use of the imagination in a situation that was probably as foreign to his experience as Greece or Rome or the lives of the worthies of English history. The imaginative effort demanded to write a lament for Niobe is exactly like that required to find words for Romeo in Friar Lawrence's cell after his banishment, and either exercise, it must be added, is about equally exaggerated and tasteless. But Shakespeare still used the conventional methods and headings even after he had learned, perhaps by his own griefs, to suggest more realistically the emotions that people actually feel. The gain was merely one of artistic skill in the use of accepted formulae. Shakespeare used art to suggest nature, not to portray it.

For the oration, the most advanced type of rhetorical exercise, Shakespeare would have turned again to the *Ad Herennium* and finally to Quintilian, of whom he had considerable knowledge.[61] Quintilian was one of the wisest men who ever wrote on education, and there is evidence that Shakespeare knew the two preliminary books which a master interested only in rhetoric might have led him to skip.[62] These discussions of the proper training of the future orator from infancy through boyhood are, in many respects, the best part of the work.

Shakespeare's probable knowledge of Greek there is no need to consider. He would have studied the familiar catechism again in a Greek version, and he seems to have had some knowledge of the Greek New Testament.[63] Greek, however, was obviously not an important element in his intellectual development, and, indeed, its influence upon Renaissance literature as opposed to philosophy and science has been much exaggerated.

Such then, in rather extended outline, was Shakespeare's grammar-school education. It is possible, perhaps, to make some generalizations as to its character and to draw some legitimate inferences as to its probable effect upon him.

We inevitably bring to an interpretation of the past the assumptions of the present, and nothing could be more dangerous. The

[61]Cf. Baldwin, *W. S. Small Latine*, II, 197-238.
[62]Ibid., 197.
[63]Ibid., 644.

first task in understanding the imprint made by Shakespeare's school upon his mind is to correct the inferences that we might draw from our own training, for the differences were fundamental. He studied much less, but far more intensively; he was taught to memorize rather than to question or discuss. He wrote according to the approved formulae and stated the sentiments of the standard authors; any originality that he might possess would find expression in the disposition of the material, not in the material itself. No one doubted that his education would mould his character, and no effort was spared to make sure that his religion was sound and his learning orthodox. Since every one of these generalizations represents the direct antithesis of modern aims, and most of them involve the opposite of modern practice, they deserve some examination.

It is no exaggeration to say that any adult who possessed the competence in Latin that Shakespeare must have had before he left school could read in two months all the books that Shakespeare studied. The contrast between the number of concepts that Shakespeare encountered and those to which a modern student is exposed was even greater, for much of Shakespeare's limited material was repetitive. Instruction in the catechism and parts of the Prayer Book and Bible was repeated in all three languages studied. Much of this material was memorized. This method had the double advantage of giving the student a thorough review of sound doctrine and of enabling him to gain confidence in a new language by working with familiar texts. It is no wonder that Shakespeare's plays show a thorough knowledge of the catechism, the Psalms, and parts of the Prayer Book. His studies of secular authors involved an equal repetition of ideas, though not of actual texts. He might encounter the same *sententia* from a Latin writer listed in Lily or *Sententiae Pueriles*, adapted in Palingenius or even Mantuan, and quoted in Susenbrotus or Aphthonius; he might even read it in the writer himself. The same mythological allusions to illustrate the same moral precepts kept recurring during his reading. And these stories from classical mythology might, in turn, be used as the basis of letters or themes that he built up from the *sententiae* so often encountered.

This repetition was also concentrated within a fairly limited range of knowledge. Many subjects which are now part of the school curriculum, and which even then existed as flourishing sciences, were deliberately left for the university or excluded altogether. The most striking omission was mathematics. Presumably Shakespeare had some training in the most elementary arithmetical processes, but very little time was spent on it. History was normally confined to a few Latin writers, and there is little evidence that Shakespeare knew even those. When we come to examine the individual plays, we shall see that he apparently knew little English history outside of the actual sources that he used for the chronicle plays. But just as he did increase his acquaintance with English history by reading in Halle and Holinshed and consulting other chronicles, so he broadened his knowledge of Greece and Rome by reading Plutarch. The social sciences were unknown as school subjects, and so were the natural sciences, although Shakespeare may have consulted Cooper's *Thesaurus*, other reference works, or even Pliny on points that occurred in his reading.

In short, Shakespeare studied the fundamentals of religion, Latin and Greek grammar, rhetoric, and Latin literature; and he studied these materials thoroughly. We shall find, furthermore, that these subjects quite literally include everything in his early plays that was not derived from the source, except for a very few possible echoes of contemporary poetry.

This concentration of material was made even more effective by prevailing methods of study. Educational techniques are notoriously conservative, as educational reformers have never ceased to point out. Shakespeare was taught by methods that developed before the multiplication of printed textbooks, when writing materials were too scarce and expensive for much note-taking and men relied primarily upon their memories. We have a striking account of a German school only fifty years before Shakespeare's student days, in which "no one had any printed books except the praeceptor, who had a Terence. What was read had first to be dictated, then pointed, then construed, and at last explained."[64] Shakespeare was probably spared the dictation, but otherwise the method was the same—thorough, but dreadfully slow. A high proportion of the grammar and rhetoric was memorized outright. So the contemporary theorists on education commanded, and the detailed following of rhetorical formulae which Baldwin and

[64]Allen, *The Age of Erasmus*, p. 35.

Sister Miriam Joseph have located in the plays shows that Shakespeare obeyed. Lily and Aphthonius summarize various kinds of rules in Latin verses to aid the memory and, one might add, to puzzle the mind. The emphasis upon sententious material both in the elementary Latin readings and in the Bible also facilitated memorizing.

This educational method had two effects, both of which appear in the plays. In the first place, Shakespeare remembered what he read. I studied in high school or college most of the classical writers that Shakespeare used. Yet I could not today recall a minute fraction of the material that he obviously remembered in writing his plays. And the difference does result, at least in some small part, from methods of study. In the second place, such detailed study and memory work become a part of the student's very life; and, perhaps in an attempt to make the process endurable, he erects upon them fantastic and pedantic jokes and witticisms. Shakespeare has at least one bad joke (*Merry Wives*, IV, i, 64-65) that amused my own classmates in beginning Latin. Several other favorites of ours were denied Shakespeare by his method of pronouncing Latin, which obviously had compensatory advantages. Another jest of ours is worth mentioning, not because it would seem witty to anyone but an adolescent Latin student, but because it perhaps illustrates the basis of some of Shakespeare's clowning. It consisted of a misapplication of several of Caesar's favorite idioms, which will be recognized by anyone who has struggled with *De Bello Gallico*. In English it would go: When Caesar was a boy, his father led him into the shed; Caesar signified by voice that the attack on the rear was successful. There is no question that schoolboys of Shakespeare's day applied the same kind of humorous perversion to their colloquial Latin (see Dull's misunderstanding of *haud credo*, *Love's Labour's Lost*, IV, ii, 12) and to the rhetorical principles that they memorized so thoroughly. Baldwin has shown how much of what the clowns say is based upon rhetorical formulae. Characteristically they get the rules more or less right, and the humor (if any) lies in their gross misapplication of the rules to the most inappropriate material or at the most inappropriate times. So Dogberry follows the formula *proposition*, *division*, and *conclusion* tying the points together; and both Don Pedro and Claudio appreciate his efforts:

Dogberry: Marry, sir, they have committed false report; moreover, they have spoken untruths; secondarily, they are slanders; sixth and lastly, they have belied a lady; thirdly, they have verified unjust things; and, to conclude, they are lying knaves.

Don Pedro: First, I ask thee what they have done; thirdly, I ask thee what's their offence; sixth and lastly, why they are committed; and, to conclude, what you lay to their charge.

Claudio: Rightly reasoned, and in his own division.

(Much Ado, V, i, 219-30)

Even Polonius wearies Gertrude by a pedantic parody of formal logic that would have delighted any bored schoolboy. There is little doubt that in many of these speeches Shakespeare the imaginative schoolboy speaks through Shakespeare the dramatist.[65] *Love's Labour's Lost* is virtually a memorial to his schooldays.

But Shakespeare's intensive study of rhetoric and Latin composition was undoubtedly a major element in developing his method of writing his plays, just as this training was an important factor in determining the characteristics of Renaissance literature as a whole. It involved, first of all, a thorough training in the art of adapting other people's ideas to his own use. A student writing a letter or a theme was given his subject by the schoolmaster. Then he hunted for the appropriate *sententiae* to use in developing his subject and amplified those sentences according to approved rhetorical principles. When Shakespeare wrote plays he usually found the subject in a source. The art of adapting the source narrative to the limits of drama he had to learn from his fellow playwrights or develop for himself. But once this cutting and selecting had been done, he could follow well recognized methods of developing the material in the source. He simply used the accepted rhetorical methods plus a large number of the actual *sententiae* or examples or mythological illustrations that he had learned in school. He was also taught to make Latin verses out of a prose passage. Ben Jonson, we know, habitually wrote English verse as his master Camden had taught him—that is, he worked

---

[65] I never read the Pyramus and Thisbe interlude of MND without thinking of the crowning achievement of my high-school Latin club, which consisted in writing a parody of the *Aeneid*. After his house in New England had burned, the hero set out for California in a broken-down Ford. He was delayed by encountering a corn-fed vamp in Oskaloosa, Kansas.

out his ideas in prose and then versified them.[66] The testimony both of Jonson and of Heminge and Condell as to the rapidity and ease with which Shakespeare worked makes it very unlikely that he used any such laborious procedure. But he did apply exactly the same method, and presumably the same training, to the considerable passages in his plays, especially those based on Plutarch, which are merely versifications of the source. His grammar-school training both justified the practice and indicated the method to be used; it also taught him to look sharply in authors that he read for details that had in them the substance of poetry. Certainly he showed uncanny skill in selecting such details from his sources. It is only fair to add that this method can lead to artificiality and insincerity and also to a plentiful use of clichés, and Shakespeare offers examples of all these faults.

Most stimulating of all, perhaps, was Shakespeare's training in adapting his letters, themes, and orations to imaginary situations. *Decorum*, a fundamental critical principle of the Renaissance, demanded that words and sentiments be appropriate to the speaker; it must often have been invoked by the master in criticizing the schoolboy's output. If the master had any judgment, it offered the best kind of training in dramatic characterization. Quintilian, in fact, would have made both master and pupil aware of the parallel between the exercise of the schoolboy and the works of the dramatic poet, for all school themes were fundamentally the impersonations of which he wrote:

Consequently I regard *impersonation* as the most difficult of tasks, imposed as it is in addition to the other work involved by a deliberative theme. For the same speaker has on one occasion to impersonate Caesar, on another Cicero or Cato. But it is a most useful exercise because it demands a double effort and is also of the greatest use to future poets and historians, while for orators it is absolutely necessary. . . . It is for this reason that Lysias is regarded as having shown the highest art in the speeches which he wrote for uneducated persons, on account of their extraordinary realism. In the case of declaimers indeed it is of the first importance that they should consider what best suits each character: for they rarely play the role of advocates in their declamations. As a rule they impersonate sons, parents, rich men, old men, gentle or harsh of temper, misers, superstitious persons,

[66] *Works*, ed. Herford and Simpson, I, 143.

cowards and mockers, so that hardly even comic actors have to assume more numerous roles in their performances on the stage than these in their declamations.[67]

Finally, many of the attitudes that seem characteristic of Shakespeare's plays are the logical outcome of the aims of grammar-school education. No writer is more moral than Shakespeare in fundamentals. His jests are often as bawdy as any, and he can hunt with a perverse pertinacity for off-color implications in familiar language. But these are on the surface of the man and of his theater. As so many critics have pointed out, there are, in his major characters, no stopping places between virtue and vice, no half tones between the white of purity and the black of sin. His villains confess their crimes to the audience if not to their victims; his good characters are sustained in adversity by an extraordinary trust in the rightness of their conduct; and his tragic heroes come to see wherein they have erred. If his morality is almost naive beside Marlowe's probing scepticism or Webster's mingling of admirable and vicious traits in the same individual, it gains strength by simplicity. It is no accident that Shakespeare wrote in *Macbeth* the most terrible of all accounts of the destruction of human greatness produced by sin, for he believed in the reality both of human greatness and of sin, as he had been taught as a child to do.

The fact that Shakespeare's religious and moral beliefs had been drilled into him as a child accounts, I think, for a paradox: Christian doctrines were so deeply and solidly embedded in his thinking that they easily escaped notice. Even a recent writer can say, in writing of *Hamlet* (italics mine): "Indeed there are ... explicit Christian overtones in this, *alone* of the tragedies."[68] Actually, *Macbeth* is based on Christian theology from start to finish. It ends with an allusion to the grace of God. *Othello* and even *Lear* have numerous doctrinal references, and so on. As one reads Shakespeare on the lookout for such matters, one constantly encounters echoes of Christian teaching, often stated in technical terms. Later chapters will argue, in fact, that the very structure of Shakespeare's tragedies is grounded in traditional Christian

[67]*Institutio Oratoria*, III, viii, 49-51 (I, 503-505).
[68]Haydn, *The Counter-Renaissance*, p. 636.

41

thought as interpreted by the greatest theologian of his age. But Shakespeare so completely assimilated religious doctrines that no strain or incongruity is felt in his use of them, and that is the secret of their failure to attract notice. The salt in food is obvious only if a lump remains unbroken. The salt of religious training was perfectly assimilated in Shakespeare's mind during his boyhood, and what he then learned was never disturbed, apparently, by a genuine skepticism. He was not, so far as we can tell, a pious man in the sense that he was concerned with externals of religious ceremonial. But he did believe profoundly that God had made man in His own image and that, as all men had fallen once in Adam, so each man might fall again if he disobeyed the fundamental laws of God. Macbeth's sin is so awful simply because, like Shakespeare, he knows and believes in the foundations of human morality and in their ultimate basis in the mind and will of God. What Macbeth knows Shakespeare began to memorize in Petty School; the poetry in which Macbeth states his knowledge is the mystery of Shakespeare's genius.

But the moral bias of Elizabethan education had another advantage. If it taught the boy to use almost fantastic ingenuity in extracting a moral lesson from everything that he read, and if it ignored many a rose of poetry while it concentrated on the moral thorn attached, it at least forced the boy to regard Greek and Roman worthies as real people whose problems were like his own. We tend to regard Caesar and Cicero as historical museum pieces; Shakespeare thought of them as men of his own time, men with whose virtues and failings he was thoroughly familiar. The priggishness to which this incessant hunt for moral *exempla* might have led was corrected by the sophisticated, almost cynical, realism of much that he read from the time when he first began to study Latin. Schoolboys who are told to write letters dissuading their comrades from visiting harlots may have to assume a serious morality unnatural to their years, but at least they are not being shielded from life. At their best, classical writers and Renaissance thinkers shared a large-minded tolerance of human failings and a considerable skepticism as to the value of virtue unaccompanied by prudence, and Shakespeare wonderfully combines this kind of sophistication with his fundamental morality.

Shakespeare also concentrated upon the character and the

motives of the heroes of Plutarch because, like his age, he felt for Rome a veneration that we find hard to understand. Actually it is no problem if we remember two things: first, the Elizabethans were almost as materialistic as we are; second, they had a far more accurate notion than we have of the scientific and technological achievements of classical civilization, for they were using Greek and Latin works as their fundamental texts on plants and animals, medicine, mathematics, architecture, and engineering. Any Elizabethan with even a grammar-school education knew that Romans of the better classes had more comfortable houses than he could ever hope to have, could travel on paved roads instead of mud, could undertake more elaborate engineering ventures, had a better chance of surviving illness or even fairly difficult surgery, and so on. Their art, their literature, and their philosophy were obviously better than his. No wonder he respected the classics! We admire success, too, especially when the successful are far enough removed not to excite our envy. Yet it is very difficult for us to grasp imaginatively the attitudes of mind resulting from the simple fact that, until a century and a half ago, western Europe could feel superior to Rome only in the possession of Christianity, printing, the compass, and gunpowder. In other respects its technology was undoubtedly inferior. In a very real sense not only Shakespeare's contemporaries but even our great-great-grandfathers were closer to Cicero culturally than they are to us; for they shared his literature and they had not bettered his technology, but we have gained a new learning and a new material civilization. And the Renaissance, at least, knew how much of its Christianity it owed to Plato, Aristotle, and the Stoics. We find it impossible to comprehend Shakespeare's attitude toward Caesar or Brutus simply because we do not comprehend the cultural inferiority of his England to their Rome as he did.

The reader has probably objected long since that the preceding summary of Shakespeare's schooling assumes a perfect teacher and a perfect student to account for the effects alleged. Certainly it does assume— with every right—a student who was very superior indeed, for the entire emphasis of the Elizabethan grammar school demonstrably lay in the direction of Shakespeare's own interests, or perhaps it even directed those interests in the direction that they took. As to the school, everyone knows Shakespeare's description of "the whining school-boy . . . creeping like a snail unwillingly to school." But, since few have reflected that he may be no more autobiographical than the soldier and justice who follow him, or may be only part of the story, it is well to state the other side of the case. About Master Jenkins and his usher, or the men who taught Shakespeare in those capacities, we know nothing. But every inference that can be drawn from Shakespeare's work indicates that he actually had unusually good teachers. Where he introduces into his plays sentences that he probably remembered from school, the English version that he used is vigorous, racy, and imaginative. He seems indebted to the most interesting and poetic passages from the Latin authors that were read in part only. He has read some of the best parts of Palingenius rather than passages that a teacher might select if he wished to cram classical commonplaces or astronomy; he knows Book I of Quintilian, which a master interested only in drill on rhetorical theory would skip. Yet he knows his rhetoric, as he knows his Latin authors, so intimately that he uses them easily and richly. He obviously retained far more of what he learned than the modern student recalls from high school. And we are perhaps justified in inferring from his comedy that he had a lot of fun out of the very drudgery of his memory work. Granted that we need much more evidence, what we do have adds up to extremely good teaching—teaching worthy to be rewarded by a really brilliant pupil. If this inference is correct, William Shakespeare may have got from his schoolmaster the interest and encouragement that many a promising schoolboy before and since has received.

CHAPTER III

The Early Chronicle Plays

AN INVESTIGATION of the development of Shakespeare's learning must obviously take as its point of departure his earliest plays, and it must attempt to find out what they show about the intellectual equipment with which he began his career. The preceding chapter has dealt in probabilities. This one should present a sounder factual basis, even though the nature of the material still makes certainty impossible; inferences must necessarily be drawn from the absence of certain ideas or references, and no man is obliged to allude to all that he knows or thinks, least of all a dramatist. But such inferences will be drawn only when the context seems to demand material that is missing, and what Shakespeare does say will always be preferred as better evidence than what he does not say.

There is still no agreement among students as to which were Shakespeare's earliest plays. The only serious claimants, however, are the Henry VI plays, *The Comedy of Errors*, *The Taming of the Shrew*, and *Titus Andronicus*. Of these the three parts of *Henry VI* have most commonly been regarded as Shakespeare's earliest work in so far as they were written by him. Assuming that Alexander has definitely established *2* and *3 Henry VI* as Shakespearean, we shall therefore take them as a point of departure, and to them we shall add *Richard III*, which obviously followed them closely both in content and in time. These three plays were probably written between 1590 and 1592, or perhaps even earlier.[1] The authorship of *1 Henry VI* must still be regarded as doubtful, and its date as in dispute, even as related to *2* and *3*

---

[1] Cf. Chambers, *William Shakespeare*, I, 270; Alexander, *Shakespeare's Life and Art*, pp. 78-79.

Henry VI. It will therefore be excluded from the generalizations to be made, although, whenever relevant, its testimony will be mentioned.

There is, in fact, every reason why Shakespeare should have begun his career by writing chronicle plays dealing with the Wars of the Roses. Plays on English history were popular. He was not a university-trained scholar, and his grammar-school education had included no English history. He would therefore think, naturally and inevitably, of events which were still the most exciting tradition of the area in which he grew up. He turned to the reigns of Henry VI and Richard III as naturally as Douglas Freeman to Robert E. Lee, and for exactly the same reasons. Many exciting incidents of the Wars of the Roses had centered in Warwick and Coventry, in the same county as Stratford-on-Avon, and the final battle of Bosworth Field had been fought only some thirty-five miles away. The oldest inhabitants of Stratford when Shakespeare was born had been children during the reign of Richard III, and not more than one hundred and five years separated Bosworth Field from Shakespeare's first plays. He was therefore only twenty years farther away from it than we are from the Civil War—with the fundamental difference that two world wars had not intervened and all England still shuddered as it remembered the anarchy of the days of Henry VI. A trip through Virginia, where every crossroad suggests its battle and "the war" is still that of 1864, should settle any question why Shakespeare began as he did and remove any temptation to conjecture, with Tillyard, that he first wrote a lost cycle on the early Lancastrian period.[2] He counted, furthermore, upon the same kind of personal interest in his audience, as he shows by his handling of one detail. At the end of *Richard III* the question whether George Stanley will survive Richard's fury is built into an important element of the plot. Doubtless one member of the audience was especially interested in the young man's fate. He was Ferdinando Stanley, Earl of Derby, great-great-grandson of this same George and patron of Shakespeare's company.

[2]*Shakespeare's History Plays*, p. 149. To extend an earlier analogy, Freeman moved from Lee back to Washington just as Shakespeare regressed from *Richard III* to *Henry V*. But earlier versions of the Lancastrian plays have also been conjectured on textual grounds. See ch. vii below.

Shakespeare's chronicle plays were therefore a dramatic treatment of something in which he and his audience had a vivid, personal interest and of which he had some immediate knowledge from local traditions in Stratford. That his interest was not the result of previous study of English history is made clear by the way in which he used his sources.

All four of the plays being considered are based upon Halle's *Union* and upon Holinshed's *Chronicle* in the second edition of 1587.[3] Since the publication of Boswell-Stone's *Shakspere's Holinshed* in 1896, it has been known that Shakespeare was indebted for many of his details to Halle rather than to Holinshed, although much of the time it is impossible to determine which of the two works he used because Holinshed is a close paraphrase or even an outright transcript of Halle. Study of variants in the two works has shown, however, that Shakespeare certainly read both of them carefully for the periods that he was treating in his plays. They, in turn, reproduced for him the content of earlier chronicles and especially of More's *History of Richard III*, which they took over in very large part.

But now we know that Shakespeare was also indebted to Halle for his concept of the entire series of wars as finally leading, by divine providence, to the happy union of England through the marriage of Henry Tudor and Elizabeth, daughter of Edward IV,[4] of which happy union Queen Elizabeth was, in the opinion of her subjects, the fairest issue. This view first emerges clearly in Richard III, and it gives to that play much of its emotional impact. When the Duchess of York and the bereaved queens of Lancaster and York unite in cursing Richard and blessing Richmond, or Richard's victims appear to him and Richmond the night before Bosworth Field, they produce two of the most moving scenes that Shakespeare ever wrote; and they must have stirred his original audience profoundly. To give Halle's theme dramatic life

[3]Page references in the following discussion have been made to conform to those in Boswell-Stone's *Shakspere's Holinshed*, since the copy of Halle consulted (see bibliography) has no page numbers.

[4]This indebtedness was demonstrated by Zeeveld ("Influence of Hall on Shakespeare's English Historical Plays," p. 343) and by C. L. Kingsford in his *English History in the Fifteenth Century and the Historical Plays of Shakespeare* (National Home-Reading Pamphlets, Historical Series, No. 1, 1916), which I have been unable to consult. Tillyard has summarized and amplified the evidence in *Shakespeare's History Plays*, pp. 40-50, 149.

Shakespeare had only to keep Queen Margaret uncowed and in England, both in violation of his sources, and to use the queens and the Duchess of York as a stylized, liturgic chorus.[5]

This interpretation Shakespeare could have obtained very easily from comments scattered throughout Halle and from his title page itself:

The Union of the two noble and illustre famelies of Lancastre & Yorke, beeyng long in continual discension for the croune of this noble realme, with all the actes done in bothe the tymes of the Princes, bothe of the one linage and of the other, beginnyng at the tyme of kyng Henry the fowerth, the first aucthor of this devision, and so successively proceadyng to the reigne of the high and prudent prince kyng Henry the eight, the undubitate flower and very heire of both the sayd linages.[6]

We know that Shakespeare did study Halle's introductory matter very carefully. He quotes a phrase from the table of contents,[7] and, in explaining the claims of the Duke of York to the throne (*2 Henry VI*, II, ii, 38), he prefers the genealogy with which Halle begins his work to that given by Holinshed in the passage upon which the scene is based. Holinshed presents no such unified view of English history.

In addition to Halle and Holinshed, details in the plays have been traced to the chronicles of Harding and Stow,[8] to Fabyan,[9] and to Grafton.[10]

Shakespeare undoubtedly took considerable pains in working up material for the chronicle plays. He might have propped Holinshed's third volume in front of him—if so undignified an expression may be used of so weighty a tome—and set to writing. But clearly he did not do so. He worked through the relevant passages of

[5]See Tillyard's admirable passage on other examples of this patterned element in *Shakespeare's History Plays*, pp. 159-60.

[6]The copy consulted, belonging to the Huntington Library, is dated 1548 on the title page, which has been inserted, and 1550 in the colophon.

[7]Cf. Halle's "The troubleous season of kyng Henry the VI" and "this troublous time," *3 Henry VI*, II, i, 159.

[8]Harding: *1 Henry VI*, III, ii, 95-96 (Arden, ed. H. C. Hart); "possibly" *2 Henry VI*, III, i, 4-8 (Boswell-Stone, *Shakspere's Holinshed*, p. 262); Stow: *2 Henry VI*, II, iv, 17, 77 (Boswell-Stone, op. cit., pp. 261-62).

[9]*2 Henry VI*, I, i, 114, 159; V, i, 83-84 (Boswell-Stone, op. cit., pp. 245, 246, 286-87).

[10]*1 Henry VI*, I, iv, 96 (Arden).

Halle and Holinshed, selecting and rearranging material; and on some points, at least, he consulted other chronicles. Had he already acquired, or was he then acquiring, a general background of English history? His knowledge, and therefore presumably his reading, was wholly limited to the period covered by the plays themselves and perhaps to the reign of Richard II and the early years of Henry IV. This remained true even when he wrote *Richard III*. Several kinds of evidence point to this conclusion.

In the first place, Shakespeare never uses details from other periods of history for illustrative purposes. An allusion to Uther Pendragon occurs in *1 Henry VI* and is therefore suspect. That is all. Yet there are constant classical references. *2 Henry VI* mentions Althaea, Aeolus, Ascanius, Dido, Iris, "Bargulus the strong Illyrian pirate," Julius Caesar, Pompey, Caesar's opinion of Kent (derived from Lily's *Euphues*), Ajax Telemonius, Achilles, Medea, Absyrtus, Aeneas, and Anchises. *3 Henry VI* is even better supplied with worthies from classical history and mythology. Even the Prince's reference to the Tower in *Richard III*, III, i, connects it with Caesar. All these are certainly not surprising in view of Renaissance habits of thought and of Shakespeare's own schooling in Ovid and Virgil. But Shakespeare's contemporaries were also in the habit of seeing in English history "mirrors" of their own problems and misfortunes or precedents for action. If we take Marlowe's *Edward II* for comparison, we reach the first parallel from English history by I, i, 109, as Kent begins: "I do remember, in my father's days." The fact that Shakespeare's characters always find analogies or illustrations in Latin writers and never in English history surely justifies an assumption that he was himself almost completely ignorant of it at the time he wrote these plays.

A second indication of Shakespeare's ignorance of history is to be found in the limited range of material that he uses. The four plays contain only the following seven historical details that do not occur in Halle or Holinshed in the contexts upon which the various scenes are based. In *1 Henry VI* (II, v, 63-91) the dying Mortimer explains to Richard Plantagenet the cause of his father's death. This involves a summary of English history since the deposition of Richard II. Most of the material is derived from the immediate sources of the scene or from Halle's prefatory genealogy. But Shakespeare mentions (1) the rebellion of the Percies against Henry IV and (2) that of the Earl of Cambridge against Henry V, and these details remain unaccounted for, although Holinshed (III, 590) tells that Cambridge was beheaded. (In the next act Bedford has the reference to Uther Pendragon, which must be derived from Harding.[11]) In *2 Henry VI*, II, ii, occurs another genealogy. This is based, for the most part, on Holinshed (III, 656-57). But Halle's genealogy goes: "whiche Roger had issue Edmond Mortimer erle of Marche, Anne and Elienor, which Edmond and Elianor died without issue. And the saied Anne was maried to Richard erle of Cambrige . . ." This sentence is clearly responsible for the line "Roger had issue, Edmund, Anne, and Eleanor" since Holinshed mentions another son. Only three items are not to be found in Halle's genealogy or in the source passages. These are the statements (3) that Richard was murdered at Pomfret "traitorously," (4) that his queen was sent to France (ll. 25-27), and (5) that Edmund Mortimer

> but for Owen Glendower had been king,
> Who kept him in captivity till he died.
> (41-42)

The quarrel between the Lancastrians and the victorious Yorkists in *3 Henry VI*, I, i, produces another historical discussion, of which the only detail not accounted for by the source passages or the genealogical tables mentioned is the information (6) that

> Richard, in the view of many lords,
> Resigned the crown to Henry the Fourth.
> (138-39)

Richard's remark that his new title of Gloucester "is too ominous" (II, vi, 107), which might seem to imply general historical information about other holders of the title, is taken directly from Holinshed (III, 627). (7) There are two references to the execution of Richard II at Pomfret Castle (*2 Henry VI*, II, ii, 26-27; *Richard III*, III, iii, 12); this is not mentioned in the immediate sources. Just before the allusion in *Richard III* Rivers describes the castle as "fatal and ominous to noble peers," which may indicate some additional knowledge of its bloody record but, on the other hand, may simply refer to the present executions. I therefore take

[11] *1 Henry VI*, III, ii, 95 (Arden).

no account of it. The statement that Richard was murdered at Pomfret "traitorously" (Halle, p. 30) indicates that Shakespeare followed the manifesto issued by the Percies at the time of their rebellion mentioned in *1 Henry VI*, II, v, 67-69, rather than Halle's earlier account of the murder. The other six details, including the rebellion of the Percies (Halle, pp. 27-30), suggest that Shakespeare sought additional information on Edmund Mortimer and Richard, Earl of Cambridge, after encountering them in the sentences quoted above from Halle's genealogy. He would have found all the facts mentioned by checking four references to the two men in Halle's indexes to the reigns of Henry IV and Henry V, provided he twice looked at the preceding page to get the context. Richard's abdication immediately precedes allusions to both Edmund and Cambridge in the first paragraph of "The Unquiete Tyme of Kyng Henry the Fourthe." The reference to the queen's being sent back to France occurs in Halle (p. 22) about twenty lines above the words "kept hym with his wife still in captivitee till he died," which Shakespeare misapplies to Edmund Mortimer, whose name occurs in the next sentence.

A final use of material extraneous to the immediate sources remains to be mentioned. Details of Cade's rebellion in *2 Henry VI*, IV, ii and vii, are derived from Holinshed's account of the rising in 1381 during the reign of Richard II.[12] They indicate that Shakespeare also checked in Holinshed.

The centering of these references in genealogical material (or at least in the first thirty pages of Halle) is doubly striking in view of the absence of allusions to other events in the reigns of Henry IV and Henry V, and especially to the wars in France. Apparently Shakespeare's knowledge of Henry V then amounted to the fact that he was a great conqueror and that he died, leaving England to be governed by a child. In general, events in *1 Henry VI*, except for the Yorkist claim to the throne, have no historical background. And this limitation must reflect Shakespeare's own ignorance rather than any fear that he might confuse his audience. The profusion of classical allusions we have already noted. In the later history plays we shall encounter numerous details so poorly assimilated to the context that they cannot be understood without

[12]Cf. Boswell-Stone, op. cit., pp. 271-72, 277-78.

reference to the source; many of these must have been completely baffling to the original spectators.

In *2 Henry VI*, III, ii, there occurs a curious substitution of Nell or Elianor for Meg or Margaret in references to the Queen. Since it happens four times, it cannot be a printer's error. As Chambers points out, it "is odd, and would be odd on any theory of authorship."[13] The simplest explanation is that the error occurred in Shakespeare's autograph, perhaps because a reference to Gloucester recalled the previous scene between Gloucester and "Nell." Yet Margaret is addressed by name in the intervening scene and indulges in considerable biographical detail in the very speech in which two of the *Elianor's* occur. The point is of minor importance, but perhaps worth mentioning because we shall encounter similar slips in *King John*, where they demonstrably result from ignorance of historical detail.

It is only fair to remark that Tillyard draws a directly contrary conclusion as to Shakespeare's knowledge of history. "Throughout the *Henry VI*'s and *Richard III*," he writes, "Shakespeare links the present happenings with the past. We are never allowed to forget that, as Hall said in his preface, 'King Henry the Fourth was the beginning and the root of the great discord and division.'" In support of his statement he cites three of the passages discussed above (*1 Henry VI*, II, v, 63-69; *2 Henry VI*, II, ii, 18-27; *Richard III*, III, iii, 9-14) and, for comparison, two from *Henry V*.[14] I can only reply that I cannot see how the evidence justifies Tillyard's claim. As a check upon my own data, I note that, according to Bartlett's *Concordance*, Henry IV is mentioned once in *1 Henry VI*, once in *2 Henry VI*, three times in *3 Henry VI*, and never in *Richard III*. The only allusion not included in the passages discussed above occurs in *3 Henry VI*, III, iii, 83, as part of a list of English kings.

Shakespeare was, to put it bluntly, profoundly ignorant of English history but a very good novice dramatist. His whole attitude toward history is indicated by the way he handles it in building his plays. He treats his historical sources almost exactly as we shall see him using the sources of his comedies. He is faithful to the main action of the source, but only to the main action. To

---

[13] *William Shakespeare*, I, 286.
[14] *Shakespeare's History Plays*, p. 147.

this narrative he gives life and dramatic effectiveness by restricting it to what he can handle in a play; he develops characters who will make it interesting and plausible, and he selects vivid details to illustrate character or enliven action—preferably to do both at once.

In selecting the material that he could cover in 2 *Henry VI*, Shakespeare took as his unit the period from Margaret's arrival in England in 1445 to the first Yorkist victory at St. Albans in 1455. In doing so, he was perhaps influenced by a passage in Holinshed:

> But most of all it should seeme, that God was displeased with this mariage: for after the confirmation thereof, the kings friends fell from him, both in England and in France, the lords of his realme fell at division, and the commons rebelled in such sort, that finallie after many fields foughten, and manie thousands of men slaine, the king at length was deposed, and his sonne killed. (III, 625)

Margaret arrives at the beginning of the play, and the first main action involves the overthrow of the good Duke Humphrey. Shakespeare may well have chosen this climax because of another passage in Holinshed (III, 627), which he wrote into Gloucester's speech:

> Ah! thus King Henry throws away his crutch
> Before his legs be firm to bear his body.
> Thus is the shepherd beaten from his side
> And wolves are gnarling who shall gnaw thee first.
> Ah, that my fear were false! Ah, that it were!
> For, good Henry, thy decay I fear.
>   (III, i, 189-94)

In building to this climax, Shakespeare rearranged history very freely. To prepare for Gloucester's downfall, he used events that happened four years before Margaret arrived: Gloucester's charges against Winchester and the conviction of the Duchess of Gloucester for sorcery, both of which occurred in 1441. For York's charge that Gloucester

> took bribes of France,
> And, being Protector, stay'd the soldiers' pay,
> By means whereof his Highness hath lost France
>   (III, i, 104-106)

Shakespeare drew upon charges actually laid by the commons against Suffolk during the events represented by III, ii, 242-99.

53

The remaining action, leading to the Battle of St. Albans, handles events with equal freedom. Cade's rebellion is much elaborated, partly, as we have noted, with material from the reign of Richard II. York's rising of 1451 is telescoped with the Battle of St. Albans in 1455 to form one climactic sequence of marching and counter-marching. In 1453, during the years thus eliminated, occurred the death of Talbot, which is the most important event of *1 Henry VI*.

The same method of treating several campaigns as one and eliminating the intervening years is used at the end of both *3 Henry VI* and *Richard III*. In the former Shakespeare has made Edward's capture, escape, and the battles of Barnet and Tewkesbury serve for interchanges involving three flights to France by Edward and two by Warwick. To one reading Holinshed all this scurrying back and forth across the Channel during the years 1469 to 1471 becomes extremely funny; on the stage it might be positively hilarious, and Shakespeare did well to simplify events. In *Richard III* the two risings of 1483 and 1485 are similarly combined, doubtless to avoid undue emphasis upon warfare in a play that had been unified about a single villain hero, perhaps under influence from Marlowe. In fact, *Richard III* is, from his point of view, merely the first of a series of experiments that Shakespeare made in adapting chronicle material to various kinds of dramatic organization, only to confess ultimate failure through the Chorus in *Henry V*.

In developing his characters, Shakespeare is somewhat more faithful to his source. He may accentuate traits, but he rarely invents them to the extent of altering the fundamental pattern. Margaret's character is much developed both to make her more interesting and to round out the chorus of queens in *Richard III*. On the basis of a reference or two in his source (Hol., III, 632) Shakespeare builds an elaborate love affair between her and Suffolk; he adds jealousy of the Duchess of Gloucester to her motives (*2 Henry VI*, I, iii, 78-90); and after the Battle of Barnet, when Halle says (p. 297) that she was dismayed with fear, he makes her boldly encourage her followers with a strong speech based upon one of Horace's odes (*3 Henry VI*, V, iv, 1-49).[15] Her strength and bitterness survive into *Richard III*, in which she is kept in England quite unhistorically. Richard's career is similarly

[15]Book I, xiv. Baldwin, *W. S. Small Latine*, II, 503.

extended, this time forward. He first appears in *2 Henry VI,* V, i, and is already the boldest of York's sons, although historically the scene occurred a good six months before he was born. To heighten his villainy, Shakespeare gives him almost full responsibility for his brother Clarence's death in a way quite at variance with the sources. But Margaret and Richard are merely accentuated and not altered. She has plenty of spirit in Holinshed, which Shakespeare merely protracts. If Richard III appears prematurely, his role as chief assistant to his father is exactly parallel to the relationship that the chronicles show between him and Edward in later battles. Details, even though unhistorical, have been invented to develop a historical character.

The best way to give a plot interest or a character life was to use striking details. For these Shakespeare had an incredibly sharp eye. Provided that he made the right side win in the end, he seldom allowed history to interfere with drama. We have already seen him misapply a striking sentence to make Edmund Mortimer die in prison. In doing so, he disregarded the account of Mortimer's rescue and life at court which occurs in the very passage on the rebellion of the Percies that he demonstrably used. Sometimes he took a minor incident and built it into an important element in his play; sometimes he made a striking episode of a mere hint. In *2 Henry VI* the Duchess of Gloucester's ambition, her use of witchcraft, and her penance are not only moved forward; they are also elaborated into three scenes and part of a fourth. The miracle at St. Albans, derived ultimately from a dialogue by More, is brought in from an extraneous source to illustrate Duke Humphrey's wisdom.[16] Richard's two bishops (*Richard III*, III, vii, 95) come from a mere phrase in Halle; the ghosts who visit Richard and Richmond are derived from Holinshed's remark that Richard, to excuse his low spirits on the morning of Bosworth Field, said that he had dreamed of being "pulled and haled" by devils (Hol., III, 755); and Richard's famous wish for a horse was suggested, apparently, by the prosaic statement that his followers brought him a horse on which to flee (Hol., III, 760).

Shakespeare also exhibited a keen sense of the dramatic or spectacular in choosing between the alternative accounts of a historical

[16]Boswell-Stone, *Shakspere's Holinshed*, pp. 253-55.

event which Halle and Holinshed so frequently offer. He read that Richard II was either murdered while fighting heroically against terrible odds or starved to death. The source regarded starvation as more likely, but Shakespeare preferred the murder, not only because it is more exciting but also because it can be staged more effectively. The same reason dictated his choice among several possible explanations why Warwick abandoned Edward—Warwick's wrath because Edward married Elizabeth while Warwick was negotiating for him a marriage with the Lady Bona. Warwick also mentions in passing one of the alternative explanations—that Edward attempted to seduce one of his wards. Of the contradictory accounts that Richard of York was killed in battle and that he survived to be crowned on a molehill and then murdered, Shakespeare obviously took the more dramatic as well as the one better calculated to reveal the characters of both York and Margaret.

All this is extremely adroit dramaturgy and shows that Shakespeare exhibited skill of a very high order even in writing his earliest plays. The primary purpose of any chronicle dramatist was, of course, to make his plays interesting.[17] Shakespeare was untypical, if at all, in skill rather than in purpose. But we are concerned with an examination of his thought rather than of his dramatic technique, although the two can hardly be separated; and his handling of his sources shows clearly that, in his hierarchy of values, fidelity to the main outline of English history as known to his audience came first, then characters that were interesting and consistent with tradition, and finally lively episodes. Fidelity to historical detail had no place in his scheme of historical drama, nor was it to be found among his contemporaries except in the unknown author of *The Troublesome Raigne*.[18] What Shakespeare did to the history in that play we shall see when we consider *King John*.

The preceding discussion has shown that Shakespeare was relatively indifferent to the chronicler's aim to narrate events in their proper order. An examination of the evidence suggests that he was less indifferent to the philosopher's problem in viewing

[17]Cf. Briggs, *Marlowe's Edward II*, p. lxv.

[18]Cf. ibid., pp. lxv-lxxv, for a discussion of the whole problem of fidelity to history in Elizabethan chronicle plays.

history—to see events in a sequence of cause and effect. To quote W. D. Briggs:

For the Elizabethan the moving forces of history were three in number: Providence, Fortune (whom we meet everywhere in Renaissance literature), and human character. The first two were unfathomable. Whoever tried really to understand a particular historical process would seek his explanation, after making all due allowance for the finger of God and for incalculable chance, in the purposes and qualities of the men concerned. It is not to be supposed that writers of plays should have looked upon history otherwise, especially since, as serious dramatists, character would be almost their chief preoccupation.[19]

This account is obviously sound. But Shakespeare's interpretation of history came almost wholly from his sources, and from them he derived a much fuller attention to the finger of God than Briggs presents as typical. From Halle came the fundamental concept of Henry Tudor's victory at Bosworth as a providential union of the houses of Lancaster and York. But even in Holinshed Shakespeare found a long account of a conference between Buckingham and Bishop Morton of Ely, then his prisoner. Buckingham explained that, "whither it were by the inspiration of the Holie-ghost, or by melancholious disposition, I had diverse and sundrie imaginations how to deprive this unnatural uncle" (III, 739). "But whether God so ordeined, or by fortune it so chanced, while I was in a maze either to conclude suddenlie on this title, & to set it open amongst the common people, or to keepe it secret a while, see the chance: as I rode betweene Worcester and Bridgenorth, I encountered with the ladie Margaret countesse of Richmond" (p. 740). Seeing her reminded him of her son's superior title to the throne. She then suggested marrying her son Henry to the King's daughter to make peace, and this inspired Buckingham with the idea of uniting the two houses by marrying Henry to Elizabeth, daughter of Edward IV. By now he (or the chronicler) rules out the possibility of Fortune: it must be Providence. "I fullie adjudged, that the Holie-ghost caused her to moove a thing ... But such a Lord is God, that with a little sparkle he kindleth a great fire, and (to the admiration of the world) of impossibilities

---

[19]Ibid., pp. xcv-xcvi. Cf. Tillyard, *The Elizabethan World Picture*, p. 48; *Shakespeare's History Plays*, p. 48.

57

he maketh possibilities." Though Shakespeare did not use this conversation dramatically, he undoubtedly read it, and it is typical of a pervasive attitude which sees the hand of God in this period of English history. (The complete passage shows, incidentally, that Holinshed was obviously thinking in terms of the three historical forces mentioned above.) The final chorus of queens (IV, iv, 9-195) is much more than a symbol of the union of Lancastrian and Yorkist hopes in Richmond; it is a religious liturgy, a kind of royal Commination Service, and the Duchess' final curse is the voice of God himself rebuking the sin of one who has falsely boasted himself the Lord's anointed. The stylized pattern of this scene comes from Shakespeare's deliberate artistic purpose to subordinate human personality in the queens, who speak for Providence. Human character in the form of Richard's sinful will encounters Providence, and God inevitably wins—God and England. The scene, like the subsequent appearance of the ghosts, was written for an audience who were Englishmen and Christians, deeply patriotic and sensitive to religious ritual. Nor should we forget that these scenes are the proper outcome of the artistic design that dominates the structure of the entire play. From the first line there is only one real character in the play, and Richard's Machiavellian will arranges and controls everything. Nothing is left to chance, and before Richard any other human will seems powerless. The Duchess makes the situation explicit when she says to Dorset: "Go thou to Richmond [in Brittany], and good fortune guide thee"; but to Anne: "Go thou to Richard, and good angels tend thee" (IV, i, 92-93). Only God and his angels can save England from Richard, and they do.

In fact, Providence in the form of divine retribution is omnipresent throughout the plays from *2 Henry VI* on, as it was in their sources. The original usurpation of Henry IV is the ultimate source of conflict, although I must insist that this theme is not stressed in these plays as it is in the later Lancastrian series. But the murder of Gloucester also sets in motion a chain of crime and retribution for crime that dominates the remaining plays, the emphasis upon this subsidiary chain of causation being, of course, inevitable because the four early chronicle plays are themselves a self-contained unit. This relationship between sin and retribution is indicated, both in the sources and in Shakespeare, by the almost monotonous regularity with which the murdered and the executed curse and recall the curses of others. His mother's final curse of Richard is merely the climax, because it is the most dreadful and unnatural, of a long series. A cynic might remark that, on this principle of delayed retribution for sin, it would be easy to account for almost any downfall in a period so perjured and so murderous. But Halle, and therefore Holinshed and Shakespeare, took Providence seriously and found ample evidence to confirm their belief.

Though Providence was responsible for the main design of the conflict, and especially for its happy outcome, the numerous battles gave Fortune ample opportunity; and Shakespeare mentions her constantly, several times complete with her wheel. The chronicles laid especial stress upon Edward's luck, and Holinshed has a long passage upon the uncertain issue of the Battle of Barnet and the way in which fortune favored Edward (III, 684-85). It is therefore no accident that *3 Henry VI* has as many references of one kind and another to fortune as *2 Henry VI* and *Richard III* combined, and that Edward's first words after Barnet are "Thus far our fortune keeps an upward course" (V, iii, 1). Toward the end of *Richard III*, however, Fortune disappears as Providence takes full control. Margaret quotes a former reference to Fortune to correct it (I, iii, 241; IV, iv, 82), but neither the united queens nor the ghosts refer to it as they pronounce Richard's doom. They speak only of God's just ordinance, of the prayers of the innocent, and of the good angels who watch over men.

Logically, of course, Fortune had little place in the Christian scheme of things. The operation of contingent causes might seem fortuitous, and man's freedom of choice introduced a minor element of chance. But what man in his ignorance called Fortune would normally be the inscrutable operation of Providence or of universal laws which govern man and non-human nature alike. In Shakespeare, however, there is as yet no trace of this level of philosophic sophistication.

Shakespeare's treatment of character as a historical force is so obvious that little need be said. "To say that he interpreted history is simply to say that he converted historical abstractions into living human beings."[20] Sir Lucy laments in words of fierce

[20]Briggs, op. cit., pp. cxiii-cxiv.

59

indignation that Talbot should be sacrificed to the "worthless emulation" and "private discord" of York and Somerset (*1 Henry VI*, IV, iv, 13-28), and in his comments upon the criminal folly of high-placed men he seems almost a preliminary study for the Bastard in *King John*. He suggests, in fact, that Shakespeare may already have been familiar with *The Troublesome Raigne*, from which the Bastard's characterization is lifted in its entirety. Winchester's haughty pride, Gloucester's choler, Margaret's proud ambition, Henry's pious weakness, Edward's lust, and Richard's evil strength and cunning are important forces shaping events in Shakespeare, as in his sources, and the reader or spectator remembers them long after details of action are forgotten.

In all these concepts Shakespeare merely bettered in emphasis and vividness of detail what he found in his sources. In one respect, he is definitely inferior to them in his concept of historical causation, and that is in exactly the realm of mundane political forces with which a modern historian would be concerned. Halle and Holinshed are, of course, without any notion of economic forces, even though they duly record the slogans and actions which a modern historian would use to demonstrate that such forces were at work. For them Cade's rebellion is simply a Yorkist plot. But the chroniclers do analyze political developments in some detail, Halle much more fully than Holinshed; and their concern with the scheming of great men is a logical result of their view of human character as a moving force in history. They explain carefully the complex motives underlying the quarrel between Humphrey of Gloucester and Cardinal Beaufort of Winchester; Shakespeare restricts the cause to the purely personal traits which he finds in the sources. They give a credible explanation why the Lancastrians released the Duke of York after his first rising. His sons were approaching with an army, and Henry's advisers did not want, by fighting them, to lose a chance to recover Aquitaine, where a number of leaders had offered to rebel in favor of England. Shakespeare merely has the sons arrive with their forces in one of his feeblest scenes (*2 Henry VI*, V, i). Richard mentions vaguely his nurturing of friction as a means to advance himself (*Richard III*, I, i, 32-35), but Shakespeare's readers hardly suspect the strong alignment into two parties that made Richard's intrigues so much simpler historically than they seem in the play and explained why men who were not fundamentally wicked would aid him. The result is to ground the entire explanation of events in Richard's own character. Shakespeare does present some scheming. But, in disregarding so many political motives in his sources, he seems not so much uncomprehending as uninterested, and one can only infer that he lacked the experience of the world necessary to develop an appreciation of political intrigue. Doubtless, too, he found it easier to characterize by creating a strong impression in a single scene than by tracing motives through several scenes.

Shakespeare's preoccupation with what might be called philosophical as opposed to political explanations of history—with Fortune and Providence rather than with intrigue—may be assigned to obvious reasons. It is, however, thoroughly consistent with a bent of mind that we shall find revealing itself in his great tragedies and is perhaps the first manifestation of it.

So far we have been concerned with Shakespeare's attitude toward his historical sources and his understanding of history itself. It is also possible to derive from the early chronicle plays some notion of the general range of his learning, in so far, at least, as it is revealed by allusions or even passages expressing contemporary ideas. The learning indicated agrees remarkably well with the inferences derived in the last chapter from his probable schooling.

Shakespeare uses the Bible so constantly that he must have known a large part of it intimately. In checking, I have taken Noble's collection of references as a basis,[21] but I have omitted multiple references to the same phrase and included a few from other sources. There are, on an average, several allusions in each scene. Apparently Shakespeare was most familiar with Matthew, the Psalms, and Luke, to which he alludes in that order of frequency in 2 and 3 *Henry VI* and *Richard III* (12, 10, 8 respectively), although Noble says that, throughout his plays, he quoted from the Psalms more often than from any other book.[22] Next comes II Samuel, largely because it furnished the key texts on the concept of the king as the "Lord's anointed." Genesis, Numbers, Proverbs, Ecclesiasticus, Isaiah, Daniel, Ezekiel, and Mark show

[21]*Shakespeare's Biblical Knowledge*, pp. 120-38.
[22]Ibid., p. 76.

more than one reference each. There are no echoes of the minor prophets or, surprisingly, of Acts and Revelation. Only Ecclesiasticus, Wisdom, and Judith occur among the Apocryphal books, and only Romans, II Corinthians, Ephesians, I Timothy, and I Peter among the epistles. There are also several references to the Catechism and to the version of the Ten Commandments used in the Catechism and Communion service, as well as scattered allusions to other services in the Book of Common Prayer.

Shakespeare's use of Biblical references apparently reveals more about his dramatic technique than about his religious views. Indeed, it shows nothing about the latter except that he knew and accepted the Book of Common Prayer. Striking phrases or ideas from the Bible or Prayer Book may occur anywhere in his plays, of course, but they tend to cluster about certain characters or situations where they serve an obvious dramatic purpose. Henry VI quotes Scripture continually as a natural outcome of—and therefore a good device for indicating—his unworldly piety. But Richard III is just as given to Biblical allusions, and they are probably the subtlest of the devices by which Shakespeare builds his character, for they make him seem possessed of all the learning of the virtuous but able to turn that learning to his own purposes. The Machiavel was expected to use religion to serve his own ends, and there is a triumphant self-assurance and cynicism about Richard's habit of employing Scriptural phrases that would be just right if only he meant them. Sometimes, too, they are instruments of the dramatic irony in which *Richard III* abounds. So Richard draws upon II Samuel (xvi, 5-14 and xix, 21) when he replies to the curses of the queens:

> A flourish, trumpets! strike alarum, drums!
> Let not the heavens hear these tell-tale women
> Rail on the Lord's anointed.
>
> (IV, iv, 148-50)

No other character approaches Henry and Richard in number of Scriptural allusions. But scenes of death inevitably lead to them, the most striking example being Clarence's murder (*Richard III*, I, iv). Not only does Clarence argue for his life with an abundance of theological and Biblical learning, but, in outrageous defiance of decorum, the murderers are quite as learned in the Scriptures and the Prayer Book as he is. The result is a very witty argument on the propriety of their killing him, but hardly a convincing murder.

Finally, like Shakespeare's figures of speech and his allusions to classical poets, his Scriptural references tend to come in clusters, one leading to another. Consequently, the presence of Henry or especially of Richard may lead to an exceptional flow of Biblical allusions from a character not normally given to them. In fact, in *Richard III*, I, ii, Anne betters Richard by a comfortable margin. This scene, incidentally, contains a phrasing in which Shakespeare may have influenced the Authorized Version. The Quarto, though not the Folio, reads: "The fitter for the King of heaven, that hath him" (I, ii, 105). All previous versions of Luke ix, 62, had read "apt to the kingdom of God," but the Authorized has "fit for the kingdom of God."[23]

The plays under discussion also offer abundant proof that Shakespeare had read the secular authors normally employed in petty and grammar schools. Clarence alludes to the horn book when he says that Edward "from the cross row plucks the letter G" (*Richard III*, I, i, 55); in the same play Queen Margaret turns the practice of declining nouns to account (IV, iv, 97), and Cade charges Lord Say with having about him men "that usually talk of a noun and a verb" (*2 Henry VI*, IV, vii, 42); and Shakespeare is not above introducing a half dozen tags of Latin and even one anglicized Greek form (*cacodemon, Richard III*, I, iii, 144). He also has several allusions to Aesop's fables and a comparison of Richard of Gloucester's deformity to Aesop's (*3 Henry VI*, V, v, 25). Baldwin has noted the influence of Susenbrotus in the phrase "bitter taunts" or "bitter scoffs" which Shakespeare several times uses to describe sarcasm and in his borrowing of "catch each other by the throat" from the discussion of allegory,[24] although this expression is certainly not beyond his unaided powers of invention. Baldwin also sees in the Scrivener's line of thought (*Richard III*, III, vi), and especially in his "mark how well the sequel hangs together," an indication that he is following Aphthonius' signs of confirmation, of which *coherence* is one, as he

[23]Ibid., p. 132. The known popularity of *Richard III* might well justify an editor in printing the Quarto text on the assumption that the Folio "better" was a misprint and the Quarto preserved the stage text that influenced the Authorized Version.

[24]W. S. *Small Latine*, II, 143-45.

reasons that he has in his hand obvious proof that Hastings' murder was planned long before the alleged treason.[25]

Much more striking are Shakespeare's continual classical allusions. Some are simple references to customs such as the triumphal chariot (*2 Henry VI*, II, iv, 13, etc.) or to mythology—a "vulture of sedition feeds in the bosom of such great commanders" (*1 Henry VI*, IV, iii, 47-48). At the other extreme are quotations in Latin from Virgil's *Aeneid* and Ovid's *Heroides* (*2 Henry VI*, II, i, 23-24; *3 Henry VI*, I, iii, 48) or considerable passages based upon Latin writers. The derivation from Horace of Margaret's speech in *3 Henry VI*, V, iii, the most extreme example of this practice, has already been mentioned. Iden's meditation on rural life (*2 Henry VI*, IV, x, 18-25) sounds to me like a recollection of an epigram of Martial's (X, 47) translated by many English poets, the first version being Surrey's "Martial, the things that do attain." The borrowing, if present, does not prove knowledge of Martial's Latin. Shakespeare perhaps added an echo of the Magnificat's "He hath filled the hungry with good things and the rich he hath sent empty away."

These allusions or echoes are distributed just about evenly among the four plays, and it is significant that *1 Henry VI*, where a more learned collaborator has often been suspected, has no more than *3 Henry VI*—sixteen each by my count, as against thirteen for *2 Henry VI* and fourteen for *Richard III*. (Such figures are obviously meaningless because they depend so largely upon the basis of the count; provided the same person does the counting, comparisons are much more meaningful than the figures themselves.) The apparent reference in *1 Henry VI*, I, v, 21, to Hannibal's trick of frightening the Romans by attaching burning twigs to oxen's horns may involve a knowledge of Livy (XXII, 16)[26] which is not paralleled in the other three plays, but Shakespeare could easily have picked up the information at second hand. Otherwise the references in the three parts of *Henry VI* follow much the same pattern. Over half the identifiable sources are in Ovid, most commonly in the *Metamorphoses*, but also in the *Heroides* and *Tristia*. A considerable number also come from

[25]Ibid., p. 327.
[26]Arden ed.

64

Virgil's *Aeneid* and from Horace, and one has been traced to Juvenal.

In view of Shakespeare's subsequent use of Plutarch, it is most interesting that the reference to the deaths of Tully, Caesar, and Pompey in *2 Henry VI*, IV, i, 135-38, is probably derived from North's *Plutarch*, which was published in 1579. "Brutus' bastard hand stabb'd Julius Caesar" looks as though Shakespeare had been reading the life of Brutus, which contains a reference to all three deaths as well as the gossip that Caesar was Brutus' real father. The inaccurate statement that Pompey was killed by "savage islanders" also suggests that Shakespeare was relying on the general statement in this life rather than on the detailed account of Pompey's death in the life of Caesar. There is no indication what caused his interest in Brutus at this time, unless possibly he may have been looking for a classical example of the murder of a ruler.

Richard III presents an altogether different situation, which makes it very likely that Shakespeare had read several of Seneca's plays in preparation for it. Baldwin concludes that Shakespeare "is not likely to have read Seneca himself in grammar school,"[27] and his view is certainly confirmed by the absence of Senecan echoes in *1* and *2 Henry VI*. But they are common in *Richard III*. Since it has recently been the fashion to minimize Seneca's influence upon Shakespeare, the evidence is worth surveying. Many of Cunliffe's parallels between Seneca and Shakespeare are so general that they probably do not prove direct borrowing, but it is significant that his examples become very much more numerous and somewhat more convincing in *3 Henry VI*. In fact, he comments "that *Henry VI* (especially Part iii) and *Richard III* have much in common with Seneca."[28] The echoes in *3 Henry VI* also involve the same plays that Shakespeare has been shown by

[27] *W. S. Small Latine*, II, 560. But Baldwin's preceding statement is simply inexplicable, unless it reflects a current scholarly fashion of minimizing Seneca's influence: "We thus have no indication that Shakspere read Seneca's plays in the original. Nor do I find any evidence worth repeating that Shakspere had read English Seneca." Surely the quotation of Seneca in Latin in a play in the First Folio is some indication, however slight.

[28] Cf. *The Influence of Seneca on Elizabethan Tragedy*, pp. 72-79, especially 73. But *3 Henry VI*, II, v, 1-12, which Cunliffe compares with Agamemnon 139-41, is derived from a hint in Halle, p. 256: "This deadly battayle and bloudy conflicte continued .x. houres in doubtful victorie, the one parte some tyme flowying, and sometyme ebbyng."

various scholars to have used in writing *Richard III*. Richard's wooing of Anne (I, ii) and of Elizabeth for her daughter (IV, iv) presents striking analogues to Lycus' wooing of Megara in the *Hercules Furens* (329-523), and another German student has found a parallel, which does not seem to me convincing, between Richard's claiming credit for sending Prince Edward to heaven and Megara's pointing out that Hercules' downfall has led to better things.[29] When Richard offers either to let Anne kill him or to kill himself if she bids him (I, ii, 174-92), he may parallel two of Phaedra's speeches, her statement to Hippolytus "I would not hesitate to offer my breast to naked swords," and her later promise to his corpse "With this hand will I make amends to thee, in my wicked heart will I thrust the sword and set Phaedra free equally from life and crime."[30] This parallel, not too convincing as just stated, becomes a certainty when we note in *Titus Andronicus* garbled quotations in Latin of lines from these same two contexts in the *Phaedra*. It should be remarked, however, that Thomas Legge's Latin play *Richardus Tertius* made the same combination of the two passages when Richard woos the Princess Elizabeth.[31] The third citizen's echo of Seneca's *Thyestes* (II, iii, 42-44) comes, as Baldwin has pointed out,[32] not directly from the Latin but from Holinshed, who took it from More, who perhaps took it from Seneca; it serves, therefore, as an excellent example of the way in which bits of the classics circulated among Renaissance writers; Richard's paraphrase of a famous *sententia* from the *Agamemnon* may belong in the same category:

> But I am in
> So far in blood that sin will pluck on sin!
> (IV, ii, 64-65)[33]

On the other hand, a reference to Medea's murder of Creusa (IV, i, 59-62), which has apparently escaped notice, is clearly derived from Seneca, since Ovid does not mention in either of his accounts

[29]Wilhelm, "Zu Seneca und Shakespeare ('Richard III')," p. 69; Vatke, "Shakespeare und Euripides. Eine Parallele," p. 67.

[30]*Phaedra*, ll. 616, 1176-77, trans. Miller.

[31]Cf. *Titus Andronicus*, II, i, 135, and *Phaedra*, 1180; *Titus*, IV, i, 81-82, and *Phaedra*, 671-72, also Boas, *University Drama in the Tudor Age*, pp. 126-31.

[32]*W. S. Small Latine*, II, 553-55.

[33]But cf. Johnson, "Shakespearian Imagery and Senecan Imitation," pp. 50-52.

of Medea both the fiery gold crown and the poisoned robe to which Shakespeare alludes.[34] Finally, the last lament of the queens (IV, iv, 1-135) is very similar to Seneca's scene of Helena, Andromache, and Hecuba in the *Troades* (861-998); and Cunliffe also compares the Duchess' words:

> Alas, I am the mother of these griefs!
> Their woes are parcell'd, mine is general
> (II, ii, 80-81)

with Seneca's: "Whosesoever woes thou weepest, thou wilt weep mine. Each feels the weight of his own disaster only, but I the disasters of them all" (*Troades*, 1060-61).[35]

In addition to these verbal echoes, three elements of Seneca's technique are especially prominent in *Richard III*: the appearance of ghosts, the soliloquy in which the villain reveals his motives and plans, and the use of stichomythia. Of these the ghosts are an omnipresent part of Elizabethan drama and have no standing whatever as evidence of Seneca's influence. The soliloquy is characteristic of the Machiavel or the villain hero wherever he appears, and Shakespeare gives the Duke of York a fine example of it (*2 Henry VI*, I, i, 214-59). Richard himself has several in *3 Henry VI* (III, ii, 124-95; V, vi, 68-93). But stichomythia, in the true classical form involving not only line-by-line dialogue but also some witty interplay of thought from line to line, first becomes prominent only in *3 Henry VI* in the scene in which Edward woos Lady Grey (III, ii), although examples occur elsewhere in the play. It is, of course, omnipresent in *Richard III*. Its appearance in *3 Henry VI*, as Shakespeare develops fully the character of Richard that will dominate the next play and as he begins to echo Seneca, suggests that it may result from his study of Seneca, if I am right in assuming that he worked through at least the *Hercules Furens, Phaedra, Medea,* and *Troades* in preparation for *Richard III*. Stichomythia is also common in *The Comedy of Errors*, which dates from the same period as *Richard III*, although there it may well reflect Latin comedy. Its relative absence in

---

[34]Cf. Seneca, *Medea*, ll. 573-74, 817-39; Ovid, *Metamorphoses*, VII, 394, *Heroides*, XII, 180-82.

[35]Cf. Koeppel, "Shakespeares 'Richard III' und Senecas 'Troades,'" pp. 188-90; Cunliffe, *The Influence of Seneca on Elizabethan Tragedy*, p. 79.

1 Henry VI would therefore suggest that this play preceded *2* and *3 Henry VI* and did not come between them and *Richard III* as some critics have thought.

To return to *Richard III* and Shakespeare's classical scholarship, it contains typical echoes of Horace and Virgil and, in addition, an interesting parallel between its four opening lines and Claudian's *De Bello Gothico* (151-53) which is hard to account for.[36]

Two lines of French (*1 Henry VI*, III, ii, 14; *2 Henry VI*, V, ii, 28) could easily have been supplied by someone else if Shakespeare wanted them for atmosphere, or Shakespeare may have been learning French, which he seems to have known by the time he wrote *Henry V*. But a number of allusions that have been traced to contemporary writers are interesting for the hints that they give of the direction of Shakespeare's interests. Unfortunately three of them, including the most likely reference to Spenser and the only probable reference to Greene, occur in one short scene of *1 Henry VI* (I, vi). We cannot be certain in attributing them to Shakespeare, especially since they occur in one of the scenes which Chambers lists as non-Shakespearean.[37] The allusion to the Garden of Adonis (I, vi, 6) might come from other writers, but the *Faerie Queene* (III, vi) was certainly the most accessible source; and Greene's *Mamillia* was similarly the most available place to find Rhodope of Memphis (22). In the same scene Astraea (4) is from Ovid's *Metamorphoses*, I, 150 (the line, incidentally, is quoted in Latin in *Titus Andronicus*, IV, iii, 4), and the "rich-jewell'd coffer of Darius" is from Puttenham's *Arte of English Poesie*.[38] Puttenham is also responsible for items in *2* and *3 Henry VI*[39] and is, with Lyly and Marlowe, Shakespeare's favorite among contemporary writers. His use suggests that Shakespeare was studying the theory of poetry, just as echoes of Marlowe[40] show his interest in its practice. Several allusions to Lyly are so definite as to admit of no doubt. When Shakespeare writes: "Drones suck not eagles' blood, but rob beehives," he

<hr>

[36]Krappe, "Shakespeare Notes," p. 174.

[37]*William Shakespeare*, I, 290-91.

[38]Arden ed.

[39]*2 Henry VI*, I, iv, 62; *3 Henry VI*, V, vi, 10.

[40]*2 Henry VI*, III, iii, 19; *1 Tamburlaine* 1452. *Richard III*, V, iii, 79, 351; *1 Tamburlaine* 596.

is hitting at a fantastic perversion of Aesop in Lyly's *Endimion*.[41] Lyly's *Euphues* supplies Caesar's opinion of Kent (*2 Henry VI*, IV, vii, 65-66), and there is a fairly clear echo of *Campaspe* (II, ii, 35 ff.) in *Richard III* (I, i, 7-8). Parallels to Spenser and other writers have been cited, but they are so inconclusive and so likely merely to indicate contemporary fashions in speech that they had better be ignored.

There is one other passage in these early plays that indicates more clearly than outright references that Shakespeare was becoming acquainted with contemporary literature. That is Richard's wooing of Anne. His "line" in this extraordinary scene is simply that Anne is a "divine perfection of a woman" who has driven him to murder that he might possess her. After suggesting that they "leave this keen encounter of our wits" (I, ii, 115) and speak more seriously, he proceeds to argue with every appearance of sincerity:

> Your beauty was the cause of that effect;
> Your beauty, that did haunt me in my sleep
> To undertake the death of all the world
> So I might live one hour in your sweet bosom.
>
> (121-24)

This rests, of course, upon the notion of beauty as the cause of love which the Elizabethans inherited, through various channels, from Platonism. But it is also a logical inference from the medieval code of courtly love. If the lover expected to serve and suffer for a season, he also expected to be rewarded in the end, and the code, at least as it appeared in medieval romance, was one of fidelity in adultery.[42] If the lady was responsible for all the lover's agony, she must accept her responsibility and make proper amends. The conclusion that the lady shared her lover's guilt in any crime to which he might be driven was, in fact, accepted and appears in medieval romances. The Renaissance moralized the code by making marriage the end of the lover's quest.[43] But

[41]*2 Henry VI*, IV, i, 109; *Endimion*, V, i, 129-34. Cf. Crundell, "Shakespeare, Lyly, and 'Aesop'," p. 312.

[42]Lewis, *The Allegory of Love*, p. 13. For a discussion of the important part played by the code of love in Shakespeare the writer is indebted to an unpublished paper by Professor Margery Bailey.

[43]Lewis, op. cit., pp. 197, 237, 242, etc.

the husband was a far more invincible barrier to marriage than to adultery, and the lady's responsibility might logically be extended to include the steps necessary to get him out of the way. So Richard argues, and it is to Love, the omnipotent god alike of the Court of Love and of the sonneteers, that he appeals. Anne yields, though doubtfully and somewhat reluctantly, to his arguments, and, as if to relate the surrender to old poetic tradition, she and Richard break into iambic trimeters that suggest, in her arch retorts, a poetic game of love. Similarly Romeo and Juliet begin their love in a formal sonnet (I, v, 95-108). We overlook the speed of their wooing because it is placed in the high tradition of poetry; Shakespeare apparently expected the same atmosphere to cover the improbability of Richard's conquest.

This use of the classics and of a few contemporary writers was doubly important because, aside from literature, Shakespeare's command of the learning of his day was still very slight indeed, far inferior both in range and in accuracy to the information displayed in his later works. He knew religious doctrine, to which he had been introduced in grammar school. Otherwise the allusions to natural history, science, and philosophy are wholly on the level of popular information (or misinformation), in some respects below the level of what he might well have learned in grammar school.

A most important part of Shakespeare's poetry came with him from Stratford in his knowledge of the country. From rural life, as Spurgeon has shown, he drew a large part of his imagery. His familiarity with coursing falcons and herding sheep also supplied major parts of two scenes (*2 Henry VI*, II, i; *3 Henry VI*, II, v, 30-54). Such material was an important part of the store of information which he used to supplement his sources in achieving the illusion of active life which drama demanded.

To the natural history of the times Shakespeare has a few references that do not derive from his own experience. They are mostly to the unnatural lore that is likely, somewhat unfairly, to be the modern reader's dominant impression of Elizabethan natural science. One encounters such material in medieval works like Bartholomaeus Anglicus' *De Proprietatibus Rerum* (which was republished in the Elizabethan period with additions drawn mostly from Cooper's *Thesaurus*), in contemporary encyclopedic productions such as Du Bartas' *Sepmaine* or Pierre de la Primaudaye's *Frenche Academie*,[44] and in numerous slighter books. It also circulated in popular literature and doubtless in popular speech. Shakespeare alludes frequently to the supposed habits of the lion as king of beasts and almost as frequently to the basilisk. He knows that the phoenix is reborn from fire (*3 Henry VI*, I, iv, 35), that the mandrake has wonderful properties derived from its resemblance to man (*2 Henry VI*, III, ii, 310), that the ostrich eats iron (*2 Henry VI*, IV, x, 30), and that the bear licks her cubs into shape (*3 Henry VI*, III, ii, 161). But these details were as much folklore as science, and he could have picked them up anywhere.

Of astronomy, as then understood, one passage in *1 Henry VI* shows a surprising knowledge:

> Mars his true moving, even as in the heavens
> So in the earth, to this day is not known.
>
> (I, ii, 1-2)

But this scene is not among those ordinarily assigned to Shakespeare, and the reference cannot be accepted as evidence of his knowledge unless we insist that he wrote the entire play.[45] It is, in fact, so completely out of line with the knowledge elsewhere displayed that I should regard it as evidence that the scene is not Shakespeare's.

Richard III shows the common knowledge of the influence of the "watery moon" upon the tides (II, ii, 69). The reference to God as "the eternal Mover of the heavens" (*2 Henry VI*, III, iii, 19) is a resounding dramatic tag which can be paralleled in Marlowe's *Tamburlaine* and in *Selimus*.[46] Otherwise Shakespeare's references are astrological rather than astronomical. To the Elizabethans the former was as good science as the latter; in fact, the distinction being made was foreign to their thought. But Shakespeare nowhere gives any evidence of understanding "scientific" as opposed to folk astrology. The first scene of *1 Henry VI*, one of those more likely to be Shakespearean,[47] opens with an astrological reference:

[44]Du Bartas was translated by Joshua Sylvester as *Bartas: His Devine Weekes and Workes*, 1605; La Primaudaye was published in English from 1586 to 1618.
[45]Cf. Chambers, *William Shakespeare*, I, 290-91.
[46]*1 Tamburlaine* 1452; *Selimus* 1440 (Arden ed.).
[47]Chambers, *William Shakespeare*, I, 290-91.

Hung be the heavens with black, yield day to night!
Comets, importing change of times and states,
Brandish your crystal tresses in the sky,
And with them scourge the bad revolting stars
That have consented unto Henry's death! ...
What! shall we curse the planets of mishap
That plotted thus our glory's overthrow?
Or shall we think the subtle-witted French
Conjurers and sorcerers, that afraid of him
By magic verses have contriv'd his end?

(I, i, 1-5, 23-27)

Later in the same play Talbot refers to "malignant and ill-boding stars" (IV, v, 6). Richard III professes his honesty by invoking "all planets of good luck" to "be opposite" if he break faith (IV, iv, 402). The first of these references—and the point is worth emphasizing because Tillyard reads an elaborate philosophic meaning into the passage[48]— places the "planets of mishap" on precisely the same level of rhetorical emphasis and decoration as "conjurers and sorcerers" and the "thread of life" (l. 34) or the "glorious star" which, according to Ovid,[49] was the final state of Julius Caesar (11. 55-56). In Shakespeare's later plays references to the influence of the stars are based on an accurate knowledge of the principle that the stars incline but they do not compel, and the speaker's view of the stars can be interpreted in the light of that principle as an indication of his own character. The attitudes of Gloucester and Edmund present a clear contrast between muddle-headed sensuality and thoroughly intelligent, although villainous, opportunism (*Lear*, I, ii, 112-45). But the frame of reference in which Edmund speaks is completely absent from the allusions to the stars in these early plays.

The same thing is probably true of Shakespeare's use of the supernatural. Demonology was an important and respectable branch of learning, despite its undoubted perils, and Shakespeare was later to show himself reasonably familiar with it. The ghosts twice invoke good angels to fight on Richard's side (*Richard III*, V, iii, 156, 175), and it is possible that Shakespeare intends a technical implication that these apparitions are "good" rather than fallen angels or demons; but, in view of the Duchess' previous prayer that good angels may protect Anne from Richard (IV, i,

[48]*Shakespeare's History Plays*, p. 150.   [49]*Metamorphoses*, XV, 840-51.

93), it is more likely that here, too, Shakespeare is thinking of guardian angels, such as Marlowe used in *Faustus*. Although certainly not at variance with the theology of the times, these are on the level of popular rather than learned allusion. On the same level are other demons, such as the Pucelle's old familiar (*1 Henry VI*, III, ii, 122) and the "busy meddling fiend that lays strong siege" upon Cardinal Beaufort's soul (*2 Henry VI*, III, iii, 21-22), or the comparisons between Richard III and the Devil.

The same observation can be made with respect to the Renaissance fusion of psychology and physiology. Allusions are predominantly popular with some evidence of knowledge at a more advanced level. The humors blood, choler, and melancholy (though apparently not phlegm) are referred to frequently, but not technically. Blood is a concomitant of battle, melancholy is a state of mind, and choler is simply a synonym for anger. Nowhere does Shakespeare so clearly imply the physiological concept of the humors as he does in the following lines from *King John*, for example:

> Or if that surly spirit, melancholy,
> Had bak'd thy blood and made it heavy, thick.
>
> (III, iii, 42-43)

But saying, even by metaphor, that melancholy, a cold and dry humor, baked the blood, which was hot and moist, suggests that Shakespeare still was not really at home in this system of learning, which organized the four elements and their compounds, including the humors, according to the possible combinations of the four contrasted qualities hot and cold, moist and dry. Two references in *3 Henry VI* indicate a similar familiarity with the principle, but uncertainty as to its detailed application. Richard says:

> I cannot weep, for all my body's moisture
> Scarce serves to quench my furnace-burning heart:
> Nor can my tongue unload my heart's great burden,
> For self-same wind that I should speak withal
> Is kindling coals that fires all my breast,
> And burns me up with flames that tears would quench.
>
> (II, i, 79-84)

Richard has in mind, quite correctly according to Elizabethan theory, that the proper function of the lungs is to cool the heart with the air breathed in, which his words will make fiery; but

73

it is much harder to explain the first two lines in terms of technical concepts, or to justify the implied comparison to putting out a fire with water. Shakespeare reverts to a similar figure later in the same scene when Warwick suggests that "the coldness of the king" "robb'd my soldiers of their heated spleen" (ll. 122, 124), identifying accurately the function of the spleen in producing choler. Shakespeare, in short, has acquired some familiarity with these concepts, but he obviously does not possess the easy knowledge that underlies the frequent and technically accurate psychological references of his later plays.

Shakespeare's ignorance was, perhaps, from the modern point of view an advantage. Richard's elaborate analysis of his own character in the opening soliloquy of *Richard III* involves none of the formal psychology of the day. It is apparently based upon the sound observation of human nature at which Shakespeare and his contemporaries were adept. But it seems to the present-day reader much more convincing than, for example, Enobarbus' technical explanation of Antony's conduct, which makes full use of passion psychology.[50]

We have noted that Shakespeare seems to have been very much interested in those passages in his sources which located historical causes in God, chance, or human character, but less concerned to reproduce in his plays accounts of political motives or intrigue. An examination of his plays for evidence of contemporary political ideas suggests that his knowledge of them was still rudimentary, but developing. The absence of political thought from Henry VI's meditation, and particularly from the famous speech during the Battle of Towton (*3 Henry VI*, II, v, 1-54), obviously shows nothing as to Shakespeare's own interests. He has been at pains to portray Henry as unworldly and unpolitical, an impractical saint at the head of a kingdom. This speech, like others given to Henry, is thoroughly in character. More significant is Shakespeare's handling of the ideas that do appear.

Richard II embodies Shakespeare's fullest treatment of the concept of the divine right of kings and will require an extended

---

[50]Tillyard has a pertinent and interesting passage on the danger of assuming that the Elizabethans were incapable of first-hand observation of human conduct because they used the formal psychology of their day (*Shakespeare's History Plays*, p. 280).

consideration of it. There are, however, enough references in these plays to show that Shakespeare already knew and accepted it. It does not occur in his sources, and his ideas very probably came from the Homilies.[51] Hart has done students of Shakespeare a real service in pointing out the importance of these pronouncements as sources of Shakespeare's thought. They stated the Government's position on religious doctrine and political theory, and they were read in rotation at church services. There is no question that Shakespeare knew them thoroughly. The absence of allusions to divine right from *1 Henry VI* perhaps results from the nature of the action or perhaps is related to the problem of authorship. In *2 Henry VI* Henry speaks of himself as the Lord's "unworthy deputy" (III, ii, 286) and stresses the sacredness of the oath of allegiance (V, i, 179-81). Reference to the anointing of the king, upon which Richard II lays such stress, first occurs in *3 Henry VI*, in a line prophetic of the great deposition scene: "Thy [Henry's] balm wash'd off wherewith thou was anointed" (III, i, 17). Later in the same play Margaret refers to Henry as "England's true-anointed lawful king" (III, iii, 29). But Richard's description of himself as "the Lord's anointed" (*Richard III*, IV, iv, 150) is surely intended to be another example of the supreme impudence of this tyrant and usurper rather than a sober statement of doctrine. In that respect it is part of his use of Scriptural allusions. It contrasts with Richmond's humbler but more sincere prayer: "O thou whose captain I account myself" (V, iii, 108).

Cade's rebellion and Shakespeare's famous scene presenting the horrors of civil war, in which a father has killed his son and a son his father (*3 Henry VI*, II, v, 55-122), may also reflect the Homilies, especially that "Against Disobedience and Wilful Rebellion" with its vivid picture of the evils of civil war.[52] Or they may be based upon *Gorboduc*, which ends with a long description of the horrors of civil war that may well be a source for the "Homily against Disobedience" itself.[53] But certainly Shakespeare

[51]Hart, *Shakespeare and the Homilies*, pp. 17-76.
[52]Ibid., pp. 53-55.
[53]Cf. *Gorboduc*, V, ii, 180-232, especially 213-14. *Gorboduc* was acted in 1561-62 and published c. 1570. This Homily was published c. 1571-73. Note that in *Richard III*, V, v, 24-26, the brothers precede father and son as in the Homily rather than Halle; but in the Homily the son first kills the father. *Gorboduc* does not mention brothers in this context. On the whole, the parallel to the Homily is the closest, but not definite.

need not have gone beyond his sources for all this material. The combats between father and son, especially, might be derived from a sentence in Halle: "This conflict was in maner unnatural, for in it the sonne fought agaynst the father, the brother against the brother, the nephew against the uncle, and the tenaunt agaynst his lord" (p. 256). Shakespeare merely selected the most unnatural of all these encounters. Richmond's lines at the end of *Richard III* may well recall either the same passage or the homily:

> The brother blindly shed the brother's blood,
> The father rashly slaughter'd his own son,
> The son, compell'd, been butcher to the sire.
>
> (V, v, 24-26)

Shakespeare seems to concentrate upon civil war as a kind of family strife and upon its destruction of decency and learning as illustrated by Cade's rebellion. He is unready, as yet, to portray the full horrors of civil war as *Gorboduc*, the Homilies, and *Richard II* describe them, or to conceive of civil disorder as a violation of universal order, in terms of the thinking that underlies *Lear* and *Macbeth*.[54]

Shakespeare's most interesting reflection of contemporary political thought is, however, his apparent identification of Richard III with the Machiavel of contemporary drama. The stage Machiavel derived, of course, not from Machiavelli's *Prince* but from Gentillet's *Discours ... Contre Nicholas Machiavel Florentin*.[55] This work excerpted Machiavelli's more sensational principles quite unfairly and blamed upon him all possible sins; but, by reducing his ideas to epigrams, it at least made them ready for popular consumption. The rather complicated history of the stage Machiavel is, however, beyond our present scope. *1 Henry VI* contains an allusion which is interesting because, if by Shakespeare, it shows that he was probably familiar, at least by reputation, with Gentillet. When the Pucelle says that Alençon is the father of her child, York retorts: "Alençon! that notorious

---

[54]Tillyard regards both the episodes just discussed as examples of the concept of universal order (*Shakespeare's History Plays*, pp. 152-53). But the speeches in themselves simply do not bear the meaning that he reads into them. Iden's speech (*2 Henry VI*, IV, x, 18-25) is, as has been noted, a commonplace classical theme. Note, too, that the two examples cited by Tillyard on p. 154 are derived directly from the source.

[55]Meyer, *Machiavelli and the Elizabethan Drama*, pp. 14-30.

machiavel" (V, iv, 74). Later in the same scene Alençon himself paraphrases one of Gentillet's maxims (ll. 159-64). The association of ideas is significant because Gentillet's ineptitude in dedicating his work to the "Machiavellian" François Duc d'Alençon was notorious, and we need not be so confident as was Meyer that Shakespeare was incapable of confusing two men with the same title.[56] In *3 Henry VI* Gloucester confesses, "And yet I know not how to get the crown"; but he then belies his words by outlining in some detail his qualifications as a Machiavel, and he boasts, not without reason, that he surpasses the prototype:

> Why, I can smile, and murder while I smile,
> And cry, "Content," to that which grieves my heart,
> And wet my cheeks with artificial tears,
> And frame my face to all occasions....
> I'll play the orator as well as Nestor,
> Deceive more slily than Ulysses could,
> And, like a Sinon, take another Troy.
> I can add colours to the chameleon,
> Change shapes with Proteus for advantages,
> And set the murd'rous Machiavel to school.
>
> (III, ii, 182-93)

It is very unlikely that Shakespeare knew Machiavelli or even Gentillet directly. Gabriel Harvey alludes several times to the interest in Machiavelli at Cambridge,[57] but there is no evidence that knowledge of Machiavelli as opposed to the popular caricature was widespread, and even Harvey's Latin poems present the caricature.[58] Simon Patrick's version of Gentillet, although its dedication is dated 1577, was not printed until 1602.[59] Actually there is nothing in Shakespeare's portrait of Richard that cannot be paralleled in earlier stage Machiavels, especially Barabas in *The Jew of Malta*, and there is very little that does not appear in the source. The influence of the conventional Machiavel appears in what Shakespeare selected and emphasized rather than in any outright invention of traits, Richard being quite consistent with

[56]Ibid., pp. 56-58.
[57]Ibid., p. 25.
[58]Ibid., pp. 22-23.
[59]Ibid., pp. 19-21. Boyer, *The Villain as Hero in Elizabethan Tragedy*, pp. 34-36. Neither Meyer nor Boyer, in my opinion, faces adequately the problem of influence presented by this date of publication. But cf. Craig, *Machiavelli's The Prince; An Elizabethan Translation.*

the generalizations about characterization laid down above. Meyer was undoubtedly right in summing up: "We can only conclude Shakspere did not know Machiavelli in the original; but drew from Marlowe, and from history."[60] One other point in this connection is consistent with Shakespeare's interests as we have inferred them. *The Prince* and even Gentillet's maxims stress statesmanship, and the Richard of the chronicles showed himself adept at it, but the play gives us no hint of this trait.[61]

As a kind of appendix to Shakespeare's political thought we might note the occurrence of *in capite* in a context that indicates some knowledge of the Latin jargon of the lawyers (*2 Henry VI*, IV, vii, 131).

There is one branch of learning in which Shakespeare displays an amount of information that seems phenomenal by modern standards, although it was probably not unusual in his own days. That is theology. His familiarity with the doctrines of the Church of England is, of course, a logical outcome of the extreme emphasis upon religious instruction that was characteristic of the grammar school. This teaching was kept fresh in mind, and probably considerably extended, by the Homilies, which were many of them popular expositions of fundamental doctrine. The Homily "Of Salvation," for example, contains an elaborate explanation of the relation of grace to good works. It may well be one basis of Shakespeare's thought, since the first of the passages to be discussed seems to reflect its detailed teaching rather than the succinct statements of the Thirty-nine Articles or the Catechism.

When Warwick rescues Henry from imprisonment in the Tower, the King says:

> But, Warwick, after God, thou set'st me free,
> And chiefly therefore I thank God and thee;
> He was the author, thou the instrument.
>
> (*3 Henry VI*, IV, vi, 16-18)

Shakespeare anachronistically makes Henry reflect orthodox Anglican doctrine as he pays Warwick an extravagant compliment. According to Protestant teachings man was incapable of doing good works unless aided by the grace of God; and, even then,

[60]Op. cit., p. 76.

[61]Boyer has noted this omission. Cf. op. cit., p. 80.

the works did not in themselves merit salvation because the credit belonged to God, by whose grace they were performed. " 'Grace,' saith St. Augustine, 'belongeth to God, who doth call us: and then hath he good works, whosoever received grace.' Good works then bring not forth grace, but are brought forth by grace.'"[62] Henry therefore implies that Warwick has done a good work of the sort which, in Catholic teaching, merited salvation, but he distinguishes in the Anglican way between God who was the author and Warwick who was merely the instrument. Hastings, before his death, thinks sorrowfully of his failure to hunt for the grace of God (*Richard III*, III, iv, 99), and the same context of ideas is surely implied by another line in the same play. Margaret, in cursing Richard, says:

> Thou elvish-mark'd, abortive, rooting hog!
> Thou that was seal'd in thy nativity
> The slave of nature and the son of hell!
>
> (I, iii, 228-30)

The last line has puzzled editors greatly, producing a long series of annotations and even emendations.[63] The obvious theological reference seems to have been overlooked completely. The ninth of the Thirty-nine Articles, "Of Original or Birth-sin," reads:

Original Sin standeth not in the following of *Adam*, (as the *Pelagians* do vainly talk;) but it is the fault and corruption of the Nature of every man, that naturally is ingendered of the offspring of *Adam*; whereby man is very far gone from original righteousness, and is of his own nature inclined to evil, so that the flesh lusteth always contrary to the spirit; and therefore in every person born into this world, it deserveth God's wrath and damnation . . .

Margaret's mind moves from Richard's physical to his spiritual deformity, and she means by "slave of nature" simply that he is in bondage to the sin which is man's fallen nature and by which he is a "son of hell" until redeemed by the grace of God. As so often, Shakespeare states the same idea in two ways. This use of *nature* as opposed to *grace* occurs throughout the period—for example, in Richard Whitford's translation of *The Imitation of*

---

[62]*Certain Sermons or Homilies*, p. 291.
[63]Cf. Furness Variorum, pp. 98-99.

Christ[64] or in George Herbert's poem "Nature," which is really a description of man in a state of sin and which, in the original manuscript although not in published editions, was followed immediately by the poem "Grace."[65] Later in the same scene Margaret reverts to this view of Richard in speaking to Buckingham, and she arranges in correct order the three elements in man's original fall: "Sin, death, and hell have set their marks on him" (l. 293). In her final scene she again calls him a servant of hell, for whose final damnation both devils and saints pray in as unnatural a union as that between the women of Lancaster and York:

> Richard yet lives, hell's black intelligencer,
> Only reserv'd their factor, to buy souls
> And send them thither; but at hand, at hand,
> Ensues his piteous and unpitied end;
> Earth gapes, hell burns, fiends roar, saints pray,
> To have him suddenly convey'd from hence.
>
> (IV, iv, 71-76)

Clarence refers to Christ's atonement in another passage where the folio prints what must be Shakespeare's text, the quarto having been altered because of the act against irreverence in plays.

> I charge you, as you hope to have redemption
> By Christ's dear blood shed for our greavous sins.
>
> (I, iv, 194-95)

The law of God forbidding marriage between uncle and niece to which Queen Elizabeth refers (IV, iv, 337-46) is still to be found in the "Table of Kindred and Affinity, wherein whosoever are related are forbidden in scripture and our laws to marry together" at the end of the English Book of Common Prayer (No. 25). In saying, "Be it lawful that I invocate thy ghost" (I, ii, 8), as she stands by Henry's coffin, Anne is using contemporary controversy between Protestants and Catholics over the invocation of saints as a way to call Henry a saint, and the implied Protestant reluctance only heightens the compulsion suggested and therefore the compliment (note that the inverted word order is imperative and not conditional—"let it be," not "if it be").

Such then, in so far as it can be inferred, is Shakespeare's intel-

---

[64]*The folowynge of Cryste*, III, liv; fol. lxxviii. Professor Louis Martz has pointed out to me this and the following example.

[65]*Works*, ed. Hutchinson, pp. liv, 45, 60.

lectual equipment as he writes his first plays. It is by no means so non-existent as was once thought; but it is little enough. Obviously he is learning as fast as possible, in no small part from the material under his hands; but these early plays are primarily a triumph of inventive ingenuity, of the ability to make much out of little. He took his sources and what learning he possessed, and with them he did the best he could. From his sources he took historical details, a scheme for organizing them, and an elementary philosophy for interpreting them. From his schooling and church-going he brought a knowledge of the Bible and religious doctrine. From his grammar-school classics he derived a fund of Latin poetry, a store of historical and mythological allusions, a sound training in composition and rhetoric, and the ability to study Seneca for hints in writing his plays. Of natural science he knew very little but what he brought from a country boyhood at Stratford. Scattered echoes show acquaintance with contemporary literature and drama, but they are confined to a few important writers. What Shakespeare did with these limited resources is a miracle that would make Anne consider invoking his ghost, too.

CHAPTER IV

The Early Comedies

IN SELECTING the four comedies to be considered in this chapter, *The Comedy of Errors, The Taming of the Shrew, Two Gentlemen of Verona,* and *Love's Labour's Lost,* I have followed Chambers' chronology,[1] although not without considering contrary opinions. Their characteristics, as seen from the point of view of Shakespeare's learning, certainly agree with a dating between 1592 and 1595 which makes *The Comedy of Errors* contemporary with *Richard III* and the rest of them a year or two later. *The Comedy of Errors* is based on Plautus with a few touches from Virgil, and it is without clear allusions to contemporary writers, unless the parallel to Nashe's *Foure Letters Confuted*[2] be a borrowing from Nashe rather than, as is more probable, a borrowing by him. *The Taming of the Shrew* has a relatively large number of classical echoes and only two or three allusions that have been traced to contemporary literature. *Two Gentlemen of Verona* and *Love's Labour's Lost,* as we shall see below, reflect a considerable knowledge of current literary movements, and the latter is a satiric play full of topical references. Furthermore, the classical details which, for obvious reasons, abound in it are likely to involve mere names rather than lines or identifiable situations. The four plays, in short, reflect a decreasing dependence upon the classics and a growing familiarity with contemporary literature. Attempts to date *Love's Labour's Lost* very early seem to have been based on the conventional metrical tests, which are obviously irrelevant in so stylized a play, especially in view of Shakespeare's

[1] *William Shakespeare,* I, 270.
[2] Wilson, New Cambridge ed., IV, iv, 84-85.

association of rhymed verse with Petrarchan love material elsewhere; and the verse of the play is certainly skillful.

Three of the plays have in their background a real or a possible old play—*The Historie of Error* (1577), *The Taming of A Shrew* (unless we accept Dover Wilson's theory that it is a bad quarto of *The Shrew*), and *Felix and Philiomena* (1585), which suggests the original names in the episode upon which *Two Gentlemen* is based. Three of them (*Two Gentlemen* being the exception) also contain passages of archaic verse which may be earlier work or may be Shakespeare's deliberate experiments with old-fashioned writing for comic effect. In contrast to *The Comedy of Errors* and *The Shrew*, which show Shakespeare's normal reliance upon a source (if *A Shrew* be a source), *Two Gentlemen* owes relatively little to Montemayor's *Diana* (only I, ii, iii; II, vii; IV, ii, iv), and no genuine source is known for *Love's Labour's Lost*. Finally, the last two plays, especially, have been much corrected and regularized by editors. A reader familiar only with the usual modern texts is likely to find some of the following statements a little startling. But, before assuming that he has found another error (of which there are undoubtedly all too many in this book), he should consult the critical apparatus in his text or a facsimile of the first folio.

Like the early chronicle plays, these four comedies represent, in general, a triumph in the use of limited resources to produce an effect disproportionate both in artistic pleasure afforded and in apparent learning. *Love's Labour's Lost*, especially, seems to involve far more intellectual sophistication than is revealed by careful examination, for its dazzling polish has been applied in large part to the same sturdy materials of which the chronicles were fashioned. The following discussion will consider, first, the survival and development, if any, of elements present in the chronicle plays and, second, those new aspects of *Two Gentlemen* and *Love's Labour's Lost* that reveal the growth and direction of Shakespeare's interests.

The Bible and Prayer Book still form an important source of Shakespeare's phraseology. It is significant, however, that in the first three comedies, where no special dramatic effect can be achieved by quoting Scriptures, Shakespeare has less than half as many echoes in each play as in the chronicles. In *Love's Labour's*

Lost, on the other hand, the baptismal service is ransacked to provide material for the opening scene, in which the young men renounce at least the world and the flesh, and Scriptural echoes help provide the atmosphere of polite learning throughout the play. There are, consequently, almost as many parallels in this play as in the other three combined. There would be more than in the other three, were it not that in *The Comedy of Errors* Shakespeare derived his notion of Ephesus, especially as a place of witchcraft, largely from Acts xix. Later in the play (IV, iii) he also became involved in a reference to angels and devils which, as so often with jokes and figures of speech, he pursued at length both through the scene and through various passages of Scripture. The references to Acts, which he did not echo in the chronicles, suggest that he consulted it at the time when he worked up material for the play.

His grammar-school texts he also continued to use. In fact, one wonders how he could have written *Love's Labour's Lost* without them, or how Baldwin could have written on his schooling without *Love's Labour's Lost*, which derives much of its material from his texts on rhetoric. From Lily's grammar he twice quoted Latin verses (*The Shrew*, I, i, 167; *Love's Labour's Lost*, V, i, 10). On the audience's memory of Mantuan depended the humor of a passage which modern editors have spoiled by correcting the Latin. Mantuan's first eclogue begins: "Fauste, precor gelida quando pecus omne sub umbra ruminat." Harvey and Nashe in their controversy, of which more below, had bandied the line about as an illustration of minimum knowledge of Latin. To quote Harvey: "He [Nashe] tost his imagination a thousand waies, and I beleeve searched every corner of his Grammar-schoole witte (for his margine is as deepelie learned, as *Fauste precor gelida*) to see if he coulde finde anie meanes to relieve his estate . . . ."[3] So Holofernes, by way of displaying his Latin, says: "*Facile precor gellida quando pecas omnia sub umbra ruminat,*—and so forth. Ah, good old Mantuan!" (IV, ii, 95-97). This is as though a modern scholar should say: "Gallia est omnes distributum in partes duo. Good old Caesar!" Except that *pecas omnia* is close to *peccas omnia*, which those in the audience used to colloquial Latin would catch as meaning "you mistake everything." In sup-

[3] *Works*, ed. Grosart, I, 195.

84

plying Mantuan's original Latin, as did the Second Folio, modern editors have simply obscured Shakespeare's joke. It is clear, furthermore, that Shakespeare expected his hearers to have had some practice in speaking Latin, for Holofernes and Nathaniel air a good many simple phrases from the standard texts. Nathaniel mistakes *haud credo* for a kind of doe (IV, ii, 11), and when he later misuses one of the first phrases that a schoolboy should have learned and says *bone intelligo* (V, i, 30-31), Holofernes has the pleasure of noting his error.

But Shakespeare made especially effective use of his rhetoric texts. Even Antipholus of Syracuse, in wooing Luciana, follows closely Erasmus' precepts for writing a love letter;[4] Armado's letter in *Love's Labour's Lost* is based on Aphthonius' treatment of narrative;[5] and Boyet's speech to the Princess follows Quintilian's division of a suasory or deliberative cause.[6] Much of the fantastic learning of the play consists simply of a literal application of the standard methods of writing themes, of construing Latin, or of achieving copiousness of diction (the term itself is used in *Comedy of Errors*, V, i, 62; the practice is illustrated in *Love's Labour's Lost*, IV, ii, 1-7).

Classical references which may be identified seem limited to Ovid, Virgil, and Horace, those to Ovid far outnumbering the rest. As is well known, *The Comedy of Errors* is based upon the *Menaechmi* and, for the twin servants and III, i, upon the *Amphitruo* of Plautus, which we need not doubt that Shakespeare read in Latin. The first scene is heavily indebted to Virgil's *Aeneid* for details of Aegeon's travels;[7] but it has not been noted, apparently, that recalling Virgil led Shakespeare into an inconsistency. In the first scene he described Aegeon as having wandered "five summers" (I, i, 133) as compared to Aeneas' "seven summers" (I, 755-56). But at the end he remembered only Aeneas, and Aegeon speaks of an absence of "seven short years" (V, i, 309).

One gets the impression, however, that Shakespeare's use of his classical background is becoming more sophisticated—that he either makes his borrowings very obvious for comic effect or

[4]*Comedy of Errors*, III, iii, 29-51; Baldwin, *W. S. Small Latine*, II, 282-83.
[5]*Love's Labour's Lost*, I, i, 232-51; Baldwin, op. cit., II, 311.
[6]*L. L. L.*, II, i, 1-8; Baldwin, op. cit., II, 92.
[7]Baldwin, op. cit., II, 485-87.

takes them in stride. They are becoming one of several resources rather than his chief resource. This tendency is observable in *Two Gentlemen of Verona*, which has less than half as many direct allusions as *The Taming of the Shrew*. *Love's Labour's Lost* offers a parade of Latin phrases, of which only the two already mentioned are quotations, and it alludes to the seven worthies and other Latin and Greek names. All these are part of the academic atmosphere. Yet it has fewer identifiable echoes of Latin poets than the other comedies; and one of these, a reference to Ajax killing sheep, is repeated from *2 Henry VI*, V, i, 26. Though Shakespeare continued to make general allusions to persons or mythological details, he was becoming less likely to write with a specific passage in a classical author in mind.

The impression that one gets of Shakespeare's general learning is about the same as that derived from the early chronicle plays. His allusions are still on the popular level, and he tends to ride a particular figure or idea in a way suggesting that it had struck his attention as an isolated concept rather than as part of a larger body of organized knowledge. The notion that overcooked, and therefore too dry, meat produces choler occurs in three passages (*Comedy of Errors*, II, ii, 58-64; *Taming of the Shrew*, IV, i, 173-75; IV, iii, 19-22), but there seems to be only one other similarly technical reference to the other humors:

> Your honour's players, hearing your amendment,
> Are come to play a pleasant comedy;
> For so your doctors hold it very meet,
> Seeing too much sadness hath congeal'd your blood,
> And melancholy is the nurse of frenzy.
> (T.S. Ind., ii, 131-35)

The concept of hair as an excrement also seems to have tickled his fancy about this time. He alludes to it in *The Comedy of Errors* (II, ii, 79) and in *Love's Labour's Lost* (V, i, 109) but elsewhere apparently only in *Hamlet* (III, iv, 121). His meaning is explained in *Batman uppon Bartholome* (1582): "... the haire of the head commeth out of fumositie thick, grose, and hot. And that fumositie commeth of hot, firie, and intensive humours, and passeth out at the pores of the head. And it is dried with aire that is without, and so tourneth into the substaunce of haire."[8]

[8]Liber V, cap. lxvi, fol. 69v.

Love's Labour's Lost contains a number of references which perhaps indicate an increasing interest in man's structure, although it is, of course, possible that the learned atmosphere of the play merely elicited information which Shakespeare had possessed for some time. When Moth speaks of the four complexions (I, ii, 82), he is stating what Shakespeare surely must have known about the humours from boyhood. Two passages, on the other hand, indicate more advanced knowledge. Nathaniel, in describing Dull as "only an animal, only sensible in the duller parts" (IV, ii, 28), refers to the fact that man shared the vegetable and sensible soul with lesser animals but was distinguished from them by his rational soul. Armado's calling Costard a "rational hind" (I, ii, 123) involves the traditional definition of man plus a double use of *copia*: "hind" for "animal," the entire definition for "man." Biron has in mind the notion that the vital spirits, agents of the sensible soul, traveled in the arteries when he says:

> Why, universal plodding poisons up
> The nimble spirits in the arteries,
> As motion and long-enduring action tires
> The sinewy vigour of the traveller.
>   (IV, iii, 305-308)

Most learned of all is Holofernes': "They are begot in the ventricle of memory, nourish'd in the womb of pia mater" (IV, ii, 70-71). This probably goes beyond what Shakespeare would have encountered in the classical-rhetorical education of the Stratford grammar school, since Palingenius has no reference to the *pia mater*.

Whether or not one is justified in assuming that Shakespeare's knowledge of human physiology and psychology was still limited because these allusions are restricted as compared to the fuller, technical references of the later plays, there is no question that he had picked up an extensive knowledge of horseflesh, doubtless at Stratford, for Biondello treats us to an elaborate description of the numerous diseases of Petruchio's horse (*T.S.*, III, ii, 49-56).

The preoccupation of *Love's Labour's Lost* with astronomical studies produced a number of general references, mostly contemptuous, but only one that indicates any specific knowledge, and that of a limited kind, when the King describes Berowne's love as an "attending star" (IV, iii, 231). Turning from astronomy to music, we find evidence of great interest and considerable knowledge. Both would be almost a professional necessity, but Shakespeare's references throughout his plays certainly indicate a genuine love of music; and it is significant that at this stage of his career he apparently knew more about it than about any other subject not studied in grammar school. Or so I infer, not because he writes technical details into his plays—that would be impossible—but because his allusions have a range and ease not to be paralleled in any other body of knowledge except religious doctrine. The joking between Julia and Lucetta in *Two Gentlemen* involves harmony and vocal singing, and we miss the point of Holofernes' display of his musical accomplishments unless we realize that, in singing "ut, re, sol, la, mi, fa" (IV, ii, 102), he has mixed up the hexachord (ut, re, mi, fa, sol, la) just as he previously misquoted Mantuan. Nothing suggests that Shakespeare was a highly trained musician, but he probably knew enough to sing his part with the rest.

Elementary references to law continue, and Shakespeare gets an improper joke out of the royal licensing of books to publishers "cum privilegio ad imprimendum solum" (*T.S.*, IV, iv, 92).

There can be no question that Shakespeare was rapidly developing an awareness of the codes of conduct of the fashionable world, to the fringes of which he had become attached. As we should expect in a period when he was beginning to write the sonnet, allusions to Petrarchism become increasingly common. In fact, he speaks of Bianca as professing "the Art of Love" (*T.S.*, IV, ii, 8). In the plays he uses the conventions as material for comedy as well as for sober conduct, just as in the sonnets he parodies them in addressing the Dark Lady but falls into them in praising "the man right fair." This ambivalent attitude toward them, like his ability both to parody and illustrate Elizabethan vices in diction, is part of the interest of his poetry. Speed's description of Proteus' love for Julia (*Two Gentlemen*, II, i, 17-33) is a kind of preliminary study for Romeo's infatuation with Rosaline; but Proteus' love, however perjured and battered, leads finally to union with Julia in a scene which relies on conventions as no other in Shakespeare, while Romeo's fades instantly and convincingly before a less artificial infatuation. Berowne's denunciation of Cupid is violent in the extreme (*L.L.L.*, III, i,

175-207); but he is falling in love, as Romeo kissed, "by the book" and his denunciation is the blasphemy, but not the apostasy, of a firm believer.

Shakespeare's use of the term "living art," a reference to the *ars vivendi* of Stoic philosophy,[9] suggests that he may have been reading in ethics and related subjects, a suspicion which *Romeo and Juliet* and *The Rape of Lucrece* will convert into a certainty. The portrayal of friendship in *Two Gentlemen* and *Love's Labour's Lost* may well derive in part from one of the standard theorists on the subject—Cicero's *De Amicitia*, perhaps, which was included in some grammar-school curricula,[10] although no definite proof has been produced that Shakespeare knew it. From this point of view an emendation in *Love's Labour's Lost* is tantalizing. Most modern editors make Berowne speak of "This senior-junior, giant-dwarf, Dan Cupid" (III, i, 182). If sound, this would be a clear reference to the tradition going back ultimately to the dispute between Phaedrus and Agathon in Plato's *Symposium*, in which they describe Love as the oldest and the youngest of the gods. But the quartos and folios read "Signior Junios"; and "signior junior," adapted by Hart, the Arden editor, and by J. Dover Wilson, involves a characteristic Shakespearean quibble on *signior*. On the other hand, the emendation is supported by a reference in *King John* to a concept also derived from the *Symposium* and part of the same tradition:

> He is the half part of a blessed man,
> Left to be finished by such as she;
> And she a fair divided excellence,
> Whose fulness of perfection lies in him.
> (II, i, 437-40)

These lines have no parallel in the source of the play and indicate Shakespeare's familiarity with Platonic theories about love.

The Prince's remarks on praise are obviously ethical commonplaces, but no definite source seems to have been found for them:

> Glory grows guilty of detested crimes,
> When, for fame's sake, for praise, an outward part,
> We bend to that the working of the heart.
> (*L.L.L.*, IV, i, 30-33)

[9]*Love's Labour's Lost*, I, i, 14; Reid, "Shakespeare's 'Living Art,'" pp. 226-27.
[10]Baldwin, *W. S. Small Latine*, II, 590-96.

Another passage on contemporary ways of life shows that Shakespeare was aware of the exploring activities of his age:

> Some to the wars, to try their fortune there;
> Some to discover islands far away.
>
> (*Two Gentlemen*, I, iii, 8-9)

It is also clear that Shakespeare had been reading on the use of arms, for *Love's Labour's Lost* (I, ii, 181-87) contains the first of several passages in his plays based upon the code of the duel, the most famous of which is, of course, Touchstone's disquisition in *As You Like It* (V, iv, 92-107). Charlton thinks that Armado must have had in mind Sir William Segar's *The Booke of Honor and Armes* (1590) in saying: "The first and second cause will not serve my turn." But Touchstone's discussion of "lies certain," "conditional lyes," and so forth, is a parody of Vincentio Saviolo's *Practice of the Rapier and Dagger*, translated from Muzio. Some pages later, in Saviolo's second book, is a section "For what causes Combats ought to bee graunted," which undertakes to "include all combats under two heads," accusation of a capital offense and dishonor.[11] There is no reason, therefore, why Armado should not have Saviolo in mind. Since Saviolo's book appeared in 1595 (Book II is dated 1594 on its title page), it could have been used only if *Love's Labour's Lost* is to be dated in 1595, and a reasonable probability of its use helps to date the play.

Love's Labour's Lost also extends considerably the evidence of Shakespeare's knowledge of religious doctrine. There is much talk of angels and devils, which results from one of his characteristic preoccupations with the contrast between evil angels and angels of light and the word play that could be based thereon. After exploiting this theme in *The Comedy of Errors* (IV, iii), he reverted to it in *Love's Labour's Lost* (IV, iii, 257). But the play of ideas involves no learned concepts. *Two Gentlemen*, on the other hand, shows some knowledge of "angelology" by a reference to *principalities*, one of the hierarchies of heavenly

---

[11] *Vincentio Saviolo his Practise*, Book II, sig. Aa2v. The objections of Furness (Variorum, I, ii, 170) and of Hart (Arden) seem to me to forget that Shakespeare was writing comedy and not a technical treatise. Saviolo uses the word *cause* in the heading and in his discussion. The parallel is closer than that between Touchstone's list of quarrels and Saviolo's kinds of lies, and accuracy is surely not characteristic of any of the fantastics in this play. Cf. also Charlton, "Notes on 'Love's Labour's Lost,'" pp. 76-78.

spirits (II, iv, 152). But Shakespeare's most revealing passages again center upon the crucial issue of justification. Berowne alludes to the Catechism and to the doctrine that the fall left man's reason, and its proper though often disobedient servant the will, unable to control the passions:

> For every man with his affects is born,
> Not by might mast'red, but by special grace.
>
> (I, i, 152-53)

He is stating the Protestant doctrine that man cannot do good works of his own volition but must rely upon God's grace working within him to master his evil affections or passions, as opposed to the Catholic position that man can himself will and do works meriting salvation. The same controversy underlies the Princess' witticism:

> *For.* Nothing but fair is that which you inherit.
>
> *Prin.* See, see, my beauty will be sav'd by merit!
> O heresy in fair, fit for these days!
>
> (IV, i, 20-22)

This quip justifies the inference that Shakespeare, although well acquainted with contemporary theological issues, was not a profoundly pious man, an inference which could also be drawn from a witticism of Berowne's:

> We to ourselves prove false,
> By being once false for ever to be true
> To those that make us both,—fair ladies, you;
> And even that falsehood, in itself a sin,
> Thus purifies itself and turns to grace.
>
> (V, ii, 782-86)

With the first passage quoted above should be compared another remark by the Princess. When Boyet says: "Proud of employment, willingly I go," she replies: "All pride is willing pride, and yours is so" (II, i, 36). She alludes, of course, to the doctrine that pride, which, as a sin, must involve a deliberate act of will, was a manifestation of man's corrupted will turned from God; it had been, in fact, the cause of all sin and the original corrupter of man's will.

Such ideas were part of the Homilies and of catechisms and confessions intended for popular use. The phrase "special grace" occurs in the Prayer Book in the Catechist's transition from the Ten Commandments to the Lord's Prayer; and, although they do not occur in the Catechism, most of the remaining ideas would doubtless have been explained to the older students when they encountered the Catechism in Latin or Greek. Any church-goer would have heard all of them explained in the Homilies. The same source of information would also account for a more explicit reference that we shall encounter in *Lucrece*. These passages are interesting because they constitute Shakespeare's first allusions to the Christian explanation of sin, which is basic to several of his greatest tragedies. But as yet they do not suggest any knowledge of philosophical and theological concepts beyond the level to be encountered by the thoughtful grammar-school student or church-goer.

So far we have been recapitulating points considered in connection with the early chronicle plays to see what additional evidence could be derived from the early comedies. Some widening of horizons seems to be indicated, but nothing startling. But upon three points these plays offer independent information of considerable significance. To begin with the least interesting, they demonstrate an ignorance of geography, and apparent indifference to it, comparable to the attitude toward historical fact revealed by the chronicles. The preceding sentence deliberately avoids the problem of distinguishing between ignorance and indifference because it would be almost impossible to draw a line. Shakespeare is careless of detail throughout his plays. Part of this apparent negligence results, of course, from a calculated reliance upon what he could expect the audience to overlook during a performance.[12] Part of it seems to come, on the other hand, from a concentration upon the central idea or impression as opposed to detail, from what we might call the philosophical as opposed to the factual temperament. It is a corollary of the tendency noted in the chronicle plays to reproduce philosophical explanations and outlines of character far more accurately than the sequence of historical events or the motivation of details. In *Two Gentlemen* Shakespeare seems never to be sure whether the ruler of Milan—if it be Milan—is a duke or an emperor, although *duke*

---

[12]This assumption underlies many of Schücking's points in his *Character Problems in Shakespeare's Plays*.

has it on points.[13] There is a similar confusion between king and duke in *Love's Labour's Lost*,[14] but here *king* wins out early in Act II.

The geographical confusion in *Two Gentlemen* is, however, so extreme that mere indifference will not account for it. In the first place, Proteus goes from Verona to Milan by ship (I, i, 71), Verona being located on a river (II, iii, 58) which has a tide (II, iii, 40)—suspiciously like the Thames at London. Nor has the industry of Shakespeare's earlier editors, who had so much to say about the system of rivers and canals in Italy, made all this plausible. After Proteus and Launce arrive at the court of the Duke (or Emperor) of Milan, Speed welcomes Launce to Padua (II, v, 1). A little later, the Duke tells Valentine: "There is a lady in Verona here" (III, i, 81). After his banishment from Milan (*alias* Padua *alias* Verona), Valentine tells the outlaws that he is headed for Verona (IV, i, 17), but perhaps he is merely tricking them, for Silvia has heard that he is in Mantua (IV, iii, 23), obviously from him before he left since he got no farther than the forest. In the final scene Valentine thinks that Thurio, Silvia's third wooer, comes from Verona (V, iv, 129), although he is apparently a native of Milan. Such is the geography of the play as the folio text presents it. William Aldis Wright remarks: "The inaccuracies are interesting as showing that Shakespeare had written the whole of the play before he had finally determined where the scene was to be laid."[15] But there are two things wrong with this theory. No sane poet would try to write without knowing what words he had to fit into the metrical pattern—at least before the days of free verse. And a writer would be most likely of all to be consistent if he went through a finished document to arrange names according to a newly determined scheme, even though he might miss a place or two along the way. Three inferences seem justified. First, Shakespeare was even more indifferent to accuracy of detail than usual. Second, he was reading, or had recently read, Arthur Brooke's *Romeus and Juliet*; and his imagination was so powerfully stimulated by its story that he introduced its geogra-

[13]For passages implying that he is an emperor see I, iii, 27-57; II, iv, 76-77; V, iv, 141.

[14]For duke cf. I, i, 182; I, ii, 132; II, i, 38.

[15]*The Cambridge Shakespeare*, I, 195, note 7.

phy (as well as numerous other details)[16] into *Two Gentlemen*. Third, he was obviously hazy as to the geography of Italy, and he did not localize events sharply in his own mind as a modern writer, using his atlas and probably recalling scenes that he had visited, would do. Shakespeare had some knowledge of Milan. At least, we are told that a St. Gregory's well mentioned in the play actually existed there.[17] But there is no evidence that he had had any instruction or done any reading in Italian geography subsequent to the Roman period, and it is very unlikely that he even had a map. The sort of simple, easily accessible geographical knowledge to which we are accustomed today simply did not exist. Even today any Westerner who travels east of the Mississippi learns to explain patiently that San Francisco and Los Angeles are as far apart as Boston and Washington, D.C., and so on. Geography was then the property of scholars, and schoolboys were not even supposed to have studied it. For the most part, Shakespeare relied on the most general information (witness his use of Acts as a source of material on Ephesus). Venice was wealthy and ornate, Padua the seat of learning, and beyond these clichés he was happy in his ignorance.

But, if Shakespeare was ignorant of geography, he was extending his knowledge of modern literature. *Two Gentlemen* and *Love's Labour's Lost* mark a notable increase in his familiarity with contemporary writers and furnish the first indication of his actual participation in the Elizabethan world of letters.

If *The Comedy of Errors* shows any definite allusions to contemporary writers, as opposed to mere parallels of language which have been cited by editors and critics to illustrate Shakespeare's usage or advanced by the more daring disintegrators in parceling out the play, they have escaped my attention. *The Taming of the Shrew* may indicate a knowledge of Gower (I, ii, 69) and Chaucer's "Clerk's Tale" (II, i, 297) but not of more recent literature. *Two Gentlemen* and *Love's Labour's Lost*, on the other hand, have a considerable number of fairly clear allusions. Puttenham we

[16]Cf. Arden *Two Gentlemen*, p. xxvii, for a list of parallels. See also Allen, "Broke's *Romeus and Juliet* as a Source for the Valentine-Sylvia Plot in *The Two Gentlemen of Verona*," pp. 25-46. Parks argues that the travel element was a later addition to a play that was originally settled throughout at Verona; cf. "The Development of *The Two Gentlemen of Verona*," pp. 1-11.

[17]IV, ii, 83. Arden note.

should expect, after the chronicle plays, and Armado's peculiar use of *dominator* (*L.L.L.*, I, i, 222) and of *passionate* (III, i, 1) has been traced to him. Parallels to Lyly's "Cooling Card" to Philautus and to *Euphues and his England* have been found in *Two Gentlemen,* and a considerable passage in the same play seems indebted to *Sapho and Phao.*[18] Its obvious geographical echoes of Brooke's *Romeus and Juliet* have already been alluded to, and numerous details might be added, such as the rope ladder, the name Friar Lawrence, and the meeting at a Friar's cell under pretence of confession.[19] A reference to Phaeton as Merops' son (III, i, 153), which might be due to Ovid but occurs much more succinctly in *The Troublesome Raigne* (Part 1, i, 333-34), confirms a suspicion, expressed in connection with Talbot's death scenes, that Shakespeare already knew the source of *King John.* The life of Caesar in North's Plutarch is quoted verbatim in *Love's Labour's Lost* (IV, i, 68-70) in that Shakespeare reproduces North's translation of *veni, vidi, vici* "came, saw, and overcame." The name Holofernes is, of course, derived from Rabelais.

The allusions so far mentioned merely show that Shakespeare had acquired some knowledge of a few contemporary books. Another group are much more interesting in that they show that he had established personal relations of some kind with the world of letters of his day. Any man could buy books, but manuscripts circulated only in a fairly limited literary circle. The probability is that, in writing *Two Gentlemen,* Shakespeare used Bartholomew Yong's translation of Montemayor's *Diana,* which was not published until 1598, although Yong says in his "Preface to divers learned Gentlemen, and other my loving friendes:" " . . . it hath lyen by me finished *Horaces* ten and six yeeres more." Yong gives no hint that the work circulated in manuscript, unless one can be read into his statement, by way of apology for errors in printing, that the copy was "verie darke and enterlined." But parallels in *Two Gentlemen* are close enough to make the use of Yong's version very likely. Editors have noted Lucia's idiom "she makes it strange" and Julia's remark

[18]With *Two Gentlemen,* I, i, 29-35, cf. Lyly, "Cooling Card," passim, *Works,* I, 246-57; with II, iv, 149-50, cf. Lyly, *Works,* II, 91-93; and with III, i, 89-103, cf. *Sapho and Phao,* I, iv, 43-47, and II, iv, 60-105, passim. See also Arden ed., pp. xxviii-xxxii.
[19]For a fuller list see Arden ed., p. xxvii.

it hath been the longest night
That e'er I watched and the most heaviest.[20]

A third parallel is clearly present. Celia commits suicide for unrequited love of Felismena, disguised as the page Valerius. (Shakespeare omitted this plot element in *Two Gentlemen*, but, as far as comedy permitted, he used both it and the name Celia in *As You Like It*). Celia's last words are: "And this for the love of thee, Valerius, and not for much for Don Felix thy master his sake, for I see how much thou lovest and tenderest his estate."[21] Compare Silvia's dismissal of the disguised Julia:

> Here, youth, there is my purse; I give thee this
> For thy sweet mistress' sake, because thou lov'st her.

It is interesting that all three of these parallels occur in a scene in Shakespeare that is not based upon the context in Yong; they reflect his tenacious memory for striking details.

The possibility that Shakespeare knew Marlowe's *Hero and Leander* in manuscript rests upon what can hardly be called evidence. Valentine's reference in *Two Gentlemen* to a story "How young Leander cross'd the Hellespont" (I, i, 22) could rest on Ovid (*Heroides*, xix) or on mere report of Marlowe's poem. The actual quotation from the poem in *As You Like It* came after its publication in 1598.

But the clearest proof of Shakespeare's acquaintance with literary circles is *Love's Labour's Lost*. The mere fact that he attempted such a play on topics fashionable at the time indicates considerable assurance, and the allusions themselves show familiarity with a number of contemporary trends. The tendency apparent in some quarters to convert the play into a kind of sustained satirical allegory of the Harvey-Nashe controversy or a School of Night, or what not, is certainly false to Shakespeare's manifest characteristics as a dramatist and to the evidence of the play itself, which is a witty comedy based upon contemporary fashions and full of allusions to a variety of topics which the more sophisticated part of the audience doubtless found amusing. Perhaps more of these are to be traced to the famous controversy

[20] *Two Gentlemen*, I, ii, 102; IV, ii, 141. Hazlitt, *Shakespeare's Library*, I (Part 1), 279, 281. Arden ed.
[21] *Two Gentlemen*, IV, iv, 181-82; Hazlitt, op. cit., I, 300.

between Gabriel Harvey and Thomas Nashe than to any other subject. The clearest occurs in an exchange between Holofernes and Costard:

Hol. Master Parson, *quasi* pers-on. An if one should be pierc'd, which is the one?

Cost. Marry, master schoolmaster, he that is likest to a hogshead.

Hol. Of piercing a hogshead.

(IV, ii, 85-88)

This Hart identified as glancing at a passage in Harvey's *Pierce's Supererogation* (1592/3), a reply to Nashe's *Pierce Peniless* (1592): "She knew what she said, that intituled Pierce, the hoggeshead of witt: Penniles, the tosspot of eloquence: & Nashe, the very inventor of Asses. She it is that must broach the barrell of thy frisking conceite, and canonise the Patriarke of newe writers."[22] Hart also noted "my tender juvenal" (I, ii, 8) as a reference to Nashe. The editors of the New Cambridge Shakespeare pointed out that *Juvenal* was capitalized in the quarto and capitalized and italicized in the folio, and therefore treated as a proper name, and they considerably expanded the evidence that Moth embodies a good deal of satire upon Nashe.[23] The selection of Moth to play Hercules in the Pageant of the Nine Worthies probably alludes to Nashe's youthful efforts as a controversialist, as does the wonderful doggerel with which Holofernes introduces him:

> Great Hercules is presented by this imp,
>   Whose club kill'd Cerberus, that three headed *canus*;
> And when he was a babe, a child, a shrimp,
>   Thus did he strangle serpents in his *manus*.
>
> (V, ii, 591-95)

But Shakespeare is quite impartial in his attitude toward the two combatants, for Harvey is parodied just as vigorously. Hart sees in Armado's demanding "l'envoy" of Moth a reference to Harvey's use of an envoy in two of his poems, one of them against Nashe, for which he was ridiculed by the latter; his identification of Harvey's "Nos'd, like to Naso" as the source of Holofernes'

[22]Harvey, *Works*, II, 91. Arden *Love's Labour's Lost*, ed. H. C. Hart.
[23]New Cambridge *Love's Labour's Lost*, pp. xx-xxiii.

97

"Why, indeed, Naso, but for smelling out the odoriferous flowers of fancy, the jerks of invention" is less convincing, although it must be remarked that Harvey's quibble is one which Shakespeare, once he saw it, would undoubtedly remember with envy until his death.[24] One recalls the story that Oscar Wilde once remarked of an epigram of Whistler's that he wished he had said it. "You will, Oscar," said Whistler, "you will." Hart identifies other echoes of Harvey and Nashe, some of them rather tenuous.

On the basis of the King's "School of night" (IV, iii, 255) and the Princess' lines

> Beauty is bought by judgement of the eye,
> Not utt'red by base sale of chapmen's tongues
>
> (II, i, 15-16)

the New Cambridge Shakespeare has detected other evidence that Shakespeare had in mind and even parodied George Chapman, whose *The Shadow of Night* appeared in 1594, and that he satirized a School of Night identified with the "School of Atheisme" headed by Sir Walter Raleigh, including Chapman, and notorious in connection with Marlowe's death.[25] Bradbrook has also found several passages that may glance at Chapman's poems.[26] Frances A. Yates goes so far as to say: "One of the best established facts about the satire in *Love's Labour's Lost* is that it had something to do with Raleigh and his friends and with the expression of their point of view which George Chapman put forward in his poem *The Shadow of Night* (1594)."[27] This is a considerable overstatement with respect both to Shakespeare and to Chapman. However probable they may be, assumptions do not form the strongest chain of evidence, and the improbability of the conclusion grows in geometric progression with each link in the chain. Proponents of the School of Night will need to meet the objections to their theory so clearly stated by Strathmann in his study of Sir Walter Raleigh.[28] They will also find it sobering to compare the quality of their evidence with that adduced by the more nearly rational

[24]*L. L. L.*, III, i, 65; IV, ii, 116. Arden ed.
[25]New Cambridge *Love's Labour's Lost*, pp. xxviii-xxxiv.
[26]*The School of Night*, pp. 162-63.
[27]*A Study of Love's Labour's Lost*, p. 83.
[28]*Sir Walter Raleigh: A Study in Elizabethan Scepticism*, pp. 262-71.

Baconians. But the preoccupation of the play with night and stars must have some basis. I find Chapman and his poems more convincing than the School of Night and its ramifications.

Yates also sees references to Giordano Bruno's new astronomy and to the anti-Petrarchan sentiments of his preface to *De gli eroici furori* (1585) in Berowne's description of his former disdain for love (III, i, 175-207); his title itself she believes to be reflected in the King's "what fury hath inspir'd thee now" (IV, iii, 229). Shakespeare's knowledge, by hearsay, of Bruno she connects with Sidney, to whose *Astrophel and Stella* she sees references throughout the play, and especially in Berowne's meditation of his lady's "blackness" (IV, iii, 257-61), which she compares with *Astrophel and Stella* vii.[29] But surely the kinship to Shakespeare's own "dark lady" sonnets is even closer.

In a more recent book Yates also suggests, without going into detail, a vast ramification of allusions to French intellectual life:

The leading male characters have names taken from the French civil wars: Navarre, Dumain, Longaville, Berowne. It is noteworthy that the opposite parties are represented in these names; as well as "Navarre," we have "Dumain," that is Mayenne, the member of the Guise family who eventually became head of the League. Shakespeare evidently knew the long tradition of "conciliatory" French fêtes, in which both "Navarin" and "Guisin" took part. They all belong to an Academy at the court of Navarre where debates on honour and virtue are in progress. They fall in love with a French queen and her ladies to whom they write sonnets and with whom they stage a masque and a measured dance. It is generally acknowledged that this seems to reflect some occasion at the court of Catherine de' Medici. And finally they join in a religious movement of penitence, retreat, and good works. It is an exposition of the relation of French academies to French fêtes; and it would not be surprising to find in such a performance allusions to differences of opinion between Protestants and Catholics and to a Neo-Pythagorean harmony of the universe.

The tracing and proving of such allusions would be much too complicated a task to enter upon here. But it can be said that the plot of this comedy of Shakespeare's, turning as it does upon a projected marriage for "Navarre," relates it to a European sequence of very great politico-religious and artistic importance.[30]

---

[29] *A Study of Love's Labour's Lost*, pp. 89-136. Cf. especially pp. 122-23, 132.
[30] *The French Academies of the Sixteenth Century*, pp. 264-65.

It must be obvious that the search for contemporary allusions in *Love's Labour's Lost* can be—and is being—carried on relentlessly. But, however many of these allusions one accepts or rejects, two conclusions are inescapable. In the first place, Shakespeare now had some connection with fashionable and literary circles in London, or at least with the area where the two overlapped. His interest in Petrarchan sonneteering and his connection with men of the court can be inferred, of course, on the basis of his own sonnets and of the dedications of *Venus and Adonis* and *The Rape of Lucrece*. But his attitude toward the Harvey-Nashe squabble is obviously one of disinterested enjoyment of the fun to be got out of the antics of both participants. Probably many other people felt the same way, and this attitude explains the extraordinary interest in a series of pamphlets that one modern reader, at least, finds insufferably dull. But Shakespeare's interest also tells us a little more about himself. So do his probable references to Chapman and his two hymns. They were first singled out by sonnet-enthusiasts pursuing the will-o'-the-wisp characters of that series, in this case the rival poet. But no one seems to have suggested that the two fantastical and obscure poems included in *The Shadow of Night* may have enjoyed a notoriety of their own, even if they failed to find an audience,[31] and that Shakespeare may have made capital of them just as every radio comedian in the United States seized upon the reputation of *Gone with the Wind*. In Shakespeare's

> Never durst poet touch a pen to write,
> Until his ink were temp-red with Love's sighs
>   (IV, iii, 346-47)

the New Cambridge editors find a probable parody of Chapman's

> No pen can any thing eternall write,
> That is not steept in humour of the Night.
>   ("Hymnus in Noctem," ll. 376-77)

If they are right, Shakespeare, unlike most modern comedians, read the work of which he made fun. His later plays show that he read a much greater and more genuinely philosophical work, Richard Hooker's *Laws of Ecclesiastical Polity*, which was pub-

[31]Cf. *The Poems of George Chapman*, ed. Bartlett, p. 4.

lished in the same year (1594). His befuddlement by Chapman perhaps resulted in brilliant comedy; his meditation upon Hooker certainly stimulated his greatest tragedy.

But, if these plays show an increasing knowledge of contemporary literature, they also show how limited Shakespeare's reading was. His triumph always lay in making a maximum use of a minimum of material. Of the small number of works which he echoes in these plays, three—*The Troublesome Raigne*, Brooke's *Romeus and Juliet*, and Plutarch's *Caesar*—he subsequently used as the basis of plays. If one adds to the *Comedy of Errors* and *Two Gentlemen* the episode of one woman's falling in love with another disguised as a page, which Shakespeare found in Montemayor's *Diana* but did not use, one already has virtually all the plot material that he used in his comedies except for what he found in the actual sources of each play or repeated from one play to another. This material he got from Plautus, Virgil, a short narrative interpolated in Montemayor, and *Euphues*, which furnished the false friend of *Two Gentlemen*. Even if we include all the suggested influences upon *Love's Labour's Lost* in addition to the works echoed in his other plays, he was still not a well-read man by the standards of his own day. It is, of course, probable that his plays do not reflect all that he read. The material that we have been accumulating has much more validity as positive proof of what he did know than as negative evidence of what he did not know. But it does have more negative value than it would if Shakespeare were habitually self-contained like most modern writers. For he is undoubtedly given to continual use of borrowed images or references, and it is significant that numerous echoes of every writer that he probably read in grammar school have been located in his works. If he borrows, as he does in *The Taming of the Shrew*, at least seven times from Ovid, as against one echo each of Virgil, Gower, and Chaucer, and none of contemporary authors, we are at least justified in suspecting that he was far more familiar with Ovid than with writers of his own day. Nor is there any evidence that he ever became a well-read man, in a scholarly as opposed to a popular sense. It is hard to see how he could have done so. He was a busy member of a dramatic company. He wrote two or three plays a year besides two narrative poems and the sonnets. He paid court to the great, became noted as a good fellow among men at the tavern, and occasionally commuted between London and Stratford. A mind of great intensity and imagination squeezed dry a limited number of sources and other books, using and reusing the same ideas. Such is the inference to be drawn. Examination of *Romeo and Juliet* will show how content he was to depend upon a single source when it was even approximately adequate and what use he could make of the virtues of such a source.

CHAPTER V

The Early Tragedies and the Poems

O F TITUS ANDRONICUS almost nothing definite is known except that on January 24, 1594, Henslowe's *Diary* reports is as "ne"—that is, new—and Meres includes it in his list of Shakespeare's plays. Scholars have disagreed as to whether it is Shakespeare's own work or his revision of an old play or even his retouching of a new play by a "private author." They have been equally uncertain as to its date. A remark by Ben Jonson in 1614 coupled it with *The Spanish Tragedy* and implied that it was then "five-and-twenty or thirty years" old—too old to fit into any accepted chronology of Shakespeare's plays. The *Titus and Vespasian* performed in 1592 also raises a problem of possible relationship between the two plays, especially since no definite source has been found for the main action of *Titus Andronicus* as distinguished from details that are imitated from Ovid and Seneca. The play is therefore not to be regarded as safe evidence of Shakespeare's thinking at any point in his career. On the other hand, it may be interesting to glance at it briefly to see whether it is consistent with what we have seen to be his practice in his other plays. In general, the learning and the marshalling of illustrative material seem thoroughly consistent with his manner.

Titus Andronicus is full of classical allusions and echoes. There are quotations in Latin from Seneca (II, i, 133-35; IV, i, 81-82), Ovid's *Metamorphoses* (IV, iii, 4), and from Horace (IV, ii, 20-21); but the last is taken from Lily's *Grammar*, for Shakespeare, like Chiron in the play, "read it in the grammar long ago." Almost all of the identifiable allusions are to Ovid and Virgil, and there are, in addition, a number of names that Shakespeare might have picked up from various sources.[1] The use of bald allusions is reminiscent of the Henry VI plays rather than of *Richard III*, but the quotations from Seneca and the obvious imitations of his *Thyestes* in the revenge banquet and of his *Troades* in the sacrifice of Alarbus link the play to *Richard III*, as we noted in discussing that play. Grammar-school material is also used in a way suggestive of the early plays, especially in connection with Titus' grandson Lucius. Tully's *Orator* (IV, i, 14) and Ovid's *Metamorphoses* (IV, i, 42) are referred to as books used by children. The tag of Horace from Lily, on the other hand, is employed as a minor detail in the plot.

There are relatively few Biblical echoes; but, in true Shakespearean fashion, three-fourths of them are concentrated in four of the fourteen scenes (I, i; III, i; III, ii; IV, ii). Titus has more of them than any other character, but even he has none of the Biblical flavor that Shakespeare gives, for different reasons, to Henry VI or Richard III. In such a play Scriptural allusions would obviously be out of place as a deliberate device to secure an artistic effect, and that fact, if the play be Shakespeare's, would undoubtedly account for their small number as compared with the echoes in other early plays. Actually there are more than in *Romeo and Juliet* and very nearly as many as in *King John*.

Most significant of all, perhaps, are the echoes of contemporary writers in the play. As usual, we shall disregard mere verbal parallels, which may mean anything or nothing. The allusion to Scythian barbarism has been traced to Purchas' *Pilgrim on Cannibalism*,[2] and Baldwin finds the influence of Greene in Marcus' reference to concealed sorrow's burning the heart, a figure which has a complicated history.[3] But these are unimportant beside

---

[1] Baker (*Induction to Tragedy*, p. 139) gives the following tabulation: "According to my count the distribution of fairly clear classical allusions is this: Ovid, sixteen (excluding the repeated references to Philomel); Virgil, fifteen; Livy-Painter, four; Horace, two (from Lyly's grammar); Seneca, two (both are short Latin tags from *Hippolytus*); and perhaps one or two from Homer, Sophocles, Euripides, Herodotus or Plutarch, and Cicero." My principle of omitting names that might have been picked up anywhere reduces the totals and almost eliminates the last group, which Shakespeare is very unlikely to have known except for Plutarch and Cicero; but the general result is the same.

[2] Arden ed., I, i, 131-32.

[3] II, iv, 36-37. Baldwin, *W. S. Small Latine*, II, 435.

a number of allusions which show clearly that Shakespeare had been reading the first part of Painter's *Palace of Pleasure* and which suggest that it was giving him suggestions for the future. References to Tarquin and Lucrece (IV, i, 63-64), to Coriolanus (IV, iv, 68), and to Virginius' slaying of his deflowered daughter (V, iii, 36-38) point to three of Painter's "novels": II, "Rape of Lucrece"; IV, "Coriolanus"; and V, "Appius and Virginia."[4] Except for a reference to Lucrece as the pattern of chastity (II, i, 108), these allusions occur in the last two acts of the play and are confined to Painter's first five novels. One suspects, therefore, that Shakespeare had just begun to read the *Palace of Pleasure* and that it may have aroused his interest in Lucrece and Coriolanus as well as in other stories which he ultimately used. Reading Painter may have recalled to him instructions for working up the story of Lucrece which he had encountered in Erasmus' *Copia* as a student and which he seems to have followed. Certainly he used Painter as an actual source for the poem, in addition to following Ovid and Livy as the *Copia* suggests.

The "learning" displayed in *Titus Andronicus*, if such it may be called, is rudimentary. It is limited to three themes that we have noted elsewhere: astrological subjects (II, i, 7; II, iii, 31); the enormity of civil war (V, iii, 73-78); and the Machiavel. Aaron is the embodiment of motiveless evil, and he has other standard characteristics, including the use of religion and honor for his own purposes (V, i, 78-80). Tamora's lines on mercy (I, i, 117-20) read like a preliminary study for Portia's great speech

---

[4]*Palace of Pleasure*, ed. Jacobs, I, 22, 29, 35. Wilson argues (New Cambridge *Titus Andronicus*, p. xxxviii) "that Shakespeare was working on *Titus* and *Lucrece* at almost the same time" and that, "when we observe that one of the most striking parallels links an early scene affected by the revision (2.4 [ll. 22-25]) with a passage (ll. 1730-43) very near the end of the poem, we may suspect the latter to have been practically complete when the former was taken in hand." But why need the better version be the earlier (cf. Wilson, pp. liii-liv)? There are plenty of examples of Shakespeare's improving his earlier handiwork. Furthermore, Wilson's view of the play would mean that, in this and several other parallels, Shakespeare perpetrated a deliberate burlesque of his own serious poetry. He was certainly given to pointing out the excesses of other dramatists; but, as a young man striving for recognition as a serious poet, could he afford, or would he be likely, to parody his own poetry, thereby putting it in the same category as the old ranting drama? Wilson's entire preface inspires me with little confidence. These remarks are intended, let me add, not as a defense of my own suggestion, which is that and nothing more, but as a general comment on Wilson's thesis. Baldwin also argues, on the basis of other parallels, that *Lucrece* is the earlier (*On the Literary Genetics of Shakspere's Poems & Sonnets*, pp. 131-32).

that comes from the same sources, although Dover Wilson, the latest editor of the play, regards them as non-Shakespearean.

All these details add up to a whole that is thoroughly consistent with Shakespeare's authorship at about the period of *Richard III*, or even a little thereafter if we assume that the setting of the play in Rome might have led him to return to his earlier manner of using grammar-school Latin authors. The quotations from Seneca tie the play to *Richard III*, and the references to Painter relate it to his future work. There is no clear reference to a classical author that is not an old favorite of his, except for Seneca, and there is no discordant note like the reference to the motion of the planet Mars in *1 Henry VI* or the same play's numerous echoes of contemporary writers in a single scene. Even the relatively high ratio of allusions to Virgil as compared to Ovid is in line with the importance of the *Aeneid* as a source for the interpolated material in *Lucrece*.

Romeo and Juliet is obviously an altogether different kind of play from *Titus*, and it shows an altogether different method of development. Like *Two Gentlemen* it has few echoes of the Latin poets and three times as many of contemporary writers. School learning no longer occurs in obvious allusions but rather as a passing and unobtrusive use of rhetorical terms or as a means, in the last scene, of creating the effect of a proper legal investigation, the material being taken from Brooke but the controlling arrangement from the *Ad Herennium*.[5]

But the play also reveals Shakespeare's increasing knowledge of contemporary poetry and an attempt to interpret his material philosophically. His control of poetry was, however, uncertain, and his fund of ideas was inadequate. These two considerations make *Romeo and Juliet* indicative of the ways in which Shakespeare's learning and thought were developing.

Stylistically the play is noteworthy for its extreme unevenness and for its experiments with various poetic forms. The range from rhetorical bombast to some of Shakespeare's greatest poetry is undoubtedly due in considerable part to the influence of Brooke's *Romeus and Juliet*, which supplied the example and even the material for some of the worst ranting. Granville-Barker notes that the hysterics of Romeo's scene with Friar Lawrence

[5]Baldwin, *W. S. Small Latine*, II, 78-80.

(III, iii) are taken, "at one point all but word for word," from Brooke,[6] and the same might be said of Juliet's preceding scene,[7] except for the wonderful epithalamium with which it opens. Obviously Shakespeare was still depending upon his source for poetic guidance. But Shakespeare quite unassisted by his source must be held guilty of the outrageous lines in which the Nurse, Paris, and Capulet lament Juliet's death, lines which have been identified as a parody of the *Spanish Tragedy*.[8] They actually differ little, if at all, from some of the outright parody that Shakespeare wrote for the "very tragical mirth" of Pyramus and Thisbe, and they, too, show how uncertain his taste must still have been. On the other hand, he has spared us some of Brooke's more maudlin poetry —for example, by restricting Romeo's final scene with Juliet to their farewell, for obvious reasons of propriety as well as of dramatic economy. The episodes of his own invention, which will be listed below, are much better poetically than those derived from the source, and, in general, the really great poetry in the play occurs in them—Mercutio's speeches, the balcony scene, and Juliet's epithalamium. Even in two scenes which as a whole follow Brooke—the meeting of Romeo and Juliet at the party and their deaths in the tomb—the best poetry is not derived from the source.

The play shows other, and less disastrous, influences of contemporary poetry than those derived from the source. As usual in his early plays, Shakespeare employs rhymed or even stanzaic verse for Romeo's purely conventional love of the shadowy Rosaline. The sonnet spoken by the Prologue perhaps reflects a similar prologue sonnet of Brooke's, but it is also an obvious and a successful effort to summarize the action of the play and establish its mood by use of a form associated with love. To achieve this same association, Romeo and Juliet meet in one sonnet[9] and begin a second, which breaks off as their love rapidly turns to something

[6]"Romeo and Juliet," *Prefaces to Shakespeare*, II, 341.
[7]Cf. especially III, ii, 97-137, with Brooke, ll. 1143-56.
[8]IV, v, 58, 62. Arden ed., p. xx. But Bethell (*Shakespeare & the Popular Dramatic Tradition*, p. 111) argues: "Its blatancy is necessary to overcome the audience's natural tendency to join the Capulets in their mourning. And the audience must not do this, because their tears are to be reserved for the last scene."
[9]Cf. Granville-Barker, *Prefaces to Shakespeare*, II, 305. But this sonnet seems to me more suggestive of the "line" of a gifted and well-bred adolescent than of a sacrament.

intense and serious (I, v, 95-112). The sonnet opening Act II is less effective, and Shakespeare uses no more. In the Queen Mab speech the whole play stops while Shakespeare and the audience enjoy a fine outburst of poetry (I, iv, 53-94), although, like Romeo, I always find myself a little impatient at the end. The epithalamium already alluded to is extraordinarily effective. It is built on a staple theme, although conventionally it was the bridegroom who was impatient; but the way in which the conventional material wanders off into arabesques of girlish fancy heightens immeasurably the irony of this joyous prelude to the awful disappointment that is to follow. Like the other passages discussed, it shows the awareness of contemporary literature and its fashions that is reflected in *Love's Labour's Lost* and reminds us that Shakespeare was now working on his own poems. It also shows, far better than they, the heights of which he was capable.

The best indication of Shakespeare's thinking (and incidentally of his artistic development) is to be found, however, in the way that he used his source in building his play. Arthur Brooke professed his poem *The Tragicall Historye of Romeus and Juliet* to be an exemplum of sound morality and of the evils of Popery, as he writes "To the Reader":

The glorious triumphe of the continent man upon the lustes of wanton fleshe, incourageth men to honest restraynt of wyld affections, the shamefull and wretched endes of such, as have yelded their libertie thrall to fowle desires, teache men to witholde them selves from the hedlong fall of loose dishonestie ... And to this ende (good Reader) is this tragicall matter written to describe unto thee a coople of unfortunate lovers, thralling themselves to unhonest desire, neglecting the authoritie and advise of parents and frendes, conferring their principall counsels with dronken gossyppes, and superstitious friers (the naturally fitte instrumentes of unchastitie) attemptyng all adventures of peryll, for thattaynyng of their wished lust, usyng auricular confession (the kay of whoredome and treason) for furtheraunce of theyr purpose, abusyng the honorable name of lawefull mariage, to cloke the shame of stolne contractes, finallye, by all meanes of unhonest lyfe, hastyng to most unhappye deathe.[10]

Actually Brooke took a considerably more charitable view of the young lovers than his preface would lead one to expect, and Walley is perhaps a little unfair to him in writing: "Romeus is

[10]Hazlitt, *Shakespeare's Library*, I (Part 1), 71-72.

an eminently proper, earnest, virtuous young man who unfortunately allows the insanity of love to betray his better judgment.
Juliet, on the other hand, is an artful coquette of Criseyde's
lineage."[11] These elements are present; but the poem contrives
to arouse real sympathy for the lovers, and it was this more charitable aspect of the story that undoubtedly fascinated Shakespeare.
We have noted that he apparently read the poem before writing
Two Gentlemen, or perhaps while writing, and that it so engrossed
his imagination that he inserted elements from it into that play
and unfortunately kept thinking of its geography in a way most
damaging to consistency of place references. In writing *Romeo
and Juliet* he paid no attention to Brooke's moralizing purpose,
but he showed how satisfying he found Brooke's poem by following it closely. Only a few scenes in the play are not based
directly on the poem, and even for these a hint is often to be
found, as the following tabulation of scenes *not* based upon the
source will show:

I, i, 1-84	(but this duplicates the brawl in III, i, which is based on Brooke.)
ii	(but cf. Brooke, ll. 161-62:
	But Capulet himself hath bid unto his feast,
	Or by his name in paper sent, appointed as a geast.)
iii	(but cf. hints in portrayal of nurse, ll. 637-73, 689-702.)
iv	
v, 1-44	
II, i	
ii	(but note Juliet's insistence upon marriage, ll. 424-28, 541-44, and Romeo's leaping the wall for his final night with Juliet, l. 830.)
iv, 1-109	
IV, i, 1-43	
iv	

Shakespeare's close following of his source makes doubly significant his deviations from it, which obviously reflect some
deliberate purpose on his part. In general, his objectives are fairly
clear, and they offer an interesting insight into his thinking. They
result either from purely dramatic considerations or from an
attempt to give the action of the play an intellectual dimension

[11]"Shakespeare's Debt to Marlowe in *Romeo and Juliet*," p. 260.

that is absent in the source. Actually, of course, Shakespeare's economy of workmanship is such that the same change often contributes to a better unified and a more meaningful action.

The most important of the changes that Shakespeare made to achieve an effective plot involved shortening the action from three months to four days. In Brooke Romeus and Juliet fall in love much as in the play; but they see each other through her window many times before they finally arrange a marriage, and, according to "The Argument," they have been married three months before Romeus' banishment. All this Shakespeare has condensed into the balcony scene, and he has even speeded up the initial wooing at the party to keep it in scale. This haste in the first part of the play is, of course, far more consistent than Brooke's leisurely narrative with the violent speed of events after Romeo's banishment, in which play and source agree closely. It also makes the lovers seem more "star-crossed," so that it contributes unity both of mood and of interpretation.

The source narrates the progress of a love affair, and many people appear in it briefly for a single function. Shakespeare therefore made numerous changes to provide a group of characters who, except when death intervenes, appear throughout the action of the play. But these adaptations do not concern us.[12]

Another and more important group of changes are intended not so much to give the action dramatic form as to give it meaning, and these are perhaps the most significant of all. Shakespeare keeps many of the conventions of romance, and we accept them willingly enough. Romeo and Juliet fall in love at sight and marry rapidly and without too much reflection (although Shakespeare gives us just enough to lull our suspicions to sleep); and they are apparently attracted only by external beauty or handsomeness. All this is made acceptable "not by analysis and realism, but by stage management, by poetry, by the fitness of the situation in the world that the poet has created."[13] But details that might

[12]For general discussions of Shakespeare's use of his sources in *Romeo and Juliet* see the following: *Brooke's 'Romeus and Juliet'* ed. Munro, pp. lv-lx and especially the tabulation of correspondences in Appendix I, pp. 131-45; Delius, "Brooke's episches und Shakespeare's dramatisches Gedicht von Romeo und Juliet," pp. 213-27; Erskine, "Romeo and Juliet," pp. 215-34; Law, "On Shakespeare's Changes of his Source Material in *Romeo and Juliet*," pp. 86-102; Moore, "Shakespeare's Deviations from *Romeus and Juliet*," pp. 68-74.

[13]Stoll, *Shakespeare's Young Lovers*, pp. 11-12, 15, 19-21.

shatter the romantic illusion Shakespeare is careful to change, and especially any note of cynical immorality. His nurse is coarse enough; but her advice to marry Paris is only cowardly opportunism, and she does not add the final outrageous detail in Brooke:

The pleasures past before, she must account as gayne:
But if he [Romeus] doe retorne, what then?—for one she shall have
   twayne.   (ll. 2303-34)[14]

Shakespeare also spares us Friar Lawrence's secret room in which in his youth he kept his fair friends. He shows us Romeo and Juliet distracted by grief, but he gives us nothing so damaging to Juliet as their final scene together in Brooke, in which Romeus comforts her and argues with her as with a spoiled little girl.

Shakespeare's principal effort, however, involved an attempt to strengthen what was, after all, a weak plot in which the lovers were defeated by a most improbable string of coincidences. This he sought to do by making the personal tragedy an inevitable part of larger conflicts—between youth and age, between individual love and family feud,[15] and between man and the universe. The extreme youth of Romeo and Juliet is, in fact, almost required by the action of the story. It is significant that Painter, following his sources, described Juliet as eighteen; Brooke, as sixteen; and Shakespeare, as fourteen. This fact seems to have been overlooked by critics who talk learnedly about the early maturing of Italian girls. In changing Juliet's age, Shakespeare was perhaps influenced by Marlowe's Abigail in *The Jew of Malta*, who is "scarce fourteen years of age."[16] But he was also attempting to create a conflict between the ardent love of youth, with all its impetuousness and lack of worldly wisdom, and the coldness of age that has forgotten what love is like. As usual, he gets his ages badly tangled, but his intention is clearer than his figures. Lady Capulet, according to her own statement, is only a little over twenty-eight (I, iii, 71-73), but she acts like a woman of advanced middle age, and Shakespeare so conceived her. She seems a little younger than her husband; but he admits to at least fifty years and probably

[14]Cf. Erskine, "Romeo and Juliet," p. 226.

[15]Erskine sees three—"the contrast of love with hate, of youth with age, of courtesy with vulgarity" ("Romeo and Juliet," p. 219). Cf. Cain, "Crabbed Age and Youth in 'Romeo and Juliet,'" pp. 186-91.

[16]Arden ed., p. xvii.

much more, since the masking at Lucentio's nuptial on which the calculation turns (I, v, 35-40) was clearly a belated fling. He acts like a very old man. Except for Friar Lawrence and the Nurse, who fails them, Romeo and Juliet are isolated in an old and unsympathetic world, and that isolation does much to explain the haste and violence of their actions, as Shakespeare intended that it should. The marriage seems to separate Romeo completely from his old friends who surrounded him in the first scene, at least as they are represented in the play by Benvolio. Shakespeare may or may not have written the poem in *The Passionate Pilgrim* beginning with the line "Crabbed age and youth cannot live to-gether" (l. 157), but *Romeo and Juliet* has the same moral.

Romeo's immaturity and his isolation, and the feeling of help-lessness which they induce, are in turn basic to Shakespeare's attempt to ground the tragedy, in part at least, in character rather than in accident. When Romeo prepares to stab himself, Friar Lawrence lectures him:

> Hold thy desperate hand!
> Art thou a man? Thy form cries out thou art;
> Thy tears are womanish; thy wild acts denote
> The unreasonable fury of a beast. . . .
> Hast thou slain Tybalt? Wilt thou slay thyself,
> And slay thy lady that in thy life lives,
> By doing damned hate upon thyself?
>
> (III, iii, 108-18)

Here Shakespeare surely meant Friar Lawrence to do more than give Romeo good advice. These lines also look forward to what Romeo ultimately does both to himself and to Juliet. They point out, furthermore, that his final suicide is both contrary to reason and a mortal sin and that he is morally responsible for the tragic outcome of the play. This speech therefore anticipates the think-ing of the mature tragedies. But its message as a judgment upon the action is not stressed, and it is, as we shall see, derived from Brooke.

Shakespeare also attempted to cover the weakness of his plot by building, from the first line of the play, a premonition of inevitable doom that hangs over Romeo and Juliet. He makes us so sure that tragedy will come and so involves our sympathies in the plight of the unhappy youngsters that we overlook the extreme improbability of the coincidences that determine their fate. This effect he creates by setting their love against the background of a family feud, so that, in our terminology though not in his, they are the victims of a hostile environment. This emphasis upon the feud is his own invention. Brooke has a sonnet "Argument" like Shakespeare's Prologue, but it is merely a resumé of the story itself:

> Love hath inflamed twayne by sodayn sight,
> And both do graunt the thing that both desyre;
> They wed in shrift by counsell of a frier;
> Yong Romeus clymes fayre Juliets bower by night.
> Three monthes he doth enjoy his cheefe delight:
> By Tybalt's rage, provoked unto yre,
> He payeth death to Tybalt for his hyre.
> A banisht man, he scapes by secret flight:
> New mariage is offred to his wyfe:
> She drinkes a drinke that seemes to reve her breath;
> They bury her, that sleping yet hath lyfe.
> Her husband heares the tydinges of her death;
> He drinkes his bane; and she, with Romeus knyfe,
> When she awakes, her selfe (alas) she sleath.

Brooke tells at the end of his poem that the tragedy ended the family feud:

The straungenes of the chaunce, when tryed was the truth,
The Mantagewes and Capelets hath moved so to ruth,
That with their emptyed teares theyr choler and theyr rage
Has emptied quite; and they, whose wrath no wisdom could asswage,
Nor threatning of the prince, ne mynd of murthers donne,
At length, (so mighty Jove it would) by pitye they are wonne.
   And lest that length of time might from our myndes remove
The memory of so perfect, sound and so approved love,
The bodies dead, removed from vaulte where they did dye,
In stately tombe, on pillers great of marble, rayse they hye.

(ll. 3005-14)

But it remained for Shakespeare to see in this story a connection with his favorite theme of the horrors of civil war, which in *Venus and Adonis* he had just equated with the worst of crimes:

> So in thyself thyself art made away;
> A mischief worse than civil home-bred strife,
> Or their whose desperate hands themselves do slay,
> Or butcher-sire that reaves his son of life.

(ll. 763-66)

He therefore set the destruction of the lovers against this background of unnatural conflict:

> Two households, both alike in dignity,
>   In fair Verona, where we lay our scene,
> From ancient grudge break to new mutiny,
>   Where civil blood makes civil hands unclean.
> From forth the fatal loins of these two foes
>   A pair of star-cross'd lovers take their life;
> Whose misadventur'd piteous overthrows
>   Doth with their death bury their parents' strife.
>   (ll. 1-8)

Shakespeare's concept was, however, far superior to his powers of expressing it, and this is the significant fact from the point of view of the development of his thought. In both *Lear* and *Macbeth* he had no difficulty in saying that the destruction of order in a kingdom produces an ever-widening destruction of the social fabric and results in time in the corruption of the family and of the very bonds of human affection.[17] Edmund in *Lear* denies specifically that the stars or fate are in any way responsible for such consequences of man's sin. But as yet Shakespeare had no terminology and no set of ideas adequate to his conception. So he fell back upon the ideas of the early chronicle plays, and of his source in Brooke. What we should call a hostile environment became in his language hostile stars and fortune, and Romeo and Juliet are in conflict with a crudely conceived universe.

Several references to the influence of the stars occur in the play, and they are regarded not as inclining but as compelling. The "star-cross'd" of the Prologue is recalled by Romeo's words as he goes to Capulet's party, and the crude fatalism of the astrology is carried over to the invocation in the last two lines:

> I fear, too early; for my mind misgives
> Some consequence yet hanging in the stars
> Shall bitterly begin his fearful date
> With this night's revels, and expire the term
> Of a despised life clos'd in my breast
> By some vile forfeit of untimely death.
> But he that hath the steerage of my course
> Direct my sail!   (I, iv, 106-13)

[17]Cf. *Lear*, I, ii, 112-45; *Macbeth*, III, ii, 16-19 ("both the worlds" are, of course, the great world of nature and the microcosm or little world of man), IV, iii, 31-137.

Upon hearing of Juliet's death, Romeo can only say: "Then I defy you, stars" (V, i, 24), again accepting by implication their control of events. And the implication would be the same if we accepted either of the original readings rather than the editorial text given: "defie my stars" with Quarto 1 or "denie you, stars" with Quarto 2 and the First Folio. Romeo sees in his suicide the only way to

> shake the yoke of inauspicious stars
> From this world-wearied flesh.
>
> (V, iii, 111-12)

The references to fortune are even more significant in that they occur at crucial points in the action of the play. "O, I am fortune's fool!" cries Romeo after he slays Tybalt (III, i, 141). Juliet's first words after Romeo bids her farewell call upon fortune:

> O Fortune, Fortune! all men call thee fickle;
> If thou art fickle, what dost thou with him
> That is renown'd for faith? Be fickle, Fortune;
> For then, I hope, thou wilt not keep him long,
> But send him back.
>
> (III, v, 60-64)

And Friar Lawrence comments on Friar John's failure to deliver the all-important letter: "Unhappy fortune!" (V, ii, 17).

Critics have been fond of complaining that the outcome of *Romeo and Juliet* depends upon a series of coincidences. An action so dominated by chance, they have argued, cannot be genuinely tragic. Probably they are right, but they have generally overlooked the importance assigned to Fortune by the language of the characters. In this respect, at least, the action of the play is in accord with its stated philosophy. But the stars, as references to them consistently imply, govern the universe, including mankind, in a fashion that is thoroughly deterministic. Determinism and blind chance cannot be reconciled. The lovers can be crossed by the stars or by Fortune, but not by both, unless Fortune is now to become a mere word to conceal man's ignorance of the inscrutable operations of astrology. That it is such the play nowhere indicates. How otherwise to reconcile Fortune and the stars I do not know. I doubt that Shakespeare knew either.

115

Romeo and Juliet therefore amounts to little as evidence of what Shakespeare believed to be man's place in the scheme of things, except to make it doubtful that at this time he had any clearly thought out view on the problem. As the opening sonnet shows, he was already groping for a more nearly adequate set of ideas, and eventually he found them. For the present, he was unable to work out and express the implications of his opening sonnet because he had no theory of causation or of social forces adequate to do so. So he fell back upon folk astrology and, as usual, upon his source material. Brooke is full of references to Fortune and her wheel, and of the three speeches instanced above, Juliet's is based directly upon words which Romeus uses in consoling Juliet:

> For Fortune chaungeth more than fickel fantasie;
> In nothing Fortune constant is save in unconstancie.
> Her hasty ronning wheele is of a restles coorse,
> That turnes the clymers hedlong downe, from better to the woorse,
> And those that are beneth she heaveth up agayne:
> So we shall rise to pleasures mount, out of the pit of payne.
>
> (ll. 1667-72)

It is interesting, incidentally, that Brooke owed "most of his frequent allusions to Fortune and her wheel" to Chaucer's *Troilus*,[18] and we have, therefore, an example of indirect influence of Chaucer upon Shakespeare.

One passage in *Romeo and Juliet* requires special comment in connection with the development of Shakespeare's thought. That is Friar Lawrence's monologue in Act II, Scene iii. Brooke provided a hint:

> Not as the most was he, a grosse unlearned foole,
> But doctor of divinitie proceded he in schoole.
> The secretes eke he knew in Natures woorkes that loorke;
> By magiks arte most men supposd that he could wonders woorke.
>
> (ll. 567-70)

But it was up to Shakespeare to fill in enough details to make convincing the Friar's reputation in Verona and his ability to provide the extraordinary sleeping potion. Into the Friar's speech Shakespeare therefore inserted a series of reasonably learned ideas

---

[18] J. J. Munro in his edition of *Brooke's 'Romeus and Juliet'*, p. liii.

dealing with nature and human conduct. Where he got them no one has suggested, but they look very much as though he had recently been reading some work which in turn combined one of Lucretius' most striking lines—*Omniparens eadem rerum commune sepulchrum* (V, 259: "the universal parent of things and their common grave")—with the well-known, but quite un-Lucretian, principle that Nature does nothing in vain. One might read a learned concept of Nature's operation into the lines about whatever "revolts from true birth" (II, iii, 17-20), but Shakespeare speaks of the revolt as "strain'd," which implies that he was thinking only of man's misuse of good things.[19] Finally, to give the Friar the necessary theological learning, he added an analogy between medicinal and poisonous plants and "grace and rude will" (II, iii, 27-28), which heal and destroy the soul. His descending sequence man, woman, beast (III, iii, 109-11), and the learning which it implies, are derived directly from Brooke:

> Art thou quoth he a man? thy shape saith, so thou art;
> Thy crying, and thy wepeing eyes denote a womans hart.
> For manly reason is quite from of thy mynd out chased,
> And in her stead affections lewd and fancies highly placed:
> So that I stoode in doute, this howre (at the least)
> If thou a man or woman wert, or els a brutish beast.

> (ll. 1353-58)

Venus and Adonis and *The Rape of Lucrece* are interesting, from the point of view of Shakespeare's intellectual development, principally because they supplement *Love's Labour's Lost* and *Romeo and Juliet* as a revelation of his interest in contemporary poetry. We noted that Shakespeare's interest in Venus and Adonis may have been aroused by Aphthonius' analysis of Ovid's treatment of the story. As is well known, the poem itself derives largely from Ovid, being a combination of elements from the account of Adonis in Book X of the *Metamorphoses*, of Salmacis and the reluctant Hermaphroditus in Book IV, and the boar from the story of Meleager in Book VIII. A few commonplaces may come from other classical writers or from Renaissance adaptations. But Shakespeare probably owed something also to Spenser's pictures of the love of Venus and Adonis in Castle Joyous (*Faerie Queene*,

---

[19]For a different interpretation see Pettet, *Shakespeare and the Romance Tradition*, pp. 118-19.

III, i, 34-38), to Lodge's *Glaucus and Scilla,* and for details to
Marlowe's *Hero and Leander.*[20] The Latin motto came from
Ovid's *Amores* (I, xv, 35-36). Reading in contemporary Latin
verse is indicated by the lines

> For he being dead, with him is beauty slain,
> And beauty dead, black chaos comes again.
> (ll. 1019-20)

These come from a *Pompa* of Buchanan's published in 1584:

> Cesset amor, pariter cessabunt foedera rerum;
> In chaos antiquum cuncta elementa ruent.[21]

(Let love give way, and the laws of the universe will likewise
give way; all the elements will collapse into the chaos of long
ago.) Most indicative of Shakespeare's knowledge of contemporary poetry is his apparent paraphrase of Ronsard's

> Les Muses lierent un cour
> De chaisnes de roses, Amour

in "Leading him prisoner in a red-rose chain" (l. 110). More
likely, however, the line is derived from the eighty-third poem
in Thomas Watson's *Hekatompathia or Passionate Century of
Love*:

> The Muses not long since intrapping Love
> In chaine of roases linked all araye.

Ronsard has also been suggested as the source for

> The tender spring upon thy tempting lip
> Shows thee unripe; yet mayst thou well be tasted.
> (ll. 127-28)

We have already noted that Shakespeare's interest in the story
of *The Rape of Lucrece* may have been aroused by reading
Painter's adaptation of Livy in the *Palace of Pleasure.* Baldwin
points out that he might have encountered in Velkirchius' edition
of Erasmus' *Copia* the following exercise appended to Chapter
xxx: "Confer historiam Lucretiae descriptam ab Ouidio in fine
2. Fast. cum narratione Liuiana in fine 1. lib." (Compare the history
of Lucretia written by Ovid at the end of *Fasti II* with Livy's

---

[20]The best summary of Shakespeare's sources for *Venus and Adonis* seems to
be in Bush, *Mythology and the Renaissance Tradition in English Poetry*, pp. 140-45.
[21]Baldwin, *On the Literary Genetics of Shakspere's Poems & Sonnets*, pp. 50-53.

account at the end of Book I.)[22] This is substantially what Shakespeare did, except that a good deal of the Livy may actually have come from Marsus' notes to Ovid.[23] Shakespeare perhaps used Chaucer's *Legend of Good Women*, and he demonstrably used Painter.[24] The painting of the fall of Troy is obviously indebted to the first two books of Virgil's *Aeneid*, and the poem owes much of its spirit to Samuel Daniel's *Complaint of Rosamond*, published in 1592.

The echo of Shakespeare's preoccupation with civil war to be found in *Venus and Adonis* has already been noted. Neo-Platonism is involved in the equation of love and beauty that Shakespeare made in adapting Buchanan, and it appears in numerous other details. But it is of the vague sort that was generally diffused throughout Renaissance literature. Two other ideas deserve comment. *The Rape of Lucrece* contains the fullest allusions to the fall of man and to its effect upon his soul that have so far been encountered. Tarquin's soul is represented as summarizing the fall of man:

> Besides, his soul's fair temple is defaced:
>> To whose weak ruins muster troops of cares,
>> To ask the spotted princess how she fares.
>
> She says, her subjects with foul insurrection
> Have batter'd down her consecrated wall,
> And by their mortal fault brought in subjection
> Her immortality, and made her thrall
> To living death and pain perpetual;
>> Which in her prescience she controlled still,
>> But her foresight could not forestall their will.
>
> (ll. 719-28)

An earlier passage reflects the conflict between man's corrupted will—"rude will," as Friar Lawrence calls it—and his reason, weakened by the fall. It also implies the ultimate overthrow by which the will, serving the passions, could master the reason and make it a servant of the will:

[22] W. S. *Small Latine*, II, 194.

[23] Cf. Baldwin, *On the Literary Genetics of Shakespeare's Poems & Sonnets*, pp. 97-153.

[24] Bush, op. cit., p. 150. Baldwin (*Literary Genetics*, p. 106) doubts that Shakespeare used Chaucer but agrees that he used Painter (p. 112).

"My will is strong, past reason's weak removing.
   Who fears a sentence or an old man's saw
   Shall by a painted cloth be kept in awe."

Thus, graceless, holds he disputation
'Tween frozen conscience and hot burning will,
And with good thoughts makes dispensation,
Urging the worser sense for vantage still;
Which in a moment doth confound and kill
   All pure effects, and doth so far proceed
   That what is vile shows like a virtuous deed.
                                        (ll. 244-52)

This is the fullest statement of these ideas to be found in his early
works, and their occurrence in *Lucrece* rather than one of the
plays is significant because Shakespeare had undoubtedly encountered them in contemporary poetry. This conflict is a major theme
of Watson's *Hekatompathia*; and it appears in Sidney's sonnets,
especially *Astrophel and Stella*, X, which turns on a similar yielding by reason that produces an extravagant compliment to Stella
rather than a more deadly sin. Spenser is full of allusions to the
same conflict as his heroes subordinate reason to one or another
of the passions,[25] and there are a number of fairly detailed allusions
in the learned Brooke, from whom Shakespeare may actually have
derived the notion of using the ideas as material for poetry.[26]

   Both *Venus and Adonis* and *The Rape of Lucrece* contain
another favorite Renaissance theme that we have not previously
encountered in Shakespeare, the conflict between art and nature.
Adonis' horse is said to excel all others as the work of a great
painter surpasses nature:

        Look, when a painter would surpass the life
        In limning out a well-proportioned steed,
        His art with nature's workmanship at strife,
        As if the dead the living should exceed;
           So did this horse excel a common one
           In shape, in courage, colour, pace, and bone.
                                        (ll. 289-94)

The reference in *Lucrece* occurs in connection with a picture of
the Greeks besieging Troy:

[25]Cf. *Faerie Queene*, I, i, 50; I, ii, 5; I, ii, 8; I, ii, 12; etc.
[26]Cf. ll. 131-32, 1355-56, 1399-1400, etc.

A thousand lamentable objects there,
In scorn of nature, art gave lifeless life:
Many a dry drop seem'd a weeping tear,
Shed for the slaughter'd husband by the wife;
The red blood reek'd, to show the painter's strife;
   And dying eyes gleam'd forth their ashy lights,
   Like dying coals burnt out in tedious nights.

(ll. 1373-79)

A few lines earlier Shakespeare had written:

To see sad sights moves more than hear them told;
For then the eye interprets to the ear
The heavy motion that it doth behold,
When every part a part of woe doth bear.

(ll. 1324-27)

This is an obvious echo of Horace's *Ars Poetica*:

Segnius irritant animos demissa per aurem
quam que sunt oculis subiecta fidelibus et quae
ipse sibi tradit spectator.

(Less vividly is the mind stirred by what finds entrance through
the ears than by what is brought before the trusty eyes, and what
the spectator can see for himself.)[27] All this looks very much as
though Shakespeare had been reading in literary criticism. Both
the comparison of poetry to a picture and the contrast between
nature and art occur in Horace (ll. 361 ff.; 408 ff.), but it is
very likely that Shakespeare had also been reading in one of
several English works that develop the themes more fully than
Horace does and point out how art can create an ideal type superior to nature, which Horace does not do. Such reading might well
have been undertaken in preparation for entry into the world
of polite letters; both of the poems belong to the type of mythological poem then fashionable and involved deliberate competi-
tion with established poets.

As negative evidence of what Shakespeare did not know we
might cite the long meditation on Opportunity, Time, and Night
which he interpolated into *Lucrece* (ll. 876-1078). Aside from
a few echoes of Ovid, it is singularly barren of interesting or
significant ideas—and, one is tempted to add, of poetry.

[27]*Satires, Epistles and Ars Poetica*, trans. Fairclough (Loeb). *Ars Poetica*,
ll. 180-82.

In conclusion it should perhaps be noted that two writers find a great deal more intellectual content in the poems than I do. Lu Emily Pearson sees in *Venus and Adonis* an elaborate philosophical allegory and in *Lucrece* Shakespeare's reflection of a Petrarchan heroine. Of *Venus and Adonis* she writes:

So Venus is shown as the destructive agent of sensual love; Adonis, as reason in love. The one sullies whatever it touches; the other honors and makes it beautiful. The one is false and evil; the other is all truth, all good. Reason in love, truth, beauty—these are the weapons with which lust must be met, or the ideals of man must go down in defeat before the appetites. Thus it is that when Adonis is killed, beauty is killed, and the world is left in black chaos, for beauty, the soul of matter, unites all parts of creation with the great God of beauty. This is the teaching of *Venus and Adonis,* as didactic a piece of work, perhaps, as Shakespeare ever wrote.[28]

Baldwin also finds philosophic meaning in the same poem:

Though the borrowed lines from Buchanan [quoted above] be but two, they are in fact the principal shaping source of Shakespeare's *Venus and Adonis.* For they generate the Platonic argument which occupies most of the poem. Adonis is Love and Beauty, and when he dies Chaos is come again. Consequently, Venus argues for procreation that Love-Beauty-Adonis may not die.[29]

All this seems over-ingenious, more like Spenser than Shakespeare. Indeed, one can do no better by way of comment than to quote Bush's comparison of the two poets:

Shakespeare doubtless knew at least two treatments of Adonis in Spenser; a few lines from one passage have already been quoted. Spenser's half-symbolic adaptation of the myth in the sixth canto of the third book is quite remote from Shakespeare's, for Shakespeare's attitude toward his material is simply that of a Renaissance Ovid; his Venus and Adonis are symbolic only in the sense that they and everything connected with them are manifestations of physical beauty.[30]

[28]*Elizabethan Love Conventions*, p. 285.

[29]*On the Literary Genetics of Shakspere's Poems & Sonnets*, p. 73.

[30]*Mythology and the Renaissance Tradition in English Poetry*, p. 144.

CHAPTER VI

King John

━━━━━━━━━━━━━━━━━━━━━━━━

D OVER WILSON remarks, quite rightly, that *King John* has never received from students of Shakespeare's dramatic technique the attention that it merits:

King John, being the only Shakespearian play the non-Shakespearian original for which has survived, offers a unique opportunity of studying the way in which Shakespeare handled the material given him, and thence of inferring to some extent his method of dealing in other plays with sources that are now lost. Strange to say, however, though there has been endless discussion of the manner in which he refashioned the plays of his predecessors, very little serious work has been done on the single instance where the refashioning is patent and indisputable.[1]

The same observation holds true for any consideration of Shakespeare's thought, and especially of his interest in and attitude toward history. *King John* gives us a chance to observe his practice when he could either have followed a non-historical source or, especially when puzzled by the old play, have referred to historical material at first hand. It should therefore enable us to check the inferences as to his knowledge of history which were drawn from the early Yorkist plays, and to see what importance he attached to the study of historical sources—that is, to check his interest in history as well as his knowledge of it. *King John* is what Bacon called a "crucial instance," and any critical theory with respect to the chronicle plays must account for the relationship between it and its source, the two parts of *The Troublesome Raigne of King John*—must, in fact, be very largely based upon that rela-

---

[1] New Cambridge *King John,* p. xxxiv.

tionship. The play therefore deserves from students of Shakespeare's thinking an attention quite out of proportion to its intrinsic merits. Such attention it has generally failed to receive, particularly from recent writers upon the chronicle plays.

Now the simple fact is that Shakespeare's mind was on character and dramatic effect. He was not sufficiently interested in English history as such to check details that confused him in his source or even to reproduce his source accurately. Nor did he develop his own interpretation of events. He was unwilling, for some reason, to accept the view that unifies *The Troublesome Raigne*. There John is a kind of pre-Reformation hero in the struggle between England and the Papacy; in his direst adversity he even prophesies the coming of Henry VIII: "A king shall reign that shall surpass them all" (*2 T.R.*, ii, 173).[2] Seeking another way of imposing unity upon the play, Shakespeare found, in the Bastard's final speech in *The Troublesome Raigne*, a theme that was an old favorite of his—the evils of civil strife. To this theme he gave much greater emphasis, and he built the Bastard into a kind of chorus, who pleads for national unity.

The preceding generalizations, the evidence for which will form the body of this chapter, obviously cannot be reconciled with the thesis of Tillyard's *Shakespeare's History Plays*: "It is indeed true that for the young Shakespeare the political theme of England, her past history and her present glory, was the theme which had the greatest surface solemnity and which he thought he minded most about."[3]

But Tillyard, whose scholarship is excellent and who has much that is brilliantly illuminating to say about the chronicles, has not failed to appreciate the test of his theories presented by *King John*. His solution of the problem is, however, more heroic than sound. In his *History of English Poetry* Courthope had argued that *The Contention*, *The True Tragedy*, and *The Troublesome Raigne* were earlier drafts by Shakespeare of plays which appear in the Folio.[4] To oppose a mass of evidence that Shakespeare

[2]References are to the text of *The Troublesome Raigne* reprinted in the Furness Variorum *King John*, pp. 471-537.

[3]Pp. 145-46.

[4]"Appendix on the Authenticity of Some of the Early Plays Assigned to Shakespeare, and their Relationship to the Development of his Dramatic Genius," *History of English Poetry*, IV, 465-66.

worked from *The Troublesome Raigne* without wholly understanding it, Courthope offered only two arguments: the excellent
construction of *The Troublesome Raigne* indicated Shakespeare's
hand, and *The Contention* and *The True Tragedy* had also been
rewritten to produce *2* and *3 Henry VI*, which were therefore
parallel instances of Shakespeare's rewriting his own earlier handiwork. This parallel disappears, of course, if it be granted that
the other two plays are bad quartos of *2* and *3 Henry VI*, as
seems to be established. As a preface to his elaborate study of the
evidence that *King John* is based upon *The Troublesome Raigne*,
Dover Wilson disposes of Courthope's theory summarily but
justly: "This is one of the curiosities of criticism, and the attribu-
tion to Shakespeare has found scant support elsewhere."[5]

But Tillyard restates Courthope's view notwithstanding the
contrary evidence, which he hardly considers, and adopts it with
an ingenious modification:

In other words, as the *Contention* and the *True Tragedy* have turned
out to be bad quartos of *2* and *3 Henry VI*, so may the *Troublesome
Reign* turn out to be a bad quarto (though perhaps in a different way
bad) not of *King John* as we have it but of an early play by Shakespeare on the same theme. This play would then be the original both
of the *Troublesome Reign* and of *King John*.[6]

But he still fails to explain how Shakespeare misunderstood details
which are correct in *The Troublesome Raigne* and which must
therefore have been correct in any earlier play of which it was
a bad quarto—a singularly good "bad" quarto, be it added. It must
be clear by now that I regard Shakespeare as subject to quite
human limitations both of comprehension and of accuracy; but
no tenable view of his mental endowment will let us assume that
he could keep details of history and of motivation perfectly clear
in *The Troublesome Raigne* or a source play for it, and then, four
or five years later, mix them up as badly as he did in *King John*,
when he obviously had the source play before him. Besides, as
we shall see, some of the confusion results from minor details
in the present text of *The Troublesome Raigne*. Tillyard's attempt
is gallant but unconvincing.

[5]New Cambridge *King John*, p. xix.
[6]*Shakespeare's History Plays*, p. 217.

In her book *Shakespeare's Histories: Mirrors of Elizabethan Policy*, Lily B. Campbell elaborates a parallel between the unhistorical treatment of Arthur in *King John* and the role of Mary Queen of Scots during the reign of Queen Elizabeth, which becomes part of the evidence for her thesis that Shakespeare rewrote English history to make it mirror contemporary events.[7] But, since relevant details in the treatment of Arthur are derived from *The Troublesome Raigne*, her evidence, if sound, relates in this instance to the writer of the old play and proves that her approach can be applied to the work of other dramatists as well. And the main argument of this chapter—that Shakespeare was uninterested in history as such—is logically inconsistent with the thesis of her entire book.

The preceding examples from two very interesting books are alleged, not to be contentious, but to illustrate the fundamental importance of *King John* to any study of Shakespeare's thought. As compared with *The Troublesome Raigne*, it reveals careful attention to dramatic effects and a skill quite consistent with the generally accepted date of 1594-1596; it also shows almost complete indifference to historical fact and historical motivation. These two generalizations will be considered in order.

The extraordinary skill which Shakespeare shows in developing character and in manipulating his material is outside the range of this study. Edward Rose has an excellent treatment of the subject in his essay "Shakespeare as an Adapter."[8] But a variety of changes, although matters of dramatic methodology, have some bearing on the development of Shakespeare's learning and thought. To begin with a familiar point, *The Troublesome Raigne* is full of crude classical allusions like those in the Henry VI plays, in which Shakespeare himself reflected an earlier dramatic style. In meditating on his doubtful paternity, Philip spouts Latin like any pedant (*1 T.R.*, i, 237-47), and most of the characters abound in classical allusions. All this Shakespeare has eliminated, although he has retained a certain amount of grammar-school material in the form of allusions to Erasmus' *Adagia* and to Aesop, and he

[7]Cf. p. 149.

[8]Reprinted in the Praetorius facsimile of Part 1 of *The Troublesome Raigne*; cf. pp. ix-xv.

makes Philip talk of a catechism in imitation of the "Absey book."[9]

More interesting are a number of changes that reflect a concern for propriety of conduct, whether in manners or morals. We have noted this concern in *Romeo and Juliet,* and it becomes increasingly important in the great comedies. But no other play reflects it in so wide a range of examples. In the opening scene of *The Troublesome Raigne* Elianor quite literally pushes John into the background in a way that violates Elizabethan (and modern) notions of deference due both to man and to king. She opens the play, introducing John to the Barons; she harangues Chatillion, the French ambassador; and she plays a much more important part in the argument over Philip's paternity than in *King John.* Shakespeare has given her the same character that she has in the source and the same role in accepting Philip, but he has seen to it that John dominates and controls the scene as a king should. In *The Troublesome Raigne* John shows his guile as he dismisses Chatillion:

> *Pembrooke,* convey him safely to the sea,
> But not in haste; for, as we are advis'd
> We mean to be in *Fraunce* as soon as he,
> To fortify such towns as we possess
> In *Aniou, Torain,* and in *Normandy.*
>
> (i, 59-63)

Shakespeare merely has John say: "An honorable conduct let him have" (I, i, 29), even though the change makes it necessary to rely improbably upon "the adverse winds" (II, i, 57) to explain how John reached France as soon as the ambassador. Shakespeare also spares Lady Faulconbridge the humiliation of participating in a public discussion of her infidelity to her late husband, whereas in *The Troublesome Raigne* she is present throughout the investigation and is interrogated. In both plays, however, her final admission of guilt is made to Philip privately.

Shakespeare shows a most romantic—and probably unrealistic —tenderness for the sensibilities of Lewis and Blanch in arranging their marriage, for John accepts the citizen's suggestion that they be married only

---

[9]Cf. Liebermann, "Shakespeare als Bearbeiter des *King John*," p. 197. For Erasmus' *Adagia* cf. II, i, 137, which, however, perhaps echoes *Spanish Tragedy,* I, ii, 172 (Anders, *Shakespeare's Books,* p. 130); Aesop, II, i, 141-42; IV, iii, 155-56 (Baldwin, *W. S. Small Latine,* I, 625, 624); Absey book, I, i, 189-204 (Baldwin, op. cit., II, 232-33; Anders, op. cit., p. 12).

If that the Dauphin there, thy princely son,
Can in this book of beauty read, "I love."
(II, i, 484-85)

Less concern is shown for Blanch's inclinations, but she seems to assent willingly. In *The Troublesome Raigne* the matter is settled more expeditiously but less romantically:

> *K. John.* Brother of *Fraunce*, you hear the citizens;
> Then tell me how you mean to deal herein.
>
> *Constance.* Why *John*, what canst thou give unto thy niece,
> Thou hast no foot of land but *Arthurs* right?
>
> *Lewes.* By'r Lady, citizens, I like your choice,
> A lovely damzel is the Lady *Blanche*,
> Worthy the heir of *Europe* for her fere.
> (*1 T.R.*, iv, 102-108)[10]

And Constance's absence from this scene of double-dealing is perhaps another example of Shakespeare's delicacy, although it also makes the scene less improbable—if degrees of improbability matter in such a scene!

A similar regard for propriety may have led Shakespeare to eliminate the attacks upon the Roman Catholic Church and the monasteries that occupied so much space in *The Troublesome Raigne*. It is possible that he had Roman Catholic sympathies, although we have noted plenty of Protestant theology in his plays. He may have wished to please the Catholic Earl of Southampton, as has been proposed; or he may have wanted to emphasize national unity rather than religious strife, as Dover Wilson suggests.[11] But it is also possible that he eliminated the low comedy scenes involving the ransacking of the monastery and convent because he found them offensive—not that he disliked low comedy but that he did avoid this particular kind of low comedy. His clowns are bawdy, but his churchmen are not clowns; rank is observed in humor as in other matters. Nor do the changes all operate in

---

[10]"In *TR* heiratete Ludwig rein geschäfstmässig; Sh. flicht ein Band der Liebesneigung hinein." Liebermann, "Shakespeare als Bearbeiter des *King John*," p. 196. Note that Shakespeare makes the same change from his source in *Romeo and Juliet* when Capulet tells Paris: "My will to her consent is but a part" (I, ii, 17). But in his subsequent actions Capulet belies his word and is quite as arbitrary as in the source.

[11]New Cambridge *King John*, pp. lx-lxi.

the same direction—that is, in favor of Roman Catholicism. It is debatable whether Shakespeare's monk who murders without any motive whatever is less of a stigma upon the church than a monk who poisons a king who has been impoverishing and persecuting his order. Shakespeare also makes Pandulph more immoral as well as more long-winded than he is in the source.[12] In fact, the Cardinal's long exposition of Machiavellian politics to Lewis is a striking exception to Shakespeare's usual indifference to political motives. Perhaps Shakespeare meant to mark John's capture of Arthur as the turning point of the play. Although he introduced no new ideas, he amplified what he found in his source, and gave Pandulph a prophecy of what very nearly happened.

It is also possible that Shakespeare took a less favorable view of John himself than *The Troublesome Raigne* both because he could not tolerate John's immoral and unkingly deeds and because he found it impossible to think of him as other than a usurper. In *3 Henry VI* Margaret argues (III, iii, 71-72) that usurpation is quite enough to prove Edward a tyrant. Certainly the argument which Arthur himself urges in *The Troublesome Raigne* that "possession of a crown is much" (*1 T.R.*, ii, 19) shows, like the rest of the play, a command of historical information of which Shakespeare nowhere gives evidence. In *King John*, on the other hand, Eleanor's blunt rejoinder to John that his holding the crown depends upon "your strong possession much more than your right" (I, i, 40) is thoroughly in accord with Elizabethan ideas of legitimate succession, which are also reflected in the Bastard's soliloquy at the end of Act IV:

> From forth this morsel of dead royalty [Arthur],
> The life, the right, and truth of all this realm
> Is fled to heaven; and England now is left
> To tug and scamble and to part by th' teeth
> The unow'd interest of proud-swelling state.
>
> (IV, iii, 143-47)

The preceding observations are not intended to imply that Shakespeare was unaware of the religious issue or that it should be overlooked in studying the play, but rather to suggest that other considerations may also have influenced him and are per-

[12]Cf. *King John*, III, iv, 107-84, with *1 T.R.*, x, 36-46.

tinent to a discussion of the problem—a discussion which I propose to avoid, since I do not have adequate evidence.

The Bastard is certainly Shakespeare's greatest dramatic achievement in the play, but he also shows how much the source stimulated Shakespeare's thinking. For Philip came from the source intact. Shakespeare gave him a much larger part in the play, but did not invent either his blunt common sense and his swaggering humor or his function as a chorus commenting upon the action.[13] He has speeches concluding Acts II, IV, and V in place of his single speech ending Part 2 of *The Troublesome Raigne*. His reflections now include the subject "Mad World! mad kings! mad composition!" and this extended treatment is new, although the puzzled note appears in the source. But the Bastard's main theme and his function as dramatist's mouthpiece are both implicit in the final lines in *The Troublesome Raigne*:

> Thus *England's* peace begins in *Henry's* reign,
> And bloody wars are clos'd with happy league.
> Let *England* live but true within itself,
> And all the world can never wrong her state.
> *Lewes*, thou shalt be bravely shipt to *Fraunce*.
> For never Frenchman got of English ground
> The twentieth part that thou hast conquered.
> *Dolphin*, thy hand, to *Worster* we will march,
> Lords all, lay hands to bear your sovereign
> With obsequies of honour to his grave:
> If *England's* peers and people join in one,
> No Pope, nor *Fraunce*, nor *Spain* can do them wrong.
>   (2 *T.R.*, ix, 42-54)

This attempt to use the Bastard to give unity and interest to the play is fundamentally a failure, as Rose comments:

The effort, too, to give the piece a hero in Falconbridge is a failure, because, as long experience teaches, you *cannot* force a character out of the position he would naturally occupy in a play. Falconbridge

---

[13]Note that Tillyard also minimizes this derivation of the Bastard from the source: "It is because Shakespeare conceived him so passionately and gifted him with so unbreakable an individuality that all these kingly qualities take on a life that is quite lacking in the character that should have been finer still: the Henry V of the play that goes under that title. In the character of the Bastard Shakespeare achieves an astonishing break-away from his official self, and through it he develops two weighty political themes which give the play its proper and effective value as part of a great historical series." *Shakespeare's History Plays*, p. 229.

is properly little more than a chorus, a cynical critic of a wicked age—he might be entirely omitted without in the least degree altering the substance of the plot—and it is therefore impossible to make the story centre in him, as should every story in some one figure, or inseparably-connected group of figures.[14]

But, though he fails to give unity, the Bastard places *King John* as one of a series of attempts that Shakespeare made to impose a dramatic structure upon refractory material from English history. After trying to unify *2* and *3 Henry VI* about Margaret and Warwick respectively and the conflicts which they dominated, he used a villain-hero in *Richard III*. The attempt made in *King John* to build a minor role into a major source of interest he repeated in *1* and *2 Henry IV*. *Richard II* is a carefully balanced conflict between two men, in which sympathy for Richard rises as his fortunes decline, and sympathy for Bolingbroke declines as his fortunes rise. *Henry V* is another one-man play, this time with a real hero, but in its chorus-Prologues Shakespeare in effect confessed ultimate failure to convert history into drama. It should also be noted that his experiments in the chronicle plays paralleled the use of similar devices elsewhere. "Shakespeare's Histories are more like his own Comedies and Tragedies than like others' Histories."[15] *1 Henry IV* has divergent plot elements from history and comedy but finally brings all characters together in the last scenes, just as the parallel threads of intrigue and romantic comedy in *The Merchant of Venice* or *Much Ado* are tied together at the end; and the emphasis upon the Bastard is not unlike the attention given to Mercutio or Jaques, which is out of all proportion to their function in carrying forward the plot. All this amounts to further evidence that Shakespeare was primarily interested in dramatic effect no matter what kind of material he was handling.

The most striking evidence of Shakespeare's indifference to historical fact and historical motivation is to be found in the mess that he made of material from *The Troublesome Raigne*, most notably in his treatment of Arthur. In the first place, he seems not to know whose son Arthur was or how he derived his claim to the throne. At the beginning of the play Chatillon demands the throne from John for "thy deceased brother Geoffrey's son"

[14]"Shakespeare as an Adapter," p. xvi.
[15]Tillyard, *Shakespeare's History Plays*, p. 3.

(I, i, 8), which is quite correct and also close to the source: "*Arthur*, Duke of *Brittaine*, son and heir to *Jeffry*, thine elder brother" (*1 T.R.*, i, 30-31). But at the beginning of the second scene *The Troublesome Raigne* neglects to say whose son Arthur is:

> *King.* Now 'gin we broach the title of thy claim,
> Young *Arthur*, in the *Albion* territories,
> Scaring proud *Angiers* with a puissant siege.
> Brave *Austria*, cause of *Cordelions* death,
> Is also come to aid thee in thy wars.
>
> <div align="right">(<i>1 T.R.</i>, ii, 1-5)</div>

Shakespeare had forgotten who the French king was; so he assigned the speech to Lewis. He had also forgotten who Arthur's father was and took the hint that Austria was atoning for killing the father by aiding the son:

> *Lew.* Before Angiers well met, brave Austria.
> Arthur, that great forerunner of thy blood,
> Richard, that robb'd the lion of his heart
> And fought the holy wars in Palestine,
> By this brave duke came early to his grave;
> And for amends to his posterity,
> At our importance hither is he come
> To spread his colours, boy, in thy behalf,
> And to rebuke the usurpation
> Of thy unnatural uncle, English John.
>
> (II, i, 1-10)

Arthur is even more explicit:

> God shall forgive you Coeur-de-lion's death
> The rather that you give his offspring life.
>
> (II, i, 12-13)

Perhaps because Chatillon's entry reminded Shakespeare that he had called Arthur Geoffrey's son, Shakespeare speaks a little later (l. 99) of Arthur as reflecting "thy brother Geoffrey's face.... That Geoffrey was thy elder brother born." Since *The Troublesome Raigne* is now heading speeches *K. Philip*, that matter is also straightened out. But later Constance tells Eleanor: "This is thy eldest son's son" (l. 177; *T.R.* has "your cousin" in the parallel speech). The only possible explanation of this mix-up is that Shakespeare had not bothered to work out the relationship of his characters.

That Shakespeare was following *The Troublesome Raigne* without any comprehension of the history upon which it was based is even more clearly demonstrated by his treatment of the attempted blinding of Arthur. *The Troublesome Raigne* narrates a sequence of events that is carefully thought out, although somewhat hurried in presentation. After capturing Arthur, John entrusts him to Hubert in the following words:

> *Hubert de Burgh*, take *Arthur* here to thee;
> Be he thy prisoner. *Hubert*, keep him safe,
> For on his life doth hang thy Sovereign's crown;
> But in his death consists thy Sovereign's bliss;
> Then *Hubert*, as thou shortly hear'st from me,
> So use the prisoner I have given in charge.
> (*1 T.R.*, ix, 29-34)

Later Hubert appears with a warrant, which he reads to Arthur, "that presently upon the receipt of our command, thou put out the eyes of *Arthur Plantagenet*" (xii, 49-50). Finally, he reports to John in the presence of the nobles, as follows:

> *Hubert.* According to your Highness' strict command,
> Young *Arthur's* eyes are blinded and extinct.
> *John.* Why, so?
> Then he may feel the crown, but never see it.
> *Hubert.* Nor see nor feel; for, of the extreme pain,
> Within an hour gave he up the ghost. . . .
> *John.* Then with him die my cares.
> (*1 T.R.*, xiii, 209-15)

All this is clear, though brief. Though he wishes Arthur dead, John dares not kill him lest he be deposed for the crime, and the nobles later react just as he had anticipated. So he plans to render Arthur unable to rule by blinding him, as he explains. But Shakespeare, who seems to have worked throughout almost on a line-by-line basis, read John's words to Hubert as a hint to murder and made his corresponding speech a perfectly unambiguous command to kill Arthur (III, iii, 59-66). We are therefore completely unprepared when Hubert appears (IV, i, 33) with a paper commanding that Arthur's eyes be burned out with hot irons, and it is from blinding him that Hubert is dissuaded. But in the very next scene Pembroke speaks of Hubert's warrant to "do the bloody deed" (IV, ii, 69-70), and the following discussion leading up to the wrathful departure of the lords is based on the assumption that Arthur has been murdered. Perhaps because all good criminal agents should report secretly (as in *Richard III*), Shakespeare suppressed the open admission by Hubert, which is very crude, and substituted Pembroke's report of seeing the warrant. But Shakespeare kept the source action, which turned on Hubert's statement that Arthur had died as a result of the blinding, forgetting that the warrant was for blinding only. So he doubled the confusion.[16]

But, if Shakespeare was unsure of facts in presenting Arthur, he knew exactly the characterization that he wanted to achieve. In *The Troublesome Raigne* Arthur generally seems an intelligent young man, although Constance calls him a boy whose years are "too green" for him to understand cares (*1 T.R.*, iv, 196-97) and Moore Smith argues that the unknown playwright actually intended to make him a child.[17] Seeing a chance for pathos, Shakespeare represented him as unquestionably a boy at all times and added an affection between him and Hubert which was not in the source. Shakespeare therefore converted his leaping from the wall, which *The Troublesome Raigne* depicted as a brave and calculated attempt to gain liberty (*2 T.R.*, i, 1-4), into the desperate act of a confused child:

> I am afraid, and yet I'll venture it.
> If I get down, and do not break my limbs,
> I'll find a thousand shifts to get away.
> As good to die and go, as die and stay.
>
> (IV, iii, 5-8)

This change is perfectly consistent with the decrease in age and is dramatically right. The contrast between Shakespeare's sound grasp of character and his indifference to historical fact and political motives is complete.

Liebermann has pointed out that Constance reflects another misunderstanding of Shakespeare's when she cries:

[16]Cf. New Cambridge *King John, pp. xxiii-xxiv*. Wilson's explanation of the final confusion differs from that given: "John and Hubert discuss the death of Arthur for sixty-six lines and assume throughout that both the warrant and the oral instructions were for death not blinding."

[17]"Shakespeare's *King John* and *The Troublesome Raigne*," p. 336. But Rose ("Shakespeare as an Adapter," p. xi) describes him as "a philosophic young man," and Smith is criticizing Rose's view.

Arm, arm, you heavens, against these perjur'd kings!
A widow cries; be husband to me, heavens!
(III, i, 107-108)[18]

In *The Troublesome Raigne* she had been reviling

This cursed country, where the traitors breathe,
Whose perjury, as proud *Briareus*,
Beleaguers all the sky with misbelief.
(*1* T.R., iv, 208-10)

Shakespeare saw the "purjury" and recalled Isaiah liv, 4-5, with
its striking figure of God as the widow's lord and husband, but he
completely forgot that the "traitors" of his source included only
one king. John, as Arthur's open enemy, was quite innocent of
perjury, if of few other crimes.

A major example of Shakespeare's lack of interest in historical
motives is to be found in his handling of John's death. In *The
Troublesome Raigne* this is carefully motivated as an outgrowth
of his exactions upon the monasteries (as well as of the dangerous
Catholic doctrine of good—that is, meritorious—works); and the
monk knows that he must die himself in effecting the murder,
since he must taste the food he offers to the king.

Monk. . . . Why, I, my lord, dare do the deed:
I'll free my country and the Church from foes,
And merit Heaven, by killing of a king.

Abbot. Thomas, kneel down, and if thou are resolv'd
I will absolve thee here from all thy sins,
For why, the deed is meritorious.
(*2* T.R., vi, 136-41)

Shakespeare introduces at least two allusions to making the monasteries pay the cost of John's wars (I, i, 48-49; III, iv, 172); but
the theme is not developed, and we are completely unprepared
for the poisoning, which is merely a minor and quite unmotivated
detail in one of the over-crowded final scenes.

The King, I fear, is poison'd by a monk. . . .
A monk, I tell you; a resolved villain,
Whose bowels suddenly burst out.
(V, vi, 23, 29-30)

---

[18]"Shakespeare als Bearbeiter des *King John*," p. 181, note 5. Cf. New Cambridge
King John, p. xxiv.

John's death, the close of the play, has no relation to the preceding action, whereas in *The Troublesome Raigne* it is a logical and dramatically appropriate outcome of the conflict between king and church that has unified the entire play. The difficulty here is not simply Shakespeare's habit of trying to wind up too much unfinished business at the very end of a play. His mind was elsewhere.

A similar indifference to the logic of historical events as presented by *The Troublesome Raigne* is revealed by John's remark:

> Some reasons of this double coronation
> I have possess'd you with, and think them strong;
> And more, more strong, when lesser is my fear,
> I shall indue you with.

(IV, ii, 40-43)

The Troublesome Raigne has two long speeches in which John explains why he thinks a second coronation necessary (*1 T.R.*, xiii, 1-31, 85-107), and it is a reasonably important incident in the play's exposition of his troubles and dangers (incidentally, the play was cut into two parts in such a way as to make it the highlight of the concluding scene of Part 1). Shakespeare, with admirable dramatic economy, kept the pageantry but shortened the action by representing the coronation as just having occurred; but, except for the extremely enigmatic remark in the last two lines quoted, he forgot all about motivating it, and it is simply another puzzling detail in his play.[19]

Shakespeare's mishandling of these matters (and of other minor points like the appearance of Peter of Pomfret that could be cited) shows two things clearly. First, he was so little interested in historical events as such that he did not keep them straight in his own mind as he reworked the old play; nor did he follow the operation of historical cause and effect, which the writer of *The Troublesome Raigne* shows remarkable skill in presenting even while he condensed his material to fashion a dramatic plot. Second, when uncertain of detail, as in the matter of Arthur's parentage, Shakespeare did not bother either to restudy his source or to refer to the chronicles. He either guessed rashly or, as in the matter of Arthur's age, chose what was dramatically most effective and developed it for maximum pathos. It is significant that, of several

[19]New Cambridge *King John*, p. xxii.

details which have been offered to prove that he did use the chronicles, the most convincing is Hubert's statement that the monk's "bowels suddenly burst out"[20]—a striking detail rather than a matter of historical importance.

It would be easy, however, to lay too much stress upon all this as evidence only of indifference to historical fact and historical motivation. In fact, I have very likely done so in an effort to combat notions of Shakespeare's historical scholarship that seem to me erroneous. For quite as many examples can be cited of his failure to keep straight the action or motivation contained in *The Troublesome Raigne* when an interpretation of English history is not involved. In the source the Bastard has two distinct and well-motivated hatreds. Austria is wearing Coeur-de-lion's famous lion skin, and it is therefore the Bastard's duty to avenge his new-found father by recapturing the skin. Elianor has promised him Blanche in marriage, together with a rich dowry (*1 T.R.*, iv, 122-24); he is naturally irritated, therefore, when the Dauphin gets her, and he roundly threatens:

> But let the frolic Frenchman take no scorn,
> If *Philip* front him with an English horn.
> (*1 T.R.*, iv, 128-29)

Shakespeare kept both hatreds while depriving them of meaning. Constance tells Austria to doff the lion's skin "and hang a calf-skin on those recreant limbs." The Bastard repeats her witticism to pick a quarrel (III, i, 129-33). His irritation at the marriage, which is completely unexplained, seems based merely on the interruption in the fighting (II, i, 455-67); and his threat to put horns on the lion's hide—that is, to cuckold Austria rather than Lewis—has no point whatever.[21]

Examples could be multiplied. In fact, if Shakespeare is even more indifferent to historical detail than he showed himself in the early chronicles, he is at least as careless in other matters as he appears in *Two Gentlemen* or *Love's Labour's Lost*. Often he seems more interested in letting a character make a momentary impression (or a bad joke) than in thorough motivation. Funda-

---

[20]This detail parallels Grafton. Cf. Anders, *Shakespeare's Books*, p. 142.

[21]II, i, 290-93. Cf. Smith, "Shakespeare's *King John* and *The Troublesome Raigne*," p. 335.

mentally, however, his mind seems to be preoccupied with a number of ideas, just as it was in some of the other chronicle plays.

On the divine right of kings he has two passages. John, like Henry VI and Richard III, thinks of himself as God's agent:

> If not, bleed France, and peace ascend to heaven,
> Whiles we, God's wrathful agent, do correct
> Their proud contempt that beats His peace to heaven.
>
> (II, i, 86-88)

And he lectures Pandulph with a discourse on the subject that goes considerably beyond anything in the earlier plays:

> What earthy name to interrogatories
> Can task the free breath of a sacred king?
> Thou canst not, Cardinal, devise a name
> So slight, unworthy, and ridiculous,
> To charge me to an answer, as the Pope.
> Tell him this tale; and from the mouth of England
> Add thus much more, that no Italian priest
> Shall tithe or toll in our dominions;
> But as we, under Heaven, are supreme head,
> So under Him that great supremacy,
> Where we do reign, we will alone uphold,
> Without the assistance of a mortal hand.
> So tell the Pope, all reverance set apart
> To him and his usurp'd authority.
>
> (III, i, 147-60)

This seems to be derived from two passages in the source. John's claim to be "supreme head" is based upon the same episode in *The Troublesome Raigne*, where John speaks with less dignity but even more vigor:

Tell thy Master so from me; and say, *John of England* said it, that never an Italian priest of them all, shall either have tithe, toll, or polling penny out of *England*; but, as I am King, so will I reign next under God, Supreme Head both over spiritual and temporal. And he that contradicts me in this, I'll make him hop headless.

> (*1 T.R.*, v, 74-78)

Other details came from Part 2 of *The Troublesome Raigne*, where the Bastard reads the rebellious nobles a lecture on the divine right of kings. It explores the doctrine a good deal more fully than Shakespeare does, and it parallels closely the teaching of the Homilies:

I say 'tis shame, and worthy all reproof,
To wrest such petty wrongs, in terms of right,
Against a king appointed by the Lord.
Why, *Salsbury*, admit the wrongs are true;
Yet subjects may not take in hand revenge,
And rob the heavens of their proper power,
Where sitteth He to whom revenge belongs.
And doth a Pope, a priest, a man of pride,
Give charters for the lives of lawful kings?
What can he bless, or who regards his curse,
But such as give to man, and takes from God.
I speak it in the sight of God above:
There's not a man that dies in your belief,
But sells his soul perpetually to pain.
And *Lewes*, leave God, kill *John*, please hell,
Make havoc of the welfare of your souls,
For here I leave you, in the sight of heaven,
A troop of traitors, food for hellish fiends.

(iii, 114-31)

Shakespeare probably owed a great deal to this speech when writing *Richard II*, as we shall see.

From the source, as we have already noted, comes the Bastard's famous concluding meditation, although the theme was an old favorite of Shakespeare's:

This England never did, nor never shall,
Lie at the proud foot of a conqueror,
But when it first did help to wound itself.
Now these her princes are come home again,
Come the three corners of the world in arms,
And we shall shock them. Nought shall make us rue,
If England to itself do rest but true.

(V, vii, 112-18)

A variant of the same theme furnishes his soliloquy at the end of Act IV.

The Bastard's great speech on Commodity at the end of Act II may well reflect, as Dover Wilson suggests,[22] English disgust with the acceptance of Roman Catholicism by Henry IV of France purely for expediency. The two references to France look like topical allusions. But it also amplifies a note of puzzled bewilderment at the strange doings of kings which is to be found in single

[22]New Cambridge *King John*, pp. lvi-lvii.

comments made by the Bastard in *The Troublesome Raigne*, although he has no formal meditation upon the theme, and the subject obviously attracted Shakespeare whether or not he intended it to reflect recent events.

The considerable increase in the amount of space allotted to this kind of material is in itself significant of Shakespeare's interest. *King John* is only about 370 lines shorter than the two parts of *The Troublesome Raigne* combined (2570 to 2942 by my count), despite its elimination of the plundering of the monasteries and its telescoping of a number of other scenes. To gain space, Shakespeare sacrificed, for the most part, the elaborate and careful motivation of the source play, motivation which was worked out in terms of historical cause and effect whether actually true to history or not. The space thus saved has been devoted largely to Arthur's scenes with Hubert, to Constance, and to the Bastard's great speeches—in other words, to development of characters and the enunciation of the themes just mentioned. Except for Arthur, Shakespeare took over and developed the characters of his source, often without their motives, for he undoubtedly preferred to build a personality by creating a series of striking impressions rather than by tracing minor motives through a number of scenes. He also concentrated his interest upon developing a few exciting ideas which he found in *The Troublesome Raigne* rather than upon tracing its careful exposition of historical cause and effect. *The Troublesome Raigne* has credible history; *King John* has living people, except, perhaps, for John himself. *The Troublesome Raigne* has ideas; *King John* has the same ideas unforgettably expressed.

Before leaving *King John*, we should note two indications of the progress of Shakespeare's thinking that are not directly connected with his handling of his source.

As befits a learned and cynical politician of the church, Pandulph gives the first statement to be found in Shakespeare of the more enlightened contemporary view on astrology:

> This act so evilly borne shall cool the hearts
> Of all his people and freeze up their zeal,
> That none so small advantage shall step forth
> To check his reign, but they will cherish it;
> No natural exhalation in the sky,

No scope of nature, no distemper'd day,
No common wind, no customed event,
But they will pluck away his natural cause
And call them meteors, prodigies, and signs,
Abortives, presages, and tongues of heaven,
Plainly denouncing vengeance upon John.

(III, iv, 149-59)

This passage, which is not paralleled in the source, does not mean
that the stars may not portend disaster or influence the affairs
of men. Indeed Constance tells Austria that he has bid her "depend
upon thy stars, thy fortune and thy strength" (III, i, 126), using
the same language that Shakespeare employed in the earlier plays
and was to continue using; and Lewis talks of

> the vaulty top of heaven
> Figur'd quite o'er with burning meteors.

(V, ii, 52-53)

But Pandulph's words strike a new note in recognizing that these
phenomena, although occasionally manifestations of the direct
intervention of Providence, are generally part of the orderly
operation of nature. These lines are far more sophisticated than
the references to the stars in *Romeo and Juliet*, and they look
forward to Edmund's speech in *Lear*, to which allusion has already
been made (*Lear*, I, ii, 127-45).

It is perhaps not too fanciful also to see in this play a new consciousness of nature itself as the operation of laws governing the
universe. Fortune appears several times in the dialogue, working
her unpredictable effect upon mankind; but so does Nature, and
her operations admit of no uncertainty, being the working out
of universal law. This contrast is implicit in what Constance says
to Arthur:

> But thou art fair, and at thy birth, dear boy,
> Nature and Fortune join'd to make thee great.
> Of Nature's gifts thou mayst with lilies boast
> And with the half-blown rose. But Fortune, O,
> She is corrupted, chang'd, and won from thee.

(III, i, 51-55)

The same certainty of nature's operations is implied by John's
words to Hubert:

Make deeds ill done! Hadst not thou been by,
A fellow by the hand of nature mark'd,
Quoted, and sign'd to do a deed of shame,
The murder had not come into my mind.

(IV, ii, 220-22)

But here the meaning is ambiguous. "Nature" may mean, as we noted in *Richard III*, man's fallen and corrupted condition as opposed to a state of grace; more likely, as in the preceding passage, it bears the significance that it so frequently has in medieval and Elizabethan thought: *natura naturans*, the principle which directs all things capable of growth or development toward fulfilling the purpose for which they were created.

These ideas are not in Shakespeare's source. Wherever he got them, they reflect a considerably more learned kind of thought than is discernible in his earliest plays.

CHAPTER VII

The Lancastrian Chronicle Plays

T HE FOUR PLAYS *Richard II, 1* and *2 Henry IV*, and *Henry V* apparently span a period of four or five years in Shakespeare's life just preceding the great tragedies. Critics generally date *Richard II* in 1595 and *Henry V* in 1599, the two parts of *Henry IV* perhaps falling in 1597 or 1598. *Richard II* obviously belongs to the same years as *King John*, to which it is linked by parallels of thought and of language;[1] and, since several passages in *John* read like preliminary studies of those in *Richard II*, it is very likely that *Richard II* is the later of the two plays, as Dover Wilson thinks.[2]

The concepts linking the two plays are important. The most obvious is, of course, the divine right of kings, which is stated in *John* with a fullness not paralleled in the earlier plays but is carried to its ultimate logical conclusion in *Richard II*. The Bastard's great final speech in *John* obviously furnished hints for John of Gaunt's even greater speech from his death-bed in *Richard II* (II, i, 31-68). The theme of order likewise develops from one play to the next, and a hesitant reference in *John* to the brain as the seat of the soul (V, vii, 1-4) gives way to Richard's unhesitating elaboration of the same idea (V, v, 6-10).

The preceding links between *King John* and *Richard II* show the importance of *The Troublesome Raigne* not only as a source for *John* but also as a stimulus to Shakespeare's future thinking. But they also underscore fundamental differences in method between the two plays—in fact, between *John* and all four of the

---

[1]Tillyard dissents: "...although *Richard II* may have been written not long after *King John*, the connections are fitful and unimportant." *Shakespeare's History Plays*, p. 234.

[2]New Cambridge *Richard II*, pp. ix-x.

Lancastrian plays. In contrast to his indifference to historical material in *John*, Shakespeare used a wide range of historical sources in these plays and worked through them carefully. Occasionally, although not always, he paid attention to historical accuracy in minute details. Though he seems to have adapted *John* from *The Troublesome Raigne* almost scene by scene, without a well-thought-out plan, *Richard II* shows that he already had in mind a scheme for plays on Henry V, and the first three of the four Lancastrian plays are carefully linked. These three differences in approach apparently reflect a change in his habits of mind, particularly in that they are progressive. The differences between *2 Henry IV* or *Henry V* and *Richard II*, intellectually as well as dramatically, are far greater than those between *Richard II* and *John*.

The four Lancastrian plays reflect careful and systematic use of a variety of sources, some of them by no means obvious. Holinshed, supplemented—except perhaps in *1 Henry IV*—by Halle,[3] furnished the main structure of all four plays. All but *Henry V* are considerably indebted to Daniel's *Civil Wars* in the first version of 1595, and the old play *The Famous Victories of Henry V* represents an important source for the three plays dealing with Hal as prince and king. In addition to these general sources, details in *Richard II* have been traced to Berner's Froissart, to *La Chronique de la Träison et mort de Richard Deux roy Dengleterre*, Creton's metrical *Histoire du roy d'Angleterre Richard II*, and to the "*Thomas of Woodstocke*, preserved in *Egerton MS*. 1994."[4] To these sources dealing with history one should also add the Bible and the Elizabethan Homilies, so important is their part in furnishing ideas and imagery. For *1 Henry IV* Sir John Hayward's *Life of King Henry IV* should perhaps be mentioned in addition to the general sources listed above, but, despite vigorous controversy among scholars, the indebtedness of the play to Hayward is by no means definitely established.[5] *2 Henry IV* reflects

[3]Hemingway writes: "I have found no passage in *1 Henry IV* which is taken directly from Hall (Variorum *1 Henry IV*, p. 364). But Zeeveld lists several minor parallels; cf. "The Influence of Hall on Shakespeare's English Historical Plays," pp. 322, 332.

[4]Cf. New Cambridge *Richard II*, pp. xxxviii-lxiv; Chambers, *William Shakespeare*, I, 352.

[5]For sources cf. Variorum *1 Henry IV*, pp. 356-94.

Stow's *Annales* and, for reasons that will appear below, probably Elyot's *Governour* as well. Elyot's *Governour*, Tito Livio's life of Henry V, the *Gesta Henrici Quinti, Regis Angliae*, and Fabyan were additional sources for *Henry V*.[6]

These plays do more than offer a complete contrast to *John* in the wide range of sources employed. Wilson remarks in connection with the problem of who escaped from the Duke of Exeter (*Richard II*, II, i, 280):

> The words just quoted from Hol. being drawn from a passage some pages distant from that used for what immediately follows, exhibit a mind respectful of the chronicle in a fashion very remote from the lordly indifference to history displayed in *K. John* or, indeed, in the treatment of the names in ll. 281-84.[7]

One might question Wilson's evaluation of this particular bit of evidence, but his generalization is sound. Witness the Earl of Cambridge's enigmatic speech:

> For me, the gold of France did not seduce,
> Although I did admit it as a motive
> The sooner to effect what I intended.
> *(Henry V*, II, ii, 155-57)

In a play devoted to glorifying Henry V, it was obviously inexpedient to explain the Earl's real motive, which was to place on the throne Edmund Mortimer, Earl of March, whose title was superior to Henry's and, through his sister, became the source of later Yorkist claims. But the fact that he was no mere traitor seduced by French gold is carefully noted.

The care expended in planning and constructing these plays is also reflected in the elaborate cross-connections. Shakespeare must have written *Richard II* after he had pretty well thought out a scheme for *1 Henry IV*. The links between these plays are more numerous and important than those between *1* and *2 Henry IV*, and they involve considerable deviations from the sources. (It should be added, however, that the differences in conception of character that will be noted also exceed any discrepancies between *1* and *2 Henry IV*.) The first appearance in *Richard II* of "young Harry Percy" (II, iii, 21 ff.), who was actually two

---

[6]Cf. Variorum *2 Henry IV*, pp. 521-57; New Cambridge *Henry V*, pp. 117-18.
[7]New Cambridge *Richard II*, note, p. 167.

years older than Bolingbroke, obviously looks forward to his role of character contrast to Hal in *1 Henry IV*. It is one of the parallels between Shakespeare and Daniel's *Civil Wars*. Hal's own part in *1 Henry IV* is clearly anticipated by Bolingbroke's inquiring for his "unthrifty son" whom he has not seen for three months (*Richard II*, V, iii, 1-22). Richard's "I wasted time, and now doth Time waste me" (V, v, 49) perhaps looks forward to the parallel between Richard and Hal that Henry IV elaborates as he lectures the Prince (*1 Henry IV*, III, iii, 93-96). Richard's prophecy to Northumberland prepares for the centering of both parts of *Henry IV* upon the revolt of the Percies:

> Northumberland, thou ladder wherewithal
> The mounting Bolingbroke ascends my throne,
> The time shall not be many hours of age
> More than it is, ere foul sin gathering head
> Shall break into corruption. Thou shalt think,
> Though he divide the realm and give thee half,
> It is too little, helping him to all;
> [And] he shall think that thou, which know'st the way
> To plant unrightful kings, wilt know again,
> Being ne'er so little urg'd, another way
> To pluck him headlong from the usurped throne.

> (V, i, 55-65)

Richard's words are actually quoted by Bolingbroke in *2 Henry IV* (III, i, 70-77). The repetition of Richard's favorite sun image by Hal as he soliloquizes on his own motives (*1 Henry IV*, I, ii, 220-26) must also be intended, as Tillyard remarks,[8] to point the contrast between the two, but this need not have been planned when *Richard II* was being written.

Linking of the two plays is not, however, complete. The change in Hal's character will be discussed below. But there are also two notable differences between the Bolingbroke of *Richard II* and the king of *1* and *2 Henry IV* that make it unwise to assume that Shakespeare had worked out his plans in detail, especially for *2 Henry IV*. In *Richard II* we are never sure whether Bolingbroke returned from France determined to seek the throne, or, as he himself asserted, he merely came to claim his rights and then availed himself of opportunities as they arose. It is significant that Daniel,

[8]*Shakespeare's History Plays*, pp. 234-35.

who discusses the problem, leaves the question in doubt.[9] There were, of course, good artistic reasons why Shakespeare should do so too. Henry IV, on the other hand, practically admits that he gained the throne by devious means:

> God knows, my son,
> By what by-paths and indirect crook'd ways
> I met this crown. . . .
>
> It seem'd in me
> But as an honour snatch'd with boist'rous hand,
> And I had many living to upbraid
> My gain of it by their assistances.
>
> (*2 Henry IV*, IV, v, 184-94)

This admission of guilt is only part of a more important contrast. Bolingbroke is a shrewd, realistic opportunist. Henry IV displays a confirmed melancholy and almost religious gravity that, like his exaggerated age, distinguish him sharply from his younger self in *Richard II*. The change was probably intended both to ennoble him and to make him remote from Hal, as it does.

The connections between *1* and *2 Henry IV* are less elaborate, and it is debatable whether Shakespeare actually prepares in the first part for the second, as opposed to carrying themes from the first part on into the second. The allusions to the crusade might be of either sort, but the dialogue on justice and hanging between Hal and Falstaff (*1 Henry IV*, I, ii, 64-82) looks like deliberate preparation for the triumph of the Chief Justice and the rejection of Falstaff. The allusions to Prince John of Lancaster in *1 Henry IV* may be intended to prepare for his role as foil to Hal in Part 2, especially the King's words:

> Thy place in council thou has rudely lost,
> Which by thy younger brother is suppli'd.
>
> (III, ii, 32-33)

And Hal's own praise may have the same intention:

> By God, thou hast deceiv'd me, Lancaster;
> I did not think thee lord of such a spirit.
> Before, I lov'd thee as a brother, John;
> But now, I do respect thee as my soul.
>
> (V, iv, 17-20)

[9] Ibid., p. 239.

But there is certainly no such preparation for John's function in *2 Henry IV* as that made in *Richard II* for Hotspur's later role. And John is completely silent in the council preceding Shrewsbury, when we might expect him to speak. Neither Tillyard nor Wilson, in arguing that the two parts were designed as one structural whole,[10] seems to have solved the problem presented by the relationship between Hal and his father. If one reads *2 Henry IV* as a continuation and development of material in the first part, one is hardly prepared, after Hal is reconciled with his father and saves his life at the Battle of Shrewsbury, for the bitter distrust that the King shows in the scene with the crown or even in his advice to Clarence (IV, iv). What happens as he lies dying is not a "final clarification"[11] of their relationship but a second reconciliation that retraces completely the ground gained in the first. Certainly the scene is less puzzling if one thinks of *2 Henry IV* as a play parallel in structure to *1 Henry IV* and developing similar themes but not necessarily integral with it as part of an artistic whole. But, either way, there are enough links between the two plays to indicate careful planning and workmanship in relating *2 Henry IV* to its predecessor.

Only the Epilogue links *2 Henry IV* to *Henry V*, and its promise was not, in fact, kept:

If you be not too much cloy'd with fat meat, our humble author will continue the story, with Sir John in it, and make you merry with fair Katharine of France; where, for anything I know, Falstaff shall die of a sweat, unless already 'a be kill'd with your hard opinions; for Oldcastle died a martyr, and this is not the man.

(ll. 27-34)

All this means that, in contrast to his practice in writing *King John*, Shakespeare took great pains both in collecting his material and in shaping it into dramatic form. The four plays show that, when he had to build his own plot instead of taking it from an earlier play, he was now prepared to do a painstaking job. They do not show that he had become a profound student of history, for the research and planning should not blind us to the survival

[10]Cf. Wilson, *The Fortunes of Falstaff*, pp. 73-81; New Cambridge *1 Henry IV*, pp. vii-xiii; Tillyard, *Shakespeare's History Plays*, p. 264.

[11]New Cambridge *1 Henry IV*, p. x. Cf. also Wilson, *The Fortunes of Falstaff*, pp. 75-78.

of habits of mind that we have encountered before. The Lancastrian plays show Shakespeare's familiar trick of seizing upon striking details and then leaving them at loose ends; they also display his old indifference to historical cause and effect and to political motives.

The kind of loose ends still to be found could be illustrated from all four plays, but *Richard II*, because of its tighter structure, will best serve the purpose. In the second act York speaks of his own disgrace and the prevention of Bolingbroke's marriage (II, i, 167-68). Neither allusion has any meaning in terms of the play. The disgrace has never been explained, in fact; but Shakespeare must have had in mind Holinshed's statement that the French king would have given his cousin to Bolingbroke in marriage had not Richard intervened.[12] The charge that Bushy and Green have "made a divorce" between Richard and his queen (III, i, 11-15) may simply echo Marlowe's *Edward II*, as has been supposed; but it may be another undigested recollection of Holinshed, who devotes a sentence to Richard's "abhominable adulterie."[13] A little later Bolingbroke says that he "must away, to fight with Glendower and his complices" (III, i, 423), of whom no more is heard until *1 Henry IV*. Holinshed tells that Glendower served Richard at Flint Castle and was captured there.[14]

A more important series of details reveals Shakespeare's indifference to historical causes and historical motives. In a scene of twenty-four lines (II, iv) a Captain tells Salisbury that the Welsh forces have dispersed. When Salisbury reports this news at Barkloughly Castle, it leads to the second in Richard's crescendo of four emotional outbursts. But the audience would hardly suspect that Holinshed regarded this departure of the Welsh forces as the main cause of Richard's downfall:

... whereas if the king had come before their breaking up, no doubt, but they would have put the duke of Hereford in adventure of a field: so that the kings lingering of time, before his comming over, gave opportunitie to the duke to bring things to passe as he could have wished, and took from the king all occasion to recover afterwards anie forces sufficient to resist him.[15]

---

[12]Holinshed, III, 495; Boswell-Stone, p. 92.
[13]Holinshed, III, 508; Boswell-Stone, p. 129.
[14]Holinshed, III, 518; Boswell-Stone, p. 105.
[15]Holinshed, III, 499; Boswell-Stone, p. 103.

This concentration upon Richard's emotional state rather than upon history continues, for no indication whatever is given of the real significance of two other details. During the deposition scene Richard accuses Northumberland of cracking "the strong warrant of an oath" (IV, i, 232-36) and laments that even "that name was given me at the font" is usurped (IV, i, 255-57). The former lines hint at an alternative account of Richard's capture in Holinshed, to the effect that Northumberland ambushed him on the way to Flint Castle after swearing an oath of safe conduct.[16] The story of his illegitimacy is contained in *Träison* and Froissart, where the point is, of course, that such a charge would call into question his right to the throne.[17]

There are, in fact, so many loose ends in all four Lancastrian plays that critics have been driven to desperate expedients to explain them. It has been argued that *1* and *2 Henry IV* and *Henry V* were derived, perhaps via an earlier Shakespearean draft, from a previous play (or plays), on which *The Famous Victories* was also based.[18] The evidence for this earlier version is primarily of the kind developed by "bibliographical" students of Shakespeare's text and does not concern us. But Dover Wilson's hypothesis of an earlier play behind *Richard II*[19] rests to a considerable extent upon an assumed contrast between the habits of thought and scholarship which it reveals and those apparent in *King John*. Actually the contradictions do not exist, and our text of *Richard* II is quite consistent with Shakespeare's methods.

Fundamentally the details just noted in *Richard II* represent the same kind of misunderstanding of source material that occurs in *King John*. In *John* the ambiguities or loose ends resulted from a misreading of the play, which Shakespeare followed carefully, because he was completely ignorant of the underlying history. He presented contradictory accounts of Arthur's parentage, for example, not because he did not follow his source but because he was dramatizing his source on a line-by-line basis and was struck by a picturesque detail that, because of his ignorance of history,

---

[16]New Cambridge *Richard II*, p. 189.

[17]Boswell-Stone, p. 118, note.

[18]Morgan, *Some Problems of Shakespeare's 'Henry the Fourth'*, pp. 42-43; Wilson, "The Origins and Development of Shakespeare's *Henry IV*," pp. 9-10.

[19]New Cambridge *Richard II*, pp. lxiv-lxxvi.

led him to infer that Richard Coeur-de-Lion was Arthur's father. Or he inserted incidents from the old play without supplying the necessary motivation for them. Now the relationship of *Richard II* to the chronicles is exactly that of *John* to *The Troublesome Raigne*. The loose ends cited in *Richard II* all involve references to a historical fact which is not otherwise a part of the action of the play and which cannot be understood without reference to the chronicles. The allusions, in other words, reflect carelessness in detail or indifference to the motivation of action, but they also display a considerable and accurate knowledge of the historical sources, which must therefore be the immediate texts from which Shakespeare worked.

Shakespeare was remarkably fond of interesting details that he encountered in his reading and had a tenacious memory for them. Just such details are involved in Bolingbroke's projected marriage, Richard's lechery, the presence at Flint Castle of Glendower, who obviously captured Shakespeare's imagination, Northumberland's oath, and Richard's illegitimacy. There should be no question by now that as yet Shakespeare was more concerned with the impression that a character makes in a scene than with analysis of historical causes or political motives. And it was just such indifference that made possible his handling of Gloucester's death.

In *Richard II* Shakespeare nowhere says clearly that Richard was responsible for Gloucester's murder, although that fact underlies Bolingbroke's charge against Mowbray and there are a number of veiled allusions to it. Holinshed relates that Richard

sent unto Thomas Mowbraie, earle marshall and of Notingham, to make the duke secretlie awaie.

The earle prolonged time for the executing of the kings commandement, though the king would have had it doone with all expedition, wherby the king conceived no small displeasure, and sware that it should cost the earle his life if he quickly obeied not his commandement. The earle thus, as it seemed, in maner inforced, called out the duke at midnight, as if he should have taken ship to passe over into England, and there in the lodging called the princes In, he caused his servants to cast featherbeds upon him, and so smoother him to death; or otherwise to strangle him with towels (as some write.)[20]

[20]Holinshed, III, 489; Boswell-Stone, pp. 82-83.

When Bolingbroke says that Gloucester's blood cries "to me for justice and rough chastisement," Richard comments: "How high a pitch his resolution soars!" (I, i, 106-109). Mowbray's words are deliberately ambiguous:

> O, let my sovereign turn away his face
> And bid his ears a little while be deaf,
> Till I have told this slander of his blood
> How God and good men hate so foul a liar.
>
> (I, i, 111-14)
>
> For Gloucester's death,
> I slew him not; but to my own disgrace
> Neglected my sworn duty in that case.
>
> (I, i, 132-34)

Knowledge that Richard is the real criminal is also needed to make intelligible remarks exchanged by him and Mowbray in the lists at Coventry:

> K. Rich.
> Farewell, my lord; securely I espy
> Virtue with valour couched in thine eye.
>
> (I, iii, 97-98)
>
> Mow.
> A heavy sentence, my most sovereign liege,
> And all unlook'd for from your Highness' mouth.
> A dearer merit, not so deep a maim
> As to be cast forth in the common air,
> Have I deserved at your Highness' hands.
>
> (I, iii, 154-58)
>
> Within my mouth you have engaol'd my tongue,
> Doubly portcullis'd with my teeth and lips.
>
> (I, iii, 166-67)

Editors and critics have repeatedly discussed Shakespeare's failure to explain a fact which underlies not only the speeches just quoted but also the whole sequence of events that begins the play. Many of them have assumed that Shakespeare expected his audience to be familiar with the circumstances of Gloucester's death, either from another play or from their knowledge of history. But this hypothesis cannot be reconciled with Shakespeare's known dramatic habits. So far as I know, not one of his plays includes, *after the second act*, action important to the plot (as opposed to picturesque details) which requires for its understanding biographical or historical information not supplied in

152

the play. This I take to prove that Shakespeare was not in the habit of relying on what the audience knew when it entered the theater. On the other hand, several of his plays—*The Merchant of Venice* and *King Lear*, for example—start with events that seem to require motivation. The opening scenes of the two plays mentioned were, in fact, carefully motivated in the sources; but Shakespeare expects the audience simply to accept them as a point of departure and to take in stride casual allusions to antecedent events, such as the fact that Lear had already worked out the division of the kingdom and had planned to give Cordelia the largest share. *Richard II* is amply accounted for if we assume the same kind of unmotivated opening action plus Shakespeare's usual indifference to tracing historical causes.

There were, moreover, very good reasons why Shakespeare should want to keep Gloucester's death in the background, reasons implicit in writing a sequence of plays involving both Richard and Hal. As everyone knows, Queen Elizabeth and her more sophisticated subjects were acutely aware of the parallel between herself and Richard. It was therefore impolitic to justify his dethronement. But sound dramatic reasons, to which Shakespeare was exquisitely sensitive, also demanded that Richard have the sympathy of the audience in the scenes of his deposition and death. The unhistorical emphasis upon the Queen and her love for Richard was surely an attempt to gain sympathy for him. Richard's murder of Gloucester, if admitted in so many words, would make it much harder to arouse that sympathy, unless the play were to be burdened with an exposition of Gloucester's treasonous plotting. Being uninterested in tracing historical motives, Shakespeare simply avoided saying who actually did kill Gloucester, but allowed references to his death to play their part in individual scenes. Sometimes, as in the passages cited, he went too far and assumed that the audience knew as much as he did, or at least he wrote in terms of what he knew rather than of what he had put into the play. But such carelessness in explaining details is, as we have seen, by no means unparalleled in *Richard II* or in his other work.

In the opening scenes of *Henry V*, Shakespeare reproduced from his source, but blandly ignored, a set of political motives as obvious as ever led a man to embrace an unsound cause. The commons (I, i, 71) are about to seize half the possessions of the church, and would have done so in the last reign had not their attention been distracted by civil war. The church's one hope now is that Henry is "a true lover of the holy Church" (I, i, 23). Henry, says the Archbishop,

> seems indifferent,
> Or rather swaying more upon our part
> Than cherishing th' exhibiters against us;
> For I have made an offer to his Majesty,
> Upon our spiritual convocation
> And in regard of causes now in hand,
> Which I have open'd to his Grace at large,
> As touching France, to give a greater sum
> Than ever at one time the clergy yet
> Did to his predecessors part withal.
>
> (I, i, 72-81)

In other words, the Archbishop seems to propose to buy the King's good will and to distract the commons with a foreign war. In the next scene he reads an elaborate lecture (from Holinshed) on the Salic Law and French genealogy and pronounces Henry's title to the French throne sound. Henry thereupon decides upon war. Incredible as it may seem, Shakespeare apparently did not intend all this as an exhibition of ecclesiastical chicanery but as a sober presentation of Henry's wonderful reformation into a pious and Christian king and of the justice of his invasion of France. The Archbishop speaks a careful exposition of Henry's new character (I, i, 38-59), such as Shakespeare habitually inserted as early in his plays as possible, and the characterization given is a key to the action of the play. It is unthinkable that Shakespeare intended to imply that Henry was a tool of the clergy or that his French war was unjust. Perhaps we should believe that Shakespeare thought the Archbishop as indifferent to monetary considerations as to sound Catholic theology; but, since even the Archbishop enunciates the Protestant doctrine that "miracles are ceas'd," we can only assume that Shakespeare shared his skepticism and regarded him as normally avaricious. The dramatist simply overlooked the obvious motives implied by the sequence of events that he portrayed. To repeat, it seems incredible—or it would seem incredible if we had not encountered the same indifference to political intrigue in the earlier history plays.

As one might expect, in view of the care and thought that went into the preparation of these plays, they contain a large number of passages summarizing contemporary learning and philosophy. They are, in fact, considerably more thoughtful than any of the plays that we have so far examined. Much of their content centers upon the nature of the kingship; and the emphasis shifts, as we progress through the plays, from the rights of the king to his duties and responsibilities. *Richard II* develops the exposition of the divine right of kings and of the evils of civil war to the ultimate form which it achieved in Shakespeare and, indeed, in Elizabethan literature. Some discussion of the source of Shakespeare's ideas is therefore in order.

In examining *King John*, we noted that its references to the doctrine of divine right seem to be derived from John's reply to Pandulph and the Bastard's lecture to the rebellious nobles in *The Troublesome Raigne*. Shakespeare's earlier plays allude to the king as God's deputy or the Lord's annointed, but *The Troublesome Raigne* very likely called to his attention the potentialities of the theme for dramatic treatment. It probably stimulated some of the passages on the subject in *Richard II*. It may also have led him to reread or recall the Homilies on the subject, which he must have encountered long before in attending church, as part of the series which were required to be read in rotation each Sunday.

As Hart first pointed out,[21] the passages in *The Troublesome Raigne* and much of what Shakespeare has to say on the subject of divine right and of the evils of rebellion are based upon two of the Homilies. The tenth in the first edition of 1547 is entitled "An Exhortation concerning Good Order and Obedience to Rulers and Magistrates." It is divided into three parts, each intended to be read at a service. In 1574 a much longer Homily in six parts "Against Disobedience and Wilfull Rebellion" was added to the collection, which had in the meantime been amplified by a second series on church discipline and ceremonial. Shakespeare obviously drew upon both of these Homilies, upon the first primarily for his concept of divine right and upon the second for material on the consequences of civil war.

[21]*Shakespeare and the Homilies*, pp. 36-76.

The Homily "Of Obedience" opens with an eloquent passage stating the principle of order in the universe and arguing that kings and other magistrates are necessary guardians of a social order which is part of the universal order. We shall have occasion to recur to it in connection with Ulysses' speech on degree in *Troilus and Cressida*, which parallels it closely. It then lays down the doctrine "that the high power and authority of kings, with their making of laws, judgments, and officers, are the ordinances, not of man, but of God" and that "they should reknowledge themselves to have all their power and strength, not from Rome, but immediately of God Most Highest."[22] They are therefore God's deputies:

We read in the Book of Deuteronomy that all punishment pertaineth to God by this sentence: *Vengeance is mine, and I will reward.* But this sentence we must understand to pertain also to the magistrates, which do exercise God's room in judgment and punishing by good and godly laws here in earth.[23]

The second part lays down the principle of passive obedience in terms used by Shakespeare:

And here, good people, let us all mark diligently, that it is not lawful for inferiors and subjects in any case to resist (or stand against) the superior powers: for St. Paul's words be plain, that *whosoever withstandeth shall get to themselves damnation*; for *whosoever withstandeth withstandeth the ordinance of God.*[24]

But "let us believe undoubtedly, good Christian people, that we may not obey kings, magistrates, or any other, though they be our own fathers, if they would command us to do any thing contrary to God's commandments." "But we must in such case patiently suffer all wrongs and injuries, referring the judgment of our cause only to God."[25] The bulk of the sermon is devoted to arguing that "even the wicked rulers have their power and authority from God. And therefore it is not lawful for their subjects by force to withstand them, although they abuse their power."[26] Although this material is reflected in *The Troublesome*

[22]*Certain Sermons or Homilies*, p. 111.
[23]Ibid., pp. 111-12.
[24]Ibid., p. 113.
[25]Ibid., pp. 117-18.
[26]Ibid., p. 114.

Raigne, Shakespeare seems, except for a speech of Gaunt's, to have used it only in so far as it enjoined obedience to the Lord's anointed; nor did he employ the third part, which argues mostly that obedience is due to the king and not to Rome.

"The Homily against Disobedience and Wilful Rebellion," which was occasioned by the rebellion of 1569 in the north, is much more violent in tone and more directly concerned with the evils of civil war. It lays down the principle "that obedience is the principal virtue of all virtues, and indeed the very root of all virtues, and the cause of all felicity."[27] After recapitulating the teachings of the earlier homily, it makes a significant addition: " . . . the princes themselves, in authority, power, wisdom, providence, and righteousness in government of people and countries committed to their charge, should resemble his heavenly governance, as the majesty of heavenly things may by the baseness of earthly things be shadowed and resembled."[28] Another reason is also given why subjects may not rebel against evil princes: "For first what a perilous thing were it to commit unto the subjects the judgment, which prince is wise and godly and his government good, and which is otherwise; as though the foot must judge the head; an enterprise very heinous, and must needs breed rebellion."[29] The third part begins the discussion of the evils of civil war. Rebellion includes all sins against God and man, a proposition which is illustrated by showing that it brings violation of all ten commandments, commission of the seven deadly sins, and finally pestilence, famine, and war. In summary of this notion occurs a passage which, though long, deserves to be quoted:

For not only those ordinary and usual mischiefs and miseries of other wars do follow rebellion, as, corn and other things necessary to man's use to be spoiled; houses, villages, towns, cities to be taken, sacked, burned, and destroyed; not only many wealthy men, but whole countries, to be impoverished and utterly beggared; many thousands of men to be slain and murdered; women and maids to be violated and deflowered. . . . when the subjects unnaturally do rebel against their prince, whose honour and life they should defend, though it were with loss of their own lives; contrymen to disturb the public peace and quietness of their country, for defence of whose quietness they

[27]Ibid., p. 588.
[28]Ibid., p. 591
[29]Ibid., p. 593.

157

should spend their lives; the brother to seek and often to work the death of his brother, the son of the father; the father to seek or procure the death of his sons, being at man's age; and by their faults to disherit their innocent children and kinsmen their heirs forever.... to turn all good order upside down; to bring all good laws in contempt, and to tread them under feet.... and so finally to make their country, thus by their mischief weakened, ready to be a prey and spoil to all outward enemies that will invade it, to the utter and perpetual captivity, slavery, and destruction of all their countrymen, their children, their friends, their kinsfolks left alive, whom by their wicked rebellion they procure to be delivered into the hands of foreign enemies, as much as in them doth lie.[30]

This passage, as well as Halle, is echoed by Henry VI at Towton (*3 Henry VI*, II, v); by the Bastard in his concluding speech in *The Troublesome Raigne* and in *King John*; and less ruefully by the Prince and Falstaff, who anticipate the deflowering if not the fighting (*1 Henry IV*, II, iv, 396-402). The remaining parts of the Homily add nothing essentially new to the discussion.

Allusions to the doctrine of divine right occur throughout *Richard II* (in addition to the passages to be discussed, compare I, ii, 4-5; II, i, 98; II, iii, 96; III, iii, 9; IV, i, 207-14). But the following are most significant. Gaunt, in refusing the Duchess of Gloucester's plea for vengeance, states explicitly the subject's duty to obey even an evil king:

> God's is the quarrel; for God's substitute,
> His deputy anointed in His sight,
> Hath caus'd his [Gloucester's] death; the which if wrongfully,
> Let Heaven revenge; for I may never lift
> An angry arm against His minister
>
> (I, ii, 37-41)

York and Bolingbroke accept the notion that rebels disobey heaven:

> *York.* Take not, good cousin, further than you should,
> Lest you mistake the heavens are o'er our heads.
>
> *Boling.* I know it, uncle, and oppose not myself
> Against their will.
>
> (III, iii, 16-19)

But Richard himself develops fully the theme that rebels bring about their eternal damnation, which, though it occurs in *The*

[30]Ibid., pp. 614-15.

Troublesome Raigne, is not present in *John.* Here it becomes a dreadful prophecy of future strife.

> For well we know, no hand of blood and bone
> Can gripe the sacred handle of our sceptre,
> Unless he do profane, steal, or usurp.
> And though you think that all, as you have done,
> Have torn their souls by turning them from us,
> And we are barren and bereft of friends,
> Yet know, my master, God omnipotent,
> Is mustering in his clouds on our behalf
> Armies of pestilence; and they shall strike
> Your children yet unborn and unbegot,
> That lift your vassal hands against my head
> And threat the glory of my precious crown.
>
> (III, iii, 79-90)

Finally, in the deposition scene the Bishop of Carlisle states the notion that subjects cannot judge a king, stigmatizes rebellion as a sin, and describes the horrors of civil war. Shakespeare used this passage to foretell the future, but it virtually recapitulates the arguments in the Homily of 1574:

> What subject can give sentence on his king?
> And who sits here that is not Richard's subject? ...
> And shall the figure of God's majesty,
> His captain, steward, deputy elect,
> Anointed, crowned, planted many years,
> Be judg'd by subject and inferior breath,
> And he himself not present? ...
> My Lord of Hereford here, whom you call king,
> Is a foul traitor to proud Hereford's king;
> And if you crown him, let me prophesy,
> The blood of English shall manure the ground,
> And future ages groan for this foul act.
> Peace shall go sleep with Turkes and infidels,
> And in this seat of peace tumultuous wars
> Shall kin with kin and kind with kind confound.
> Disorder, horror, fear, and mutiny
> Shall here inhabit, and this land be call'd
> The field of Golgotha and dead men's skulls.
> O, if you raise this house against this house,
> It will the woefullest division prove
> That ever fell upon this cursed earth.
> Prevent it, resist it, let it not be so,
> Lest child, child's children, cry against you "woe!"
>
> (IV, i, 121-49)

But Shakespeare also develops two logical implications of the doctrine of divine right that are apparently not present in the Homilies. The first of these is the paradox inherent in the contrast between the king's divine authority and his human needs:

> Throw away respect,
> Tradition, form, and ceremonious duty;
> For you have but mistook me all this while.
> I live with bread like you, feel want,
> Taste grief, need friends; subjected thus,
> How can you say to me I am a king?
>
> (III, ii, 172-77)

The second of these is the more daring parallel between the king, as the Lord's anointed, and Christ, to whom the same term is applied in Scriptures. Wilson finds the source of this analogy in the *Träison*,[31] but it is also a logical inference from the teaching of the Homilies which Shakespeare might easily have made. Richard speaks of his supposedly false friends as "three Judases" (III, ii, 132) and compares the fidelity of Christ's disciples with the falsehood of his subjects:

> Did they not sometime cry, "All hail!" to me?
> So Judas did to Christ; but He, in twelve,
> Found truth in all but one; I, in twelve thousand, none.
>
> (IV, i, 169-71)

Later he thinks of the trial of Christ:

> Nay, all of you that stand and look upon me
> Whilst that my wretchedness doth bait myself,
> Though some of you with Pilate wash your hands
> Showing an outward pity; yet you Pilates
> Have here deliver'd me to my sour cross,
> And water cannot wash away your sin.
>
> (IV, i, 237-42)

The reference to sin also links this passage with the reasoning in the Homilies.

In one respect *Richard II* follows the teaching of the Homilies to an extent not typical of other plays. Gaunt, as we have noted, accepts the full doctrine of passive obedience as it was laid down in the Homily "Against Disobedience": ". . . indeed a rebel is worse than the worst prince, and rebellion worse than the worst

[31]New Cambridge *Richard II*, p. lviii.

government of the worst prince."[32] Elsewhere Shakespeare seems to hold the doctrine that subjects are justified in rebelling against a tyrant. At least, his characters regularly justify their acts of rebellion and regicide by stigmatizing their opponents as tyrants, and this is equally true no matter where his own sympathies seem to lie. In *Julius Caesar*, Cassius asks why Caesar should be a tyrant (I, iii, 92, 103); Cinna hails Caesar's death with the words "Tyranny is dead!" (III, i, 78); and even the First Plebian grants, "This Caesar was a tyrant," as though that clinched the argument (III, ii, 74). Shakespeare's sympathies, at least on this point, can hardly have been with the conspirators. Not only Margaret but also Buckingham and Richmond call Richard III a tyrant (IV, iv, 52; V, iii, 168, 246). As a preliminary to taking up arms, Lenox, Malcolm, and Macduff all describe Macbeth's tyranny (III, vi, 22, 25; IV, iii, 12, 32, 45, etc.); indeed, proof that Macbeth is a tyrant seems a major purpose of the scene between Malcolm and Macduff. The doctrine that subjects were justified in rebelling against a tyrant was held by Aquinas and other medieval thinkers and, among Shakespeare's contemporaries, by Buchanan, the Huguenot writers of the *Vindiciae contra Tyrannos*, the Jesuits, and numerous others.[33] Good and bad characters alike show by their use of the word *tyrant* that Shakespeare was familiar with this doctrine; the care with which Richmond and Malcolm submit evidence against Richard III and Macbeth certainly suggests that Shakespeare himself believed that tyranny justified rebellion, at least against usurpers.

The meaning that Shakespeare attached to *tyrant* is abundantly clear from *Richard III* or *Macbeth* as well as from his frequent metaphorical uses of the word: it is the one commonly accepted by his contemporaries. Occasional injustices or crimes do not convict a king of tyranny. He must willfully and consistently violate most of the fundamental laws of God and man. Only at one point does Shakespeare imply a different view, and that, significantly enough, involves his first use of the word in a political context. In *3 Henry VI*, III, iii, both Margaret and Warwick describe Edward as a tyrant, grounding their use of the term

[32]*Certain Sermons or Homilies*, p. 594.

[33]Cf. Allen, *A History of Political Thought in the Sixteenth Century*, pp. 337, 340, 320-28, 360, etc.

simply upon his usurpation of the throne rather than upon his conduct:

> To prove him tyrant this reason may suffice,
> That Henry liveth still.

(III, iii, 71-72; cf. 206)

All this implies that Shakespeare's knowledge of political thought grew rapidly after *3 Henry VI*. The inconsistency between the unqualified language of *Richard II* and his practice in some other plays may only prove that the needs of a particular dramatic situation loomed larger in his mind than consistent adherence to a political doctrine or careful qualification of his language. Or it may indicate that he followed the Homilies without regard to consistency of thought, as he so often took details from his sources. For one cannot discover any sharp distinction on Shakespeare's part between a divine right derived by legitimate succession, to which absolute obedience was due, and a *de facto* sovereignty achieved by force, which would justify rebellion if it became tyrannous. Lancaster describes Henry IV as God's substitute, and the rebellious Archbishop himself describes his own action as "this monstrous form" (*2 Henry IV*, IV, ii, 28, 34). Note that for an Elizabethan *monstrous* means contrary to nature as well as having its modern force.

The doctrine of divine right continues to be important in Shakespeare's plays—for example, in *Hamlet* and *Lear*. It is fundamental to an understanding of *Julius Caesar*. The parallel theme of the evils of civil war also continues throughout Shakespeare's plays (cf. *2 Henry IV*, I, i, 193-200; *Henry V*, II, pro. 16-35; *Julius Caesar*, III, i, 259-75). But he never again developed either concept so elaborately as in *Richard II*.[34] In the following chronicle plays, he moved on to a richer theme, which also grew out of *The Troublesome Raigne* and the Homilies and perhaps other sources as well—namely, the cares and responsibilities of the king.

In his final speech in *The Troublesome Raigne* the Bastard proclaims:

> Let England live but true within itself,
> And all the world can never wrong her state.

(*2 T.R.*, ix, 45-46)

---

[34]But an interesting case could be made out that only Shakespeare's failures and criminals (Richard II, Henry VI, Richard III) invoke their divine right, whereas his strong kings are silent on the subject.

This speech is developed by Shakespeare in *John*, as has been noted, but it also lies back of John of Gaunt's great speech in *Richard II* (II, i, 31-68). Wilson suggests[35] that another source is to be found in Berners' Froissart, where a speech of Gaunt's "to suche as he trusted best" is given as one of several examples of men's comments upon the "defyaunce bytwene the erle of Derby and the erle Marshall." There is a general similarity of theme but no direct parallel in words.[36] Be that as it may, Gaunt certainly adds to what the Bastard said a new implication which is to be found in the Homilies: namely, that the king, like his subjects, must be true to his trust if the kingdom is to be safe. The notion was, of course, a Renaissance commonplace. Shakespeare may well have encountered it in Elyot's *Governour*, from which, as we shall see, he took the speech on obedience in *Henry V* (I, ii, 183-206):

This notable sentence is nat only to be imprinted in the hartes of governours, but also to be often tymes revolved and called to remembraunce.

They shall nat thynke howe moche honour they receive, but howe moche care and burdene. Ne they shall nat moche esteme their revenues and treasure, considerynge that it is no buten or praie, but a laboriouse office and travaile.

Let them thynke the greatter dominion they have, that thereby they sustayne the more care and studie. And that therfore they muste have the lasse solace and passetyme, and to sensuall pleasures lasse opportunitie.[37]

Several of the best speeches in *Henry IV* and *Henry V* dwell upon the cares of a king, notably in Hal's meditation upon the crown, which is not without a note of exultant possession:

> Lo, where it sits,
> Which God shall guard; and put the world's whole strength
> Into one giant arm, it shall not force
> This lineal honour from me. This from thee
> Will I to mine leave, as 'tis left to me.
> *(2 Henry IV, IV, v, 43-47)*

This possessive pride is completely absent from Hal's finest development of the theme in his soliloquy before Agincourt (*Henry V*, IV, i, 247-301).

[35]New Cambridge *Richard II*, pp. lvi-lvii.
[36]*The Chronicle of Froissart*, VI, 310-11. [37]Ed. Croft, II, 4 (Book II, ch. i).

But the duties of a king do more than provide occasional speeches in *1* and *2 Henry IV*. They form the background of the plays themselves, for both parts of *Henry IV* may be regarded as tracing the evolution of Hal from madcap prince to king and as depicting the qualities essential to the kingship. In planning to present Henry V as a great king, Shakespeare reflected upon the troubles and the responsibilities of the kingship, and he became keenly aware of the qualities needed by a great ruler and leader of men. All this he wrote into Hal's speeches. But he must also have seen that the characteristics of Henry V as a hero king simply could not be squared with the madcap prince of tradition and of *The Famous Victories*. Hal must have grown in skill and in moral stature.

Popular tradition, which was again reflected in *The Famous Victories of Henry V*, represented Hal as having undergone a kind of conversion. Such sudden changes of character could be explained by an Elizabethan either on religious grounds or in terms of the humors, which produced a psychology that at times was almost mechanistic in its determination of human character. Timothy Bright seems, in fact, to have been conscious of the danger that the theory of the four humors might lead to determinism.[38] But Shakespeare chose the alternative, sounder both artistically and in its agreement with man's observable behaviour, of presenting Hal as developing from wild, though never vicious, youth into pious but hearty maturity, from the member of a band of reprobates to England's great leader.[39] Perhaps this choice was related to his interest in a new theory of causation, which dominates the mature tragedies and to which allusions appear in *2 Henry IV*. These ideas will be discussed below. For the present, we may observe that Shakespeare undertook to trace growth of character in Hal, and this meant that, for the first time, he attempted to follow character evolution throughout a play. To solve this problem, he fell back upon a more primitive dramatic technique than he had used in *Richard II*.

Shakespeare actually had few models in attempting to present an evolving human personality. Growth of character is certainly present in Greek drama. The process by which Admetus has

[38]Cf. his *Treatise of Melancholy*, pp. 122-23.
[39]Cf. Hudson, *Shakespeare*, II, 68, 78-79.

become worthy of Alcestis by the time she is restored to him by Apollo is one of the elements that make the *Alcestis* technically one of Euripides' most interesting plays. But such development of personality is rare in Greek drama, and there is no evidence that Shakespeare knew a single Greek play even in translation. It is non-existent in Seneca. In English drama it was probably confined to Marlowe's *Faustus* and *Edward II* and Shakespeare's own *Romeo and Juliet,* in which Juliet, especially, matures markedly before her death. But in *Romeo and Juliet* the effect was easy to achieve, perhaps in part accidental. In the first part of the play, in which he followed Brooke more freely, Shakespeare made his lovers younger than they were in his source, in action as well as in Juliet's stated age, and then he automatically took over their greater maturity by following Brooke as closely as he did in the last half of the play. But, as we have noted, he did strengthen the effect by eliminating Juliet's whimpering during her last meeting with Romeo.

Hal was therefore a much tougher problem, for which Shakespeare could find no guidance in his sources or in Marlowe, by whom he was influenced in *Richard II*. He apparently attempted to solve the problem about as follows. He had planned, even when writing *Richard II*, to devote *1 Henry IV* to Hal as a military figure, which was indeed to be his most glorious role. Hotspur was therefore built into a dramatic foil for Hal, an incredibly engaging combination of reckless bravery and hot-headed stupidity. King Henry repeatedly emphasizes the contrast between the two, beginning with his fourth speech in the play; and the reconciliation between father and son, the climactic scene of the play, turns on the King's restatement of this contrast and Hal's promise that he will outdo Hotspur (III, ii, 93-161). Hal's final victory over Hotspur marks his achievement of maturity as a soldier.

Next, Shakespeare made Hal's wild oats palatable, to him and to his audience, by presenting, in the person of Falstaff, temptations to which any man might be forgiven for yielding. In fact, critics from Maurice Morgann on have themselves been so seduced that they have condemned Hal, not for dissipating with Falstaff as prince, but for rejecting him as king—for yielding, not to vice, but to virtue.

Finally (and admiration for Falstaff has too often obscured

this fact), Shakespeare attempted to show that Hal was always superior to his surroundings. There is actually a marked change between the "preview" of Hal in *Richard II* and his role in *1 Henry IV*. In the former he is completely dissolute:

> *Boling.* Inquire at London, 'mongst the taverns there,
> For there, they say, he daily doth frequent,
> With unrestrained loose companions,
> Even such, they say, as stand in narrow lanes
> And beat our watch and rob our passengers;
> Which he, young wanton and effeminate boy,
> Takes on the point of honour to support
> So dissolute a crew....
>
> *Percy.* His answer was, he would unto the stews,
> And from the common'st creature pluck a glove
> And wear it as a favour; and with that
> He would unhorse the lustiest challenger.
>
> (V, iii, 5-19)

His scenes with Falstaff are never on this level, and the difference in the two concepts of Hal may indicate that Shakespeare did not decide to make Hal evolve before he began writing *1 Henry IV*. Hal's very first speech in this play shows—and, since Shakespeare was very careful of initial impressions, was obviously intended to show—that he knows what kind of a man Falstaff is. An examination of his scenes with Falstaff will reveal that he never fails to recognize Falstaff's conduct for what it is, far more clearly and uncharitably than we are willing to do, and to call it unhesitatingly by its right name. To make assurance doubly sure, Shakespeare gave him, at the end of his first scene, a soliloquy in which he seems to analyse his motives with a calculating hardness worthy of his father at his worst. But Shakespeare undoubtedly intended the speech to be a simple statement of fact no different in kind or effect from many other characterizing soliloquies in his plays. The trouble was, of course, that he had made Falstaff too ingratiating and he now loaded upon an essentially artificial device a dramatic function too heavy for it. It is certainly plausible that an introspective character like Hamlet or an imaginative one like Macbeth should soliloquize; we are even prepared to assume, to make matters easier for the dramatist, that a cold-blooded villain like Richard III or Iago would analyze his own motives in terms of our standards of right and wrong. But it is simply incredible that a lusty young playboy, as he might be called today, would polish off a gay escapade by examining his deviation from the path of virtue and charting the way by which he would return. Hal tells of Hotspur's good qualities while the audience sees Hotspur's weaknesses. This is obviously sounder artistry than making Hal talk of his own good intentions while the audience watches his dissipations, and Hotspur is much the more convincing character. Hal's soliloquy fails, and with it falls Shakespeare's artistic design.[40] Even Vernon's description of his martial bearing (IV, i, 97-110), though the testimony of an enemy, leaves us unconvinced.

In *2 Henry IV*, Shakespeare apparently attempted to repeat essentially the same formula. This time the theme was to be Hal's rehabilitation as a political leader, and Prince John of Lancaster was to be the foil, as Falstaff makes clear in his great speech comparing the two (IV, iii, 92-135). In addition, the Chief Justice would illustrate Hal's acceptance of sound guidance. In *1 Henry IV* Hal had proved, by killing Hotspur, that he had acquired valor; he would now prove, by not killing the Chief Justice, that he had acquired virtue. To prepare for the rejection of Falstaff—a rejection which, by every law of folklore, is inevitable the minute a Chief Justice appears who has jailed the Prince— Shakespeare made him more dissolute and more remote from Hal.[41] Lines like the King's "up, vanity! Down, royal state!" (IV, v, 120-21), the formality of the final scenes between Hal and the Chief Justice, and the rejection of Falstaff all support the suggestion that the play is a morality treatment of the conflict between justice and vice,[42] a theory which seems much more nearly convincing as applied to this play than to Part 1. Finally, the scene with the crown balances the reconciliation scene of Part 1. But Henry speaks to Hal as though the previous reconciliation scene

[40]For a somewhat different estimate of this soliloquy see Schücking, *Character Problems in Shakespeare's Plays*, pp. 217-21. Bethell (*Shakespeare & the Popular Dramatic Tradition*, pp. 68-71) compares the technique of Hal's soliloquy with "the conventionalism of the medieval miracles."

[41]Cf. Matthews, *Shakspere as a Playwright*, p. 130. Bradley also recognizes this deterioration clearly (*Oxford Lectures on Poetry*, p. 272).

[42]Quiller-Couch, *Shakespeare's Workmanship*, p. 115; Wilson, *The Fortunes of Falstaff*, passim.

and the Battle of Shrewsbury had never occurred, and Shakespeare avoided the problem of the Prince's previous regeneration only by leaving him out of every serious scene up to this point, although some of the comedy scenes present the old Hal.

Henry V is a still different kind of play. In its simple narrative it returns to the Henry VI plays; in its spontaneity and its rich comedy it recalls *1 Henry IV;* in its meditation upon the kingship it continues the thoughtful vein of *2 Henry IV*. Except possibly for *1 Henry VI* its chauvinism is unique in its extent. Its chorus confesses Shakespeare's feeling that the chronicle play was itself inadequate as a dramatic genre.

As the preceding paragraphs have indicated, *1 Henry IV* is, in some ways, dramatically crude. It represents, despite its brilliant minor characters, the same kind of reversion to an earlier dramatic technique that we shall find Shakespeare making in the great tragedies as he tries to present mental conflict and moral choice. Despite the loose ends that have been discussed, *Richard II* is skillfully done. It shows great technical dexterity, and it is hard to imagine Shakespeare doing a much better job of that particular type of play. It is fundamentally a contrast between two characters, both of them rich but static. For Richard cannot be regarded as developing. His death illustrates the courage of a desperate man, as well as Shakespeare's habit of making an English king die as a king should, rather than any strengthening of his character, although critics have sometimes read into his lines the development of character which Marlowe's Edward II certainly does undergo. The play therefore involves, as even its imagery emphasizes, a formal balance between Bolingbroke and Richard, in which one rises as the other falls and gain of power is matched by loss of the audience's sympathy, or vice versa. The background for Richard's self-dramatizations is as richly patterned as can well be imagined. The whole complex design is worked out with extraordinary technical mastery. Richard's character, though not that of a Hamlet or a Macbeth, is subtle enough, and it is revealed solely by what he does or what he says to other people. He needs no asides, and his only soliloquy is spoken in the solitude of prison, where a man might surely indulge in self-communion if ever. There are few characterizing speeches by others, and none remotely comparable in crudeness to Vernon's praise of Hal as prince (*1 Henry IV*, V, ii, 52-79) or the Constable of France's praise of him as king (*Henry V*, II, iv, 30-40), in both of which his enemies are used to exalt Hal in defiance of all probability.[43] The scene growing out of Aumerle's conspiracy may be a weakness; but it does contrast Bolingbroke's handling of a crisis with Richard's, and it prevents the death scene from following too soon after the deposition. Certainly *Richard II* has no artistic error comparable to Hal's characterizing soliloquy. Of its kind it is a very finished play indeed. The virtuosity of *1 Henry IV* consists in the vitality of its characters; it cannot pretend to technical finish. But who would trade the depth of perception in *1 Henry IV* for the surface polish of *Richard II*?

In enunciating another set of ideas, *2 Henry IV* and *Henry V* remind us that we are approaching the mature tragedies. It is probable, in fact, that *Henry V* and *Julius Caesar* were only a year apart in composition. *2 Henry IV*, despite its parallels of structure, contains statements of contemporary learning of a kind which is completely absent from Part 1, so that it seems to have been written from Shakespeare's intellect, whereas Part 1 came from his heart. Even the parody in the comic scenes becomes the delight of the annotator rather than of the audience. An important part of this learning is the concept of order and of natural law. For the first time the vague hints of the earlier plays give way to explicit statement. These ideas, as we shall see, play a fundamental part in the problem comedies and the tragedies, and they serve to link both *2 Henry IV* and *Henry V* with later plays.

The first important passage is probably derived from the account of the creation in Genesis, as the references to Cain and to darkness show.

> Let heaven kiss earth! Now let not Nature's hand
> Keep the wild flood confin'd. Let order die!
> And let this world no longer be a stage
> To feed contention in a ling'ring act;
> But let one spirit of the first-born Cain
> Reign in all bosoms, that, each heart being set
> On bloody courses, the rude scene may end,
> And darkness be the burier of the dead!
>
> (I, i, 153-60)

[43]Cf. Schücking's treatment of this point, which is, however, confined to the villains: *Character Problems in Shakespeare's Plays*, pp. 59-66.

Later on Falstaff speaks glibly of "the law of nature" (III, ii, 356).

Another very significant passage shows that Shakespeare had been thinking about the application of laws of nature to the history upon which he was building his plays and that he shared the accepted theory of his day that history had a practical use because it repeated itself.[44]

> There is a history in all men's lives,
> Figuring the nature of the times deceas'd
> The which observ'd, a man may prophesy,
> With a near aim, of the main chance of things
> As yet not come to life, which in their seeds
> And weak beginnings lie intreasured.
>
> (*2 Henry IV*, III, i, 80-85)

The "seeds" are, of course, Lear's "germens" "that makes ingrateful man" (III, ii, 8-9) and the "seeds of time" of which Banquo speaks (*Macbeth*, I, iii, 58). As Curry has shown, they are the *rationes seminales*, the essences in things which lead to the working out in nature of the archetypal pattern in the mind of God the creator. Shakespeare may have derived the term and even the concept from Timothy Bright.[45] History is therefore a record of the way in which these seeds have germinated into events of the past, and it is thereby a means of foretelling how they will determine future growth. How long Shakespeare had held such a concept we cannot tell. This is certainly the first explicit statement of it in his works and apparently the first implication as well. We have noted how indifferent he seemed to political motives and historical causes as they were stated in his sources. The broad philosophic pattern of crime and retribution which he took intact from Halle involved, as he presented it, rather the direct intervention of Providence than a fulfillment of God's purpose through the steady operation of laws laid down by Him at the time of creation. The seeds imply a view of events that is at once more sophisticated and more genuinely philosophic. It leads directly to the major change of method that we shall encounter in Shakespeare's use of his sources in the period of the great tragedies. Its first appear-

[44]Cf. Tillyard, *Shakespeare's History Plays*, pp. 54-58; Campbell, *Shakespeare's Histories*, pp. 18-22, 67-84.

[45]*Shakespeare's Philosophical Patterns*, pp. 29-49; Elton, "Timothy Bright and Shakespeare's Seeds of Nature," pp. 196-97.

ance may also have had something to do with Shakespeare's attempt to show Hal as developing into a great king rather than undergoing a conversion. But the connection would be impossible to prove.

The well-known discourse on obedience by the Archbishop of Canterbury in *Henry V* is clearly derived from Elyot's *Governour*, as a comparison will show. Since the passage is a long one, involving parts of two chapters, relevant sentences have been selected:

More over take away ordre from all thynges what shulde than remayne?...But they that be governours (as I before sayde) nothinge do acquire by the sayde influence of knowlege for theyr owne necessities, but do imploye all the powers of theyr wittes, and theyr diligence, to the only preservation of other theyr inferiours: amonge which inferiours also behoveth to be a disposition and ordre accordynge to reason, that is to saye, that the slouthfull or idell persone do nat participate with hym that is industrious and taketh payne: wherby the frutes of his labours shulde be diminisshed: wherein shulde be none equalitie, but therof shulde procede discourage, and finally disolution for lacke of provision....Wherfore to conclude, it is onely a publike weale, where, like as god hath disposed the saide influence of understandyng, is also appoynted degrees and places according to the excellencie therof; and therto also wold be substance convenient and necessarye for the ornament of the same, which also impresseth a reverence and due obedience to the vulgare people or communaltie; and without that, it can be no more said that there is a publike weale, than it may be affirmed that a house, without his propre and necessarye ornamentes, is well and sufficiently furnisshed.[46]

After several intervening pages, there follows, by way of analogy, an extended discussion of the bees which is very like that in Shakespeare:

<blockquote>
Therefore doth heaven divide
The state of man in divers functions,
Setting endeavour in continual motion,
To which is fixed, as an aim or butt,
Obedience; for so work the honey bees.
</blockquote>

(I, ii, 183-87)

Another passage links the law of nature and of nations in a way reminiscent of Elyot and more especially of Hooker, but the juxtaposition of the two probably comes accidentally as Exeter

[46]Ed. Croft, I, 3, 6-8 (Book I, ch. i).

enumerates the bases of Henry's claim to the French crown, thinking of primogeniture as a universal law and of the Archbishop's pronouncement upon the Salic Law:

> He wills you, in the name of God Almighty,
> That you divest yourself, and lay apart
> The borrowed glories that by gift of heaven,
> By law of nature and of nations, 'longs
> To him and to his heirs; namely, the crown . . .
>
> (II, iv, 77-81)

It is apparent that the passages just cited contain all the ingredients of Ulysses' famous speech on degree in *Troilus and Cressida*, which outlines a universal hierarchical scheme stretching from God through all nature and including rank in man's political organization as a part of a universal principle. Certainly the entire scheme appears both at the beginning of the Homily "Of Obedience" and in Elyot's *Governour*, as well as in Hooker, to whom as yet there has been no demonstrable allusion. This scheme underlies the imagery in *Richard II*, where the king is elaborately compared with the highest-ranking members of various natural hierarchies—not only with his symbol the sun, the king of planets, but also with fire, the ranking element (III, iii, 58), the eagle (III, iii, 69), the lion, and the rose (V, i, 8, 29). Each of these is king of its kind, and both the Queen and Richard play with the idea that the lion is the king of beasts. These comparisons were all part of Renaissance symbolism, and Shakespeare might have picked them up anywhere. He shows more clearly that he was familiar with the notion of a relationship between the natural and political order by the comic use to which he puts it in *A Midsummer-Night's Dream*, where Titania tells Oberon that, because his brawls have disturbed her sport, the winds howl, the fields do not yield, and the seasons have got all mixed up (II, i, 87-117).

It seems a reasonable inference that Shakespeare had read the relevant passages some time before and had grasped their meaning superficially. On the other hand, he had been deeply impressed by the teaching of the Homilies and Elyot on the need for order within a kingdom and the horrors of civil war. Indeed, no Elizabethan surveying his country's past could fail to be profoundly moved by such ideas, especially as he reflected upon the Queen's advancing years and the unsettled succession. But there is no evidence whatever that Shakespeare had previously grasped the profound implications of the relationship between man and the universe or the notion of forces operating throughout nature and society which was basic to it. In 2 *Henry IV* and *Henry V* he was just coming to grips with these ideas. It is one thing to see that civil war leads to murder, rape, and destruction of property. These evils he portrayed vividly throughout the chronicle plays. It is another to see that the very emotional and intellectual stability of the individual, as well as his fulfilling his potentialities as a rational creature, depends upon his being part of a stable moral order that derives from a stable universe. That concept he did not write into his plays until *Hamlet* and *Troilus and Cressida*, and he waited until *Lear* to give it ultimate expression. We must assume that he first developed the full idea in *Troilus and Cressida* rather than in the chronicle plays, in many of which it would have been even more appropriate, because he had only recently come to feel its compelling significance. By contrast, even in *Henry V* he took from Elyot's complete exposition of universal order only the sentences on doing one's work and obeying authority.

These last chronicle plays also provide interesting evidence of further mastery of three kinds of material that we have previously encountered. Shakespeare's interest in the Bible and religious doctrines had not ceased. Richard and Falstaff are, in their respective ways, two of Shakespeare's most Biblical characters. Richard's scriptural allusions are a reflection of the divinity that he feels hedging himself as king, and Falstaff's are a sign of his ability to misapply a good education as he does his quotations. But the fact that, as Noble testifies,[47] the Genevan version begins to furnish most of the Biblical echoes in 2 *Henry IV* suggests that Shakespeare continued to read the Bible, since the Genevan translation was never used in churches officially, although it undoubtedly crept into some unofficially. In *Henry V* (III, vii, 68-70) the Dauphin, if one makes a reasonable allowance for printer's errors in setting French, quotes the French Olivetan version of II Peter, ii, 22, which Shakespeare must have looked up.[48] Noble also points out that *Henry V* contains an interesting example of

[47]*Shakespeare's Biblical Knowledge*, p. 174: "This is the earliest play in which Genevan readings show a decided preponderance over Bishops'."
[48]Ibid., pp. 86-87.

Shakespeare's checking a Biblical reference in his source. After Agincourt Holinshed says that Henry commanded the troops to sing the psalm "In exitu Israel de Aegypto" and to kneel at "non nobis, Domine," which was, in fact, the title of the next Psalm (cxv), the Anglican Psalter having separated into two psalms what appeared as one in the Vulgate and in Catholic usage. Shakespeare therefore concluded that his source was in error and made Henry say: "Let there be sung *Non nobis* and *Te Deum*" (IV, viii, 128).[49]

In contrast to Shakespeare's continuing study of the Bible, the five theological allusions that I have noted in *1 Henry IV* (I, ii, 119) and *Henry V* (I, i, 28-31, 67-68; I, ii, 31-32; V, ii, 216), except for the Archbishop's doubt of miracles, are all concerned with the fall and salvation of man and do not indicate any advance of knowledge or interest beyond the references in the early plays.

Two important applications of contemporary psychology deserve mention. Richard's discussion of "still-breeding thoughts" begotten by brain upon soul (*Richard II*, V, v, 6-10) has been noted in passing and need not concern us further. But Falstaff's comparison of Hal and Prince John is of great importance both dramatically and as an indication of Shakespeare's learning. It is a deliberate statement of the reason why Hal can become a great leader but Prince John never could.[50] With consummate skill it has been adapted to the speaker and has been centered upon an essentially comic theme, the drinking of sack, which is so appropriate to Falstaff's bibulous nature that even Ben Jonson must have regarded it as a prime example of *decorum*. But the fun should not blind us to the fact that Falstaff is talking sound learning as the Elizabethans understood it. Of John he says: "There's never none of these demure boys come to any proof; for thin drink doth so over-cool their blood, and making many fish-meals, that they fall into a kind of male green-sickness; and then, when they marry, they get wenches" (IV, iii, 96-101). According to *Batman uppon Bartholome*, published in 1582, Falstaff has selected for comment the essential quality of a man: "And therefore through the great abundance of spirits and hot bloud, a man is

[49]Ibid., pp. 80-81.
[50]Wilson comments briefly on the importance of this speech (*The Fortunes of Falstaff*, p. 74).

more hardy then a woman."[51] The prophecy that John will get wenches also has a sound basis: "Therefore the seede that the male commeth of, is more stronger and more hot, and in more hotter place received, than the seede that the female commeth of."[52] "Hereof comes it," says Falstaff, "that Prince Harry is valiant; for the cold blood he did naturally inherit of his father, he hath, like lean, sterile, and bare land, manured, husbanded, and till'd with excellent endeavour of drinking good and good store of fertile sherris, that he is become very hot and valiant" (IV, iii, 126-32). The rest of the lines could be similarly analysed to show how Shakespeare has merely livened up the best learning of his day with Falstaff's inimitable manner of speech. The passage is a milestone marking the progress of Shakespeare's knowledge as well as of his comedy.

That Shakespeare had also been reading on military theory and history may be indicated by Fluellen's disquisitions in *Henry V*. As so often, however, he creates an atmosphere of much greater erudition than he actually displays. Fluellen's stipulation "concerning the disciplines of the war, the Roman wars" (III, ii, 103) results in a suspicious parallel between his interests and most of Shakespeare's early training and reading.

The preceding discussions of the various chronicle plays must have made it perfectly clear that I distrust current theories that Shakespeare incorporated into the chronicle plays either a profound philosophic concept of a universal order governing the affairs of men or deliberate reflections upon contemporary statecraft. Toward a more philosophic view Shakespeare was certainly moving—very rapidly from *King John* on; but his thought was still developing. The following diagnosis of his method in writing the history plays is offered in the hope that it will explain the observable facts as well as the theories just mentioned. It also attempts to take into account Shakespeare's experiments and his growth in dramatic technique, which are sometimes ignored.

(1) Shakespeare worked backward from the more recent and familiar Yorkish period to the reigns of the Lancastrians and of King John.

[51]Liber VI, cap. xiii, fol. 74ᵛ.
[52]Liber VI, cap. iv, fol. 72.

(2) He was several times led to his choice of subjects by earlier plays which had treated the same material.

(3) He used Halle and Holinshed where an old play was not available or adequate, and he followed them, like all his sources, closely. Consequently the "Tudor myth," which was present in Halle, appears in his plays.

(4) Not being an historical scholar, he interpreted what he read in the light of events and ideas with which he was familiar, and was not above pointing an obvious parallel or introducing a contemporary allusion like that to Essex in the Prologue to Act V of *Henry V*. He applied the concept of the divine right of kings to all previous English history, whether it was in his sources or not, simply because he took it for granted. Hart points out that Shakespeare shares his allusions to the divine right of kings with his contemporaries but goes far beyond them in applying the doctrine to all ages and climes.[53] His doing so seems to reflect his relative ignorance rather than design, for Shakespeare's fellow dramatists when he was writing the history plays were most of them university-trained scholars, even if not his equals as dramatists.

(5) He inserted into his histories, as into his other plays, the commonplaces of his age or reminiscences of what he had read or heard. The passages on civil war belong in this category.

(6) Above all, he was interested in writing effective plays. His deviations from history, like those from other sources, were dictated by his desire to build an effective plot or interesting characterization, especially by means of character contrast. So Hotspur was made younger to provide a foil for Prince Hal, as part of an attempt to make the Prince convincing despite the traditional change from madcap to model king. Theodore Spencer summarizes Shakespeare's principal concern admirably:

His greatness consists—and no historian of ideas should forget it for a moment—in his ability to create characters in whom we can believe, and it is only in so far as we are helped toward an understanding of how he does this, that a study of the conventions of his time is really useful.[54]

[53]*Shakespeare and the Homilies*, pp. 27-28.
[54]*Shakespeare and the Nature of Man*, p. 73.

In short, Shakespeare's general procedure in writing the history plays was very much the same as that in writing the early tragedies and the comedies. He merely used different kinds of source material and adapted his dramatic treatment to his sources. Despite his vivid pictures of the disorders of civil war, and his acceptance of the "Tudor myth," his main interest lay in character and in ideas, and both his material and his thought were on a relatively popular level, although in the later plays he was moving rapidly toward a more genuinely philosophical point of view.

CHAPTER VIII

The Romantic Comedies

THE COMEDIES to be considered in this chapter span the same period as the Lancastrian chronicle plays and the earliest of the mature tragedies. *A Midsummer Night's Dream* belongs to the same year as *King John* and *Richard II*. *Twelfth Night* and *The Merry Wives of Windsor* parallel *Julius Caesar* and *Hamlet* in 1599 and 1600.

In contrast to the histories, which show clearly the increase in Shakespeare's learning and the rapid maturing of his thought, the romantic comedies have relatively little evidence to offer. Titania's long description of the way in which Oberon's brawls have upset the weather has been mentioned. Portia's great speech on mercy (*Merchant of Venice*, IV, i, 184-205) is derived from Seneca's *De Clementia*,[1] with details from Ecclesiasticus xxxv, 19, and the Communion Service; Touchstone's remarks on quarreling by the book (*As You Like It*, V, iv, 94-108) parody Saviolo's elaborate discussion "Of the manner and diversitie of Lies," in which he distinguishes "Lies certaine," "conditionall Lyes," "the Lye in generall," "the Lye in particular," and "foolish Lyes."[2] The *Merry Wives of Windsor* is full of elementary medical lore. Otherwise the allusions in the various plays add nothing to what has already been discussed.

The comedies do show, however, the perfection of Shakespeare's earlier manner of constructing his plays. Dramatic technique, as such, is obviously irrelevant to this discussion, although any interpretation of meaning, even in details, is unsafe unless it

---

[1]Cf. letter from Sonnenschein in *Times Literary Supplement*, Sept. 16, 1904; and New Cambridge *Merchant of Venice*, p. 164.

[2]*Vincentio Saviolo his Practise*, paragraph headings, fols. S2v-T2.

is kept in mind. But the case for a fundamental enrichment of Shakespeare's thought after 1600 rests, in considerable part, upon contrasting techniques in constructing the plays. The earlier plays merely adapt a source narrative to stage presentation. The problem comedies try to superimpose philosophic interpretation upon material developed by the same easy-going methods, and trouble results. The tragedies, on the other hand, reshape the plot to fit a predetermined character problem. It will therefore be necessary to analyse Shakespeare's method of constructing the comedies, both to show how much and what kind of thought he put into writing them, and to furnish a basis for future comparison. If the material of this chapter seems, for the moment, irrelevant, I hope that its bearing will become clear in succeeding chapters. Since the sources of *A Midsummer Night's Dream* and *Merry Wives* are so fragmentary that they do not furnish adequate bases for comparison, these plays, like *The Tempest*, must be regarded as exceptions to Shakespeare's usual method, and they will be omitted from the following discussion.

Of the remaining plays *The Merchant of Venice* clearly rests upon the first tale of the fourth day of *Il Pecorone* of "Ser Giovanni" of Florence. Being unable (for reasons to be discussed later) to use its device by which the suitor wins the lady, Shakespeare substituted the casket story from Robinson's version of the *Gesta Romanorum*.[3] The two sources may have been linked in the old *Iew* mentioned in 1579 by Stephen Gosson in his *School of Abuse;* but Shakespeare rarely used such outdated dramatic material, and the possibility need not worry us. *Much Ado About Nothing* is derived primarily from Bandello's Twenty-second Story of Part 1, although the scene at Hero's window may have been taken from the Fifth Book of Ariosto's *Orlando Furioso* or from Book II, Canto iv, of Spenser's *Faerie Queene.*[4] *As You Like It* is based directly upon Thomas Lodge's pastoral romance *Rosalynde, or Euphues' golden Legacie,* published in 1592.[5] For

[3]Chambers, *William Shakespeare,* I, 373. The stories are reprinted in Hazlitt, *Shakespeare's Library,* I (Part 1), 319-66.

[4]The sources are reprinted in the Furness Variorum, pp. 295-329. Furness' conclusion that Bandello's original rather than Belleforest's French version was Shakespeare's source has been accepted by Grace R. Trenery, the Arden editor (p. xiii), but Quiller-Couch (New Cambridge, p. ix) and Chambers (*William Shakespeare,* I, 387-88) regard the two versions as alternate sources.

[5]Reprinted in Hazlitt, *Shakespeare's Library,* II (Part 1), 13-144.

Twelfth Night Shakespeare seems to have used *Gl' Ingannati*, a play acted by the Intronati at Siena in 1531 and much reprinted, Bandello's Novella xxxvi of Part 2 (No. 28 in Payne's translation), and Barnabe Riche's story of Apolonius and Silla in *Riche his Farewell to Militarie profession.*[6] The plot is obviously closer to Riche's version than to the others, and I should regard it as the main source. But the minor characters seem to owe a good deal to the other versions.

Shakespeare's primary aim seems to have been to tell a good story. When he found a narrative that he regarded as suitable basis for a play, he therefore followed it as closely as possible.[7] To the fundamental outline of the plot he was likely to be faithful, even though it was completely improbable as it stood. Often, in fact, when he felt compelled to change details to achieve propriety of morals or manners, he introduced new improbabilities into the source plot, but still he followed it. Whenever possible, he also used the characterization or even details of language in the original. Both Rosalind and Celia are considerably indebted to Lodge's Rosalynde and Alinda for their personalities and even for repartee, and Luce has shown that several unexplained allusions in *Twelfth Night* can be made clear by referring to Bandello.[8] But Shakespeare was ordinarily compelled to develop or alter characters to make the source story acceptable, and his normal procedure was to accept the source plot and to adapt characterization and details to it. An examination of the kinds of adaptation that he made therefore becomes a clue to what he was trying to accomplish, as well as to how he went about achieving his goals.[9]

Shakespeare's first task was obviously to condense the source material for dramatic treatment. However far the Elizabethan play may have departed from the unity of time insisted upon by

[6]Cf. Arden *Twelfth Night*, pp. 177-90; *The Novels of Matteo Bandello*, trans. John Payne, IV, 121-56; and for Riche, Hazlitt, *Shakespeare's Library*, I (Part 1), 387-412.

[7]Cf. Schücking, *Character Problems in Shakespeare's Plays*, pp. 147, 190; Ashley H. Thorndike, "Shakspere as a Debtor," p. 166; C. C. Stopes, *Shakespeare's Industry*, p. 16.

[8]Arden *Twelfth Night*, p. 184.

[9]The following discussion revises material from my "Shakespeare's Use of his Sources." The techniques which I attributed to all Shakespeare's plays at the time when I wrote that article I now regard as characteristics only of the plays before 1600, at least in so far as they involve fundamental acceptance of the source narrative.

neo-classic critics, it was still impossible for him to duplicate the rambling structure of his sources. He could indeed present an entire life from birth to death; but he had to keep the action crowded and exciting, and the introductory narratives in the tales that he used were commonly neither. As his first operation in constructing a plot, he therefore eliminated all the source narrative up to the immediate causes of the real excitement—which meant, in a love story, the occasion when boy met girl and the action headed, although never directly, toward marriage.

Sometimes omitting the background in the source made no great difference. In *Rosalynde,* the source of *As You Like It,* Lodge tells how Sir John of Bordeaux divided his property among his three sons and how Saladin, the eldest, then treated Rosader, the youngest, as a servant for a period of years, until finally he plotted to have Rosader killed in a wrestling match just as in Shakespeare. At the match Rosader and Rosalynde exchanged the same fatal glances as Orlando and Rosalind. No harm was done, therefore, if the play began with the wrestling. Overlooking the lands of which Saladin defrauded Rosader actually made his final repentance less implausible, and the boorish upbringing that Lodge describes at length would have been most unlikely to endow Rosader with the overmastering charm that he displayed.

In *The Merchant of Venice* and *Twelfth Night,* on the other hand, this same omission of preliminaries deprived the action of adequate motivation. In *Il Pecorone* Gianetto's father had given Ansaldo his start in life, and at the father's death Ansaldo therefore received Gianetto as his son, with all the obligations that such a relationship implied. Ansaldo fitted out three ships to set up Gianetto as a merchant, two of which Gianetto lost in making trial of the siren of Belmont; to find money for the third, Ansaldo proposed the terrible bond, since he had nothing left but his flesh to offer as security. For the source relationship Shakespeare substituted mere friendship,[10] perhaps adding Antonio's melancholy not only to foreshadow ensuing dangers but also to make convincing his dependence upon the younger man for companionship. This made the bond even more improbable, and Shakespeare tried to meet part of the difficulty by letting Shylock propose the terms "in a merry sport." In both *Gl' Ingannati* and Bandello, the equiva-

10Cf. Walley, "Shakespeare's Portrayal of Shylock," p. 229.

lents of Orsino and Viola have been in love, and he has transferred his affections during her absence. In Riche she has fallen in love with him when he visited her father's home and has followed him to Constantinople. All three versions give her a definite reason for serving him as page, and the first two make much more plausible his final marriage to her. This omission of the source motivation for the opening action of the plays is, of course, exactly what we have already seen in *Richard II*, and by a similar process Shakespeare produced even more startling results in *King Lear*.

A second obvious device for condensing the plot consisted in omitting unexciting sections within the segment selected for the play, just as Shakespeare habitually combined several battles in the chronicle plays to telescope years of civil war. After the wrestling match, he omitted a reconciliation, final quarrel, and a pitched battle between Rosader and Saladin, and the action leading up to Rosalynde's banishment. Eliminating all this speeded the play from falling in love to love-making as rapidly as possible.

Finally, Shakespeare apparently stopped at no improbability to wind up a play in a hurry. To eliminate a pitched battle in Lodge, *As You Like It* tells that the usurping Duke has been converted by "an old religious man" and has restored his possessions to the rightful Duke.

Shakespeare also had to fit the action for dramatic as opposed to narrative presentation and to adapt it to Elizabethan stage conventions.

He first had to fill in the minor characters logically implied by the source narrative. Lodge could say that the banished Duke had a group of followers in Arden; Shakespeare had to present that group on the stage, or at least a few representatives of it, and to give them enough to say to suggest a real court. Portia must have servants, and a young man of marriageable age like Bassanio should have a few friends. Jaques, Nerissa, Gratiano, and the rest are therefore not changes of the source but rather a working out of the source narrative in its own terms.

Other types of adaptation to the stage might involve departing from the source. To begin with, a universal marrying off was as inevitable in comedy as a general slaughter in tragedy. Shakespeare's sources generally observed the same principle; so he needed to provide only for characters that he himself introduced, such as Lorenzo and Jessica or Touchstone and Audrey, or for occasional matrimonial arrangements in the sources that he found unsuitable, such as the socially impossible marriage between Ansaldo and the maid corresponding to Nerissa. This characteristic may explain why Adam disappears in *As You Like It*. Shakespeare perhaps found his presence awkward in pairing off the characters,[11] Jaques and the Duke being, in their respective ways, necessary though unmarriageable.

It was also dramatically convenient that each major character have a confidant, whether friend or servant, and the source was less likely to provide this arrangement. In narration, the writer himself can impute motives or emotions to his characters; if the dramatist is to avoid soliloquies or asides, he must make his points through dialogue between two persons who enjoy each other's confidence. Shakespeare either developed a minor character in the source into this role of confidant or provided a new person altogether. Nerissa he developed from a maid in the source who certainly did not deserve her mistress's confidence. But he gave her no character of her own, and she is only a support for Portia.[12] Gratiano and Tubal were invented. No additional characters were needed in *As You Like It* and *Much Ado*; but in *Twelfth Night* the Sea Captain and Antonio were provided for Viola and Sebastian, and Maria, who derives from Bandello's maid, was given an important part in the subplot.

Another group of conventional characters plays an important part in the technique of the histories and tragedies. Shakespeare frequently found it necessary to personify a political party or a point of view or to guide the spectators in interpreting what occurred on the stage. We have noticed how Tybalt was developed into a kind of incarnation of the feud between the Capulets and the Montagues and how the Bastard at times stood apart and commented upon the action as an interpreter or dramatist's mouthpiece. Such characters are almost unrepresented in the comedies. There seems to be no occasion for someone to represent a faction, as Tybalt does. Jaques and Touchstone, as the latter's name suggests, come close to being the voice of cynicism and of normal

[11]Albert H. Tolman wonders what happens to Adam in his "Shakespeare's Manipulation of his Sources in *As You Like It*," pp. 68-69.
[12]S. A. Small, *Shakespearean Character Interpretation*, p. 113.

183

common sense, respectively. They comment on the fantastic make-believe of the Duke's court and on Arcadianism and literary pastoralism in general.[13] Touchstone's relations with his Audrey also raise some questions as to romantic love-making.

Finally, Shakespeare had to keep in mind the members of his own company. The clowns had to be provided for. Launcelot Gobbo and Dogberry gave Kemp a chance to perform. Robert Armin's excellence as a court fool is reflected in Touchstone and Feste. But more important roles had also to be adjusted to the personnel of the company, and Shakespeare's women, especially, reflect the boys who played them. Their characteristics and mannerisms had to be adapted not only to the capacities of highly trained boy actors but also to the particular boys immediately available. Shakespeare's habit of pairing a serious and a somewhat gayer woman in the same play—Celia and Rosalind, Hero and Beatrice—may well have resulted from the presence of two leading boys who specialized in the two kinds of roles. Baldwin remarks that Juliet and Portia were adapted to Robert Goffe, Nerissa to William Eccleston; and several scholars have noted that the women come in cycles according to the development of various generations of apprentices.[14]

Elizabethan plays were subject, of course, to licensing by the Master of the Revels, who would be on the lookout for dangerous political doctrine or personal satire. The act against stage profanity was not passed until the reign of James, and oaths or irreligious Biblical allusions were not the source of trouble that they later became. But the Act of Uniformity at the beginning of Elizabeth's reign provided severe penalties "if any Person or Persons whatsoever, after the said Feast of the Nativity of St. *John Baptist* next coming, shall in any Enterludes, Plays, Songs, Rhimes, or by other open Words declare or speak any thing in the derogation, depraving, or despising of the same Book, or of any thing therein contained. . . ."[15] This made it impossible to use portions of the services of the church, or anything approximating them, in a play; and the marriage ceremony, so long favored by Hollywood as the

[13]Cf. Quiller-Couch, *Shakespeare's Workmanship*, p. 96.
[14]Baldwin, *The Organization and Personnel of the Shakespearean Company*, pp. 274-5. Cf. this entire chapter, pp. 229-83.
[15]Cf. Noble, *Shakespeare's Biblical Knowledge*, p. 82. I give the version still printed in the preface to the English *Book of Common Prayer*.

final scene in a moving picture, could not be suggested. This fact explains Shakespeare's use of classical wedding masques in several plays and the appearance of Hymen to perform the wedding in *As You Like It* (V, iv, 114-52).

In addition to endowing the story with the necessary characters and to obeying the law, Shakespeare tried, in adapting his material to the stage, to please the fancies of his audience by providing them with as much action as possible and by reflecting current fashions. Both *The Merchant of Venice* and *Much Ado* have parallel plots, the subplot of *Twelfth Night* is very nearly as important as the main plot, and *As You Like It* has a total of four weddings, of which two involve considerable subplots. *Il Pecorone* provided Shakespeare with the material for both main plots of *The Merchant of Venice*, although he added the Lorenzo-Jessica subplot to tie the two together, and Lodge furnished all but one of the marriages in *As You Like It*. The sources of the other two plays provided only the Claudio-Hero story and the serious plot involving Viola, Orsino, Olivia, and Sebastian. Shakespeare therefore had to add a good deal of new material to both plays. But, however much new material he had to provide for the different plays, he characteristically found it by doubling episodes in the source or repeating episodes or characters from his earlier plays. In *The Merchant of Venice* he doubled the ring trick, which was confined to Gianetto and the Lady of Belmont in the source, and he devoted two scenes to Shylock's outcry over Jessica's flight, although the first prepares for the second and shows the audience how it is to be taken.[16] *Much Ado* presents several well-tried comic formulas, including a friar descended from Friar Lawrence and a reincarnation of Berowne and Rosaline in Benedick and Beatrice.[17] *Twelfth Night* is a perfect anthology of plot elements from the earlier plays. Commentators, struck by this phenomenon, have sometimes forgotten that the parallels to *The Comedy of Errors*, *Two Gentlemen*, and *As You Like It* came from the source; but Shakespeare himself was responsible for the devoted merchant friend even named Antonio and for the resemblance between Sir Toby and Sir John Falstaff.

Current interests and fashions appear in a number of details. *The*

16Cf. Walley, "Shakespeare's Portrayal of Shylock," p. 239.
17New Cambridge *Much Ado*, pp. xxvi-xxvii.

Merchant of Venice seems to reflect both the trial of the unfortunate Dr. Lopez and the popularity of Marlowe's *Jew of Malta*. The former underlies Gratiano's lines at the trial, as Wilson points out:

> Thou almost mak'st me waver in my faith
> To hold opinion with Pythagoras,
> That souls of animals infuse themselves
> Into the trunks of men. Thy currish spirit
> Govern'd a wolf, who, hang'd for human slaughter,
> Even from the gallows did his fell soul fleet,
> And, whilst thou lay'st in thy unhallow'd dam,
> Infus'd itself in thee; for thy desires
> Are wolfish, bloody, starv'd, and ravenous.
>
> (IV, i, 130-38)[18]

Lopez is derived, of course, from Latin *lupus* for *wolf*. Schücking comments upon the indebtedness of Shylock to Marlowe's Barabas:

Indeed, we may be sure that the witnessing of a good representation of *The Jew of Malta* had made him independent of all the models in the world. Marlowe's play was all the more useful as its hero already possessed, to a very noticeable degree, that quality of Shylock which most critics agree in overlooking, viz., his servile and repulsive politeness, which so surprisingly appears in the scene with Antonio (I, iii).[19]

Jessica's pointless action in handing her money out the window when she is about to walk down the steps probably imitates a scene in Marlowe: Abigail does the same thing for the excellent reason that she cannot come out to her father.[20] It was perhaps this combination of popular excitement and dramatic influence that led Shakespeare—and this fact has often been overlooked—to make Shylock more villainous and unpitying than is the usurer in *Il Pecorone*.[21]

Jaques was undoubtedly intended to make fun of the affectation of melancholy which had become fashionable,[22] and Malvolio

[18]New Cambridge *Merchant of Venice*, p. xvii.

[19]*Character Problems in Shakespeare's Plays*, p. 92.

[20]New Cambridge *Merchant of Venice*, p. xix.

[21]Stoll notes this increase in villainy so far as the penalty is concerned, but he overlooks the essential increase in the cruelty of Shylock's action before the trial. Cf. *Shakespeare Studies*, p. 263.

[22]G. B. Harrison discusses this fashion in "An Essay on Elizabethan Melancholy" appended to his edition of Nicholas Breton's *Melancholike Humours*. Cf. especially pp. 67-70.

may possibly glance at the Jonsonian humour character[23] as well as satirize the Puritans. Quiller-Couch speaks of Shakespeare's aping the elaborate and affected speech of the court in *Much Ado*,[24] but surely the same comments would be more pertinent if applied to Viola's extraordinary diction in her interviews with Olivia. This last touch does not alter the fundamental structure of the play, as does the insertion of Malvolio, but it shows that Shakespeare was keenly alive to fashions prevalent among all levels of his audience.

A final category of changes in the source, some of them of great importance, resulted from Shakespeare's attempts to create socially impeccable but interesting characters. If the characterization of the source was suitable, he accepted and developed it. If, as sometimes happened, it outraged morality or decorum, he must create a new character better adapted to the basic plot which he had taken over. In either event, he had to make his intentions clear to the audience and arouse its interests.

As told in *Il Pecorone*, the wooing of the lady of Belmont outraged not only morality but also consistency.[25] With each suitor she made a bargain that he was to go to bed with her. If he could possess her, she would marry him. If not, he was to depart and leave her in possession of his belongings. Twice Gianetto went soundly to sleep, and when he awoke in the morning his ship had already been stripped. The third time a maid warned him to beware of drugged wine. He stayed awake, possessed the lady to their mutual enjoyment, was married to her, and lived so happily that he forgot all about Ansaldo's bond until reminded of it by seeing a religious procession on the feast day on which it became forfeit. This episode could not be presented on the stage; furthermore, it would have left both Portia and Bassanio without a shred of character or sympathy. So Shakespeare fell back upon the casket story, and, with the assistance of Morocco and Aragon, established Portia as both a spirited young woman and a great lady. This careful rewriting was clearly intended to forestall the point of view that regards the young Venetians as "wasters," and those

---

[23]P. Mueschke and Jeanette Fleisher, "Jonsonian Elements in the Comic Underplot of *Twelfth Night*," pp. 722, 737.

[24]New Cambridge *Much Ado*, pp. xxi-xxii.

[25]Cf. New Cambridge *Merchant of Venice*, p. x.

who, like Quiller-Couch, hold to it must be prepared to argue that Shakespeare failed to achieve his intentions.[26]

Bandello's cynical atmosphere, in which Don Timbreo decided to marry Fenicia only after he was unable to seduce her, is completely absent from *Much Ado*, and regard for morality may have prevented Shakespeare from effectively motivating Margaret's part in Don John's plot and her silence when Hero is accused. In Ariosto and Spenser, the maid is the villain's lover and dresses in her lady's clothes to make herself more attractive to him; she does not dare reveal her part in the deception. In *Twelfth Night* Shakespeare stopped relations between Olivia and Sebastian, after she had mistaken him for Cesario, considerably short of the point to which they developed in any of the three possible sources.[27]

Concern for social proprieties as well as for consistency of character perhaps prevented Shakespeare from following *Il Pecorone* in marrying Antonio to Nerissa. Antonio's conversion to matrimony would probably have caused Shakespeare few qualms in the final scene of a play—witness the usurping Duke in *As You Like It*. But a gross breach of rank was involved in marrying him to Portia's maid, even though Nerissa is obviously closer to a lady-in-waiting than to a mere servant.

Shakespeare used a variety of methods for conveying to the audience the impression of a character that he intended. Among these were discussion by other characters, significant dialogue or action, and contrast between characters. He also used conversations, asides, and soliloquies to explain motives, and motives, in turn, reveal character.

Shakespeare never made a minor figure in the comedies responsible for speeches so badly out of character as some that he used to develop Hal, and he was less careful than in the tragedies to prepare for the appearance of the hero by conversation among subordinates.[28] But a variant of the latter device is used. The appearance of Claudio and Benedick in *Much Ado* is preceded by a scene in which Leonato and the rest describe them fully, and the important facts about Olivia and Portia are revealed to the audi-

[26]Ibid., pp. xxiii-xxiv.

[27]Shakespeare's acceptance of conventional morality is, of course, the theme of Alfred Harbage's *As They Liked It*. Cf. Whitaker, "Shakespeare's Use of his Sources," pp. 385-86.

[28]Cf. Bradley, *Shakespearean Tragedy*, p. 44.

ence before they appear. In general, one might say that in the comedies Shakespeare presented some of the key figures immediately and then allowed them to prepare the way for the rest. After the opening of the play, discussion of one character by others is used in the comedies exactly as in the other plays. As if anticipating the harsh judgment of Bassanio already mentioned, Shakespeare was at particular pains to make Portia, Nerissa, and his friends at Venice all speak in praise of him.[29]

In all these plays Shakespeare made brilliant use of significant speech or action as a means of revealing character. He was especially skillful in writing opening speeches that established a basis for the entire characterization: "In sooth, I know not why I am so sad," says Antonio (I, i, 1); "My little body is aweary of this great world," says Portia (I, ii, 1). Orsino's "If music be the food of love, play on" (I, i, 1) is, however, the most brilliant beginning of them all. But for Beatrice's most revealing line we must wait until her simple "Kill Claudio" (IV, i, 291), in which she shows the courage to stake everything upon her faith in Hero. Shylock is, of course, Shakespeare's greatest triumph in the invention both of a significant manner of speech, based upon the Old Testament, and of significant actions. Many of these center upon the stolen wealth and especially the turquoise, which were Shakespeare's invention.

The comedies do not present any deviation from the sources so obviously intended for character contrast as the change of Hotspur's age, but they do make effective use of complementary pairs. The Benedick-Beatrice plot of *Much Ado*, an addition of Shakespeare's that very nearly supplanted the source, provided a triple contrast between men, between women, and between Benedick and Beatrice herself, whose swifter mind is set off by his. Rosalind and Celia also afford a somewhat clearer contrast than in the source, where Alinda is more echo than contrast to Rosalynde.

So far we have been considering the devices which Shakespeare used in shaping the source story into a dramatic plot, in adapting it to the techniques and fashions of his stage, and in endowing it with effective characters. We have noted, however, that his elimination of introductory material often involved a sacrifice of motives that gave to the actions in the source such plausibility as they possessed. There was, of course, no chance whatever of making

[29]Cf. Small, *Shakespearean Character Interpretation*, p. 103.

most of the plots possible in realistic terms; but the impossible might at least be made probable according to the fairy-tale logic of romance, and such it was Shakespeare's task to accomplish. In our world no sane merchant would make a bond for a pound of flesh, and no wise father would leave his beloved daughter the prize in a lottery of caskets. But such a world would at least be entertaining as compared to our humdrum existence. We should doubtless adapt ourselves to it easily enough, and the same motives would continue to determine our conduct among its exciting new surroundings. In a society where a girl could pursue her beloved disguised as a page, she would still be as careful to preserve her reputation as in our own, provided that marriage was her goal. Conventions may change, but human nature is human nature. Shakespeare had, therefore, to make his characters convincing even in his world of romance.

Actually his comedies, like his histories, are far more indifferent than their sources to motivation of action. We have noticed how carefully *Il Pecorone* explains Ansaldo's bond, and the same care is bestowed upon its other episodes. The siren of Belmont's scheme for defrauding her suitors of their wealth at least involved greed, a recognizable motive, and the drugged wine which she gave them should have kept her in control of the bestowing of her person. After Gianetto remembers Ansaldo's discomfiture, she goes to Venice, lodges at an inn, draws the landlord into conversation about the sensational case of the merchant, tells him that she can solve the problem of the bond, and in effect gets him to suggest to Ansaldo that the case be referred to the young lawyer who has just arrived. All this has some resemblance to a plausible line of procedure even if it is much too involved for a crowded play. At all crucial points, and in minor matters as well, *Il Pecorone* at least makes an attempt to give probability to its actions. Shakespeare often gives no explanation or depends upon an extreme coincidence, such as Portia's going to her cousin, the learned Bellario, whom, as it turns out, the Duke has already summoned to give advice. Shakespeare's handling of Don John's plot and of Margaret is far more implausible than either of the two versions in his sources, and so is Viola's role in *Twelfth Night. As You Like It,* however, is about on a par with Lodge's *Rosalynde,* except for the usurping duke's conversion at the end.

The most extreme examples of Shakespeare's failure to explain events are to be found, however, in Leonato's acceptance of Hero's guilt in *Much Ado* and in the lapsing of the bond in *The Merchant of Venice*. Allusion has already been made to the clumsy manipulation of Don John's plot, but that is as nothing beside the spectacle of a father who believes, even without really careful investigation, the most damaging charges against his own daughter. Stoll demonstrates that Shakespeare accepted in a number of plays an old plot convention by which a slanderer's charges were believed, in defiance of all probability, primarily to simplify matters for the dramatist.[30] Such ready acceptance was obviously necessary in the crowded action of Shakespeare's plays. Adequately motivating Leonato's attitude toward Hero, like explaining Medea's killing of her children, would require an entire play in itself.

Shakespeare's failure to account for the lapsing of the bond can only be regarded as capitulation to an insuperable difficulty in plotting his play. As has been noted, the source explained that Gianetto forgot about the bond. This explanation was consistent enough with his previous selfishness, but it was impossible if his character was to be salvaged and the play made to conform to accepted moral standards. On the other hand, he had to make his choice speedily, both because real lovers always move fast in Shakespeare and because any delay would involve further diverting of the audience's interest from Belmont to the exciting events in Venice. The elaborate pageantry of the casket scenes is an obvious attempt to keep the two plots equal in interest. How to reconcile the few days' action at Belmont with the three months provided by the bond Shakespeare was apparently unable to puzzle out. The excitement attendant upon Jessica's elopement helped to conceal the exact number of days involved and to distract attention. He was, furthermore, extremely careless of details of time and place, and he doubtless expected his audience to be like himself. So he simply ignored the problem!

So far we have been concerned with probability of events; but, save for two notable exceptions, the same generalization holds true of motivation of characters. "Who ever lov'd, that lov'd not at first sight?" wrote Marlowe, and this simple axiom solved most of Shakespeare's problems. His women, especially, are wonderful

[30] *Shakespeare Studies*, pp. 93-94.

creations, people whom we know intimately and whom we come to admire as human beings. But a little reflection will show that, for the most part, we have no more idea why they do things than they seem to have themselves. Their individuality rests upon the rich wit of their speech and the spirit with which they act, not upon our comprehension of their motives, except in so far as love itself is an all-sufficient motive. Portia obviously loves Bassanio, but critics are still wondering why. We know that Rosalind wants Orlando, but we have no idea what she hopes to accomplish, beyond keeping Orlando with her, by her wooing game. And Viola is an even more passive beneficiary of circumstances. Like the nineteenth-century critics, we can play a fascinating game of inferring motives and character from what these women do and say, just as we habitually make the same inferences about our friends. But when we come to the great figures of tragedy, such inference is unnecessary and, in fact, will lead us astray, for Shakespeare tells us what they think as well as what they do.[31]

To the generalization just laid down the villains and the characters that Shakespeare himself invented are, to some extent at least, an exception. They are also exceptional in that they, alone of the characters in the comedies, use asides and soliloquies, important devices for revealing motives. One is tempted to suggest that, in the ideal world of the comedies at least, villainy was so abnormal that it required motivation, but the explanation is probably the more prosaic fact that Shakespeare drew upon the tradition of the villain hero who explained himself in asides and soliloquies and who therefore formulated his motives. Shylock explicitly states that he desires to cause Antonio's death because the merchant is a Christian and brings down the rates of interest in Venice (I, iii, 42-46); and, when Jessica carries off some of his money, she only increases his wrath at the losses that Antonio has caused him (note that, in his final speeches on the subject, he is clearly enraged by the loss of his money rather than by the flight of his daughter; cf. III, i, 132-34).[32] Don John's villainy is less elaborately motivated, but it is surely a mistake to argue, as does Quiller-Couch, that he

[31]On this point cf. Pettet (*Shakespeare and the Romance Tradition*, pp. 85-86): "...motivation is often weak and sometimes lacking altogether." "In the main ... [Shakespeare] was not much interested in the comedy of character."

[32]*Shakespeare Studies*, pp. 265-66.

has no reason for what he does.[33] He has just rebelled against his brother Don Pedro and been defeated, as Conrade makes clear (I, iii, 22); he himself explains: "That young start-up [Claudio] hath all the glory of my overthrow: if I can cross him any way, I bless myself every way" (I, iii, 67-70).

The most careful motivation in the comedies is to be found, however, in the Benedick-Beatrice plot and in the comic subplot of *Twelfth Night*, both invented by Shakespeare. The final capitulation of Benedick and Beatrice is prepared for from her first line, and it seems the inevitable result of their characters rather than of the obvious trick that is played upon them. The trick is, in fact, convincing only because it compels them to admit their own feelings. Furthermore, each of them explains his reasons for yielding in a soliloquy that looks forward to the method of Shakespeare's later plays (II, iii, 228-55; III, i, 107-16). If Malvolio's immediate obedience to the letter seems a little improbable, even by comic standards, Sir Toby's hatred of him is abundantly motivated; and Maria's reasons for plotting against him are made clear, at least in retrospect, by her marriage to Sir Toby, her elevation from maid to Lady Maria being an achievement almost equal to Malvolio's fondest dreams of being a count. It was in handling these two intrigues of his own invention that Shakespeare showed what he was, in fact, already doing in the tragedies, for it must not be forgotten that *Twelfth Night* belongs to the same years as *Hamlet*.

[33]New Cambridge *Much Ado*, p. xviii. But cf. Arden *Much Ado*, p. xxii.

CHAPTER IX

Troilus and Cressida
and Measure for Measure

ROILUS AND CRESSIDA probably dates from 1602.[1] In
the sequence of Shakespeare's plays, it follows *The
Merry Wives of Windsor* among the comedies, *Julius
Caesar* and *Hamlet* among the tragedies. *Measure for
Measure* has generally been assigned to 1604, about the time of
Othello, although some critics have regarded one or two references in the play as indicating a later date.[2] Considering the two
plays ahead of the first great tragedies therefore moves them out of
their proper order. This placing violates the principle of arrangement observed throughout this book and requires explanation.

The reason for considering the two plays so soon lies in their
content. Both are radically faulty as drama, but they are, in their
respective ways, the most explicitly learned plays that Shakespeare ever wrote. A system of philosophical and theological
concepts can be inferred to underlie the tragedies; "in *Troilus
and Cressida* the story is an excuse for thought rather than the
embodiment of thought. The metaphysical problems of the tragedies must, from the first, have presented themselves to Shakespeare in terms of concrete experience; but in *Troilus and Cressida*
he pursues philosophical abstractions with the impassioned eager-
ness of Donne."[3]

[1]Chambers, *William Shakespeare*, I, 443-44. I hope shortly to investigate the
possibility that Shakespeare may have derived from Robert Greene's *Euphues
His Censure to Philautus* (1587) the notion of subjecting the Troilus and Cressida
story to ethical analysis, and even considerable guidance in doing so.

[2]Ibid., 453-54.

[3]Bethell, *Shakespeare & the Popular Dramatic Tradition*, p. 99.

Troilus and Cressida is, in fact, the keystone in the arch of Shakespeare's intellectual development, however rough-hewn and misshapen it may be. Considering it immediately after the last histories and the romantic comedies will show how rapidly his thought matured. Examining it before the tragedies will provide us with clues that we need to understand them. It would certainly have been very handy for students if Spenser had paused between the third and fourth books of *The Faerie Queene* to write a philosophic poem expounding the ideas fundamental to his allegory. That is exactly what Shakespeare did for his tragedies in *Troilus and Cressida*. The following discussion will try to isolate the philosophic passages in this play and then to point out related theological principles in *Measure for Measure*. Succeeding chapters will show how the same concepts work out in the tragedies.

In surveying the Lancastrian chronicle plays, we observed that references to the doctrine of an ordered universe became increasingly numerous, and led finally to an explicit statement of a theory of causation. There was a parallel development of dramatic technique. In *Henry IV* Shakespeare tried to show Hal's development in valour and virtue; in the last of the romantic comedies he attempted to work out what the characters did as an effect of their personalities and of their thinking. This kind of motivation was without precedent in his earlier plays, and it related the operation of the human mind to a universal chain of cause and effect. For Providence, Fortune, and human character, the forces determining events in his early history plays, he seemed to be substituting a notion of laws of nature which organized God, natural phenomena, and man himself into a related whole. Although the word *Fortune* still appeared, it tended to mean man's lot as opposed to the cause of that lot, and its role was subsidiary to a view of events that was at once more sophisticated and more philosophic. The metaphysics behind this development of Shakespeare's ideas finally comes to explicit statement in Ulysses' speech on degree in *Troilus and Cressida*.

This speech is actually out of all proportion intellectually and dramatically to its setting, which is a council of Greek leaders to discuss their lack of success. Achilles is sulking in his tent with Patroclus, Ajax is becoming vainglorious, and the war is indecisive. But, when Ulysses finally gets down to cases after his philosophizing, his complaints are a complete anticlimax. Achilles and Patroclus are using the achievements and problems of the Greeks as stuff "to make paradoxes" (I, iii, 184), and Ajax and Thersites "count wisdom as no member of the war" and "esteem no act but that of hand" (I, iii, 198-200). And the scene itself, which is the longest in the play, is out of all proportion to the relatively unimportant scheme which it initiates. The inference seems inevitable that in this and in the parallel council of the Trojan leaders Shakespeare was more interested in the ideas themselves than in the movement of his plot.

Ulysses' speech has already been quoted all too often, but excerpts, at least, are required for comparison:

> The specialty of rule hath been neglected;
> And, look, how many Grecian tents do stand
> Hollow upon this plain, so many hollow factions.
> When that the general is not like the hive
> To whom the foragers shall all repair,
> What honey is expected? Degree being vizarded,
> The unworthiest shows as fairly in the mask.
> The heavens themselves, the planets, and this centre
> Observe degree, priority, and place,
> Insisture, course, proportion, season, form,
> Office, and custom, in all line of order....
>
> But when the planets
> In evil mixture to disorder wander,
> What plagues and what portents! what mutiny!
> What raging of the sea! shaking of earth! ...
>
> O, when degree is shak'd,
> Which is the ladder to all high designs,
> Then enterprise is sick! How could communities,
> Degrees in schools, and brotherhoods in cities,
> Peaceful commerce from dividable shores,
> The primogenitive and due of birth,
> Prerogative of age, crowns, sceptres, laurels,
> But by degree, stand in authentic place?
> Take but degree away, untune that string,
> And, hark, what discord follows! Each thing meets
> In mere oppugnancy. The bounded waters
> Should lift their bosoms higher than the shores
> And make a sop of all this solid globe.
> Strength should be lord of imbecility,
> And the rude son should strike his father dead.

Force should be right; or rather, right and wrong,
Between whose endless jar justice resides
Should lose their names, and so should justice too.
Then everything includes itself in power,
Power into will, will into appetite;
And appetite, an universal wolf,
So doubly seconded with will and power,
Must make perforce an universal prey,
And last eat up himself. Great Agememnon,
This chaos, when degree is suffocate,
Follows the choking.

(I, iii, 78-126)

There are three obvious sources for this speech.[4] All of them were well known to Shakespeare, and he seems actually to have used all three. At the beginning of *The Governour* (first published in 1531) Sir Thomas Elyot based the need for government among men upon the principle of universal order. From part of this passage Shakespeare derived the Archbishop's speech in *Henry V*, I, ii, as we noted, and from the same context comes the reference to bees here. Elyot does not parallel Shakespeare in detail, but he is the only one of the three writers who uses the word *chaos* as Shakespeare does. The following extracts will perhaps illustrate his possible influence:

More over take away ordre from all thynges what shulde than remayne? Certes nothynge finally, except some man wolde imagine eftsones *Chaos*: whiche of some is expounde a confuse misture. Also where there is any lack of ordre nedes must be perpetuall conflicte: and in thynges subjecte to Nature nothynge of hym selfe onely may be norished; but when he hath distroyed that where with he dothe participate by the ordre of his creation, he hym selfe of necessite muste than perishe, wherof ensuethe universall dissolution. . . .

Hath nat he set degrees and estates in all his glorious workes?
Fyrst in his hevenly ministres, whom, as the churche affirmeth, he hath constituted to be in divers degrees called hierarches. . . .
Beholde the foure elementes wherof the body of man is compacte, howe they be set in their places called spheris, higher or lower, accordynge to the soveraintie of theyr natures. . . .
Beholde also the ordre that god hath put generally in al his creatures, begynning at the most inferiour or base, and assendynge upwarde.[5]

[4]Cf. Deutschberger, "Shakespeare on Degree: A Study in Backgrounds," pp. 203-206.
[5]*The Governour*, I, 3-4.

To "An Exhortation Concerning Good Order and Obedience to Rulers and Magistrates," the tenth of the first book of Homilies, Shakespeare perhaps owed a good deal more, including the combination of cosmic and social order.

Almighty God hath created and appointed all things, in heaven, earth, and waters, in a most excellent and perfect order. In heaven he hath appointed distinct (or several) orders and states of archangels and angels. In earth he hath assigned and appointed kings and princes, with other governors under them, all in good and necessary order. The water above is kept, and raineth down in due time and season. The sun, moon, stars, rainbow, thunder, lightning, clouds, and all birds of the air, do keep their order. The earth, trees, seeds, plants, herbs, corn, grass, and all manner of beasts, keep themselves in their order. All the parts of the whole year, as winter, summer, months, nights, and days, continue in their order. All kinds of fishes in the sea, rivers and waters, with all fountains and springs, yea, the seas themselves, keep their comely course and order. And man himself also hath all his parts both within and without, as soul, heart, mind, memory, understanding, reason, speech, with all and singular corporal members of his body, in a profitable, necessary, and pleasant order. Every degree of people, in their vocation, calling, and office, hath appointed to them their duty and order. Some in high degree, some in low; some kings and princes, some inferiors and subjects; priests and laymen, masters and servants, fathers and children, husbands and wives, rich and poor; and every one have need of other. So that in all things is to be lauded and praised the goodly order of God: without the which no house, no city, no commonwealth can continue and endure (or last); for, where there is no right order, there reigneth all abuse, carnal liberty, enormity, sin, and Babylonical confusion. Take away kings, princes, rulers, magistrates, judges, and such estates of God's order, no man shall ride or go by the highway unrobbed; no man shall sleep in his own house or bed unkilled; no man shall keep his wife, children, and possessions in quietness; all things shall be common; and there must needs follow all mischief and utter destruction both of souls, bodies, goods, and commonwealths.[6]

The clearest statement of the central thesis of Ulysses' speech is to be found in Richard Hooker's *Of the Laws of Ecclesiastical Polity*, where it occurs as a kind of demonstration that the alternative to Hooker's position is impossible to contemplate. In eloquence and in poetic imagery it perhaps surpasses Shakespeare's lines; it certainly is their superior in clarity and in concentration upon the logical point.

[6]*Certain Sermons or Homilies*, pp. 109-10.

Now if nature should intermit her course, and leave altogether though it were but for a while the observation of her own laws; if those principal and mother elements of the world, whereof all things in this lower world are made, should lose the qualities which now they have; if the frame of that heavenly arch erected over our heads should loosen and dissolve itself; if celestial spheres should forget their wonted motions, and by irregular volubility turn themselves any way as it might happen; if the prince of the lights of heaven, which now as a giant doth run his unwearied course, should as it were through a languishing faintness begin to stand and to rest himself; if the moon should wander from her beaten way, the times and seasons of the year blend themselves by disordered and confused mixture, the winds breathe out their last gasp, the clouds yield no rain, the earth be defeated of heavenly influence, the fruits of the earth pine away as children at the withered breasts of their mother no longer able to yield them relief: what would become of man himself, whom these things now do all serve? See we not plainly that obedience of creatures unto the law of nature is the stay of the whole world?[7]

One idea in Ulysses' speech is not to be found in any of the immediate sources quoted. That is the reference to "appetite, an universal wolf," which must at last "eat up himself." This is, incidentally, a poetic statement of the view which Bradley regards as fundamental to all Shakespeare tragedies,[8] that evil is ultimately self-destructive. It is a logical result of the concept of universal order, although Bradley did not recognize it as such but inferred it from the plays themselves.

But, if obedience to nature's laws is the "stay of the whole world," why do the Greeks disobey? Ulysses does not explain. But in the next act there follows a parallel council of Trojan leaders in which Hector makes a speech that is of equal importance, dramatically and intellectually, and it is given an even more emphatic position at the climax of its scene. It involves explaining the basis of law and the reason for sin:

> Nature craves
> All dues be rend'red to their owners: now,
> What nearer debt in all humanity
> Than wife is to the husband? If this law
> Of nature be corrupted through affection,
> And that great minds, of partial indulgence,
> To their benumbed will, resist the same,
> There is a law in each well-ord'red nation

[7]*Laws of Ecclesiastical Polity*, I, iii, 2; *Works*, I, 207-208.
[8]*Shakespearean Tragedy*, pp. 31-39 and especially pp. 34-35.

To curb those raging appetites that are
Most disobedient and refractory.
If Helen then be wife to Sparta's king,
As it is known she is, these moral laws
Of nature and of nations speak aloud
To have her back return'd. Thus to persist
In doing wrong extenuates not wrong,
But makes it much more heavy.   (II, ii, 173-88)[9]

The passage may perhaps be paraphrased as follows in terms of the ideas upon which it rests. The law of nature, which God has established to control the operation of the universe, demands, among other things, that all possessions be returned to their owners, and therefore a wife to her husband. But men sometimes sin against the law of nature. Since man's reason naturally chooses what seems good, evil cannot be desired as evil but must be accepted because it is, to some extent and in some way, a good; "there was never sin committed wherein a less good was not preferred before a greater, and that wilfully."[10] This false choice may be made (1) because of ignorance (which is not involved in this passage); (2) because the affections or passions have solicited man's will and prevailed against reason; or (3) because a habit of indulging the will has made reason "partial"[11] to it and therefore ineffective in controlling it. Since minds so governed by man's "benumbed" will resist the law of nature, well-ordered nations have established statutory laws. These are "ordained for external order and regiment amongst men, [and] are never framed as they should be, unless presuming the will of man to be inwardly obstinate, rebellious, and averse from all obedience unto the sacred laws of his nature."[12]

Shakespeare, in short, sees human actions and human society as part of a universal system governed by laws laid down by God

[9]In contrast to the emphasis placed upon Ulysses' speech, this one has apparently gone almost unnoticed by students of Shakespeare's thought. Deutschberger cites the allusion to laws "of nature and of nations" to prove Shakespeare's knowledge of Hooker ("Shakespeare on Degree," p. 206), and Spencer quotes it without noting its implications (*Shakespeare and the Nature of Man*, pp. 112-13). Haydn, however, quotes it as "a definitive statement of the traditional humanistic view" (*The Counter-Renaissance*, p. 608).

[10]Hooker, *Laws of Ecclesiastical Polity*, I, vii, 7; *Works*, I, 224.

[11]If "partial" could only mean "in part" the passage would describe exactly the tragic hero as opposed to the villain, whose indulgence is complete. But the word occurs in Shakespeare only in the sense taken.

[12]Hooker, op. cit., I, x, 1; *Works*, I, 239-40.

at the time of creation. Human excellence lies in conformity to these laws. To act virtuously is to act according to that nature which is God's plan and his instrument. Sin consists in willful disobedience to these same laws either because man's reason, made less effective by his fall, fails to see clearly what is his highest good or because it fails to control the will, which the fall turned from God and left unable to prevent the passions from being aroused. To sin is therefore to act according to man's fallen nature, which is apart from God. Both natures appear in Shakespeare's language, and it is important to keep them straight. From this point of view certain consequences follow.

The first of these is the importance of man's reason. Even Cressida remarks: "Blind fear, that seeing reason leads, finds safer footing than blind reason stumbling without fear" (III, ii, 76-79). By reason Shakespeare means primarily the capacity for making value judgments rather than for systematic thinking. The two meanings are not contradictory. In his day they very nearly merged, and they both appear in his plays as aspects of the one concept. But modern usage is likely to center the word upon thinking logically, whereas medieval and renaissance writers concentrated upon making a judgment. As Milton puts it: "Reason also is choice." (P.L., III, 108). The technical term for reason directing man according to the laws of nature is right reason, but I believe that Shakespeare never uses it.

This meaning gives added significance to the emphasis upon reason in the great tragedies. In part Shakespeare's heroes fall through a failure of what we should call intelligence. In Hamlet the tragedy centers, at least to some extent, in the mind's inadequacy to solve the problem. In all but Hamlet the tragic failure is accompanied by and dependent upon a failure to think clearly. Othello refuses to ask simple and obvious questions; Lear's folly is pointed out to him on the spot by Kent and later by the Fool; Macbeth knows what is right and imagines with terrible clarity the consequences of sin, but he yields to Lady Macbeth's sophistic arguments; Menenius Agrippa and Enobarbus are like philosophers serving as a chorus to point out the blindness of Coriolanus and of Antony. But "reason also is choice." And it is man's fundamental duty as a rational animal to choose correctly—that is, according to the laws of nature. Life may be thought of as a lengthening series of alternatives, and each act of choice is central in this ethical system. But, for simplicity, Shakespeare concentrates upon a single choice and its results. A whole list of characters in the tragedies explain the weaknesses which predispose the hero to choose irrationally: Cassius, Iago, Lady Macbeth, Goneril and Regan, Menenius Agrippa, and Enobarbus. Still others are used to point out the hero's folly at the time of his false choice or later: Antony in *Julius Caesar*, Emilia, Banquo, Kent and the Fool, and Volumnia. If the hero has knowledge adequate for right choice, or the means of acquiring such knowledge (and he always has in Shakespeare), his failure is sin. *Unnatural, irrational,* and *immoral* become synonymous as applied to conduct, and tragedy is grounded in moral choice.

If tragedy results from irrational or immoral choice, the reasons for the false choice are of vital importance. They are those implied by Hector. Sin, as we have seen, always involves a false choice of a lesser instead of a greater good. Sometimes reason's error is due to an inability to distinguish between appearance and reality. "Goodness," wrote Hooker, "doth not move by being, but by being apparent; and therefore many things are neglected which are most precious, only because the value of them lieth hid."[13] Shakespeare had much to say on this point. Hamlet alludes to it constantly.[14] The contrast between the outward beauty of both Helen and Cressida and their inward foulness is fundamental to the present play, and the same contrast underlies another well-known speech by Ulysses:

> O, let not virtue seek
> Remuneration for the thing it was;
> For beauty, wit,
> High birth, vigour of bone, desert in service,
> Love, friendship, charity, are subjects all
> To envious and calumniating Time.
> One touch of nature makes the whole world kin,
> That all, with one consent, praise new-born gawds,
> Though they are made and moulded of things past,
> And give to dust that is a little gilt
> More laud than gilt o'er-dusted. (III, iii, 169-79)

[13]Ibid., I, vii, 6; *Works,* I, 223.

[14]Spencer has an interesting discussion of this element in Hamlet, but he misses, I think, the philosophic basis of Hamlet's preoccupation and therefore produces a distorted impression (*Shakespeare and the Nature of Man,* pp. 106-109).

And the nature that touches the whole world, like that to which Richard III was slave, is man's fallen nature.

The reason's false choice of gilded dust instead of dusty gold is more likely to result from man's "disobedient and refractory" appetites than from mere ignorance, although the effects of the two are in practice often indistinguishable.

The object of Appetite is whatsoever sensible good may be wished for; the object of Will is that good which Reason doth lead us to seek. Affections, as joy, and grief, and fear, and anger, with such like, being as it were the sundry fashions and forms of Appetite, can neither rise at the conceit of a thing indifferent, nor yet choose but rise at the sight of some things. Wherefore it is not altogether in our power, whether we will be stirred with affections or no: whereas actions which issue from the disposition of the Will are in the power thereof to be performed or stayed. Finally, Appetite is the Will's solicitor, and the Will is Appetite's controller; what we covet according to the one by the other we often reject; neither is any other desire termed properly Will, but that where Reason and Understanding, or the show of Reason, prescribeth the thing desired.

Sensible Goodness is most apparent, near, and present; which causeth the Appetite to be therewith strongly provoked. Now pursuit and refusal in the Will do follow, the one the affirmation the other the negation of goodness, which the understanding apprehendeth, grounding itself upon sense, unless some higher Reason do chance to teach the contrary. And if Reason have taught it rightly to be good, yet not so apparently that the mind receiveth it with utter impossibility of being otherwise, still there is place left for the Will to take or leave.[15]

Just such a choice in which the reason finally grounds itself upon sense is illustrated by the Trojan council of which Hector's speech is a part. Until the end Hector speaks as the voice of true wisdom and of nature's laws, stating principles of conduct that are sound but abstract and a trifle remote from every-day experience. Troilus appeals to the sensations that he knows and has encountered. He converts his brother's principles into the cowardice that he has seen; and he prefers honor and Helen's beauty, good things that appeal to the senses, above cold reason:

---

[15]Hooker, *Laws of Ecclesiastical Polity*, I, vii, 3, 6; *Works*, I, 221, 223.

You fur your gloves with reason. Here are your reasons:
You know an enemy intends you harm;
You know a sword employ'd is perilous,
And reason flies the object of all harm. . . .
        Nay, if we talk of reason,
Let's shut our gates and sleep. Manhood and honour
Should have hare hearts, would they but fat their thoughts
With this cramm'd reason. Reason and respect
Makes livers pale and lustihood deject. . . .
Is she [Helen] worth keeping? Why, she is a pearl,
Whose price hath launch'd above a thousand ships,
And turn'd crown'd kings to merchants. . . .
        O theft most base,
That we have stol'n what we do fear to keep!
        (II, ii, 38-41, 46-50, 81-83, 92-93)

The workings of Troilus' appetite are recognized by Hector:

        Or is your blood
So madly hot that no discourse of reason,
Nor fear of bad success in a bad cause,
Can qualify the same?   (II, ii, 115-18)

So far the debate has been exactly like that between the virtues and the vices in a morality play, except that the psychological basis is made absolutely explicit; but, in this most cynical of plays, the virtues lose. Hector betrays his own principles. After demonstrating that the "moral laws of nature and of nations" demand that Helen be returned, he goes on:

        Hector's opinion
Is this in way of truth; yet ne'ertheless,
My spritely brethren, I propend to you
In resolution to keep Helen still,
For 'tis a cause that hath no mean dependence
Upon our joint and several dignities.
        (II, ii, 188-93)

After all, the war had to go on, or there would be no play. But Shakespeare had at least worked in a considerable outline of the ethics which Christianity inherited from Plato, Aristotle, and the Stoics.

In the scene just outlined Troilus and Hector make the same kind of moral choice as Shakespeare's tragic heroes. But, unlike the heroes, they explain their thinking in the technical terminology of contemporary ethics and psychology. As antagonists presenting the conflicting claims of appetite and reason, they also personify a conflict which, in the tragedies, is internal and which we must infer from soliloquies that indicate the working of the hero's mind.

This internal conflict is the subject of a book by Lily B. Campbell, in which she studies Hamlet, Othello, King Lear, and Macbeth as examples of grief, jealousy, wrath, and fear respectively.[16] In *Othello* and *Antony and Cleopatra*, at least, Shakespeare provides his own interpretation by making Iago describe the operation of jealousy in Othello, and Enobarbus tells us that Antony "would make his will lord of his reason" (III, xiii, 3-4). Here, as elsewhere, Shakespeare may simply be using *will* loosely for man's fallen will dominated by appetite, just as he and his contemporaries used nature in a similar double sense. Or he may be using the word to mean man's sensible appetite itself, as Calvin does: "But instead of the word 'appetite'. . . I use the word 'will', which is more common."[17] This would explain, of course, how "will" can mean the satisfaction of lust, as it does in the punning sonnets.

But one indulgence may lead to another, and the reason may become wholly "partial" to the will—become, in fact, its instrument. "Custom," says Hooker, "inuring the mind by long practice, and so leaving there a sensible impression, prevaileth more than reasonable persuasion what way soever."[18] Shakespeare's great example of a reason subservient to man's "benumbed" will is, of course, Macbeth as he sinks from crime to crime after his murder of Duncan. But the sisters in *Lear* would serve almost as well. *Lear* and *Macbeth* are, in fact, simply full-scale studies of the ideas in the two key speeches in *Troilus and Cressida*. Both depend upon the entire complex of ideas that lies back of the two speeches, and both exemplify the principle of order and the disturbing effects of human sin. But *Lear* might be described as primarily a development of Ulysses' ideas, *Macbeth* of Hector's, in that the former is centered in the disintegration of social and then universal order because Lear's own irrationality is abetted by the folly and sin of many people, while the latter

[16]*Shakespeare's Tragic Heroes*, pp. 109-239.
[17]*Institutes*, I, xv, 7; 7th Amer. ed., I, 214.
[18]*Laws of Ecclesiastical Polity*, I, vii, 6; *Works*, I, 223-24.

is worked out in terms of the causes of a single sin and its consequences for the individual and only incidentally for the social order.

If the preceding observations are sound, it may follow that Richard Hooker was to a considerable extent responsible not only for the thought but also for the very structure of some of Shakespeare's greatest plays. *Of the Laws of Ecclesiastical Polity* first appeared in 1594, and Shakespeare had therefore had ample time to digest it, as well as to reflect its growing impact upon his mind in plays from *King John* on.

There is no reason to suppose that all the ideas just discussed, or even a large part of them, were derived only from Hooker. Most of them were commonplaces of the age. But Shakespeare demonstrably knew Hooker. The parallel in Ulysses' speech on degree is obvious and has long been recognized. Hector's statement that human law is intended "to curb those raging appetites that are most disobedient and refractory" is also very close to Hooker's explanation of why laws are ordained. This is, furthermore, one of two points in which Hooker differs from his later medieval predecessors. Aquinas argues that human laws are needed to supplement the laws of nature because man's natural aptitude for virtue needs to be developed by training and discipline and because it is easier for a few wise men to frame laws in advance than for individuals to judge rightly in particular instances and under the pressure of an emergency.[19] "Hooker gives a more affirmative attention to the thesis that men must frame their laws with post-lapsarian corruption in mind," returning to the emphasis of thinkers earlier than Aquinas.[20] A second difference lies in the concept of natural law itself. Aquinas defines it as "nothing else than the rational creature's participation of the eternal law."[21] Hooker unfortunately uses natural law in a double sense. Sometimes it means "that manner of working which God hath set for created things to keep"—that is, what he also calls God's second law eternal (the first law eternal is the perfection imposed upon God by his own being). But Hooker also restricts natural law to that part of the second law eternal which

---

[19]*Summa Theologica*, Ia-IIae, Q. 95, A. 1; *Basic Writings*, II, 783.

[20]Haydn, *The Counter-Renaissance*, pp. 137, 169.

[21]*Summa Theologica*, Ia-IIae, Q. 91, A. 2; *Basic Writings*, II, 750.

binds those things "which keep the law of their kind unwittingly" —that is, to involuntary agents. The law "which bindeth creatures reasonable in this world" he calls the law of reason.[22] The contrast between the two thinkers is by no means so sharp as the preceding summaries might imply, since Aquinas means by law of nature God's eternal law as it is apprehended by rational creatures, not just that part which applies exclusively to them. But there is a difference, nevertheless, and Shakespeare seems always to regard laws of nature simply as forces working through all creation, including man. His view is closer to Hooker's.

Whether Shakespeare was indebted to the *Ecclesiastical Polity* for details is, however, unimportant. Furthermore, reliance upon parallels as evidence is risky. In *Measure for Measure*, for example, Angelo urges upon Isabella the principle that "our compell'd sins stand more for number than for accompt" (II, iv, 57-58). Exactly this same point is made by Hooker in the context that I believe Shakespeare to have used.[23] But the remark is probably derived from *Promus and Cassandra*, the source play, where it also occurs. The really significant consideration is that the ideas enunciated by Ulysses, Hector, and others in the play are presented systematically and briefly by Hooker, and by Hooker alone, among writers that Shakespeare might reasonably have encountered. As Trevelyan writes:

Some idea of the solid reading of an ordinary man, not specially literary or poetical, but anxious to instruct himself, may be gathered from the following list, recommended by an old gentleman (born 1580) to his grandson, as having formed the library of his youth (*Harl. Misc.*, ix, p. 592). After the Bible he recommends Hooker's *Ecclesiastical Polity*, Sir W. Raleigh's *History of the World*, Plutarch's Lives, Camden's *Brittania*, "my friend Sir Richard Baker's *Chronicle*," Xenophon's *Cyrus*, Tully's *Offices*, James I's *Basilicon Doron*.[24]

The fact that Shakespeare's first systematic statement of this whole complex of ideas so obviously came straight out of Hooker gives us every reason to suppose that it was Book I of *Of the Laws of Ecclesiastical Polity* that first awakened him to the full significance of laws of nature and of nations and furnished him

[22]*Laws of Ecclesiastical Polity*, I, ii, 2; I, iii, 1, 2; *Works*, I, 204-206.
[23]Ibid., I, ix, 1; *Works*, I, 237-38.
[24]*England under the Stuarts*, p. 55, n. 1.

with a tragic interpretation of life. Man, he seems to say, may violate the laws of nature through some failure of his reason. His sin causes a convulsion of nature, whether in the social or the universal realm, during which not only the guilty but the innocent as well may perish. But in this struggle evil inevitably destroys itself, being contrary to universal law; and, at whatever cost in suffering, order returns. This is approximately the view that Bradley ascribes to Shakespeare when he comes to grips with the kind of moral order that lies behind the tragedies; and his account is, in effect, as clear a summary of Hooker as the speeches of Ulysses and Hector. The fact that he is apparently unaware of any possible connection between Shakespeare and Hooker makes his testimony the more significant.[25] Quite apart from the evidence presented, it is intrinsically probable that a mind as penetrating as Shakespeare's, and as philosophic in inclination as even his first plays show it to have been, would seize upon Hooker's work, which was one of the greatest achievements of the age and which was also marked by the same large-minded tolerance that we associate with Shakespeare.

Hooker was also of great value to Shakespeare in another way. He organized into a coherent system both the religious doctrines that Shakespeare had learned in school and church and the psychology of which increasing fragments appear in the earlier plays. Seeing this body of learning as an integrated whole must have given it more meaning for Shakespeare and have enabled him to use it with more confidence. So, at least, one infers from his increased dependence upon technical psychology in explaining characters in the tragedies. Whenever he reflects contemporary intellectual fashions in the later plays, he seems to assimilate them to this system and to understand them in its terms. When he refers to the new naturalism, he sees it as the working of man's fallen nature. When he encounters Stoicism in his sources, he blends it with the Stoic elements in his Christianity. He is on firm ground in handling the orthodox demonology of *Hamlet* and *Macbeth*, but he is badly confused when he introduces neo-

[25]Bradley does not mention *Troilus and Cressida* in elaborating Shakespeare's notion of tragedy (*Shakespearean Tragedy*, pp. 31-39), nor does he mention Hooker. But elsewhere (ibid., p. 268) he cites Ulysses' speech for its notion that evil is self-destructive. For his interpretation of nature and a reference to Hector's speech cf. ibid., pp. 301-302.

Platonic white magic into *The Tempest*. His understanding even of Hooker apparently had limitations. Hector says, "There is a law in each well-ord'red nation" and then refers to "these moral laws of nature and of nations." The *each* makes it doubtful that he really understood Hooker's notion of a generally accepted body of law equivalent to the Roman *ius gentium*, as distinguished both from special laws of particular nations and from international law in the modern sense. There is also something a little too pat about the relationship between man's sins and universal disorder as Shakespeare presents it. Macbeth violates the law of nature by murdering a man who is his king, his kinsman, and his guest. At once all nature behaves unnaturally. What the plays give us is at times closer to the pathetic fallacy than to a genuinely philosophic view of the interrelationship between man and the rest of creation. These qualifications need to be made, lest, in our enthusiasm for Shakespeare the thinker, we forget the limitations imposed by the myriad activities of Shakespeare the practical dramatist. They should not blind us to the intellectual achievement represented by the tragedies.

But, if these ideas bore wonderful fruit in the tragedies, they were less beneficial to the comedies, where they subjected the traditional situations and characters of romance and *novella* to a kind of moral analysis that they were quite unable to bear. In *Troilus and Cressida* it is impossible to tell how much of the present play was due to popular developments of the old story, how much to Shakespeare's artistic purpose, whatever that may have been, and how much to the philosophy with which Shakespeare has loaded it. Certainly both popular tradition and undigested learning had a share in producing a drama that was probably a failure on the Elizabethan stage[26] and has certainly not endeared itself to modern audiences.

Shakespeare's previous allusions to Troilus had reflected a reasonably charitable view of his character. In *The Merchant of Venice* Lorenzo tells Jessica that Troilus

> mounted the Troyan walls,
> And sigh'd his soul toward the Grecian tents,
> Where Cressid lay that night.
> (V, i, 4-6)

[26]Lawrence, *Shakespeare's Problem Comedies*, p. 125.

Rosalind calls him "one of the patterns of love" (IV, i, 100). Cressida, on the other hand, figures in *Henry V* (II, i, 80) as a symbol of syphilis and leprosy as the penalty of harlotry.[27] Such she had become in Henryson's sequel to Chaucer's poem. Shakespeare reflects the same views in his play. Troilus is an inexperienced idealist. He loves as young men were expected to love (even the temperate Sir Guyon lets Verdant go from the Bower of Acrasis with a moral lecture), but he is profoundly shocked by Cressida's betrayal; Cressida is well started on her downward path, and her hesitancy in yielding is artful coyness, no more. Medieval romance was generally pro-Trojan, furthermore, and the English nation rejoiced in an alleged descent from Brutus of Trojan stock. English writers were therefore prone to make Homer's heroes somewhat less heroic, and Shakespeare had precedent for the view that he takes of the Greeks. O. J. Campbell has argued convincingly that *Troilus and Cressida* was intended as a learned but bawdy satire upon current thought for some festive occasion at one of the Inns of Court.[28] But whether Shakespeare was merely following tradition or was trying to write satire, either purpose would have been easily achieved by analysis of the accepted story in terms of the system of ideas outlined above. That is apparently just what happened, for the plot as a whole and the actions of individuals are subjected to a ruthless moral scrutiny the results of which are written into the text of the play—at length! As Thersites inelegantly but graphically says of the war: "All the argument is a cuckold and a whore; a good quarrel to draw emulous factions and bleed to death upon" (II, iii, 78-79). Diomedes says the same:

> For every false drop in her bawdy veins
> A Grecian's life hath sunk; for every scruple
> Of her contaminated carrion weight,
> A Troyan hath been slain. Since she could speak,
> She hath not given so many good words breath
> As for her Greeks and Troyans suff'red death.
>
> (IV, i, 69-74)

And the Trojans can do no better at justifying themselves. Troilus at least admits their dilemma honestly in a passage already cited:

[27] C. J. Sisson is clearly wrong in thinking that Shakespeare echoed conflicting aspects of the story (*The Mythical Sorrows of Shakespeare*, p. 19).
[28] *Shakespeare's Satire*, pp. 98-120.

Nay, if we talk of reason,
Let's shut our gates and sleep. Manhood and honour
Should have hare hearts, would they but fat their thoughts
With this cramm'd reason. Reason and respect
Makes livers pale and lustihood deject.   (II, ii, 46-50)

The entire Trojan council, as we have seen, is a ruthless moral
dissection of honor and therefore of a war waged on grounds of
honor rather than of fundamental morality. In short, the war
stands on a rotten foundation, and Shakespeare makes that fact
devastatingly clear.

Love itself is subjected to an equally thorough and destructive
examination in terms of the conflict between appetite and reason.
Chaucer himself may have stimulated ethical scrutiny of his story
both by his failure to make convincing Cressida's yielding to
Diomedes and by two stanzas defending Cressida from the charge
of falling into love with Troilus at first sight (II, 666-79):

Now myghte som envious jangle thus:
"This was a sodeyn love; how myght it be
That she so lightly loved Troilus,
Right for the firste syghte, ye, parde?"
Now whoso seith so, mote he nevere ythe!
For every thyng, a gynnyng hath it nede
Er al be wrought, withowten any drede.

For I sey nought that she so sodeynly
Yaf hym hire love, but that she gan enclyne
To like hym first, and I have told yow whi;
And after that, his manhod and his pyne
Made love withinne hire herte for to myne,
For which, by proces and by good servyse,
He gat hire love, and in no sodeyn wyse.

Shakespeare's Cressida, like the heroines of the romantic comedies, confesses that she loved at first sight (III, ii, 125-26), but
at that point the parallel ceases. The swift falling in love that
is characteristic of romance could be justified in terms of the
court of love or even of Renaissance Platonism but was contrary
to Christian ethics and psychology. Worthy love presumably
would result from a choice by the reason of a real good; but the
reason would require time to evaluate. Love at sight must rest
upon sense and therefore appetite; and it must be a triumph of
passion in defiance of reason, a sin. And such it is throughout this
play, where each mood is elaborately dissected. Cressida says:

                              for to be wise and love
          Exceeds man's might; that dwells with gods above.
                                        (III, ii, 163-64)

Or, at the end of the play:
          Ah, poor our sex! this fault in us I find,
          The error of our eye directs our mind.
          What error leads must err; O, then conclude
          Minds sway'd by eyes are full of turpitude.
                                        (V, ii, 109-12)

For Troilus love is an exhilaration of the flesh. We are, in fact,
back of the whole medieval and renaissance tradition of romantic
love and in the classical world, where Sappho's love brought
flesh afire, dim eyes, sweat, and trembling limbs, or Catullus cried
in despair: "I hate and love.... I know not why, but I feel it
happen, and I am tortured."[29] So Troilus speaks of his anticipation
in terms that Sappho might have used:
          I am giddy; expectation whirls me round.
          Th' imaginary relish is so sweet
          That it enchants my sense; what will it be,
          When that the wat'ry palates taste indeed
          Love's thrice repured nectar? Death, I fear me,
          Swooning destruction, or some joy too fine,
          Too subtle, potent, tun'd too sharp in sweetness
          For the capacity of my ruder powers.
                                        (III, ii, 19-26)

And to Cressida he is even more brutally realistic: "This is the
monstruosity in love, lady, that the will is infinite and the execution confin'd, that the desire is boundless and the act a slave to
limit" (III, ii, 87-90). Most fatal of all to romance is Troilus'
reflection that the consequence of such yielding to the appetites
is permanent:
          I take to-day a wife, and my election
          Is led on in the conduct of my will,
          My will enkindled by mine eyes and ears,
          Two traded pilots 'twixt the dangerous shores
          Of will and judgment: how may I avoid,
          Although my will distaste what it elected,
          The wife I chose? There can be no evasion
          To blench from this and to stand firm by honour.
                                        (II, ii, 61-68)

[29]Sappho, "*Phainetai moi*," preserved by Longinus; Catullus lxxxv, "Odi et amo."

Whatever Shakespeare's intentions in *Troilus and Cressida*, this skeptical view of love at first sight was no passing mood of cynicism or satiric *jeu d'esprit*. When next he portrayed genuine and worthy love, he made absolutely clear that it had not come at first sight and that it did not rest merely upon appearances. In *All's Well* Helena has grown up with Bertram, and her love is at least rooted in long and intimate acquaintance. Even so, at least one critic writes that her "degradation springs from the irrationality of love," and the play "is a reading of love that has no place whatever in the romantic tradition."[30] The love between Othello and Desdemona, noble and rational if ever love was, grew slowly as he visited her father and she listened to his experiences; in fact, Desdemona instances this slow development and Othello's unattractive "visage" as proof that their love is rational and pure (I, iii, 249-55). Imogen and Posthumous have grown up together. How Perdita and Florizel fell in love we are not told precisely. Only Miranda, under stress of unity of time, falls in love at sight; and she is protected by an omniscient magician father, who subjects Ferdinand to ordeal by woodpile to try his love. Antony, in contrast, succumbs to his first ravishing sight of Cleopatra in her barge. In other words, worthy love at first sight very nearly disappeared from Shakespeare with *Twelfth Night*.

What would have happened if the standards of *Troilus and Cressida* had been applied to Rosalind, who was infatuated by a handsome face and a superior display of muscles at a wrestling match? Or to Portia or Olivia? Or, conversely, to Orlando or Sebastian, although the latter was at least consulting his financial interests? We need not speculate what would happen to whole plots, for, in the preface to the New Cambridge *Merchant of Venice*, Sir Arthur Quiller-Couch has examined the play in terms of realistic moral standards with results as devastating as they are false to Shakespeare's intentions. In *Troilus and Cressida* Shakespeare did the examining himself.

There was, in short, a fundamental contradiction between the unmoral, fairy-tale world of Shakespeare's sources and the elaborate Augustinian ethics that he was now applying. Stouter material than the story of Troilus and Cressida would have collapsed under the strain. These observations do not explain the

[30]Pettet, *Shakespeare and the Romance Tradition*, p. 138.

play, of course, and they are not intended to. Shakespeare was responsible for choosing his material if not for originating it, and he presumably knew why he was attracted to it. Perhaps his intentions were satiric, and he was exposing the results of rejecting the accepted moral system. But there is just a possibility that he let his philosophy get the better of his intentions, whatever they were. Certainly he incorporated into *Troilus and Cressida* the most ruthless and cynical analysis of human motives to be found in his plays—but also the most pedantic and verbose. The talkiness and lack of proportion are quite as fatal to the play as the apparent absence of a controlling purpose. And, if Homer could nod, why could not Shakespeare philosophize, especially if he were just assimilating his ideas and had not wholly brought them under control?

Whatever were the motives and the explanation, Shakespeare's ruthless dissection of love and honor in *Troilus and Cressida* left man in a perilous state indeed. For, assuming that man is a fallen creature whose will is turned from God and whose reason is more or less befuddled,—a Catholic might call it "clouded," an Anglican "far gone from original righteousness," a Calvinist "deformed and ruined,"[31]—what hope has he in this troubled life? The Christian answer, limited by Calvinists to those predestined to salvation, would have been that God's grace can aid man and his mercy can forgive. Christian doctrine would be an anachronism in *Troilus and Cressida*, even though an allusion to a state of grace does occur as the basis of a joke (III, i, 15). The same is true of the tragedies that have a pre-Christian setting. But even in plays dealing with Christian times and countries the chief emphasis is upon man's responsibility. Man seems to be left to stand or fall with his reason, a point of view that might look forward either to the religious despair of the seventeenth century or the rationalism and optimism of the eighteenth, depending on whether one regarded the reason as inadequate or adequate. (In this respect, too, Shakespeare is like Hooker, who was severely attacked for paying insufficient attention to the role

[31]Cf. St. Thomas Aquinas, *Summa Theologica*, Ia-IIae, Q. 82, A. 3 (*Basic Writings*, II, 676-77), and note that the will rather than the reason is corrupted. The extent of the damage done by original sin was, of course, a fundamental issue between Catholics and Protestants. Thirty-nine Articles, No. IX. Calvin, *Institutes*, II, ii, 12; ed. cit., I, 292-93.

of grace, which plays no part in Book I, upon which Shakespeare seems to have leaned.)[32] But *Hamlet* has several references to grace, and *Macbeth* concludes with a promise that it will be restored to Scotland. *Measure for Measure* is therefore important because it is, with *Macbeth*, the most specifically Christian of Shakespeare's plays and presents human sin in relation to the mercy of God and of man. So far as its thought is concerned, it is a kind of supplement to *Troilus and Cressida;* and it shows that Shakespeare was surveying the whole of Christian teaching as well as the problem of sin.

Once again Shakespeare based his play upon an earlier one, George Whetstone's *Promos and Cassandra* of 1578, which was in turn derived from Geraldi Cintio's *Ecatommiti*, the source of *Othello*.[33] Shakespeare's main adaptations were three in number. For the low comedy subplot abundantly illustrating the city's immorality he substituted a much more effective one constructed on the same general principles. Whetstone's Promos, the equivalent of Angelo, first appears reading a proclamation naming him deputy, and the king himself does not appear until the end of the second part of the play, where he is merely a judge of appeal and *deus ex machina* rather than a participant in the action. Cassandra actually yields to Promos, who then sends her brother's supposed head to her. At the end the King sentences Promos to marry Cassandra and to be beheaded the next day. She pleads for him and, at the risk of his own life, her brother Andrugio, who has escaped from prison to the woods, reappears to prove that he is alive and to join his prayers to hers. The king then pardons them all. Mariana is Shakespeare's invention to save Isabella's chastity and, incidentally, to reserve her for the Duke.

Out of this play, unpromising except for its emphasis upon mercy, Shakespeare made a drama that explicitly involves fundamental Christian doctrines. Recent critics have gone very far indeed in attributing to it a Christian meaning. For G. Wilson Knight it is to be read "on the analogy of Jesus' parables"; "the

[32]Hooker was charged in *A Christian Letter* (1599) with neglecting grace in a way inconsistent with the Thirty-nine Articles, and his statement of his own "orthodox" position occurs in a fragment printed by Keble as Appendix 1 to Book V (*Works*, II, 537 ff.). Cf. the prefatory account (*Works*, I, xvii-xix).

[33]Chambers, *William Shakespeare*, I, 457. For *Promos and Cassandra* see Hazlitt, *Shakespeare's Library*, II (Part 2), 207-304.

ethical standards of the Gospels are rooted in the thought," and the final scenes suggest the Last Judgment.[34] S. L. Bethell distinguishes between "two diverse aspects of the same character: the representational and the symbolic." In the former the Duke is a human being; in the latter he suggests the Deity.[35] For Roy W. Battenhouse the play has been "formed" "after the pattern of the Christian doctrine of the Atonement," although "the Atonement theme is thus present not as a preconceived design impressed from without upon recalcitrant materials, but as a formal principle allowed to mold the action from within, according to what will forward the total end of a happy denoument despite the tragic 'flaws' of several of the characters."[36] The views cited represent an extreme position, but evidence to support them can certainly be adduced from the language of the play, whether it be conclusive or not. I should prefer personally to stick to the point of view embodied in R. W. Chambers' British Academy Shakespeare Lecture of 1937, "The Jacobean Shakespeare and *Measure for Measure*," which seems to me one of the masterpieces of modern Shakespearean criticism. This sees the action as turning upon fundamental Christian doctrines rather than as being itself a kind of allegory of Christianity.

Early in the play the Duke places the entire action in a framework of mercy and justice. His own policy has been one of mercy if not of indulgence, but it may not have involved real kindness:

> so our decrees,
> Dead to infliction, to themselves are dead,
> And liberty plucks justice by the nose,
> The baby beats the nurse, and quite athwart
> Goes all decorum.
>
> (I, iii, 27-31)

But the Duke cannot punish for what he has in effect encouraged:

> 'Twould be my tyranny to strike and gall them
> For what I bid them do; for we bid this be done,
> When evil deeds have their permissive pass
> And not the punishment.
>
> (I, iii, 36-39)

[34]*The Wheel of Fire*, pp. 73, 83.

[35]*Shakespeare & the Popular Dramatic Tradition*, p. 107.

[36]"*Measure for Measure* and Christian Doctrine of the Atonement," pp. 1058-59.

So he proposes to see what strict justice, as administered by Angelo, will accomplish and incidentally to test Angelo's own righteousness under the temptation of power:

> Lord Angelo is precise,
> Stands at a guard with envy, scarce confesses
> That his blood flows, or that his appetite
> Is more to bread than stone; hence shall we see,
> If power change purpose, what our seemers be.
>
> (I, iii, 50-54)

Let us pass over the ethics of this strategem, as Shakespeare evidently intended that we should, and grant that the play is concerned not only with the relative claims of justice and mercy but also with the soundness of the position of those who judge. Texts from the New Testament begin to occur even to the modern reader, and Shakespeare's brain was undoubtedly teeming with them.

As Isabella begins to plead for Claudio, she first applies the Golden Rule to human justice:

> If he had been as you and you as he,
> You would have slipt like him; but he, like you,
> Would not have been so stern.   (II, ii, 64-66)

Then she relates the play to the justice of God and to the Atonement itself:

> Why, all the souls that were were forfeit once;
> And He that might the vantage best have took
> Found out the remedy. How would you be
> If He, which is the top of judgement, should
> But judge you as you are? O, think on that;
> And mercy then will breathe within your lips,
> Like man new made.   (II, ii, 73-79)

Angelo answers on her own grounds by stating a fundamentally sound argument that legal justice is, in effect, mercy to all rather than to the criminal:

> I show it [pity] most of all when I show justice,
> For then I pity those I do not know,
> Which a dismiss'd offence would after gall;
> And do him right that, answering one foul wrong,
> Lives not to act another.   (II, ii, 100-104)

There is no need to pursue the interpretation of the play further, since I should merely be repeating R. W. Chambers. Enough has perhaps been said to make possible the development of two generalizations. First, in this play Shakespeare develops and applies several key principles from the New Testament quite as rigorously as he employed the Christian interpretation of sin in *Troilus and Cressida.* Second, the result is an equally fatal conflict between the thought and the unsophisticated plot material upon which it is superimposed.

Much of the dismay with which modern readers view *Measure for Measure* is certainly due to its uncompromising adherence to fundamental Christian doctrines that we like to forget. First of all, it insists that the soul is of infinitely more importance than the body: "What shall it profit a man if he gain the whole world and lose his own soul?" Claudio's life or Isabella's is as nothing beside the salvation of their souls.[37] She says of her own life:

> O, were it but my life,
> I'd throw it down for your deliverance
> As frankly as a pin.
>
> (III, i, 104-106)

But of her soul she has said to Angelo:

> Better it were a brother died at once,
> Than that a sister, by redeeming him,
> Should die for ever.
>
> (II, iv, 106-108)

And her terrible dialogue with Claudio must be read against the full realization, perfectly obvious to any Elizabethan, that in demanding the life of his body at such a price Claudio is condemning his own soul to death as well as hers. "Mercy to thee would prove itself a bawd," she cries (III, i, 150), and it would indeed, prostituting his immortal soul to his body as hers to Angelo. A few minutes later Claudio himself realizes that his demand is outrageous, and, as he prepares for death, he says to the disguised Duke: "Let me ask my sister pardon" (III, i, 173). This is a stern code, the code of the martyrs in the Roman arena, but it is undoubtedly Christianity.

But why, in her final words to Claudio, does Isabella so firmly reject all thought of mercy, after her eloquent plea to Angelo for mercy? The answer involves not only the point just made

---

[37]Cf. Chambers, "The Jacobean Shakespeare," pp. 37-40.

but also a second Christian principle—the reality of sin and of absolute standards of right and wrong. "Sure, it is no sin," says Claudio; "or of the deadly seven it is the least" (III, i, 110-11). "Which is the least?" replies Isabella, and, if sin is an absolute, her argument is unanswerable. Shakespeare has sharpened the issue further by making her a votaress of St. Clare and writing a scene (I, iv) to make sure that the audience understood exactly what that involved. Though she has not taken the vows, she is already on probation—that is, on trial before God and man.

Because sin is an inescapable fact and its wages are death, punishment is certain in this world, as well as in the life to come. Shakespeare makes this clear. Lucio must marry his whore and live with her, but his real punishment lies in his own character, which he cannot escape and which is utterly despicable, however amusing we may find it in the play. Of the life to come Shakespeare gave Claudio the most vivid and horrible description that he ever wrote. Claudio's words gain horror, not so much from the threat of death which hangs over him as from the sure damnation which he will incur if his attempt to escape a physical death succeeds. In trying to escape Hell, he falls into it even as he describes its horrors. His real choice is between death of body and soul. This he cannot see in his terror, but Isabella can; and to be true to her Christian duty to her brother she must reject his plea. It is in this realm of absolute moral standards and of final and absolute punishment—final and absolute because they have been established by God and not by fallible man—that Angelo's logic is sound and justice is the highest mercy. Angelo's mistake lies in confusing his justice with God's, but Isabella makes no such error in saying, in the presence of the law of God,

> Mercy to thee would prove itself a bawd;
> 'Tis best that thou diest quickly.
>
> (III, i, 150-51)

It is, on these principles, unquestionably mercy that he should die, lest, by living, he gain eternal death.

But, if the justice of God is absolute, so, for those who do truly and earnestly repent, is his mercy. This is the fundamental paradox of the Atonement, to which Isabella alludes. Shakespeare prayed: "Forgive us our trespasses, as we forgive them that trespass against us." He therefore pushed to its logical extreme the granting of mercy on the human level as well as the divine. Of Angelo's penitence he tries to leave us in no doubt:

> I am sorry that such sorrow I procure;
> And so deep sticks it in my penitent heart
> That I crave death more willingly than mercy.
> 'Tis my deserving, and I do entreat it.   (V, i, 479-82)

But even before this Isabella, after some hesitation while Mariana pleads,[38] has added her supplication that the Duke be merciful. So Angelo escapes being judged with the judgment that he meted out, and he receives not the "mercy of the law" for which he argued but the mercy of Christianity. When Angelo says,

> When I perceive your Grace, like power divine,
> Hath look'd upon my passes,   (V, i, 374-75)

his words seem to imply a parallel between the Duke's justice and God's, whether we wish to push the analogy farther or not; and the Duke's reference to the "mercy of the law" involves not only Angelo's earlier argument but also the distinction between the unyielding law of the Old Testament and Christ's gospel of mercy, which extends even to Angelo. This mercy, Shakespeare seems to say, is the universal need of sinful and imperfect man, whose own judgments must therefore be tempered with mercy.

If we find these elements of the play unacceptable, Shakespeare might argue, as R. W. Chambers argues for him, that the fault is not in the play but in our unwillingness to face the implications of Christianity. To a degree that is true; but it is not, I submit, the whole truth. Something else is wrong. My first reaction to Battenhouse's study, "*Measure for Measure* and the Christian Doctrine of the Atonement," was, I confess, to reflect that, if Shakespeare intended to mirror the process of the Atonement, he had involuntarily produced a parody upon which a skeptic might pounce as revealing all the weaknesses of this central Christian doctrine. Why, for example, did the Duke make a mess of his administration and then turn it over to Angelo to straighten out while he spied from concealment? Why did he appoint a deputy knowing that he had been faithless to his

[38]Cf. Chambers' excellent interpretation of this scene (ibid., pp. 48-50, 51-52).

betrothed? And difficulties could be multiplied. Similarly, no argument can make acceptable the device by which Mariana substitutes for Isabella.[39] Nor is the trouble centered in the plot material as such. In trying to preserve Isabella's chastity, as he reformed many another unchaste character in his sources, Shakespeare introduced the "bed trick" and made the Duke a kind of continuous *deus ex machina* to settle difficulties in the plot. But both of these were familiar devices which he had used in *All's Well that Ends Well* and *Romeo and Juliet* respectively, and we are bothered neither by Helena's deception nor by Friar Lawrence's stratagems. We also accept without hesitation inconsistencies in other plays as glaring as those in the Duke's conduct. One difficulty lies, as in *Troilus and Cressida*, in the incongruity between the Christian framework of the characters and the folk materials of the plot.

Angelo—at least in the first part of *Measure for Measure*—is a convincing character in whom Shakespeare has represented a subtle, complicated working of lust; and Angelo is quickened into life precisely because Shakespeare was vitally interested in that form of wickedness. But barely has life been breathed into Angelo when he has to be distorted to the necessities of a romantic story.[40]

We can readily enough accept a fairy-tale lady who changes beds to gain a worthy objective or an omniscient friar who resorts to white lies to avoid difficulties. But a woman, confronted with as dreadful a choice as we can well imagine, who works out her conduct according to fundamental Christian principles and discusses them fully while so doing, is not a fairy-tale character even for the most skeptical of us; and she sheds upon her surroundings the cold light of her own standards of conduct.

In short, the folk elements in the plot do not explain away the difficulty. They create it. There was a fundamental antipathy between Shakespeare's new learning and his old plot situations, and *Measure for Measure* failed of being as a whole what individual scenes undoubtedly are—as wonderful in its affirmation of charity and mercy and other Christian principles as *Macbeth* is in its presentation of the Christian view of sin. A radical revision of his sources such as Shakespeare had begun to make in

[39]Cf. ibid., pp. 31-32.
[40]Pettet, *Shakespeare and the Romance Tradition*, p. 158.

Hamlet was required. That adjustment of plot to philosophy he achieved triumphantly in *Lear* and *Macbeth* and even in *Othello*.

Two other possible interpretations of these plays are tempting but, I believe, probably unjustified. The alternative to order, as Ulysses makes clear, is chaos. It follows, therefore, that if man deliberately violates the laws of nature the result may be a disruption of the entire chain of being, extending from the social sphere even into that of inanimate nature. That is exactly what happens in *Lear* and, to a lesser extent, in *Macbeth*. In *Troilus and Cressida* both the Greeks and the Trojans are certainly at cross purposes. In *Measure for Measure* the characters in the main plot are redeemed from the consequences of their sins by grace and forgiveness, and the social order is restored. But parallel to the main plot is a most unpleasant low-comedy subplot. When it is first introduced in the second scene of the play, Shakespeare describes its characters as villains "despite of all grace" (I, ii, 25-27). Unlike Angelo, Lucio, the most important figure in the subplot and its link with the main action, finds no forgiveness. Though he escapes hanging, he must face the consequences of his sins, including marrying a whore. One is tempted to see in these two plots a contrast between a world in which order, though violated, can be restored and the social chaos that follows complete violation of the moral laws of nature. But, so far as I can discover, there is no language in the play to justify that interpretation, and Shakespeare is not in the habit of leaving his meaning in doubt.

During the Renaissance the Christian scheme of things outlined by Ulysses and Hector was being attacked from a number of directions.[41] Machiavelli proclaimed that "there is such a distance between how men doe live, and how men ought to live; that hee who leaves that which is done, for that which ought to bee done, learnes sooner his ruine, than his preservation";[42] and he based his statecraft upon what men do. Thinkers like Henry Cornelius Agrippa, Montaigne, and Francis Bacon brought contemporary learning under philosophic attack because of its dependence upon reason. Calvinism, and indeed most Protestantism, denied that man's fallen reason could achieve moral conduct.

[41]Cf. Haydn, *The Counter-Renaissance*, pp. 87-111, 139-66.
[42]*The Prince*, ch. xv (p. 69).

For a Calvinist poet and thinker like Fulke Greville, morality and even knowledge of nature are possible only when grace and faith begin to work in those whom God has elected.[43] Calvin's whole system rests upon the premise that God is will rather than reason and that man can only prostrate himself before this arbitrary deity and obey his revealed commands. What is right is right because God wills it, not because man's reason recognizes it as the rational law of a rational God. Certainly the Trojans in *Troilus and Cressida* decide quite deliberately and explicitly to follow will in defiance of reason, and it is possible that Shakespeare was showing the consequences of such conduct. The play would then become his defense of reason and the traditional order against the new skeptical naturalism and the new voluntarism. This view is extremely tempting. But actually nothing in the action of the play except the continuation of the war depends upon the decision of the Trojan council, and again I am unable to find a single passage in the play which would in so many words support the proposed interpretation. Surely, when Shakespeare has himself so richly and so explicitly indicated his meaning as he has in this play, we need not try to add further riches to what he offers.

[43]"Treatie of Humane Learning," st. 149, in *Poems and Dramas*, I, 191.

CHAPTER X

Julius Caesar and Tragedy of Moral Choice

ULIUS CAESAR, the first of Shakespeare's mature tragedies, can be very confidently dated in 1599, just after *Henry V* and alongside *As You Like It* and *Twelfth Night*. It is a landmark in the development of Shakespeare's thought. Its very structure results from applying to the sources in Plutarch two postulates that we have encountered in the earlier plays—namely, that monarchy is necessary to social order and that wrong conduct results from a failure of reason. This structure, in turn, became a formula which Shakespeare used in building all the great tragedies except *Hamlet*. The evidence for these generalizations will form the bulk of this chapter. Since the interpretation of the play to be presented runs counter, in important respects, to the opinions of several well-known editors, the evidence will first be presented, and then an attempt will be made to evaluate it. The best clue to the meaning of the play lies, of course, in comparing it with its sources.

The principal sources of *Julius Caesar* were obviously Plutarch's lives of Brutus, Caesar, and Antonius in North's translation. Where the lives of Brutus and Caesar gave divergent accounts of details connected with the murder of Caesar, Shakespeare followed the "Brutus." He drew relatively little from the "Antonius." A few details seem to have come from other writers, mostly classical.[1] In handling accounts of the prodigies preceding

---

[1]Sykes (to cite an extreme view) maintained that Shakespeare also "knew and used Appian, Dio, Ovid, and possibly Suetonius, Valerius Maximus, Virgil's *Georgics*, Boccaccio's *Life of Caesar*, and Eedes' Latin play" (Furness Variorum,

Caesar's death, for example, Shakespeare added details from Ovid, taking them from the same context in *Metamorphoses* XV from which he derived the reference to Caesar's becoming a star in *1 Henry VI* (I, i, 55-56).[2] The contributions of writers other than Plutarch amounted, in any event, only to details such as in his earliest plays he borrowed from the Bible and classical authors and in later plays from contemporaries as well. The fundamental plot structure and the characterization of individuals were due to Plutarch, and any inferences as to Shakespeare's thought must therefore rest upon a comparison between the play and the lives of Brutus and Casear.

In building his plot, Shakespeare followed events in Plutarch closely, partly for the very good reason that they had already been arranged to form an interpretation of character and motives by a writer whose primary interest was in ethical analysis rather than in factual biography. In beginning his life of Alexander the Great, Plutarch tells us candidly:

... I will use none other preface, but only desire the readers not to blame me though I do not declare al things at large, but briefly touch divers, chiefly in those their noblest acts and most worthy of memory. For they must remember, that my intent is not to write histories, but only lives. For, the noblest deedes doe not alwayes shew mens vertues & vices, but oftentimes a light occasion, a word, or some sporte makes mens naturall dispositions & maners appeare more plaine, then the famous battells wonne, wherein are slaine tenne thowsande men, or the great armies, or cities wonne by siege or assault. For like as painters or drawers of pictures, which make no accompt of other partes of the bodie, do take the resemblaunces of the face and favor of the countenance, in the which consisteth the judgement of their maners and disposition: even so they must geve us leave to seeke out the signes and tokens of the minde only, and thereby shewe the life of either of them, referring you unto others to wryte the warres, battells, and other great thinges they did.[3]

---

p. 295). But no translation of Dio Cassius into English was available, and it is very unlikely that Shakespeare would have consulted a Greek writer. Since Eedes' play is lost (cf. Boas, *University Drama in the Tudor Age*, pp. 163-65), any conclusions about it must be purely conjectural, and the case of Suetonius and Valerius Maximus cannot be regarded as proved. MacCallum (*Shakespeare's Roman Plays*, pp. 644-47) quotes and discusses possible parallels in Appian.

[2]Shackford, "*Julius Caesar* and Ovid," pp. 172-74. She seems to have overlooked the allusion to Ovid in *1 Henry VI*.

[3]*The Lives of the Noble Grecians and Romanes*, V, 164-65.

Attempting to present men's "vertues & vices" inevitably involves formulating a view of their motives. Shakespeare therefore found Plutarch an admirable source for tragedy, and the *Lives*, like some of the other sources, may actually have stimulated his interest to take the direction it did.

Plutarch, broadly speaking, presented Caesar as the destroyer of Roman liberty and Brutus as the noblest Roman of them all, a man of almost flawless character. But, for reasons that I hope will appear during the following discussion, Shakespeare was not prepared wholly to accept either Caesar or Brutus in these terms. He therefore made a number of changes in detail which altered the two men fundamentally, and for the first time he reshaped events to fit a predetermined characterization. There is no better example of this skill to be found than the economy with which he managed to alter Plutarch's design by a few strokes. These strokes are therefore the best clue to his intentions, which were, in turn, the result of his political thinking. Let us first consider Caesar.

When Shakespeare first read Plutarch, presumably while he was writing the Henry VI plays, he obviously did not approach the life of Caesar without preconceptions. He had doubtless already encountered two contrasting views of the man. The first was that exemplified by Dante, who placed Brutus and Cassius along with Judas Iscariot in the lowest circle of hell. For him the murder of Caesar by his friends was the second greatest crime recorded in history. The other interpretation was derived from Plutarch himself and from later Roman writers. It portrayed Caesar as a commanding genius but fundamentally an evil man. In later tradition he had become vainglorious as well. Several writers have argued that Shakespeare accepted this second concept. I believe, however, that a careful examination of the evidence shows that he came close to sharing that illustrated by Dante. I must apologize for once again inflicting a series of details upon the reader, but I know of no other way to demonstrate why the position taken by many critics seems to me ill-considered. Since Dover Wilson presents an admirable summary of their position as his preface to the New Cambridge *Julius Caesar*, I have used his arguments in planning my own discussion.

To begin with, Shakespeare frequently mentions Caesar in

such a way as to show his attitude. One should probably leave out of account *Antony and Cleopatra* as well as *Julius Caesar,* since the references are entangled in the action of the play. A number of the remaining allusions occur in comic scenes and show nothing about how Shakespeare regarded the man. Pompey in *Love's Labour's Lost,* for example, elicits the inevitable jokes about what Caesar did to him. But a number of really significant references remain. Two of these may reflect the vainglorious Caesar. In *As You Like It* (V, ii, 33-34) Rosalind speaks of "Caesar's thrasonical brag of 'I came, saw, and overcame.' " Partly in quotation of Plutarch, the ship which bore "Caesar and his fortune" is called proud and insulting (*1 Henry VI*, I, ii, 138). But every other allusion places Caesar on the highest possible pedestal. Caesar's death by "Brutus' bastard hand" is instanced as proof that "great men oft die by vile besonians" (*2 Henry VI*, IV, i, 134). What is more, Suffolk urges the comparison upon the pirate who is about to kill him. Queen Margaret, under similar stress, clearly echoes the same view. To the still-bleeding body of her son Edward, she says in the first fury of her grief:

> O traitors! murderers!
> They that stabb'd Caesar slew no blood at all,
> Did not offend, nor were not worthy blame,
> If this foul deed were by to equal it.
> (*3 Henry VI*, V, v, 52-55)

That she used the word "traitors" advisedly is proved by another passage in the same play that explicitly attributes to Caesar the divine right of kingship:

> Thy place is fill'd, thy sceptre wrung from thee,
> Thy balm wash'd off wherewith thou was anointed.
> No bending knee will call thee Caesar now.
> (III, i, 16-18)

There is no indication in the later plays that Shakespeare's attitude changed. Caesar remains the type of the invincible conqueror and great man. Most revealing is Macbeth's remark about Banquo:

> Under him
> My Genius is rebuk'd, as, it is said,
> Mark Antony's was by Caesar. (III, i, 55-57)

227

Throughout the play Banquo has been established, in direct contrast to Macbeth, as the pattern of rationality and virtue. Just before the lines quoted, in fact, Macbeth speaks of the dauntless temper of his mind and of his wisdom.

In short, the evidence available outside the present play indicates that Shakespeare took a high view of Casear indeed.[4]

Let us now turn to Shakespeare's handling of his source material in *Julius Caesar*. Again contradictory indications appear; but the preponderant evidence indicates that Shakespeare, while in the main accepting Plutarch's account, attempted to reconcile it with his notion of a great man and ruler.

In Plutarch's "Caesar" Shakespeare found a portrait that emphasized the man's courage, his ambition, his vanity, and his superstition but did scant justice to his greatness as a statesman. Beginning his play in the last days of Caesar's life further emphasized this bias of his source. The conquests were past, and Plutarch gives no adequate indication of the statesmanlike schemes for the government of Rome that we know Caesar to have formulated during his last months. Shakespeare found only one element in his source that he recognized as commensurate with the greatness of Caesar's influence—namely, the omens which marked his approaching death. To these he gave maximum emphasis. There is no reason to doubt that Shakespeare, like his contemporaries, accepted these details in classical writers as historically accurate. The achievement of pagan gods and of oracles Christian theory explained by assuming that the fallen angels had masqueraded as gods to work the further damnation of man. But Shakespeare perhaps had no need to rely upon such an explanation of these omens, for subsequent history amply demonstrated Caesar's place in the divine scheme of things; Providence might be expected to intervene directly to foretell his death. As Calphurnia tells him: "The heavens themselves blaze forth the death of princes" (II, ii, 31). Shakespeare therefore seized upon these details and emphasized them as properly indicating Caesar's surpassing greatness. Furthermore, he was careful to rule out specifically the possibility, mentioned by Pandulph in *King John*, that they might be manifestations of the normal

---

[4]MacCallum summarizes the evidence of Shakespeare's attitude towards Caesar (*Shakespeare's Roman Plays*, pp. 177-80).

operation of nature. His use of omens is deliberately and explicitly given the greatest possible significance by being worked out in terms of the learning of his day. Casca is his mouthpiece:

> But never till to-night, never till now,
> Did I go through a tempest dropping fire.
> Either there is a civil strife in heaven,
> Or else the world, too saucy with the gods,
> Incenses them to send destruction.
>
> When these prodigies
> Do so conjointly meet, let not men say,
> "These are their reasons; they are natural";
> For, I believe, they are portentous things
> Unto the climate that they point upon.
>
> (I, iii, 9-13, 28-32)

In finding a second means of squaring his source with his own notion of Caesar's greatness, Shakespeare was perhaps guided by a passage in the life of Caesar, much as he apparently used passages in Holinshed as a basis for the structure of individual chronicle plays:

But his [Caesar's] great prosperity and good fortune, that favoured him all his lifetime, did continue afterwards in the revenge of his death, pursuing the murtherers both by sea and land, till they had not left a man more to be executed, of all them that were actors or counsellors in the conspiracy of his death.

This sentence, which has a marginal gloss "The revenge of Caesar's death," is followed by the information that Cassius "slew himself with the same sword, with the which he strake Caesar" and an account of various prodigies of nature. Plutarch then continues:

But, above all, the ghost that appeared unto Brutus showed plainly that the gods were offended with the murther of Caesar. . . . looking towards the light of the lamp that waxed very dim, he saw a horrible vision of a man, of a wonderful greatness, and dreadful look, which at the first made him marvellously afraid. But, when he saw that it did him no hurt, but stood by his bedside and said nothing, at length he asked him what he was. The image answered him: "I am thy ill angel, Brutus, and thou shalt see me by the city of Philippi."[5]

---

[5]"Julius Caesar," *Four Lives from North's Plutarch*, p. 110.

Shakespeare had only to convert Plutarch's evil genius into the ghost of Caesar to achieve not only a perfect dramatic revenge ghost but also a personification of the greatness of the man, whose influence Brutus himself confesses on the battlefield:

> O Julius Caesar, thou art mighty yet!
> Thy spirit walks abroad, and turns our swords
> In our own proper entrails.
>
> (V, iii, 94-96)

In addition to selecting his material carefully, Shakespeare attempted by changing various details to alter the impression created by the source. First of all, Caesar is a weaker man physically than in the source. Wilson has an excellent summary of what has happened to him:

Shakespeare adds to the infirmities in Plutarch a deafness in one ear; and makes "the falling sickness," which Plutarch does not mention, seize him at the most awkward and humiliating moment—when being offered a crown. Worse still, he substitutes for the pluck, resolution, and endurance often praised by Plutarch, a "feeble temper"; and derives the three examples of this from passages in North which show the exact opposite. Cassius is here, indeed, the speaker, and the points illustrate his malice; but Brutus does not reply to the charge, and it is fully borne out by stroke after stroke later. Cassius begins by hinting at the great man's sensitiveness to "the winter's cold," whereas Plutarch, while admitting a delicate constitution, gives instances of his hardiness in ignoring it. Cassius tells a story of a swimming match in which Caesar has to cry to him for help; Plutarch on the contrary stresses his strength and skill in swimming and tells of a wonderful aquatic feat. Lastly, of Caesar's "fever in Spain," when according to Cassius his "coward lips" cried out for water "as a sick girl," Plutarch writes:

"Yet therefore [he] yielded not to the disease of his body, to make it a cloak to cherish him withal, but contrarily took the pains of war as a medicine to cure his sick body, fighting always with his disease, travelling continually, living soberly, and commonly lying abroad in the field."[6]

When Caesar bids Calphurnia station herself in Antony's way among women who would "shake off their sterile curse" (I, ii, 9), Wilson remarks that "Elizabethans would be quick to set their own interpretation" on his words.[7] Perhaps. But the less carnally-

---

[6]New Cambridge *Julius Caesar*, pp. xxvii-xxviii.
[7]Ibid., p. xxix.

minded among the audience might also see in them the very proper foresight of a newly established ruler worried about a stable succession. That subject was in everyone's mind when the play first appeared.

Wilson, like other critics who stress Caesar's weakness, also minimizes an even greater body of evidence that Shakespeare tried to make Caesar a model ruler.[8] Antony's testimony that Caesar wept over the poor is perhaps suspect, but the will, which is Shakespeare's invention, displays a similar solicitude for them. In Plutarch Caesar, who is himself superstitious, is frightened by the prodigies of nature and by Calphurnia's dream, whereas she "until that time was never given to any fear or superstition."[9] He has to be shamed out of his decision to stay home by Decius Brutus. Shakespeare presents him as without superstition and gives him bravery. In the play Caesar at first refuses to heed warnings that he stay home, and the fears are Calphurnia's. His words during this episode have been taken as boasting, vacillating, and rationalizing; but they are more likely to be simple statements of fact, such as Shakespeare gives to his great men even though in lesser men they might seem immodest. They are further justified in that they involve a clever reinterpretation of the omens taken by the augurers to be unfavorable:

> Caesar should be a heart without a heart,
> If he should stay at home today for fear.

> We are two lions litter'd in one day;
> And I the elder and more terrible:
> (II, ii, 42-43, 46-47)

But he yields to his wife's entreaty, and Shakespeare gets the same suspense that he found in his source. Even so, Caesar refuses to lie, despite his first impulse to say that he is sick:

> Cannot, is false, and that I dare not, falser;
> I will not come today.   (II, ii, 63-64)

Decius then persuades him to go to the Senate by arguing that his yielding to Calphurnia will seem not gallantry but petticoat domination.

---

[8]For a summary of this evidence cf. Phillips, *The State in Shakespeare's Greek and Roman Plays*, pp. 176-79.

[9]"Julius Caesar," *Four Lives from North's Plutarch*, p. 105.

This reading of the scene as fact and not vainglorious rationalizing is true to Shakespeare's dramatic method. It is also supported by contemporary evidence. Jonson wrote in *Timber*: "Many times hee [Shakespeare] fell into those things, could not escape laughter: As when hee said in the person of *Caesar*, one speaking to him; *Caesar thou dost me wrong*. Hee replyed: *Caesar did never wrong, but with just cause* and such like: which were ridiculous." The line is indeed ridiculous, but it does not stand in the play. Jonson's anecdote itself shows that he never suspected the Caesar of the play of being a braggart—what more appropriate to a "thrasonical" character than the line he quotes! Nor can I imagine even gentle Will Shakespeare removing a line under Jonson's taunts if it showed that the learned Ben had completely missed the point.[10]

I should perhaps add that I have been fortified in my interpretation of this scene by seeing a recent college production based on the view of Caesar's character summarized by Wilson. It was a failure, and it showed clearly the danger of selecting a few passages and giving them an emphasis contrary to the intention of the whole play. To regard Caesar as a hollow shell is to inflict upon him, for reasons also growing out of modern sympathies, the fallacy of the romantic interpretation of Shylock. Caesar's ghost at Philippi is an unsubstantial being. But he needs a very substantial background to make him credible.

Events on the way to the Senate have also been changed to ennoble Caesar. In Plutarch he "many times attempted" to read the crucial message from Artemidorus warning of the conspiracy, but he could not because of the people who pressed about him. Shakespeare gives the soothsayer significant motives:

> My heart laments that virtue cannot live
> Out of the teeth of emulation.   (II, iii, 13-14)

Caesar refuses to read the paper because Artemidorus urges that it touches him personally: "What touches us ourself shall be last serv'd" (III, i, 8). (Notice, incidentally, that in a public pronouncement he uses the royal "us.")

---

[10]For Jonson cf. Chambers, *William Shakespeare*, II, 210. Schücking has an admirable discussion of this scene (*Character Problems in Shakespeare's Plays*, pp. 40-52). The views against which I am arguing are summarized by Wilson, New Cambridge *Julius Caesar*, pp. xxvi-xxvii.

Most meaningful of all, perhaps, is Shakespeare's handling of Brutus' crucial soliloquy (II, i, 10-34). This will need to be discussed at length in connection with the structure of the play. But we may note here that it is apparently based in part upon Plutarch's introductory summary of Caesar's character:

His enemies, judging that this favour of the common people would soon quail, when he could no longer hold out that charge and expense, suffered him to run on, till by little and little he was grown to be of great strength and power. But in fine, when they had thus given him the bridle to grow to this greatness, and that they could not then pull him back, though indeed in sight it would turn one day to the destruction of the whole state and commonwealth of Rome: too late they found, that there is not so little a beginning of anything, but continuance of time will soon make it strong, when through contempt there is no impediment to hinder the greatness. Thereupon Cicero, like a wise shipmaster that feareth the calmness of the sea, was the first man that, mistrusting his manner of dealing in the commonwealth, found out his craft and malice, which he cunningly cloaked under the habit of outward courtesy and familiarity.[11]

What the source states as fact, the play develops as a hypothesis, and Brutus says explicitly that it is a hypothesis unsupported by past conduct.

How is one to reconcile these contrary changes from the source, which make Caesar more subject to physical infirmities but also more careful and unselfish as a ruler? In part, probably, Shakespeare is actually trying to contrast human weakness and royal power. But the obvious explanation is to be found, I think, in Plutarch. Shakespeare took Caesar as one who "yielded not to the disease of his body," but triumphed by the strength of his will and intellect as well as by his bravery:

> What can be avoided
> Whose end is purpos'd by the mighty Gods? . . .
> Cowards die many times before their death;
> The valiant never taste of death but once.
> (II, ii, 26-27; 32-33)

To magnify Caesar's achievements, Shakespeare presented him as weaker of body than in the source, and therefore stronger of will. No one ever regarded Franklin D. Roosevelt's paralysis

11"Julius Caesar," *Four Lives from North's Plutarch*, pp. 47-48. Note that this invalidates Wilson's reading of the soliloquy (New Cambridge *Julius Caesar*, pp. xxx-xxxi).

as detracting from his greatness. Quite the contrary. His triumph over it was part of his hold upon men. Shakespeare expected those who were without Cassius' envy to take the same view of Caesar. He was a great and good ruler. To kill him was regicide.

The ennobling of Caesar is paralleled by a similar strengthening of his chief partisan, Antony. Plutarch tells us that Antony urged the Senate to bury Caesar in order to placate the people and that he delivered an oration; but he is neither brave enough, as in the play, to confront the conspirators immediately after the murder, nor strong enough to meet them on their own terms. His part in the dramatic structure we shall want to consider later.

There may be question as to what Shakespeare was trying to accomplish by the changes he made in portraying Caesar. There can be no doubt whatever as to what he was trying to do to Brutus. To Plutarch Brutus was an almost perfect example of the antique and heroic republican mould. To Shakespeare he was a very great man, but, because of fundamental defects in his own mind and character, he made a horrible and tragic error—in short, he was a tragic hero.

Shakespeare therefore emphasized both Brutus' self-righteousness and his impractical and muddled head. His deviations from his source indicate that such was his intention. In the meeting of the conspirators that occupies the latter half of Act II, Scene 1, Brutus overrules three suggestions by Cassius.[12] The first is an outright invention, and the other two involve significant divergences from the account of Brutus' reasoning in the source. Cassius first proposes an oath, which Brutus rejects on the grounds that it would "stain the even virtue of our enterprise" (II, i, 132-33). Cassius then suggests that they invite Cicero to join them. Plutarch implies that the conspirators agreed to omit Cicero "for they were afraid that he being a coward by nature, and age also having increased his fear, he would quite turn and alter all their purpose, and quench the heat of their enterprise, the which especially required hot and earnest execution, seeking by persuasion to bring all things to such safety, as there should be no peril."[13] For this general distrust of a born politician Shakespeare substituted a rejection by Brutus alone

[12] Tassin, "Julius Caesar," pp. 259-60.
[13] "Brutus," *Four Lives from North's Plutarch*, p. 121.

234

on grounds more indicative of his own vanity than of Cicero's incompetence:

> O, name him not; let us not break with him,
> For he will never follow anything
> That other men begin.
>
> (II, i, 150-52)

In Plutarch Brutus' reasons for refusing to kill Antonius, as Cassius wishes, at least show genuine idealism:

But Brutus would not agree to it. First, for that he said it was not honest; secondly, because he told them there was hope of change in him. For he did not mistrust, but that Antonius, being a noble-minded and courageous man, (when he should know that Caesar was dead) would willingly help his country to recover her liberty, having them an example unto him, to follow their courage and virtue.[14]

Shakespeare makes his motives reflect both self-righteousness and a lack of worldly experience. He argues that, because Antony is given to wild living, he is not dangerous:

> If he love Caesar, all that he can do
> Is to himself—take thought and die for Caesar;
> And that were much he should, for he is given
> To sports, to wildness, and much company.
>
> (II, i, 186-89)

Later, when Antony asks to deliver a funeral oration over Caesar's body, Shakespeare attributes to Brutus himself the very arguments for granting the request which Plutarch makes Antony advance. Coming from Antony they were crafty; coming from Brutus they are fatuous. Brutus also demands the impossible in the following proviso: praise Caesar without dispraising us!

> You shall not in your funeral speech blame us,
> But speak all good you can devise of Caesar.
>
> (III, i, 245-46)

Shakespeare tried so obviously to accentuate Brutus' self-righteousness in the quarrel between Brutus and Cassius just before Philippi that his writing is actually clumsy. In Plutarch Brutus gets money from Cassius while they are at Smyrna. Some time later, during the quarrel upon which Shakespeare's scene

[14]Ibid., p. 127.

is based, he reproves Cassius for his way of exacting money. But Shakespeare so arranges matters that Brutus first reproves Cassius for his methods of getting money (the speech is a direct paraphrase of North) and then, all the while protesting his own superior virtue, upbraids Cassius for not sending him some of the ill-gotten wealth:

> I did send to you
> For certain sums of gold, which you deni'd me;
> For I can raise no money by vile means.—
> By heaven, I had rather coin my heart
> And drop my blood for drachmas than to wring
> From the hard hands of peasants their vile trash
> By any indirection.—I did send
> To you for gold to pay my legions,
> Which you deni'd me.
>
> (IV, iii, 69-77)

These lines suggest that Shakespeare took more pains to emphasize Brutus' self-righteous inconsistency than to construct a credible speech.[15]

Finally, Shakespeare made Brutus alone responsible for the disaster at Philippi by attributing to his order (V, iii, 5) the fatal premature charge which lost the battle. Plutarch says that it was caused by the impatience of the troops. Brutus' failure is further emphasized by Cassius' speech protesting that he fights against his will (V, i, 71-89). The protest is taken from the source; but this speech, being much the longest in the entire act, focuses attention upon what Plutarch mentions in passing.

Brutus therefore emerges from Shakespeare's hand considerably shorn of the perfection which Plutarch gave him. The importance that one attaches to this shift of emphasis depends, of course, upon the view that one takes of the structure of the play. I must therefore confess my conviction that *Julius Caesar* is a well-constructed tragedy of which Brutus is the hero. The name is obviously irrelevant; for the respect due kingly rank made Shakespeare name a serious play after the reigning monarch as inevitably as his first printers placed a king's name at the head of the *dramatis personae*, no matter how slight his part in the

[15]Hunter calls Brutus "noble-hearted and sincere" but "intellectually dishonest." Cf. "Politics and Character in Shakespeare's 'Julius Caesar,' " p. 124.

action of the play, and we have noted that Shakespeare thought of Caesar as a ruler. In addition to the chronicle plays, one thinks of *Cymbeline* in this connection. *Hamlet* is no exception because, for Shakespeare, Claudius was a usurper and Hamlet, the rightful king. Caesar's share in the total action of the play does not prove him the hero, for it is no greater than Duncan's part before Macbeth murders him, seizes the throne, and incidentally gives his own name to the play. The watch of Caesar's ghost over the destruction of the conspirators might be likened to the lingering effects of Duncan's blood, not to mention Banquo's ghost. Tassin seems to me to summarize the matter very well, except that I should call the "great daemon" of Caesar the antagonist rather than the "spiritual hero," Antony being its subsidiary in the last as in the first half of the play:

That he [Shakespeare] intended Brutus to be regarded as the actual hero is obvious as early as the second scene of the first act. Instead of following Caesar to the games and beholding the superlatively picturesque and dramatic scene of the enforced refusal of the crown (a scene which must have required much self-restraint on Shakspere's part to forego), we get the effect of Casca's narration of it upon the two principal characters of the future conspiracy. Moreover, all the sympathetic side scenes, those apart from the main dramatic action, concern Brutus and are largely invented by Shakspere; and no dramatist so persistently builds the sympathy of his audience for anyone but his hero. Yet though Brutus is the actual and visible hero, it is not at all far-fetched to say, as has been said, that the spiritual hero is the "great daemon" of Caesar. And this interpretation Shakspere himself urges frequently by the mouth of his actual hero.[16]

Hunter seems at first glance to offer a valid objection to this view:

In the first scene of each of the great normal tragedies, the leading personage, if not brought directly on the stage, is introduced so prominently in the dialogue, as to leave the audience in no doubt as to the character on behalf of whom their interest and sympathies will principally be engaged. In the opening scene of "Julius Caesar" Brutus is not so much as mentioned; everything that is said or done has reference to Caesar.[17]

But examination will show that the opening scene and the first twenty-five lines of the second, before the stage is left to Brutus

---

[16]"Julius Caesar," pp. 255-56.
[17]"Politics and Character in Shakespeare's 'Julius Caesar,'" pp. 115-16.

and Cassius, actually constitute the scene of excitement and bustle with which Shakespeare liked to open his plays and which normally precedes the appearance of the hero. One misses only the usual preliminary discussion of the hero by minor characters, and such a discussion would be pointless without the exposition which is contained in the opening scene. In *Hamlet*, too, we hear nothing but the name of the hero before his appearance in the second scene.

If it be granted that Brutus is the real hero, the changes in characterization fit into an orderly pattern, and the play proves to be worked out in terms of two sets of ideas that we have already encountered: Shakespeare's political theory and his concept of moral choice.

The very first scene develops the political background for the play. In Plutarch the images were decked by Caesar's flatterers "to allure the common people to call him king, instead of dictator." The tribunes, "meeting with them that first saluted Caesar as king . . . committed them to prison." The people rejoiced at this defence of Roman liberty.[18] For Shakespeare all this simply had no meaning. The images are decked for Caesar's triumph over Pompey, and the tribunes are moved by loyalty to the fallen leader. The people are a fickle rabble, as in so many of the plays. As Sir Mark Hunter observed in a stimulating essay on "Politics and Character in Shakespeare's 'Julius Caesar,'" "Liberty" as an end in itself had no meaning for Shakespeare, obedience being the chief virtue in his political philosophy. Brutus' reliance upon liberty as the basis of his own thinking and in his appeal to the people is simply self-deception. This the people themselves make clear when they respond to his oration by saying, "Let him be Caesar" (III, ii, 56), and Antony's oration depends for its effect upon the contrast between his appeal to Caesar's good deeds and Brutus' nebulous charge that Caesar was ambitious.

As the play progresses, we are introduced to a Roman state organized in the hierarchical fashion that Tudor theory prescribed. Phillips calls attention to what Artemidorus is thinking of when he speaks of

---

[18]"Brutus," *Four Lives from North's Plutarch*, p. 119; "Julius Caesar," ibid., p. 102. Cf. MacCallum, *Shakespeare's Roman Plays*, p. 206.

The throng that follows Caesar at the heels,
Of senators, of praetors, common suitors.

(II, iv, 34-35)

Here we have the degrees of society that should wait upon a
monarch, arranged in proper order.[19] Caesar is still, in fact though
not in name, what Margaret called him in *3 Henry VI* (III, i, 17)
—a king. And he has for Shakespeare the sanctity that surrounds
a king.

Antony's soliloquy after the assassination therefore parallels,
both in its thought and in its correct forecasting of events, the
Bishop of Carlisle's great speech in *Richard II* (IV, i, 114-49).
Antony speaks more briefly and with some adjustment of his
words to a Roman and non-Christian world, but his thought, too,
is based on the Homilies:

> O, pardon me, thou bleeding piece of earth,
> That I am meek and gentle with these butchers!
> Thou art the ruins of the noblest man
> That ever lived in the tide of times.
> Woe to the hands that shed this costly blood!
> Over thy wounds now do I prophesy
> Which, like dumb mouths, do ope their ruby lips
> To beg the voice and utterance of my tongue:
> A curse shall light upon the limbs of men;
> Domestic fury and fierce civil strife
> Shall cumber all the parts of Italy;
> Blood and destruction shall be so in use
> And dreadful objects so familiar
> That mothers shall but smile when they behold
> Their infants quartered with the hands of war;
> All pity chok'd with custom of fell deeds;
> And Caesar's spirit, ranging for revenge,
> With Ate by his side come hot from hell,
> Shall in these confines with a monarch's voice
> Cry "Havoc," and let slip the dogs of war,
> That this foul deed shall smell above the earth
> With carrion men, groaning for burial.

(III, i, 254-75)

This civil strife involves even Brutus and Cassius, and it is no
accident that our first view of them after Caesar's funeral finds
them involved in a bitter quarrel and that their final defeat results
from their inability to work together.

[19]*The State in Shakespeare's Greek and Roman Plays*, p. 179.

The conspirators also add their testimony that Shakespeare regarded Caesar as a monarch. They do not justify their attack, as in Plutarch, only on the grounds that he wanted to be king. They repeat the word "king," it is true; but, like all Shakespeare's regicides, they add "tyrant" and "tyranny." "And why should Caesar be a tyrant then?" asks Cassius (I, iii, 103).[20] "Liberty! Freedom! Tyranny is dead!" proclaims Cinna as Caesar is stabbed (III, i, 78). The first plebian concedes, "This Caesar was a tyrant" (III, ii, 74). And young Cato boasts three distinctions: he is "the son of Marcus Cato, ho! a foe to tyrants, and my country's friend" (V, iv, 4-5).

Shakespeare's Tudor absolutism was therefore at complete odds with Plutarch's idealization of Brutus as the epitome of the old republican virtues. That Shakespeare approached his source with the presuppositions of his own times is not surprising. What does mark his intellectual development is the fact that he was able to read Plutarch with such sympathetic understanding and to portray Brutus, not as a villain, but as a tragic hero, whose sin was the error of judgment of a great and virtuous man. Brutus is the first of Shakespeare's superb tragic figures who fail through false moral choice.

In attempting to dramatize a moral choice, Shakespeare was breaking new ground, just as he had done in trying to show the development of Hal from hellion to worthy king. But this time he had adequate precedent, which he used. Later on, in discussing *Macbeth*, we shall have occasion to note that, in its treatment of sin in conventional Christian terms, it ends a line of progression from the late medieval moralities through Marlowe's *Faustus*. I do not mean to assert that Shakespeare knew and used one of the moralities, but rather that a living dramatic tradition leads from them to him. There is a similar progress in dramatic technique from the moralities through *Faustus* to *Julius Caesar*. The moralities were fundamentally allegories of moral choice. In *The Castle of Perseverance*,[21] for example, mankind enters describing his birth "this night." He is attended by a good and a bad angel, who debate for control of him. He yields to

[20]Cf. also I, iii, 93, 99, and the whole purpose of Cassius' speeches.

[21]Reprinted in part in Adams, *Chief Pre-Shakespearean Dramas*, pp. 265-87; the entire text appears in *The Macro Plays*, ed. Furnivall and Pollard, pp. 76-186.

the bad angel and accepts the seven deadly sins. But Shrift and Penance win him back to the Castle of Perseverance, which is assaulted by Pride, Wrath, and Envy, who conduct a running debate with the virtues Meekness, Patience, and Charity until they are beaten back. The subsequent action, in which all ends happily and virtuously, need not concern us. Enough has been said to show several things. A conflict is presumed to go on in the soul of any man confronted with a choice between moral conduct and temptation. This conflict is presented in the form of a debate between good and bad angels and between virtues and vices, who personify and externalize the *psychomachia* which descended to Christian ethics from Plato and Aristotle. This concept of morality is implicit in the New Testament word for sin, *hamartia* ("missing the mark"), which is, incidentally, the term used by Aristotle for the tragic hero's flaw. The psychology involved was formulated in Christian terms, I believe, by Augustine in his *De Libero Arbitrio*, and from him it descended to subsequent thinkers, among them Hooker. To return to drama, the next important step in the treatment of this "war of the soul" was taken by Marlowe, who attempted in *Faustus* to present the spiritual biography of a scholar driven by the sin of despair to ultimate damnation. The good and evil angels still appear, but the good angel states sound doctrine, which Faustus does not understand. It is likely, therefore, that the angels are now intended to present the struggle between God and Satan for the soul of man rather than to externalize moral tension. Marlowe keeps within the mind of his hero the conflict that leads to false choice. He presents it in a long soliloquy. Since Shakespeare probably borrowed his technique in *Julius Caesar* from this soliloquy, it is worth examining.

Faustus is presented in his study. After rejecting philosophy, physic, and law as pursuits, he turns to divinity.

> When all is done, Divinitie is best.
> *Jeromes* Bible, *Faustus*, view it well.
> *Stipendium peccati mors est*: ha, *Stipendium, &c.*
> The reward of sinne is death: thats hard.
> *Si peccasse negamus, fallimur, & nulla est in nobis veritas.*
> If we say that we have no sinne,
> We deceive our selves, and theres no truth in us.
> Why then belike

We must sinne, and so consequently die.
I, we must die an everlasting death:
What doctrine call you this, *Che sera, sera,*
What wil be, shall be? Divinitie, adieu,
These Metaphisickes of Magicians,
And Negromantike bookes are heavenly:
Lines, circles, sceanes, letters and characters:
I, these are those that *Faustus* most desires.   (ll. 65-80)

In choosing magic in preference to divinity and therefore committing his soul to Lucifer, Faustus of course sins, though not irreparably as he imagines. Marlowe presents him as making this wrong choice because of fallacious reasoning based upon culpable ignorance. He ignores the grace and mercy of God, and his ultimate destruction comes about because he continues to despair of God's mercy. This emphasis upon the danger of despair was, of course, a medieval and Renaissance commonplace. In *The Faerie Queene* Despair personified urges upon Red Cross exactly the same arguments that Faustus uses, and Una, in her only outburst of anger, exposes their falsity: "In heavenly mercies has thou not a part?" (I, ix, 53). Marlowe has a subtler way of implying the same fallacy. As a basis of his reasoning, Faustus quotes part of two key texts, which the audience undoubtedly knew. But they also knew the rest of the texts, which Faustus does not quote. Completing his quotations exposes his error. "The reward of sin is death, (but the gift of God is eternal life, through Jesus Christ our Lord"—Romans vi:23). "If we say that we have no sin, we deceive ourselves, and there is no truth in us. (If we confess our sins, he is faithful and just to forgive us our sins, and to cleanse us from all unrighteousness"—I John i: 8-9.)[22] From Faustus' false choice in this passage, and from his failure to correct it, resulted his final descent to Hell.

Shakespeare presents Brutus' false choice in a famous soliloquy (II, i, 10-34) that has been a puzzle to scholars.[23] But it does not seem to me particularly difficult if Marlowe's technique and Shakespeare's political views are kept in mind. Like Marlowe, Shakespeare expected his audience to detect a fallacy in reasoning. Many other writers of his time expected the same thing, includ-

[22]Cf. Mahood, *Poetry and Humanism*, p. 69.
[23]Note Charlton's sound reading of the soliloquy (*Shakespearian Tragedy*, p. 77).

ing Spenser, Chapman,[24] and Milton. A very instructive essay could be written, in fact, on the use of the logical fallacy by Renaissance authors as an expository device, and on the resulting confusion of modern readers less trained in dialectic. But Shakespeare was unable to place such clear signposts within Brutus' soliloquy as Marlowe had provided for Faustus; so he warned the audience in advance. Cassius plies Brutus with suggestions throughout a scene which is punctuated by shouts as Caesar is being offered the crown offstage; then he concludes with a soliloquy in which he explains how he proposes to win Brutus over to his scheme:

> Well, Brutus, thou are noble; yet, I see,
> Thy honorable metal may be wrought
> From that it is dispos'd; therefore it is meet
> That noble minds keep ever with their likes;
> For who so firm that cannot be seduc'd?
> Caesar doth bear me hard, but he loves Brutus.
> If I were Brutus now and he were Cassius,
> He should not humour me. I will this night,
> In several hands, in at his windows throw,
> As if they came from several citizens,
> Writings all tending to the great opinion
> That Rome holds of his name; wherein obscurely
> Caesar's ambition shall be glanced at;
> And after this let Caesar seat him sure,
> For we will shake him, or worse days endure.
>
> (I, ii, 312-26)

In short, Brutus is noble but proud of his reputation as a descendant of the Brutus who expelled the last kings of Rome, and pride is the most insidious of the passions that spring from man's sensible appetite. Upon that vanity Cassius proposes to work by throwing into Brutus' window messages purporting to come from various citizens. By the time of Brutus' soliloquy his scheme is taking effect.

As numerous writers upon Shakespeare and poetic drama have reminded us, quite rightly, his technique is one of suggestion rather than of complete representation. There was no need for him to portray the entire mental struggle leading up to a crucial

[24]With Faustus and Julius Caesar, cf. Bussy D'Ambois, where the initial exposition of Bussy's character depends on the fact that he states sound moral doctrine in his opening soliloquy (I, i, 1-33) and then violates these principles as soon as Monsieur offers him gold.

choice, but he did have to imply how it came about convincingly enough to stimulate the imagination of his audience. He might attempt to parallel all stages of the inner conflict. That he did in *Othello*, with somewhat doubtful success. Or he might present the climax of the struggle, giving only a hint of what had gone before. This is his method in *Julius Caesar*, as it is in *Macbeth* and, with variations, in *King Lear*. The first line of Brutus' soliloquy resumes an interrupted process of cogitation. "It must be by his death." Two assumptions are implicit in this remark. Caesar can be prevented from being king only by killing him, and killing a ruler is justified only if he is a tyrant. The former was axiomatic to anyone with a knowledge either of English history or of Machiavelli, and it is explicit in Brutus' first words. The latter should have been clear to the audience, since Cassius had just harped throughout the preceding scene on the weakness of those who submit to tyrants. It is clearly implied by the reasoning throughout the soliloquy. Having established his premises, Brutus continues:

> It must be by his death; and for my part,
> I know no personal cause to spurn at him
> But for the general. He would be crown'd:
> How that might change his nature, there's the question.
> It is the bright day that brings forth the adder,
> And that craves wary walking. Crown him? That—
> And then, I grant, we put a sting in him
> That at his will he may do danger with.
> Th' abuse of greatness is when it disjoins
> Remorse from power; and, to speak truth of Caesar,
> I have not known when his affections sway'd
> More than his reason. But 'tis a common proof
> That lowliness is young Ambition's ladder,
> Whereto the climber-upward turns his face;
> But when he once attains the upmost round,
> He then unto the ladder turns his back,
> Looks in the clouds, scorning the base degrees
> By which he did ascend. So Caesar may;
> Then, lest he may, prevent. And, since the quarrel
> Will bear no colour for the thing he is,
> Fashion it thus: that what he is, augmented,
> Would run to these and these extremities;
> And therefore think him as a serpent's egg
> Which, hatch'd, would, as his kind, grow mischievous,
> And kill him in the shell.   (II, i, 10-34)

His meaning is somewhat as follows. I have no personal grievance; so, if I act, it must be for the Roman people. The question that I must answer is whether crowning Caesar might change his nature. If we crown him, we give him the power to do great harm. But he will do harm and abuse his greatness only if he uses power without remorse (that is, without a moral sense). But, to speak truthfully, Caesar has never let his affections win control over his reason (in other words, he has never shown any inclination to irrational and immoral conduct). But it is common experience that humility is merely the ladder to ambition (ambition was for the Elizabethans a vice). Once the climber has achieved his ambition, he scorns the humility by which he ascended. Caesar may do so; therefore anticipate him. And, *since his present conduct gives no warrant whatever* for concluding that he will be a tyrant and therefore for killing him, assume that, once he gains absolute power, he will proceed to extremities; and kill him to prevent what he may become, as one would destroy a serpent's egg because a serpent is, by nature, dangerous.

Shakespeare has done his best to make the fallacies in the reasoning obvious. Brutus says explicitly that he has no evidence to support the conclusion that Caesar will become immoral and that he must kill on an assumption without basis; he ends by remarking that one destroys a serpent's egg because it is the "kind" (nature) of a serpent to be poisonous, but he has opened by observing that Caesar will be a tyrant only if crowning him changes his nature. His error in assuming that he is acting for the Roman people is proved by later events.

I take it that Brutus' doubling back upon his previous reasoning, as he does in the last seven lines, is intended by Shakespeare to suggest that his mind is still not made up at the end of the soliloquy. But there follows an appeal to his fatal weakness. Lucius reenters with another letter. Logic yields to pride, and reason becomes the tool of appetite. Brutus resolves upon action, and Caesar's doom is sealed. But Brutus has one further revelation to make. The process of choice has been agonizing:

> Since Cassius first did whet me against Caesar,
> I have not slept.
> Between the acting of a dreadful thing
> And the first motion, all the interim is

Like a phantasma or a hideous dream.
The Genius and the mortal instruments
Are then in council; and the state of a man,
Like to a little kingdom, suffers then
The nature of an insurrection.   (II, i, 61-69)

To make assurance doubly sure, Shakespeare, through Brutus, points out that an insurrection has occurred: passion has overturned reason. But this agony in retrospect is a little unconvincing. In *Othello* and *Macbeth* Shakespeare showed, during the choice itself, the full agony that his heroes suffered.

From Brutus' decision followed action. As a result of the killing of Caesar chaos engulfed all Rome, and discord and then death overwhelmed Brutus and Cassius themselves.

This kind of scene was new to Shakespeare and indeed, so far as I know, to all drama except for *Faustus*. A choice that involves moral issues is, of course, fundamental to most serious action. It underlies Antigone's defiance of Creon or Bolingbroke's deposition of Richard II. What was new was the attempt to make the act of choice an important part of the play and to work it out in detail according to accepted psychological theory. Shakespeare motivates his action by a formal scene of moral choice.

In comparison with the chronicle plays just preceding it and even with the comedies contemporary with it, *Julius Caesar* is remarkable as being the first Shakespearean play in which the motivation is really adequate and in which we become acquainted with the characters through their mental processes as well as through their actions. There are a few loose ends such as Brutus' unexplained and very imprudent departure before Antony's funeral oration. But Brutus nearly always has reasons for what he does, and those reasons, whether sound or unsound, reveal his character and carry forward the action of the play. The same generalization might be made about both Caesar and Cassius. This change has been accomplished partly by concentration upon a smaller body of events and especially by giving a new importance to the soliloquy in the structure of the play. In fact, if the preceding analysis of Shakespeare's thinking is sound, the interpretation of the play as a whole turns upon the three key soliloquies by Cassius, Brutus, and Antony, and upon Antony's conventional summary speech over Brutus' body. Antony, in fact, is a little torn between his roles as dramatist's mouthpiece and as practical politician, and we are in danger of underestimating the significance of his soliloquy because we assign it only to the politician. For the same reason critics have generally overlooked the parallels between his funeral oration and Brutus' soliloquy. He actually uses the same evidence that Brutus mentions, and the people accept his conclusion as logical—which it is. In fact, Shakespeare failed to make his meaning as clear in this play as it is in *Lear* or *Antony and Cleopatra* or *Coriolanus*. Antony is too involved in the action to be an effective guide to the audience, and there is no chorus character to underscore the folly of the hero as do Kent and the Fool or Enobarbus or Menenius Agrippa. Perhaps Shakespeare also relied too heavily upon character contrast. For Cassius seems constantly to be used as a foil to Brutus, illustrating by contrast both the latter's virtue and his lack of worldly wisdom. Tassin writes that Shakespeare "seems much to have admired this vigorous, impulsive, and generous man."[25] So it seems in the final scenes of the play, but not in those before Brutus joins the conspiracy, where Cassius is motivated by envy. I suspect, therefore, that Cassius is the beneficiary, not of Shakespeare's affection but of his artistic design. He was trying primarily to illustrate Brutus' weaknesses by contrasting them in the final scenes with Cassius' practical ability and his generosity, just as in the early scenes and in Antony's final summary he used the dishonesty of Cassius' motives to emphasize Brutus' nobility.

The play is less clear than the later tragedies in another respect. Othello, Macbeth, and Lear not only confess that they have sinned but also recognize in specific terms the weakness that led them to err. Brutus acknowledges the might of Caesar before he dies, but he never sees how his own pride has helped to make that might effective.

Despite these defects, which Shakespeare learned to remedy, he showed magnificent control in working out his ideas by a slight manipulation of Plutarch's material. The same skill is illustrated by the play's easy command of a good deal of learning. Details from a variety of minor sources have been employed so

[25]"Julius Caesar," p. 268.

skillfully that one is unconscious of their intrusion. In addition to those already mentioned, an interesting echo of one of Montaigne's essays has been found in the last part of Brutus' oration,[26] although like all the suggested examples of Montaigne's influence before *The Tempest*, it is only close enough to be tantalizing but not to be indubitable. The rhetoric from Shakespeare's school days is used with extraordinary effectiveness both in fashioning the orations and in creating a style that "counterfeited that brief compendious manner of speech of the Lacedaemonians" to which Plutarch says that Brutus was addicted.[27] Whether Brutus' style also reflects the Stoic prose becoming fashionable in reaction against Ciceronianism there is no way of telling. In addition to handling the omens accurately in terms of the best contemporary learning, Shakespeare was careful to distinguish between their influence and men's free will. Cassius' famous lines are absolutely sound:

> Men at some time are masters of their fates;
> The fault, dear Brutus, is not in our stars,
> But in ourselves, that we are underlings.
>
> (I, ii, 139-41)

Cassius also delivers a string of Renaissance commonplaces on death (I, iii, 91-97) that remind one vaguely of Donne's sonnet "Death, be not proud." Finally, it is probable that Shakespeare intended to characterize Cassius as a melancholy malcontent of the type much discussed at the time and familiar enough in drama. Plutarch applies Caesar's remark that he feared "lean and whitely-faced fellows" (which is given in the lives of both Caesar and Brutus) to Brutus and Cassius jointly, but Shakespeare applies it only to Cassius and adds details that were appropriate to the malcontent (cf. I, ii, 194-210).[28]

But the significance of *Julius Caesar* for the development of Shakespeare's thought lies not in these details but in its use of a formula which appears in all the great tragedies except *Hamlet* —a formula for tragedy of moral choice, which is somewhat as follows. During the dramatic exposition three things are accomplished. The dilemma facing the hero is explained, as in *Julius*

[26]Arden *Julius Caesar*, III, ii, 27.
[27]"Brutus," *Four Lives from North's Plutarch*, p. 113.
[28]Cf. Harrison, "An Essay on Elizabethan Melancholy," pp. 64-67.

Caesar, or a situation is developed which will confront the hero with the necessity of making a fundamental choice, as in the remaining plays. A character is presented who for his own reasons wishes the hero to make a false choice. He may be the antagonist, as are Iago and, in a sense, the tribunes in *Coriolanus* and Goneril and Regan in *Lear;* or he may be a collaborator like Cassius, Lady Macbeth, or Cleopatra. This character explains, generally in a soliloquy, the weakness that predisposes the hero to make a false choice (in *Antony and Cleopatra* this function is given to Philo in the opening speech). As the next step, in violation of all probability the actual choice is made in a single scene, the most improbable of all being that in which Othello enters speaking of his devotion to Desdemona and exits resolved to murder her. The false moral choice then leads to a decisive act, and from that act results the hero's downfall. Every hero except Brutus recognizes and states explicitly the full extent of his error.

That the hero's downfall results from irrationality Shakespeare is at pains to make clear. One or more characters repeatedly point out the folly of the hero's ways. In *Julius Caesar* Cassius and Antony both do so, as we have noted; in *Othello* Iago and Emilia (at the end of the play); in *King Lear* Kent, Goneril and Regan, and the Fool; in *Macbeth* Banquo; in *Antony and Cleopatra* Enobarbus; in *Coriolanus* Menenius Agrippa and Volumnia. One of these figures—Antony, Emilia, Banquo, Kent, Enobarbus, and Volumnia—stigmatizes the choice itself as false either when it is made or shortly thereafter. It is also interesting that, as we move from concern with the individual in *Othello* to *Macbeth,* which emphasizes the individual but presents the social order, to *Lear,* which considers both social and universal order, the scene of moral choice moves forward. In *Othello* it is Act III, scene iii, the climax of the play; in *Macbeth,* Act I, scene vii; in *Lear,* Act I, scene i, which telescopes exposition of the false choice, decisive act, and explanation of character weaknesses into the opening scene, so that the entire play may be devoted to consequences. There is, furthermore, a technical development in these tragedies paralleling that in the early chronicles. The plays up through *Macbeth* depend heavily on self-revelation through soliloquies and asides; *Antony and Cleopatra* and *Coriolanus* are almost free of these devices. *Antony and Cleopatra* is carelessly put together in other respects, but *Coriolanus,* though lacking power to grip the audience, is one of Shakespeare's most carefully constructed plays. This formula that was worked out in *Julius Caesar,* and even the elaborate use of self-revelation, grew out of the system of ideas to which Shakespeare was to give expression in *Troilus and Cressida.* It enabled the tragedies to absorb the learning which was too much for *Troilus and Cressida* and to achieve a perfect fusion of thought and action.

CHAPTER XI

Hamlet

I N *Julius Caesar* Shakespeare worked from a superb source
which furnished him both a scheme for his plot and elaborate
characterization. He was therefore able to devote his full
attention to a kind of character motivation that he had not
achieved before and to building one of his most carefully constructed plots. To his audience he presented not only the actions
but even the very soul of his hero. In *Hamlet* he worked with a
source that probably had less character analysis to offer but more
action. He kept the action, but upon it he superimposed a hero
whose inner struggle was more profound than Brutus' and even
more fully displayed to view.

This change in Hamlet's character completed the evolution in
Shakespeare's method of building a play that had begun in *Julius
Caesar*. Even in that play, he had followed the main outline of
the story in his source, with only enough changes to adapt the
action to his view of Caesar and Brutus. He had also found an
inner conflict in Plutarch and had merely altered the moral issues
to fit his own preconceptions. But in *Hamlet* he decided what
kind of a character he wanted and adapted his source to it, making
fundamental changes in the structure of the plot itself. In *Hamlet*
this process is, of course, hypothetical, being based upon a reconstruction of the source; but it is remarkably confirmed by *Macbeth* and *Lear*, for which the sources are available and in which
the alterations made to produce an internal conflict within the
hero are so obvious as to be inescapable. This change of method
was of such importance that it will be necessary to consider in
some detail what Shakespeare probably did to his source in
Hamlet. The following discussion will therefore rest upon my

reconstruction of the old play from extant versions. But before one can attempt to infer the content of the *"Ur-Hamlet,"* one has to work out the relationship among the surviving versions of the story. I have followed the theory most commonly accepted, but, as always in Shakespearean criticism, there are dissenters of such standing that their objections require consideration. Both arguing and reconstructing involve an enormous mass of detail. I have therefore tried to spare the long-suffering reader by taking my reconstruction of the lost play for granted in the present chapter, except that I have illustrated the main points by occasional references to the different extant versions of the Hamlet material. More curious or less trustful readers will find the reconstruction worked out in an Appendix.

Our knowledge of the background of Shakespeare's *Hamlet* rests upon the following facts, which it will be necessary to recapitulate before discussing the play. The non-dramatic source seems to have been Belleforest's *Histoires Tragiques* (1582), which derived the story from the *Historiae Danicae* of Saxo Grammaticus. Since the earliest English translation of Belleforest's version appeared in 1608 and contained echoes of our present play, Shakespeare must have used the French if, as is unlikely in view of his handling of *The Troublesome Raigne,* he consulted a non-dramatic source. There are references to a Hamlet play in Nashe's "Epistle" to Greene's *Menaphon* (1589); in Henslowe's *Diary* under date of June 11, 1594, where it is not indicated as new; in Lodge's *Wit's Miserie* (1596); and in a number of subsequent references to the ghost's "Hamlet, revenge," which is not paralleled in the extant *Hamlet* and seems to have become a byword.[1] On the basis of Nashe's allusion to "the Kidde in Aesop" this play has often been ascribed to Kyd. In 1603 there was published a quarto *The Tragicall Historie of Hamlet Prince of Denmarke* by William Shakespeare. This text (Q1) is now universally regarded as one of the "stolne, and surreptitious copies" to which Heminge and Condell alluded. It abbreviates and perverts or even replaces the accepted text, but it seems to be derived from that text or one parallel to it. It calls

[1] Cf. Chambers, *William Shakespeare,* I, 411-12; New Cambridge *Hamlet,* pp. xv-xxi.

the chief counselor Corambus, however; and it differs in three important details of plot, two of which involve a different view of Gertrude's character. In 1604 came a second quarto (Q2) giving the fullest text of the play that we have. It was reprinted several times. The folio version (F1) was obviously not printed from the quarto both because it differs constantly in verbal detail and because it omits several hundred lines in Q2 and adds somewhat less than one hundred that are not in Q2. Finally, there is a German *Tragoedia Der bestrafte Brudermord oder Prinz Hamlet aus Dännemark*, which survives in a manuscript dated 1710 but may well be derived from a Hamlet play presented by English players "at Dresden in 1626, and possibly at Danzig in 1616."[2]

In discussions of *Hamlet* and its relationship to the old play, two pertinent facts have often been lost sight of. Shakespeare's plays all present so many loose ends that no hypothesis could possibly explain every puzzling detail in our text of *Hamlet*. Our best guide to his probable rehandling of the source play is what he did in deriving *King John* from *The Troublesome Raigne*. His practice in *Measure for Measure* is less significant, because *Promus and Cassandra* was an older and inferior play. The slighter evidence that it provides confirms the inferences drawn from *King John*. Their bearing will become apparent during what follows. As a matter of fact, while Shakespeare was making Hamlet the most interesting character in all literature, he also made as bad a mess of the motivation in his source as he did in converting *The Troublesome Raigne* into *King John*.

Both Q1 and Q2-F1 share four principal differences from other versions of the Hamlet story. Each of these changes has implications for the development of Shakespeare's thought, but each has left its scar upon the play. (1) External barriers to Hamlet's revenge have been removed. (2) Hamlet has been isolated. (3) The ghost has been Christianized and made to contribute to Hamlet's mental conflict by its very nature as well as by its revelations. (4) Polonius, Ophelia, and Laertes have been developed as a family group. The old play related them but never showed all three of them together.

[2]Chambers, op cit., I, 408-409, 422.

(1) Removing the guards upon which the Hamlet of the *Brudermord* lays such stress was, of course, Shakespeare's fundamental change. Karl Young has summarized admirably what Shakespeare did, although he has perhaps overstressed the effect of Gertrude's adultery and minimized Hamlet's other problems:

For Shakespeare's Hamlet the essential dramatic conflict is no longer with external circumstances but with inner distress. The external obstacles are gone. Hamlet explicitly assures us that he has the strength and means, and he repeatedly denounces himself for not using them. The essential consideration for Hamlet, then, is not the physical pursuit of Claudius and the achieving of vengeance upon his murderer. Hamlet's problem is how to readjust oneself to a world in which one's mother can commit adultery. For a son in this predicament what is the remedy? What will repair for him the ruined moral order? Surely not vengeance. The darkness that has settled over the beauty of Hamlet's world cannot be dispersed by the mere destruction of a life or two —or by any other means. For Shakespeare, then, the external matter of revenge has receded into unimportance. Shakespeare's passion is spent not in curious devices showing how an avenger might *act*, but in appalled contemplation of what an injured soul must *endure*.[3]

But Hamlet not only feels and endures; he thinks. And Shakespeare has made him see his problems in terms of the moral order of the universe and of the theology and psychology of his day. In his intellectuality and in his inner struggle he is allied to Brutus, and in the vividness with which he describes that struggle he is akin to Macbeth.[4] But he far surpasses all Shakespeare's great tragic characters in his wonderful combination of feeling and thought as he faces his mother's sin, the ghost and all that it implies, and finally his own nature. We shall presently consider the fund of ideas that he uses.

Removing the guards made Hamlet a much subtler character, but it also eliminated all reason for the assumed madness, which the source motivated as an attempt on his part to get past the king's guards by seeming a harmless lunatic. As a heritage from the riddling Hamblet of Belleforest, there was method in the madness. It therefore aroused Claudius' suspicions and was actually a source of danger. It is no wonder that critics have argued

[3]"The Shakespeare Skeptics," p. 387. Charlton M. Lewis puts it: "He [Shakespeare] was interested in effects of character and will, not of muscle and agility" (*The Genesis of Hamlet*, p. 81).

[4]Cf. Bradley, *Shakespearean Tragedy*, p. 82. The parallel to *Macbeth* is notorious.

either that the madness was real or that it was feigned because Hamlet felt his reason giving way.[5] The feigned madness is as unmotivated as the poisoning of King John, and for a similar reason.

(2) In *Der bestrafte Brudermord*, Horatio is Hamlet's confidant and support from the first appearance of the ghost. It is clear that such was the situation in the old play and that Shakespeare deliberately increased Hamlet's physical and spiritual isolation from his fellows by depriving him of Horatio's sympathy and understanding in the crucial scenes of the play. In Shakespeare's first scene Horatio's function parallels that in the old play. He is familiar with the armor that the late king wore when he fought Norway, and he gives Marcellus and Bernardo (and the audience) a long account of "our late king." Yet in the very next scene Hamlet asks him three times why he has come from Wittenberg (I, ii, 164, 168, 174), repeating the question as though his presence were quite inexplicable; and, speaking of the dead king, Horatio says, "I saw him once," as though it were not to be expected that he had done so. Later he repeats "I knew your father" as though Hamlet would be in doubt of the fact. In short, Shakespeare is now thinking of Horatio as a college friend of Hamlet's whose presence in Denmark requires explanation. Later Hamlet tells Horatio that he disapproves of the heavy drinking at court "though I am native here" (I, iv, 14). He refuses, furthermore, to confide what the ghost has said (I, v, 117-40). Yet just before the play scene he speaks to Horatio of "the circumstance which I have told thee of my father's death" (III, ii, 81-82).

It is customary to speak of Horatio as "plot-ridden" and to explain these inconsistencies as resulting from his function as dramatist's mouthpiece in interpreting the play to the audience. I should prefer to say that he is "source-ridden," the victim of Shakespeare's failure to assimilate all the elements in the old play to his new design, so that Horatio is a stranger when Hamlet is to be isolated, but resumes his former role just before the public revelation of Claudius' guilt makes possible conversation about it. Hamlet's loneliness after he has seen the ghost is emphasized by

[5]Cf. Wilson, *What Happens in Hamlet*, p. 92; Granville-Barker, *Prefaces to Shakespeare*, I, 30-31.

the successive betrayals of Rosencrantz and Guildenstern and of Ophelia. But his isolation produces another and more important effect. Being unable to confide in anyone, he must speak to the audience in soliloquies, and the inevitable result is that he seems the most introspective, as well as the most intellectual, of Shakespeare's characters. It might be argued whether he seems introspective because he soliloquizes or soliloquizes because Shakespeare meant him to be introspective. Obviously Shakespeare intended the latter, for he deliberately deprived Hamlet of the customary confidant furnished by the old play. In the *Brudermord* Hamlet discusses with Horatio each step that he takes.

(3) Modern critics have said so much about the theological background of the ghost that no explanation is necessary here.[6] By converting the revenge ghost of his source into a figure to be dealt with in terms of the best learning of the day—the only one in Elizabethan drama—Shakespeare showed how much of that learning he was mastering himself. But he also produced two important effects upon his play. First, he enormously increased its impact upon the audience. Schücking comments upon Shakespeare's failure to use his customary technique of having other characters prepare for the hero's appearance.[7] This omission was doubtless intended to increase Hamlet's isolation when he first appears in black in contrast to the whole court, but it also enabled Shakespeare to concentrate all his energies upon building up the effect produced by the ghost.[8] He gave the audience a series of shocks. He replaced his usual opening bustle by an appearance of the ghost, which must have been at least equally effective in capturing attention. Then, instead of proceeding immediately to the ghost's revelation, he brought forward the first court scene, which made it abundantly clear that all was not well. The effect of the ghost's second appearance—this time to an audience curiously aware that something is wrong—is so powerful that the most blasé modern spectators will start. But Hamlet's ensuing words must have given the original audience a final and overwhelming shock:

[6]Cf. Chapter i. See also Spalding, *Elizabethan Demonology*, pp. 53-61.
[7]Cf. Schücking, *The Meaning of Hamlet*, pp. 71-72.
[8]C. S. Lewis has an appreciation of the horror and mystery of the ghost in *Hamlet: The Prince or the Poem*, p. 11.

> Angels and ministers of grace defend us!
> Be thou a spirit of health or goblin damn'd
> Bring with thee airs from heaven or blasts from hell,
> Be thy intents wicked or charitable,
> Thou com'st in such a questionable shape
> That I will speak to thee.　　　　(I, iv, 39-44)

This was no stage convention but either an angel or a devil, almost certainly the latter; and, like Hamlet, the spectators were face to face with hell itself—a hell in which they really believed.[9] Horatio emphasized the effect still further by enumerating the various devices by which a devil masquerading as a ghost might be expected to lure body to death and soul to damnation (I, iv, 69-78).

But in bringing into his play the Christian scheme of salvation and damnation Shakespeare also compelled Hamlet to reckon with it, and that was certainly his primary motive. The problem was no longer merely that of the *Brudermord* and presumably of the old play—whether the ghost was right. Hamlet had to dovetail his conduct into the Christian scheme of life and death and retribution. He must keep in mind

> The indiscover'd country from whose bourn
> No traveller returns

(including the real spirits of the dead, as he well knew); and the fearful prospect of punishment to which every man's own conscience bears witness "does make cowards of us all" (III, i, 79-83). Hamlet returned to the point just before the play, as he had done several times before:

> If his occulted guilt
> Do not itself unkennel in one speech,
> It is a damned ghost that we have seen,
> And my imaginations are as foul
> As Vulcan's stithy.　　　　(III, ii, 85-89)

The old problem whether the ghost was right had become a problem whether the ghost was damned—a shift of emphasis and especially of implication. But Hamlet's first rational words after the play scene accept only the ghost's veracity: "O good Horatio,

---

[9] On the audience, cf. Dover Wilson, *The Essential Shakespeare*, pp. 17-18. Schücking contrasts Hamlet's horror and the violence of his reaction with the calmness of Shakespeare's other heroes in the presence of ghosts (*The Meaning of Hamlet*, p. 84).

I'll take the ghost's word for a thousand pound." In short, giving the ghost a Christian context added immeasurably to Hamlet's inner conflict. In my opinion, in fact, Hamlet's language in the first three acts shows that the ghost is the primary source of his inner conflict, not so much because of its revelation that his father has been murdered as because of the undiscovered country, the world of ultimate values, with which it keeps him face to face. At any rate, this new kind of ghost gave to the play a moral dimension of which previous revenge plays had been innocent, if a thoroughly unmoral kind of drama may be described as innocent of anything.

But here again Shakespeare did not completely adapt the source action to his new design. The ghost, after all, told the truth. Logically, if Hamlet was to be morally bound to follow its instructions, it must be an angel masquerading as a ghost or the spirit of the dead divinely permitted to return from Purgatory, and one must admit that its tender and charitable concern for Gertrude hardly seemed diabolical. But somehow it is unthinkable that an angel should command revenge, and the play seems never to contemplate that possibility. The ghost itself spoke as the *bona fide* spirit of the departed; but that meant nothing, for it had to do so as a condition of its pretending to be a ghost, which was by definition, though not by theology, the soul of the dead. But no Protestant could admit that the spirit of the dead might return, since Purgatory was ruled out and heaven and hell were closed to departure. Dover Wilson argues that Shakespeare intended to entertain as a possibility the Catholic view that the real ghost might return from Purgatory,[10] but Hamlet's express words seem to refute that argument, since he always thinks in terms of the alternative "spirit of health or goblin damned" and of a hereafter "from whose bourn no traveller returns." The explanation seems to be that once again Shakespeare altered his source enough to make his point but not enough to achieve complete logical consistency. In the source the ghost told the truth. Shakespeare failed to work out in theological terms why the theological ghost that he presented should have done so. Why should he worry about consistency when no one in the audience would have time or energy to do so?

[10]*What Happens in Hamlet*, pp. 61-71.

But there was perhaps a genuine reason why he did not work out all the implications of his Christian ghost—and let me warn the reader that I am embarking on mere speculation. What would have happened to Hamlet's inner conflict if Shakespeare had taken a definite position? If the ghost was indeed the spirit of a loving father or an angel from heaven, Hamlet's delay involved disobeying the command of God as well as the conventions of men, and his continued inner turmoil was physical cowardice, no more. Nor does this tragic life ordinarily furnish us with such certainty. Hamlet knew only that the ghost was honest in that it told the truth, and his inner distress manifestly continued, whatever view one takes of the prayer scene or of his actions after his return. Perhaps for the same reason Shakespeare avoided facing a related problem—namely, the righteousness of the revenge itself. Belleforest is careful to explain at length that Hamblet was justified in killing Fengon despite the Christian veto of revenge: "... but if I lay handes upon Fengon, it will neither be fellonie nor treason, hee being neither my king nor my lord, but I shall justly punish him as my subject, that hath disloyaly behaved himselfe against his lord and soveraigne prince."[11] Later Belleforest discusses at some length Biblical precedents for avenging injuries done to a king. In making the uncle a usurper as in the *Brudermord* rather than a joint ruler as in Belleforest, the old play had made the issue much clearer; and it may be that Shakespeare expected the audience to take for granted that Hamlet, as the rightful king, was executing retributive justice upon Claudius and not the sort of revenge prohibited by his religion.[12] Perhaps, on the other hand, Shakespeare wished to leave open another area of mental conflict. Hamlet's words to Horatio, spoken at the very end of the play, imply doubt rather than certainty:

> Does it not, thinks 't thee, stand me now upon—
> He that hath kill'd my king and whor'd my mother,
> Popp'd in between th' election and my hopes,
> Thrown out his angle for my proper life,
> And with such cozenage—is't not perfect conscience,
> To quit him with this arm?   (V, ii, 63-68)

[11]*The Sources of Hamlet*, pp. 224-27.
[12]On Hamlet's right to the throne cf. Wilson, *What Happens in Hamlet*, pp. 30-37.

(4) About Shakespeare's change in showing Polonius, Laertes, and Ophelia as a family group little need be said. It was in line with his habit of giving all his characters as much humanity as possible, and it strengthened the parallel between the main plot and the subplot by establishing Laertes as Polonius' son and preparing for the violence of his reaction to his father's death. Shakespeare seems also to have been responsible for Laertes' instigating a revolt instead of coming directly to the king, as in the *Brudermord*. If so, he added both a further revelation that there were no external barriers to Hamlet's revenge and a proof by contrast that caution showed wisdom. But the new family ties aroused a sympathy for Ophelia that laid emphasis upon the problem of Hamlet's attitude toward her, so that his language to her seems justified by her role in Belleforest rather than by her character in the play. Her appearances in the *Brudermord* suggest that Shakespeare must have made considerable changes from the source play; he obviously changed her death from suicide to drowning and forgot to alter the priest's remarks (V, i, 249). We may perhaps speculate that her part was at one time less inconsistent with Hamlet's insults or with some of her own lines in the mad scene. Shakespeare's handling of his sources in the comedies demonstrates that he would probably have eliminated any implication of immorality in a woman occupying an important role.

So far we have been considering changes common to Q1 and Q2-F1. It is, of course, impossible to compare the two versions in details of text, because of the way in which Q1 was put together. In addition to the name Corambus for Polonius, as in the *Brudermord*, it shows three major differences: (1) the nunnery scene immediately follows its planning and precedes Hamlet's dialogue with Polonius (II, ii, 170-223), appropriate changes being made in the linking dialogue; (2) during the closet scene Hamlet reaches an understanding with his mother, who promises to aid him; (3) in place of IV, vi, where Horatio reads Hamlet's letter, and of V, ii, 1-74, where Hamlet narrates his escape, Q1 substitutes an account of Hamlet's journey which Horatio gives the Queen. Since this scene assumes Gertrude's knowledge and approval of Hamlet's plans for revenge, the third change is a corollary of the second if Q1 represents an earlier version.

It seems reasonable to assume, for reasons explained in the Appendix, that the arrangement of the *Brudermord* and Q1 obtained in the source and in a first Shakespearean draft. If so, Shakespeare's subsequent rearrangement of the nunnery scene was a logical extension of his isolation of Hamlet and his development of Ophelia, for it made her treachery to him follow the betrayal by Rosencrantz and Guildenstern as his climactic disappointment. It also separated preparation for the play within a play from the performance, thereby building suspense, and it made possible a swift reversal from disappointment to triumph of the sort that Shakespeare loved. The fact that the present arrangement seems exactly right should not blind us to the possibility that it may once have been otherwise. Many another playwright has improved his play after seeing it staged. But these improvements left the inevitable loose end. As I argue in the Appendix, Hamlet calls Polonius a bawd and refers insultingly to his daughter (II, ii, 174-87) because he is continuing the imagery and the insults of the nunnery scene, which in Q1 just precedes the conversation with Polonius. This is a much simpler explanation than the lost entry on the inner stage which Wilson assumes at II, ii, 158, so that Hamlet can hear Polonius speak of "loosing" his daughter to him and make that the basis of his innuendos.

Shakespeare's revision of the Q1 closet scene to eliminate Hamlet's understanding with his mother only carried to its logical conclusion the artistic design which underlay all his revisions. It made Gertrude consistently weak and sensual, it eliminated an important episode in the play which suggested that fear of external danger was a deterrent to Hamlet's revenge, and it extended his isolation from the first half of the play on into the final scenes by limiting him to one confidant (Horatio) instead of two. But, above all, it concentrated a key scene of the play upon the nature and cause of sin itself. This emphasis reflects the relationship between *Hamlet* and *Troilus and Cressida*. It also adds another intellectual dimension to the play.

The cumulative effect of all Shakespeare's changes was therefore to make Hamlet the man more thoughtful and *Hamlet* the play more thought-filled. Of the four original changes from the source play only the consolidation of Polonius' family failed to contribute markedly to these effects. The others—removing the guards that barred Hamlet from revenge, partly separating Horatio from Hamlet, and giving the ghost a theological background —all gave the story new intellectual depth. The revisions made by Shakespeare for his second version (Q2-F1) further isolated Hamlet and centered a key scene on an ethical problem rather than on plot development. It is no wonder that the play reveals a good deal of Shakespeare's knowledge and that ideas are an inseparable part of the action.

The atmosphere of thought which pervades *Hamlet* is really due to four inter-related systems of ideas: the Christian scheme of reward and punishment to which the ghost belongs; the ordered universe which it calls into question; the traditional interpretation of sin; and the Tudor concept of the kingship. The last three of these have been considered in connection with other plays; but the first, or at least an extensive use of it, is a new element in Shakespeare's thought. It immediately raises two problems which must be considered as a preliminary to discussing the ideas themselves —the unknown influence of the old play upon Shakespeare's thinking and the distinction between what his characters say and what he himself believes.

No lost document would add so much to our understanding of Shakespeare as the old *Hamlet*. Not only would it be an invaluable clue to his dramatic technique, but it would also enable us to see what kind of stimulus produced the *Hamlet* that we know. Several of the ideas that seem to us most characteristic of Shakespeare were almost certainly in the old play. The closet scene occupies an even more important part in Belleforest's narrative than in our play, and its influence can be traced in four of Shakespeare's scenes.

Hamlet's disillusionment and his disgust at his mother's conduct, as well as the concept of sin that is so prominent in his thinking, are summed up in his first soliloquy:

> Why she, even she—
> O God! a beast, that wants discourse of reason,
> Would have mourn'd longer—married with mine uncle,
> My father's brother, but no more like my father
> Than I to Hercules.   (I, ii, 149-53)

This comparison of Gertrude's action to that of a beast parallels Belleforest's closet scene closely: "Is this the part of a queene, and daughter to a king? to live like a brute beast (and like a mare that yieldeth her bodie to the horse that hath beaten hir companion awaye), to followe the pleasure of an abhominable king that hath murthered a farre more honester and better man than himself in massacring Horvendile, the honor and glory of the Danes."[13] Hamblet returns to the analogy with beasts twice again. There is, however, no reference to "discourse of reason." The *Brudermord* contains still another parallel to Hamlet's first soliloquy: "How could you, then, so soon forget him? Fie, for shame! Almost on the same day you had the burial and the nuptials."[14] But this speech also occurs in its closet scene. The implications of this fact are important. Obviously the old play had an elaborate closet scene that retained much of Belleforest's material and added striking points of its own. Shakespeare probably drew the parallels to Belleforest in his four soliloquies from the closet scene of the old play. This would mean, in turn, that a powerful scene in his source stimulated his thinking in *Hamlet* much as the Bastard's final speech in *The Troublesome Raigne* was elaborated in *King John* and *Richard II*.

To return to the three remaining passages that reflect Belleforest, Hamlet's words to Gertrude during Shakespeare's own closet scene resemble the French in emphasizing both her sensuality and the contrast between the two men and in exhorting her to repent. Q1 still further parallels Belleforest in making her promise to aid Hamlet, although she swears that she knew nothing of the murder, whereas in Belleforest, where the murder is public knowledge, she says that she acted under compulsion. Hamlet's soliloquy "How all occasions do inform against me" (IV, iv, 32-66) contains references to Fortinbras which Shakespeare must have introduced. Otherwise it parallels the last part of Hamblet's speech to his mother. But in the French he tells her that he "must stay the time, meanes, and occasion."[15] Shakespeare, having removed all external barriers, writes: "I have cause and will and strength and means" (IV, iv, 45). Hamlet's only discussion of the propriety of his taking revenge (V, ii, 63-70) seems once again to reflect Belleforest. In his final speech to his mother Hamblet sums up his reasons for

---

[13]*The Sources of Hamlet*, pp. 210-11.

[14]III, v. Variorum *Hamlet*, II, 133. Note also that here *B.B.* cannot derive from Q2-F1, as Greg and Wilson argue. Cf. Appendix A.

[15]*The Sources of Hamlet*, pp. 216-17.

revenge and then argues that he may properly kill Fengon in just punishment.[16] In short, a considerable part of Hamlet's soliloquies, the very essence of Shakespeare's interpretation of his character, was apparently derived from the closet scene in the old play. Belleforest, however, does not display the preoccupation with the psychology of sin, with death and the life after death so characteristic of Shakespeare, although he taxes Gertrude with being "a vile wanton adultresse" and enlarges upon her sensuality. One speech from the *Brudermord* considers the possibility of death and may be related to "To be or not to be." How much of this element was in the old play, and how much did Shakespeare add? There is no telling.

Another major element in Hamlet's character is shown by the *Brudermord* to have been part of the old play. Just after he first appears and before he sees the ghost, Hamlet says to Horatio: "Alas, Horatio! I know not why it is that since my father's death I am all the time so sick at heart, while my royal mother has so soon forgotten him, and this King still sooner."[17] In the scene equivalent to Shakespeare's second the King tells Hamlet: "See here, how your lady mother is grieved and troubled at your melancholy."[18] Hamlet's melancholy is alluded to several times again, but he and Horatio never use it, as Hamlet does in Shakespeare, as a basis for the doubt of the ghost which in the *Brudermord* they both express. It is certainly not improbable that a play written about 1589 should exploit melancholy. The doctrine of the four humours was as old as Greek medicine, and the publication of Bright's *Treatise of Melancholie* in 1586 shows that interest in the subject had begun to increase well before 1589. Melancholy was characteristic of Hamlet in the old play. How much use was made of it, and whether it was tied in with his doubt of the ghost, we shall probably never know.

It is very likely, therefore, that the old play stimulated Shakespeare to develop an intellectual element in *Hamlet* and that it furnished a good many of the ideas that he used. It is even possible that Gertrude's sensuality interested him in the technical examination of love that is so important a part of *Troilus and Cressida*.

---

[16]Ibid., pp. 224-27.
[17]I, iv. Variorum *Hamlet*, II, 124.
[18]I, vii. Ibid., II, 126.

To many lovers of Shakespeare these suggestions would seem both heresy and blasphemy; but they should not surprise anyone who recognizes the stimulus to his thought demonstrably furnished by *The Troublesome Raigne*. There is a real possibility that the old *Hamlet* faced some of the moral and intellectual problems that it raised as soon as it combined a doubtful ghost, a melancholy son, and a sinful mother, and that it led Shakespeare to face still more. That possibility is tantalizing.

The fact that important elements in the play are derived from the source should also put us on our guard against confusing what Hamlet said with what Shakespeare thought. If Hamlet takes a gloomy view of the contrast between man's deeds and his capacities, we can be sure that Shakespeare was familiar with similar ideas that were current in his age, but we cannot infer that he accepted them. Hamlet's melancholy is to be fathered, not upon him, but upon the writer of the old play. Nor can we infer that Shakespeare expressed all his learning upon any point. One could make a very good case for his being a Puritan on the basis of the concept of God implied by this play, but *Measure for Measure* would destroy one's case completely. Shakespeare states as much, and only as much, as is appropriate to the action of his play. The kind of ratiocination by which one develops the thought of a philosopher has no place in the exposition of *Hamlet*. Yet a tendency to read their own philosophizing into the play seems to overcome some modern critics as insidiously as a disposition to make Hamlet a victim of their own neuroses possessed the romantics.[19]

Turning to the ideas expressed in *Hamlet*, we have already noticed how the ghost becomes a key to the moral order of the play. Having explained it in Christian terms, Shakespeare was compelled to reconcile as much of the remaining action as possible with Christian values. Hamlet is deterred from suicide by the Almighty's "canon 'gainst self-slaughter"; he ponders his revenge and its attendant dangers with reference to an afterlife in which the guilty are punished; and his earth is set perilously between the immensities of heaven and hell. But important areas of Christian

[19]This tendency to develop implications of Shakespeare's thought seems to be a weakness in Theodore Spencer's otherwise excellent discussion of *Hamlet* in *Shakespeare and the Nature of Man*, pp. 93-109. Note especially his treatment of melancholy, pp. 98-99.

thought are missing completely. Hamlet invokes the grace and mercy of God in binding Horatio and Marcellus with an oath (I, v, 180); but elsewhere in the play neither God nor man knows mercy, and except in Claudius' prayer there is not a trace of the Christian doctrine that the grace of God is available to support feeble man in his warfare with the world, the flesh, and the devil. Here again the ghost is the key. However Christian his geographical background may be, his ethical climate is still the unmoral, or even immoral, world of the revenge play. As we have noted, only in one passage does Shakespeare face the fundamental clash between Christian ethics and revenge (V, ii, 63-70), and then inconclusively. The prayer scene brings his dilemma to a focus. The King reasons out in orthodox terms the religious basis of his prayer, and all that he says can be paralleled in the "Homily of Repentance."[20] God's mercy is available to wash away even a brother's blood, and prayer itself is but a request that God's grace may keep us from sin or bring forgiveness for sins committed. But God's pardon is contingent upon true repentance and upon restitution and reconciliation with the person wronged. Claudius is "still possessed of those effects" for which he murdered, and his "limed soul" therefore struggles in vain, as he well knows (III, iii, 36-72). His words are a kind of summary of what happened to Macbeth, but Macbeth becomes a great tragic figure because he foresees even before he murders what Claudius learns only by experience. But, even as Claudius prays, Hamlet stands with drawn sword, and his thinking has nothing to do with the essentials of Christianity. He dares not kill a praying man lest he run some chance, however slight, of saving that man from torment through all eternity. Revenge must be not only for this world but for the world to come, and the teachings of Christianity are merely rhetoric for giving a horrible exaggeration to the theme of vengeance. Shakespeare could not resolve the contradiction, even supposing that he faced it, without depriving himself of his play. But he could make Hamlet seem Christian, and he could use that illusion of religion wonderfully to motivate his inner conflict, just as he could use it to give his hesitancy a rightness and a moral basis in contrast to the unthinking blasphemy with which Laertes rushes on:

[20]Cf. *Certain Sermons or Homilies*, pp. 573-80.

To heel, allegiance! Vows, to the blackest devil!
Conscience and grace, to the profoundest pit!
I dare damnation. To this point I stand,
That both the worlds I give to negligence,
Let come what comes; only I'll be reveng'd
Most throughly for my father.

(IV, v, 131-36)

Despite his interest in ideas, Shakespeare was a dramatist and not a philosopher.

The ghost also brought Shakespeare face to face with universal order, although negatively. Horatio, the scholar, twice expounds the conventional view that the ghost, as a violation of the order of nature, portends some dire calamity. "This bodes some strange eruption in our state," he says (I, i, 68). Ghosts and other omens preceded the death of Caesar,

And even the like precurse of fierce events,
As harbingers preceding still the fates
And prologue to the omen coming on,
Have heaven and earth together demonstrated
Unto our climatures and countrymen.

(I, i, 121-25)

And, as everyone knows, Hamlet tells Horatio that there are even more things than his philosophy encompasses.

We feel, as I have several times remarked, that the entire play moves against the whole universe and heaven and hell as a background. More than the time is out of joint. It is therefore a little surprising to find that there are fewer explicit references to the concept of universal order in *Hamlet* than in the later chronicle plays. Laertes, as we have just seen, desires revenge to the extent "that both the worlds I give to negligence." Hamlet uses the same concept in trying to impress upon Rosencrantz and Guildenstern his melancholy. He paraphrases the conventional exaltation of both macrocosm and microcosm, and, as a melancholic should, he announces that he likes neither. I shall not do more than refer to Theodore Spencer's brilliant discussion of this passage (II, ii, 304-20),[21] except to point out that the view of man—"How like an angel in apprehension! How like a God!"—is a link between Shakespeare and Renaissance neo-Platonism. It reflects the concept of emanation from God to angels to men and on down to

---

[21]*Shakespeare and the Nature of Man*, pp. 98-100.

lower forms rather than scholastic doctrine, which made a sharp break between angels and even the rational soul.[22] It also suggests another Renaissance view that regarded the rational soul as completely separate from the sensible soul (sense and motion) whereas the scholastic tradition regarded it as containing within itself the two lower souls. The two notions are themselves inconsistent, although both are apparently of Platonic origin;[23] but Shakespeare's language itself is neither clear nor consistent, and I doubt that he had thought the matter through as opposed to reflecting popular ideas. He has, furthermore, assimilated the ideas to the medieval synthesis that was central to his thinking. Tillyard goes so far as to say of the passage: "Actually it is in the purest medieval tradition."[24] I think that he is wrong, but his error, if such it be, proves my point. How many modern dramatists, for that matter, keep their Freud straight? To take the entire passage too seriously is to miss its function in the play: one young college man is supposed to be impressing two others with a display of the latest jargon, and he is feigning a learned madness at the same time! Where Shakespeare got the jargon there is no telling. None of it suggests that he looked very far.

Roughly the same generalization can be made about the echoes of Stoicism in the play. Stoic thought appears in the Renaissance on two levels. In its more pervasive form it was an inseparable part of the synthesis that survived from the Middle Ages. It furnished, in fact, two fundamental concepts of morality: obedience to the laws of nature and subordination of the passions to reason. These notions, and also the medieval preoccupation with Fortune, were clarified and fortified for Elizabethans by their reading of Stoic writers, especially Seneca and Cicero's *Offices*, the standard school text on ethics. On the one point where Cicero differed from the Stoics—the duty of a good man to take part in public life— Shakespeare's contemporaries almost unanimously followed Cicero. But Stoic writings also caused a more definite reflection of

[22]Cf. St. Thomas Aquinas, *Summa Theologica*, Ia, Q. 75, A. 7; *Basic Writings*, I, 693-94. For Shakespeare's view cf. Robert Allott, *Wits Theater of the little World*, fol. 37ᵛ, where the rational soul is compared to an angel.

[23]In distinguishing between the reasonable soul as "bodilesse, and spirituall" and the other souls Juan Huarte takes Plato as his point of departure. Cf. *Examen de Ingenios. The Examination of mens Wits*, p. 88. But Bacon derived his similar separation from Telesius. Cf. *De Augmentis*, VII, iii (Vol. IV, 396-97).

[24]*The Elizabethan World Picture*, p. 1.

their attitudes and, at times, self-conscious adherence to their principles. Of this development the later plays of George Chapman—especially *The Revenge of Bussy D'Ambois* and *The Tragedy of Caesar and Pompey*—are examples.[25] But even professed exponents of Stoicism like Justus Lipsius adapt it to orthodox doctrines of God and causation,[26] so that its more specialized form also presents little conflict with traditional Christianity.

In his *The Counter-Renaissance* Haydn finds a great deal of Stoicism in the tragedies from *Hamlet* on. The preceding chapters have demonstrated, I hope, that much of what he regards as evidence is simply part of the system of ideas now fundamental to Shakespeare's thinking. Horatio says, to indicate that he plans suicide, "I am more an antique Roman than a Dane" (V, ii, 352). But this is probably an allusion to common Roman practice rather than to a doctrine. A few specific references do appear, but even these merge rapidly into the general pattern. In the following passage "readiness is all" is certainly Stoic doctrine, but Providence is hardly the Stoic Destiny. Lipsius, in fact, discusses the difference and, in an effort at reconciliation, regards Destiny as itself determined by God's providence (but hardly by special providence!):

There's a special providence in the fall of a sparrow. If it be now, 'tis not to come; if it be not to come, it will be now; if it be not now, yet it will come; the readiness is all. Since no man has aught of what he leaves, what is't to leave betimes? (V, ii, 230-35)

The associations of this passage are predominantly Christian, as Cunningham notes in his illuminating discussion of it. The same blending appears in the soliloquy "To be, or not to be," of which Haydn has an excellent explication.[27] To suffer the "slings and arrows of outrageous fortune" with constancy of mind and to find in death a relief from heartaches and shocks are Stoic commonplaces. "To sleep? Perchance to dream." And that thought brings Hamlet back to the Christian scheme of heaven, hell, and conscience (III, i, 56-88). In other passages that reflect doctrines once Stoic but now universal, he never leaves it.

[25]Cf. Wieler, *George Chapman—The Effect of Stoicism upon his Tragedies*, pp. 3-17, especially p. 9.

[26]Cf. Lipsius, *Two Bookes of Constancie*, ed. Kirk, pp. 37-46.

[27]Cf. Cunningham, *Woe or Wonder*, pp. 10-12; Haydn, *The Counter-Renaissance*, pp. 628-30.

The doctrine that right conduct consists in following reason is almost as fully developed as in *Troilus and Cressida*, and there is considerably more technical psychology than in the later play. Some of it is used with extraordinary power. Hamlet has found in Horatio a friend whose passions are under control:

> for thou hast been
> As one, in suffering all, that suffers nothing,
> A man that Fortune's buffets and rewards
> Hath ta'en with equal thanks; and blest are those
> Whose blood and judgment are so well commingled,
> That they are not a pipe for Fortune's finger
> To sound what stop she please. Give me that man
> That is not passion's slave, and I will wear him
> In my heart's core, ay, in my heart of heart,
> As I do thee. (III, ii, 70-79)

This passage, like that from Laertes cited above, is used to indicate a contrast of character fundamental to the play, this time between Horatio as a norm and Hamlet himself. But the play's use of this aspect of the psychology of the passions[28] appears, for the most part, in the closet scene, where Hamlet tries to analyse his mother's conduct. He finds it incredible for two reasons. First, she has made a false choice even on the level of sensual appetite, since his father was the better man. Since she can move and motion is a faculty of the sensible soul, her senses are still functioning. But even madness could not account for their causing such a false choice as she has made. Second, it is incredible that a woman of her age should let her passion—that is, lust—sway reason as it has done.

> Rebellious hell,
> If thou canst mutine in a matron's bones,
> To flaming youth let virtue be as wax
> And melt in her own fire. Proclaim no shame
> When the compulsive ardour gives the charge,
> Since frost itself as actively doth burn,
> And reason panders will. (III, iv, 82-88)

[28]For an analysis of Hamlet in terms of grief, cf. Campbell, *Shakespeare's Tragic Heroes*, pp. 109-47. She regards the passage just quoted as an expression of Shakespeare's theory of tragedy. But Paul (*The Royal Play of Macbeth*, pp. 10-13) prefers as a theory of tragedy a passage discussed below (I, iv, 23-36). Anderson has an interesting discussion of the occasions when Hamlet yields to passion in *Elizabethan Psychology and Shakespeare's Plays*, pp. 162-69.

All this is merely a more vivid statement of ideas that Shakespeare had used many times before, but another remark to Gertrude shows that he had really come to grips with the theory of sin before writing *Troilus and Cressida*:

> Assume a virtue, if you have it not.
> That monster, custom, who all sense doth eat
> Of habits evil, is angel yet in this,
> That to the use of actions fair and good
> He likewise gives a frock or livery,
> That aptly is put on. (III, iv, 160-65)

Shakespeare first states, and then reasons from, the doctrine that each false choice makes the next one easier and that a series of sins may therefore make the reason so liable to succumb to appetite that sin itself becomes a habit. This is the third of the three traditional reasons for sin, and it becomes the basis for Macbeth's actions during the last half of that play. Hamlet's exposition is specific where Hector's is general.

But the clearest proof that Shakespeare had been thinking deeply about the reasons for human sin is to be found in Hamlet's famous speech to Horatio just before he confronts the ghost:

> So, oft it chances in particular men,
> That for some vicious mole of nature in them
> As, in their birth—wherein they are not guilty,
> Since nature cannot choose his origin—
> By their o'ergrowth of some complexion
> Oft breaking down the pales and forts of reason,
> Or by some habit that too much o'er-leavens
> The form of plausive manners, that these men,
> Carrying, I say, the stamp of one defect,
> Being nature's livery, or fortune's star,—
> His virtues else—be they as pure as grace,
> As infinite as man may undergo—
> Shall in the general censure take corruption
> From that particular fault. (I, iv, 23-36)

Perhaps Shakespeare meant to imply by his confused and tortured sentence structure that Hamlet was baffled. Perhaps he was also a little puzzled himself. Notice how he considers the various possible causes of the "particular fault": first, a defect of birth— and he is clearly thinking not of original sin, wherein men *are* guilty, but of some defect of soul or body with which an individual is born; then a dominance of one of the four humours that breaks down reason; and finally habit. Forces breaking down the reason would lead to its loss of control, and therefore the last two causes that he imagines parallel two of the traditional explanations of sin—subordination of reason to appetite and a habit of sinning. "Nature's livery, or fortune's star" pairs natural law with a capricious astrological determinism as alternative explanations of the fault. "Fortune's Star" means the star that determines man's lot, and there is no such contradiction as we noticed in *Romeo and Juliet*. But the passage as a whole does not come to clear focus.

Shakespeare makes surprisingly little use in *Hamlet* of the views of the kingship that he developed in *Richard II, Henry IV,* and *Henry V*. A theory of social order is certainly implicit in the play, mostly in allusions to ways in which Denmark falls short of the ideal and in the atmosphere of watchful tension that surrounds so much of the action. But in this, as in so many respects, *Hamlet* stimulates interest by what it suggests rather than by what it explains. There is a reference or two to the king as the head of the state, and Claudius states in familiar terms the conventional doctrine of the divine right of kings (IV, v, 122-25). (Why, one wonders again, is it always Shakespeare's weak kings or his usurpers who appeal to their divine right? Is it merely coincidence, or was he skeptical of the doctrine?) Hamlet's father was a great warrior, but otherwise we learn remarkably little about his record as king.[29] Hamlet talks primarily of the difference between his father and Claudius as men rather than as rulers, perhaps because he is concerned with Gertrude's inexplicable conduct and he regards her as having judged sensually and therefore on the basis of personal appearance. Ironically enough, Claudius always shows himself an able and efficient king, and in handling Laertes he demonstrates both bravery and self-possession. Shakespeare needed to provide a formidable antagonist for his hero, even though, in doing so, he very nearly invalidated what Hamlet says about his uncle.

But enumerating lines of thought which Shakespeare devel-

---

[29] I cannot agree with Spencer that "Shakespeare deliberately puts Hamlet's situation in a political environment" (*Shakespeare and the Nature of Man,* p. 103). The source put Hamlet in a political setting which Shakespeare, except that he possibly added Fortinbras' appearance, did little if anything to develop.

oped in *Hamlet* obviously fails to account for the atmosphere of ideas which pervades the play. Only the treatment of the ghost, furthermore, opens a new vista in Shakespeare's learning, and only man's relation to sin and death is elaborated philosophically. The effect of thoughtfulness is probably to be explained by the large proportion of the play devoted to soliloquy and by the considerable number of lines that have no function except to express ideas. In many of them Shakespeare seems to be pursuing his own thought and to forget that he is writing for the stage. Apparently his company took a similar view, for it is interesting to examine the differences between Q2 and F1 on the assumption, which is very generally accepted, that the latter was cut down for stage performance. In F1 oaths have been toned down in accordance with the law of 1606 against stage profanity. A little of Polonius' verbiage has been excised, the speaking parts have been reduced in one scene, and a few other lines have been omitted for various reasons. But the bulk of the omissions consist of passages in which the words that advance the action have been retained but the philosophic digressions have been eliminated. These include the discussion between Bernardo and Horatio on omens (I, i, 108-25), the whole passage on reveling and "some vicious mole of nature" (I, iv, 17-38), Hamlet's psychological reasoning in the closet scene (III, iv, 71-76, 78-81), and his discussion of habit (III, iv, 161-65, 167-70). His promise to watch his two schoolfellows (III, iv, 202-10), a matter of action rather than thought, may have been removed when someone saw how inappropriate it was to the new version of the closet scene in which Hamlet did not trust Gertrude. The only considerable cut not so far listed is that in the fantastic dialogue between Hamlet and Osric (V, ii, 110-50). The new matter in F1 may have been omitted from Q2 for reasons of tact (e.g., II, ii, 244-76, 352-79). None of it is at all like the cuts in F1, which certainly suggest that someone thought that the philosophy got in the way of the drama. Incidentally, most of the passages that I have discussed in connection with the ideas in the play were among those cut.

It should now be apparent that *Julius Caesar* and *Hamlet*, which came close together in Shakespeare's development, are not only contrasting but complementary. In writing the former, he found in Plutarch an inner conflict leading to a fateful decision and a final downfall resulting from that decision. This material he built into a brilliantly constructed play by adjusting Brutus' character to his own view of history and working out his conception in soliloquy, dialogue, and action with an attention to motivation that he had not shown before. For *Hamlet* he found an old play with a wonderful plot, plenty of blood and noise, and a healthy young extrovert pitted against a villainous uncle surrounded by guards. There was, moreover, enough thinking to stimulate more. He must have wondered how he would feel if he saw his throne usurped, watched his mother sink to adultery and incest, and then heard, from a ghost who was probably a devil, that his father had been murdered and his uncle must be killed. (A good many critics might also wonder. Timorous college professors have been known to talk of Hamlet's delay as though they were Hotspurs accustomed to kill some six or seven dozen Scots at a breakfast.) As Shakespeare thought about the old play, he brought to bear upon it all that he had seen of human nature and all that he had heard or read about demonology, religion, and ethics. He soon realized that the guards amounted to nothing beside the moral difficulties —that Hamlet was in the same predicament as Brutus, except that his problem was infinitely more complicated. The issues were less clearly drawn, and there were more choices to be made. So Shakespeare changed the conflict from eluding the king's guards to the struggle of a human soul. That soul was perplexed by a lost throne, a sinful mother, and a murdered father; he was face to face with heaven and hell, but unsupported by a stable moral and social order or even by friends. The action was much too complicated to be worked out in terms of the neat formula that had been developed for *Julius Caesar*, where the outcome resulted from a single moral choice. In this fundamental respect, the source did determine the nature of the play and produce its greatness. Hamlet's world, like our own, was a series of confused and interacting choices made by a group of people. The play therefore fascinates us, even while it defies clear-cut interpretation. The other tragedies suggest laboratory experiments in their artistic—and artificial —concentration upon a single problem. *Hamlet* suggests the complexity of life.[30]

[30]Cf. Fergusson, *The Idea of a Theater*, pp. 98-115.

CHAPTER XII

Othello, Macbeth, King Lear

THE THREE tragedies which form the subject of this chapter are all worked out according to the formula used in *Julius Caesar*. But the weaknesses of method present in that play have largely been eliminated. Expository characters are unmistakable, and the heroes come to recognize their own shortcomings. *Othello*, *Macbeth*, and *King Lear* therefore show increasing technical virtuosity. Their significance for the development of Shakespeare's thought also lies in the skill with which they use ideas already familiar but do not break new ground. For the fusion of thought and action is achieved without the unresolved difficulties of *Hamlet*, and it is even more intimate than in *Julius Caesar*. The dramatist seems more at ease in handling his material. The three plays are based upon the "moral laws of nature and of nations" which Shakespeare outlined in *Troilus and Cressida*. Among them they cover the entire range of ideas involved, and, since *Othello* came first and the relative dates of *Macbeth* and *King Lear* are purely conjectural, they will be discussed in the order of their ascent from the particular to the general.

Othello is a study of sin in the private individual, worked out in terms of the theory of reason, will, and appetite. The larger context of this theory as part of a universal order is missing, except in so far as it is implied by two of Othello's speeches:

> Excellent wretch! Perdition catch my soul,
> But I do love thee! and when I love thee not,
> Chaos is come again.
>
> (III, iii, 90-92)

I have no wife.
O, insupportable! O heavy hour!
Methinks it should be now a huge eclipse
Of sun and moon, and that th' affrighted globe
Did yawn at alteration.

(V, ii, 97-101)

The first of these, like the similar line in *Venus and Adonis*
(1020),[1] paraphrases a Latin couplet of the Scottish humanist
Buchanan and would be without philosophical significance, were
it not made explicit by the second.

In *Macbeth* Shakespeare is again concerned with the causes
and consequences of an individual's sin. But the emphasis in the
first half is placed upon the false choice of an apparent good rather
than upon the passions as such, although they are, of course, involved; and the relentless tracking down of Macbeth's degeneration, as fear grips him and one crime leads to another and finally
to a "custom of evil," makes the play a unique study of sin itself.
Macbeth's sin is also shown as attended by a convulsion in nature
and as disrupting the social order in his kingdom. In *Lear* individual sin is seen primarily in terms of social disintegration and
violation of the fundamental laws of nature themselves; and man,
kingdom, and the universe all participate in the resulting chaos.
Lear removes us, furthermore, from the specifically Christian
atmosphere of *Macbeth* and even *Othello* to a world in which,
except for a few anachronisms, morality is based upon nature as
apart from Christian revelation.

Paralleling this movement from sin in man to chaos in nature is
a progression from the causes of sin to its consequences. In *Othello*
the act of moral choice comes at the climax of the play and the
crime itself in the last scene, so that consequences must be indicated swiftly. *Macbeth* is divided about equally between the
causes of sin and the degeneration of man and society to which it
leads. *Lear* presents the irrational act in the opening scene, and the
fundamental moral choice—the decision to divide the kingdom—
is revealed in retrospect even as Lear rushes on to a further immoral act, the disinheriting of Cordelia. This brilliant combination of exposition and action dominates the first scene, and the

---

[1]Baldwin, *On the Literary Genetics of Shakspere's Poems & Sonnets*, pp.
50-51.

play becomes an account of retribution and, in Lear himself, of regeneration. But, however different the focus of the plays, Othello, Macbeth, and Lear all come to realize the enormity of their mistake, Lear most fully of all.

The three plays have all been elaborately studied from the present point of view, and no attempt will be made to interpret them in detail or to appreciate their amazing richness of expression and of technique. Emphasis will be placed, rather, upon aspects of the individual play which illustrate the continuity or development of Shakespeare's thought. I hasten to add that I realize very well that Shakespeare was writing plays and not philosophic treatises and that character and action were more important to him than abstract ideas. I can only hope that I shall not mislead myself or the reader, and that it will become apparent that Shakespeare used ideas to interpret character and action and to give them meaning, just as we do habitually, even in our most aimless gossip.

For the story of Othello Shakespeare went to Giraldi Cintio's *Ecatommiti*.[2] The Moor's jealousy would have seemed to an Elizabethan a probable outcome of his heritage from a hot climate, and Shakespeare accepted the fact without stressing it. But he did try to make Othello's jealousy still more credible by one fundamental alteration. In the source the Moor and Disdemona have lived together happily for years, whereas Othello has had no time to acquire the intimate knowledge and trust which a happy marriage should bring. This change also enabled Shakespeare to introduce an account of their courtship, the implications of which we shall discuss later. His other important change is interesting in that it in effect cancelled the first. By adding the detail that Cassio had been given a promotion which Iago wanted, Shakespeare motivated Iago's jealousy of Cassio and his hatred of Othello, whereas in Cintio the Ensign was merely trying to discredit Disdemona so that he could have her for himself. But this variation also added a reason why Othello should suspect Iago to which no attention is paid in the play. Perhaps Shakespeare expected the insistence upon Iago's honesty to cover this difficulty; more likely he simply overlooked it as he did so many similar problems. From the source he derived an astonishing amount. Most of what he tells us about

[2]Chambers, *William Shakespeare*, I, 462. For reprints see Variorum *Othello*, pp. 377-89; Hazlitt, *Shakespeare's Library*, II, (Part I), 285-308.

Othello is there, and, aside from the additional motive for jealousy, Iago's distinguishing traits are all in the *Ecatommiti*.[3] Shakespeare's management of the handkerchief is much clumsier than Cintio's, but he undoubtedly substituted his version to save time and to avoid extra characters.

By reshaping the opening scenes of the play, Shakespeare also made possible the psychological analysis which underlies the action. Othello commits not only a murder but also a mortal sin, as he well recognizes:

> Will you, I pray, demand that demi-devil
> Why he hath thus ensnar'd my soul and body?
> (V, ii, 301-302)

This sin Shakespeare explains as resulting from a subversion of the reason by passion so that Othello believes Desdemona unchaste and then kills her on the false assumption that he is executing justice. As in *Measure for Measure*, the principles underlying the action are pushed to logical extremes, so that the psychological pattern is perfectly clear even if the resulting lack of plausibility has often puzzled critics thinking in more nearly modern terms. Three definite relationships of reason, will, and appetite are presented in the play. At the beginning Othello and Desdemona represent the ideal state of virtue in which reason controls the will. Iago represents a state of sin in which the will is in control and the reason is subservient to it. Other characters and finally Othello himself illustrate the working of the passions. The treatment of Iago comes, of course, primarily from dramatic tradition, and the passions are depicted with the conventional characteristics which Shakespeare could have derived from a number of works popular at the time.[4]

Shakespeare is at pains to establish the norm of rational control upon which "hell and night" in the person of Iago work, and he uses Iago himself for the purpose:

> The Moor is of a free and open nature,
> That thinks men honest that but seem to be so,
> And will as tenderly be led by th' nose
> As asses are.   (I, iii, 405-408)

[3]Cf. Schücking, *Character Problems in Shakespeare's Plays*, pp. 63-64.
[4]Cf. Campbell, *Shakespeare's Tragic Heroes*, pp. 148-74.

Schücking is right, of course, in remarking that these lines are intended simply to characterize Othello and show nothing about Iago's own moral capacities.[5] Equally significant are the comments which Shakespeare assigns to a number of characters toward the end of the play. After Othello strikes Desdemona, Lodovico exclaims:

> Is this the noble Moor whom our full Senate
> Call all in all sufficient? Is this the nature
> Whom passion could not shake? whose solid virtue
> The shot of accident nor dart of chance
> Could neither graze nor pierce?   (IV, i, 275-79)

Still later he says to Othello:

> O thou Othello, that wast once so good,
> Fall'n in the practice of a cursed slave.
>
> (V, ii, 291-92)

In the very presence of death Othello so describes himself:

> one not easily jealous, but, being wrought,
> Perplex'd in the extreme.   (V, ii, 345-46)

And Cassio echoes: "For he was great of heart" (V, ii, 361).

But the important thing is what is said at the beginning to guide the audience in interpreting the action, and Shakespeare is extraordinarily careful to show that Othello was not "passion's slave" by making clear that the love between Othello and Desdemona was governed by reason and not appetite.[6] It developed slowly as Desdemona came to know Othello and to value his worth so much that she overlooked his appearance. To this "marriage of true minds" blackness was no impediment. But Othello held back, and Desdemona finally took the initiative and gave him what, by understatement, he calls a "hint":

> Upon this hint I spake:
> She lov'd me for the dangers I had pass'd
> And I lov'd her that she did pity them.
>
> (I, iii, 166-69)

---

[5]*Character Problems in Shakespeare's Plays*, pp. 64-65.
[6]Cf. Campbell, *Shakespeare's Tragic Heroes*, pp. 155-56.

Most of Shakespeare's heroines have to bring their men to the point, but Othello's slowness was perhaps intended to reflect the unsureness upon which Iago was later to work. For the time being, however, Shakespeare used Othello's looks only to raise the love above the level of sense—and, of course, to give strangeness and romance to his play. Brabantio argued that it was incredible that Desdemona should "fall in love with what she fear'd to look on!" (I, iii, 98). And, as if to answer him, she explained:

> I saw Othello's visage in his mind,
> And to his honours and his valiant parts
> Did I my soul and fortunes consecrate.   (I, iii, 253-55)

Othello also went out of his way to explain that there was nothing sensual in his desire to take her with him to Cyprus:

> Vouch with me, Heaven, I therefore beg it not
> To please the palate of my appetite,
> Nor to comply with heat, the young affects
> In my defunct and proper satisfaction,
> But to be free and bounteous to her mind.   (I, iii, 262-66)

All this, and especially the technical language of the last passage quoted, can only mean that Shakespeare was trying to make sure that his audience regarded Othello as no slave of passion but a man whose reason was in complete control of his acts, a man who would be a test case of the power of jealousy. The logic is the same that was used to stigmatize the love of Troilus and Cressida as unworthy. Its use here further proves an awareness that the manner of falling in love had implications as to the kind of love involved.

Against Othello is pitted a "demi-devil"—that is, one in whom evil has become the controlling principle of conduct. Theologically this would have to mean one of two things. Either the individual had resisted the call of grace and had remained in a state of sin, so that the will had become habituated to evil and able to bend the reason to its own ends, or a series of sins had produced the same effect. This perversion of the reason to the service of the will constituted a state of mortal sin.[7] But actually the dramatic villain or Machiavel was simply assumed to be an absolute villain whose intelligence was directed toward achieving his evil purpose. Such a man was Richard III:

[7] Cf. Campbell, *Shakespeare's Tragic Heroes*, pp. 99-101, 157.

And therefore, since I cannot prove a lover
To entertain these fair well-spoken days,
I am determined to prove a villain
And hate the idle pleasures of these days.

(I, i, 28-31)

Shakespeare's growth in thought is therefore to be inferred from the difference between the lines just quoted and Iago's account of himself:

I have look'd upon the world for four times seven years; and since I could distinguish betwixt a benefit and an injury, I never found man that knew how to love himself.

Virtue! a fig! 'tis in ourselves that we are thus or thus. Our bodies are our gardens, to the which our wills are gardeners; so that if we will plant nettles or sow lettuce, set hyssop and weed up thyme, supply it with one gender of herbs or distract it with many, either to have it sterile with idleness or manured with industry, why, the power and corrigible authority of this lies in our wills. If the balance of our lives had not one scale of reason to poise another of sensuality, the blood and baseness of our natures would conduct us to most preposterous conclusions; but we have reason to cool our raging motions, our carnal stings, our unbitted lusts, whereof I take this that you call love to be a sect or scion. . . . It is merely a lust of the blood and a permission of the will.   (I, iii, 312-40)

Iago's character is founded upon pride or self-love, the very source of all sin. To quote the Homily for Whitsunday: "As for pride, St. Gregory saith 'it is the root of all mischief.' And St. Augustine's judgment is this, that it maketh men devils." Hooker, speaking of angels, explains why sin ultimately rested upon self-love: "It seemeth therefore that there was no other way for angels to sin, but by reflex of their understanding upon themselves; when being held with admiration of their own sublimity and honour, the memory of their subordination unto God and their dependency on him was drowned in this conceit; whereupon their adoration, love, and imitation of God could not choose but be also interrupted. The fall of angels therefore was pride."[8] With a nice sophistication Iago readjusts the accepted philosophy to his own wilfulness: reason must control the appetites, but so that they do

---

[8]*Certain Sermons or Homilies*, p. 497; Hooker, *Laws of Ecclesiastical Polity,* I, iv, 3; *Works,* I, 214.

not interfere with the will, to which the reason is therefore a servant. For him love can only be sensual, and it is he and not Othello who injects sensuality into the play.[9] Against Othello's rational good is counterpoised Iago's rational evil. This analysis of Iago's character also explains why his motives are so little stressed that some critics—quite unsoundly, I think—have doubted their validity. Reason needs only the flimsiest pretext—"the show of Reason," in Hooker's terms—for yielding its habitual assent; and there is no need to stress Iago's passions, since his will is already turned to evil and no struggle like Othello's is involved in his formulation of his schemes. In a sense, his role is like that of a Vice in the morality play to which Shakespeare's tragic scheme is analogous. Shakespeare assumes his villainy as a postulate of the play, just as he assumed Richard III to be wholly evil; but he gives a theologically tenable explanation of Iago's state of sin.

Upon the other characters Iago works by stimulating their passions. Roderigo becomes his dupe because love for Desdemona leads to jealousy and hatred of Othello and later of Cassio. Cassio is choleric and needs only to be persuaded to drink in defiance of his better judgment. Cassio's brawling leads, in turn, to Othello's first loss of control as he gives way to anger,[10] and he recognizes the danger of what is happening:

> Now, by heaven,
> My blood begins my safer guides to rule;
> And passion, having my best judgement collied,
> Assays to lead the way.
>
> (II, iii, 204-207)

Iago himself states with perfect simplicity and clarity his problem in attacking Othello. Incidentally, the first part of his statement looks like a survival of the source, since he makes no attempt upon Desdemona in the play:

> And nothing can or shall content my soul
> Till I am even'd with him, wife for wife;
> Or failing so, yet that I put the Moor
> At least into a jealousy so strong
> That judgement cannot cure.
>
> (II, i, 307-11)

[9]Stoll, "Othello the Man," p. 119.
[10]Campbell, *Shakespeare's Tragic Heroes*, pp. 160-61.

This preliminary exposition of Iago's scheme corresponds, of course, to Cassius' outline of his plan for seducing Brutus to his purpose; and, in depicting the actual overthrow of Othello's reason by jealousy, Shakespeare fell back upon much the same technique that he had used in *Julius Caesar.* Yet the difficulty of compressing into a single scene an intellectual choice in which vanity played a part was slight indeed beside that of showing the change from devoted and rational love to insane jealousy. Iago's first stroke comes immediately after Othello's strongest statement of his love for Desdemona—"when I love thee not, chaos is come again"—and by the end of the scene (III, iii) chaos has indeed come. Othello has given orders for Cassio's death, and he withdraws to find "some swift means of death for the fair devil" (III, iii, 477-78). This too swift reversal is, of course, another example of the play's tendency to push to their logical extremes the philosophic principles upon which it is based. Iago's method consists in repeated stimuli to Othello's imagination. This technique was thoroughly in accord with accepted ideas of the operation of jealousy.[11] But Shakespeare did try by a number of devices to make Othello's jealousy less improbable, and it has sometimes been overlooked how much he was concerned to provide acceptable motivation.

As in *Romeo and Juliet,* he first tried to cover any possible weakness in his plot by foreshadowing. Brabantio warns Othello:

> Look to her, Moor, if thou hast eyes to see;
> She has deceiv'd her father, and may thee.
>
> (I, iii, 293-94)

But here the foreshadowing is also the first incitement to jealousy and is correspondingly more effective than the Prologue in the earlier play. Shakespeare's departure from his source in making Othello newly married we have already noted, and Iago urges home the fact that Othello does not understand Venetian women and their ways and then adds another barb by citing as proof of their subtlety the skill with which Desdemona deceived her father (III, iii, 201-12).[12] Iago also urges upon Othello the unnaturalness of Desdemona's choosing him:

[11]Anderson, *Elizabethan Psychology and Shakespeare's Plays,* pp. 107-10.
[12]Bradley, *Shakespearean Tragedy,* pp. 192-93.

Not to affect many proposed matches
Of her own clime, complexion, and degree,
Whereto we see in all things nature tends—
Foh! one may smell in such, a will most rank,
Foul disproportion, thoughts unnatural.

(III, iii, 229-33)[13]

In arguing about Othello's race, it seems to me, critics have often missed the two effects which Shakespeare intended to get from Othello's color and which involve rather a barrier of sense than of race. Brabantio regards Othello as repulsive, as we have noted, and Desdemona, in turn, alludes more delicately to his "visage" as proof that her love is rational rather than sensual. Now, at least in Othello's poisoned mind, his color becomes a barrier between them that increases in importance exactly as his thinking moves from the plane of reason to that of appetite. For if Desdemona's love were governed by sense, then her affection for him would indeed be incredible, and Iago's constant sensual insinuations operate to increase the importance of Othello's blackness. That Othello's appearance is now weighing on his mind and that he thinks of Desdemona's love in terms of appetite rather than of reason he shows by his soliloquy after Iago's first departure:

If I do prove her haggard,
Though that her jesses were my dear heartstrings,
I'd whistle her off and let her down the wind
To prey at fortune. Haply, for I am black
And have not those soft parts for conversation
That chamberers have, or for I am declin'd
Into the vale of tears,—yet that's not much—
She's gone. I am abus'd; and my relief
Must be to loathe her. O curse of marriage,
That we can call these delicate creatures ours,
And not their appetites!

(III, iii, 260-70)

Finally, Othello's honor is at stake, and the importance of honor Shakespeare stresses continually. Cassio laments his loss of reputation rather than of his commission, and Iago's obviously cynical attempts to comfort him only emphasize his words. Iago urges the importance of honor upon Othello as part of his temptation:

[13]Cf. ibid., p. 201.

Good name in man and woman, dear my lord,
Is the immediate jewel of their souls. . . .
But he that filches from me my good name
Robs me of that which not enriches him,
And makes me poor indeed.   (III, iii, 155-56, 159-61)

To the connection between a man's honor and his wife's reputation all Elizabethan literature bears witness. Othello himself upbraids Desdemona for depriving him of honor before men and of
his own self-esteem (IV, ii, 48-62).

Shakespeare therefore tried valiantly to make Othello's jealousy convincing, and Stoll's argument that he relied upon a plot
convention by which the "calumniator" was believed seems to me
far less true of this play than of *Much Ado* or *Cymbeline*, where
the action turns upon statements of fact.[14] Here it rests upon the
plausibility of Iago's suggestions plus his statements of fact, and
the suggestions work far more powerfully than the facts, which
seem, indeed, to be confirmed by the rather unsatisfactory business of the handkerchief. Note, furthermore, that Othello accepts
such shaky evidence because it seems so probable. Once his thinking becomes centered upon sensual considerations, the probabilities are all against him, and that shift Iago achieved by his insinuations. Reason becomes the tool of passion, and Othello is, for the
time being, the counterpart of Iago in that his reason obeys his
passion-driven will. He even duplicates Iago's misdirected pride
and self-esteem. For, by the highest philosophic irony that Shakespeare ever achieved, the reason is still Othello's and preserves its
usual characteristics even while it "panders will." He talks about
justice and sacrifice (V, ii, 17, 65); he hates the deed that he must
do, and he wishes to avoid cruelty and to care for Desdemona's
soul (V, ii, 1-22). His methods are right, but his end is horribly
wrong. Once jealousy has been equated with justice, all follows
logically. And Shakespeare, as usual, labels Othello's error clearly.
In the very next scene after his moral choice Emilia attributes it
to jealousy (III, iv, 155-62), and Desdemona describes his symp-
toms all too clearly as he prepares to smother her (V, ii, 43-44).
Emilia is also used in the final scene to drive home the point that
Othello's crime has involved a failure of his reason: "O gull! O
dolt! As ignorant as dirt!" (V, ii, 163-4); "O thou dull Moor"

[14]*Othello: An Historical and Comparative Study*, pp. 15-23.

(225); "What should such a fool do with so good a wife" (233-34). The final scenes of *Othello* are almost a contrast to those of *Measure for Measure*, in that both plays illustrate the dreadful fallibility of human justice in the presence of human passions; but in the one mercy intervenes, in the other it fails. The parallel is a minor one, but perhaps worth noting as indicating the continuity of Shakespeare's thinking. In its main emphasis *Othello* returned, of course, to the theme which Shakespeare introduced in *Julius Caesar* and which he continued to exploit in the remaining tragedies, the importance of obedience to reason in all human conduct.

In *Othello* Shakespeare depicted the operation of jealousy so clearly that critical controversies have been confined to details. *Macbeth*, on the other hand, has been fundamentally misinterpreted by a majority of modern critics, because they were unaware of its philosophic basis. But Walter Clyde Curry's *Shakespeare's Philosophical Patterns*, one of the landmarks in the modern study of Shakespeare, has removed all excuse for misunderstanding the play, even though one may dissent from his interpretation in some details.

To the story of Macbeth Shakespeare was perhaps directed by Banquo's position as mythical ancestor of James I, just as he certainly drew upon the King's alleged experiences with witches for details of the witch scenes. He followed Holinshed closely for the opening events of the play, including the battles and the encounter with the "weird sisters," and for the downfall of Macbeth after the murder of Banquo. But, according to Holinshed, Macbeth was heir to the throne under Scottish law until Malcolm came of age and was supplanted by Duncan's nomination of Malcolm as his successor. Furthermore, Duncan was incompetent. Encouraged by the three weird sisters and by his wife, who "was verie ambitious, burning in unquenchable desire to beare the name of a queene,"[15] Macbeth consulted with his friends, including Banquo, rebelled with their aid, and killed Duncan openly. He reigned justly for ten years before he attempted to murder Banquo and Fleance. To make the crime secret and the murder therefore a matter of moral choice rather than of physical safety, Shakespeare introduced an earlier episode from Holinshed, in which one Don-

[15]Holinshed, II, 170; Boswell-Stone, *Shakespeare's Holinshed*, p. 25.

wald was urged by his wife to murder King Duff, who "was accustomed to lie most commonlie within the same castell, having a speciall trust in Donwald, as a man whom he never suspected."[16] They murdered Duff much as in the play, and Donwald attracted suspicion by killing the chamberlains and too vigorously protesting his horror of the deed. Important details in the characterization of both the principals—his secret ambition and his torturing conscience, her nagging and her first description of him—came from the accounts of Macbeth and of his great-great grandfather Kenneth in Buchanan's *Rerum Scoticarum Historia*.[17]

But Shakespeare did more than introduce a problem of moral choice such as he had used in *Julius Caesar* and *Othello*. Stimulated, perhaps, by the evil implications of the weird sisters, he made the play something very close to a study of sin itself, and he ended it with a promise by the new king to depend upon "the grace of Grace" (V, viii, 72-73). The phrase is an obvious paraphrase of "grace of God" made necessary by the law of 1606,[18] and it is Shakespeare's clearest reference to man's dependence upon God's co-operative grace sustaining him and working with him if he is to do good works. Malcolm declares, in effect, that Scotland has been delivered from the reign of sin. The pattern of the play is certainly illuminated—and may well have been suggested—by a passage in Hooker which has already been quoted in part but will stand repetition to develop the whole scheme:

For there was never sin committed, wherein a less good was not preferred before a greater, and that wilfully; which cannot be done without the singular disgrace of Nature, and the utter disturbance of that divine order, whereby the preeminence of chiefest acceptation is by the best things worthily challenged. There is not that good which concerneth us, but it hath evidence enough for itself, if Reason were diligent to search it out. Through neglect thereof, abused we are with the show of that which is not; sometimes the subtilty of Satan inveigling us as it did Eve, sometimes the hastiness of our Wills preventing the more considerate advice of sound Reason, as in the Apostles, when they no sooner saw what they liked not, but they forthwith were desirous of fire from heaven; sometimes the very custom of evil making the heart obdurate against whatsoever instructions to the contrary, as in them over whom our Saviour spake weeping, "O Jerusalem, how often, and thou wouldest not!"[19]

[16]Ibid., II, 150; p. 27.   [17]Paul, *The Royal Play of Macbeth*, pp. 213-19.
[18]Ibid., pp. 312-14.   [19]*Laws of Ecclesiastical Polity*, I, vii, 7; *Works*, I, 224.

In deciding to show not only how the "subtilty of Satan" and "hastiness" of will led to sin and to the "utter disturbance" of nature, but also how "the very custom of evil" hardened Macbeth's heart, Shakespeare committed himself to paying as much attention to the consequences of sin, both for the individual and for the order of nature, as to its causes, although he did not fail to demonstrate that what was good had "evidence enough for itself." The easiest way to illustrate the working out of these ideas in *Macbeth* is to analyse the development of the play. A kind of summary and commentary will therefore be attempted, at least for the first part, but it will be restricted to the underlying thought and will in no sense be a general interpretation of the play.

The management of the two witch scenes parallels strikingly the handling of the ghost scenes in *Hamlet*. The first merely opens the play and establishes its atmosphere of gloom and unnatural horror. As Spalding long ago pointed out, it portrays

the fag-end of a witches's sabbath, which, if fully represented, would bear a strong resemblance to the scene at the commencement of the fourth act. But a long scene on such a subject would be tedious and unmeaning at the commencement of the play. The audience is therefore left to assume that the witches have met, performed their conjurations, obtained from the evil spirits the information concerning Macbeth's career that they desired to obtain, and perhaps have been commanded by the fiends to perform the mission they subsequently carry through. All that is needed for the dramatic effect is a slight hint of probable diabolical interference, and that Macbeth is to be the special object of it; and this is done in as artistic a manner as is perhaps imaginable. In the first scene they obtain their information; in the second they utter their prediction. Every minute detail of these scenes is based upon the broad, recognized facts of witchcraft.[20]

This account is obviously right. Spalding argues that Shakespeare, although he retained the term "weird sisters" from Holinshed, thought of the creatures simply as witches; and his evidence seems to me conclusive both against the view that they are goddesses of destiny and against Curry's conjecture that they are devils impersonating witches.[21]

The witches owe their knowledge of the future and their power

[20]Spalding, *Elizabethan Demonology*, pp. 102-103.

[21]Cf. Spalding, op. cit., pp. 97-102. With Curry, *Shakespeare's Philosophical Patterns*, pp. 60-61, cf. Spalding, op. cit., pp. 100-102.

over the elements to the devils who are their familiars—Grey-malkin (cat), Paddock (toad or hedge-pig), and Harpier (owl). The owl had been associated with witchcraft by Ovid, and its shriek punctuates the play (II, ii, 3; II, iii, 63-64). The Old Man tells Ross that a mousing owl hawked at and killed a falcon, an obvious bit of symbolism since the falcon was a royal bird.[22] Actually the play ascribes to the witches, and therefore to the devils who serve them, a power that exceeds what orthodox demonology would allow. Demons could conjecture the future through their ability to "look into the seeds of time" (I, iii, 58), but they could not know it certainly or read men's minds. But Shakespeare uses only a slight exaggeration that is dramatically effective. The real significance of the witches in the play, however, is that they are agents of the external forces of evil. Human sin, as Hooker implies in the passage quoted, is caused either internally by the appetite or externally by the solicitation of Satan or of other men. Devils could not directly cause men to commit sin, which must involve the consent of the will, but could work only by suggesting an object to the appetite—that is, they operated by stimulating the internal causes of wrong-doing.[23]

The second witch scene, like the second ghost scene in *Hamlet*, carries the real burden of exposition. It is very carefully worked out. Banquo states the proper reaction to the witches and, in contrast to Macbeth, illustrates the rational norm somewhat as Horatio does in *Hamlet*. He continues this function until his murder, but in this scene he is also used to make sure that the audience does not miss any significant details. He first points out that the creatures cannot be women since they have beards, a distinguishing trait of witches (compare *The Merry Wives of Windsor*, IV, ii, 202-205). Next he calls attention to Macbeth's start at their prophecies and identifies accurately the source of their knowledge:

> If you can look into the seeds of time,
> And say which grain will grow and which will not,
> Speak to me, who neither beg nor fear
> Your favours nor your hate.   (I, iii, 58-61)

[22]Cf. Paul, *The Royal Play of Macbeth*, pp. 195, 265-68.

[23]Cf. St. Thomas Aquinas, *Summa Theologica*, Ia-IIae, Q. 80, A. 2-3; *Basic Writings*, II, 660-62.

When the witches' first prophecy is confirmed by the arrival of Ross, he comments: "What, can the devil speak true?" (I, iii, 107). And his words to Macbeth indicate the proper interpretation of what has happened:

> But 'tis strange;
> And oftentimes, to win us to our harm,
> The instruments of darkness tell us truths,
> Win us with honest trifles, to betray 's
> In deepest consequence.
>
> (I, iii, 122-26)

Macbeth's speech that follows establishes two significant things: first, his failure to brand the "supernatural soliciting" as absolutely evil, as Banquo has done, shows that the wiles of Satan and his legions, who work through the witches, are producing their intended effect; second, Macbeth's own appetite is powerfully stimulated, and the possibility of murder is already present in his imagination. Both external and internal causes of sin are therefore at work upon Macbeth. In short, Shakespeare took the fundamental knowledge of demonology which he displayed in *Hamlet*, details from witch trials in Scotland in which James was involved, and ideas from James's own *Daemonologie*; and he combined them to build for *Macbeth* a background of evil forces so explicitly defined that they center the play upon a moral problem just as the theological ghost intruded moral considerations into *Hamlet*.[24]

From the dilemma posed by his powerful desire to become king, Macbeth still has one escape: "If chance will have me King, why, chance may crown me without my stir" (I, iii, 143-44). This outlet is closed to him by Duncan's nomination of Malcolm as Prince of Cumberland and heir to the throne, and his temptation arises with renewed force:

> The Prince of Cumberland! That is a step
> On which I must fall down, or else o'erleap,
> For in my way it lies. Stars, hide your fires;
> Let not light see my black and deep desires;
> The eye wink at the hand; yet let that be
> Which the eye fears, when it is done, to see. (I, iv, 48-53)

[24] Cf. Spalding, *Elizabethan Demonology*, pp. 111-18. The *Daemonologie* and *Newes from Scotland* have been reprinted as Bodley Head Quarto No. IX.

In this aside, as throughout the play, Macbeth exemplifies a somewhat subtler and more sophisticated development of the same convention that Shakespeare used in portraying Richard III, who avowed his evil designs and labeled himself a villain in his opening soliloquy. Experience teaches that life's real criminals rationalize their actions somehow and do not regard themselves as especially sinful. But Macbeth is just as revealing as Richard, although somewhat less naïve in his analysis, in describing the progress of his temptation and in weighing his motives with a logical thoroughness more consistent with Shakespeare's interpretation of sin than with realism of character.[25] Some such convention was, of course, inevitable if drama was to be used for philosophic analysis of the actions of its characters or even if the dramatis personae were to explain their motives in terms intelligible to the audience.

Shakespeare next followed exactly the same pattern of moral choice that he had used in *Julius Caesar* and *Othello*, except that it was necessary to put the crucial scene earlier in the play. Lady Macbeth, like Cassius and Iago an agent of temptation, has a soliloquy in which she interprets Macbeth's character and builds a plan of attack. We must, I think, take her words at their face value. Macbeth is fundamentally great and good, in so far as mortals may be, and the greatness of his fall is commensurate with the greatness of his temptation. He is drawn in the same strong primary colors as Othello. He has already been established as brave; Lady Macbeth, in effect, adds the data that he is ambitious but is humane and has moral standards, qualities which are abundantly evident as he approaches his first crime even if they are not apparent in his soliloquy debating the murder (I, vii, 1-28). These qualities she recognizes without any appreciation of them, just as Iago describes Othello's virtues only to sneer at them. But we must never forget that, except for ambition, they are virtues. Macbeth is a great play precisely because it presents, with incredible imaginative intensity, the spectacle of a human being who is potentially both great and good and who, deliberately and in agony, chooses evil despite the most powerful warnings of his own conscience.

That Macbeth was intended by Shakespeare to have a con-

[25]Cf. Bethell, *Shakespeare & the Popular Dramatic Tradition*, pp. 73-75.

science there can be no doubt. In the passage from which came the voice that cried, "Sleep no more," Buchanan explains that Kenneth was disturbed by consciousness of his crime (*conscientia sceleris*).[26] Critics who deny Macbeth a conscience, furthermore, ignore the system of thought which underlies the play. They point out that his reasons for not killing Duncan involve fear of the consequences (I, vii, 7-25) and a desire for men's good opinion (I, vii, 31-32) rather than any aversion to the crime as such. Bradley makes a subtle distinction which involves the same fallacy: "His conscious or reflective mind, that is, moves chiefly among considerations of outward success and failure, while his inner being is convulsed by conscience."[27] But this contrast is based upon the ethics which Protestantism inherited from Luther and Calvin, who regarded man's nature as so totally depraved that moral conduct was possible only in the elect in whom God had implanted a new nature. Morality was therefore the result of a spiritual state. For Shakespeare this notion would have been meaningless (unless he had encountered it in Calvinist preaching). His moral system is based upon the operation of human reason, which, though fallen from its first perfection, is not ruined. For such an ethic prudential motives are as moral as any other—are, in fact, preeminently moral. Shakespeare learned as a boy that prudence was one of the four cardinal virtues, and his constant emphasis upon intelligence and right choice shows how completely he accepted that doctrine.

Macbeth, in short, has a conscience. He would not play false and yet would wrongly win, and therein lies his tragedy. He is not good enough to escape sin, but he is good enough to feel its horror and to imagine its consequences. Compared to him Lady Macbeth—if not, as Dr. Johnson called her, "merely detested"—is endowed with less intelligence and less goodness rather than with more strength. At the beginning of the play she accepts the witches' prophecy without a moment's reflection as to its implications; she counters Macbeth's horror after the murder with "a little water clears us of this deed"; at the end she lapses into sleep-walking while slowly and painfully he pays the full wages of sin. She is superbly drawn, but she is no

[26]Paul, *The Royal Play of Macbeth*, p. 216.
[27]*Shakespearean Tragedy*, p. 353.

titaness; she is a moral imbecile. To regard him as weak because he hesitates or to think her the greater of the two, as many writers have done, is a monstrous perversion both of Shakespeare's intentions and of the fundamental morality of any civilization.

Lady Macbeth, to whom morality means little, sees the problem of murdering Duncan primarily as one of wifely nagging:

> Hie thee hither
> That I may pour my spirits in thine ear,
> And chastise with the valour of my tongue
> All that impedes thee from the golden round
> Which fate and metaphysical aid doth seem
> To have thee crown'd withal.
>
> (I, v, 26-31)

But she does have some compunctions, as the violence of her next soliloquy seems to indicate. Curry argues that she is to be thought of as technically possessed by a demon.[28] This seems to me improbable because other characters who describe her — the physician, Macbeth, Malcolm — seem never to contemplate the possibility. The physician says merely that her heart is "sorely charg'd" and her mind infected by its secrets (V, i, 60, 80). His added "God, forgive us all" seems to imply that she needs a divine for absolution rather than for exorcism. Malcolm, in his final summary, calls her "fiend-like," and likeness logically excludes identity.

The scene of moral choice (I, vii) opens with a soliloquy which centers the action upon the subversion of reason into a false choice rather than upon the "soliciting" of ambition, which serves merely as a background. It also indicates that the process is already well under way in that Macbeth is prepared to "jump the life to come." But even the wisdom of this world—and, let it be said for him, its morality—argues against the deed: he is obligated to protect Duncan as his kinsman, his guest, and his king, and murder will provoke universal horror. Lady Macbeth enters and he therefore informs her: "We will proceed no further in this business" (I, vii, 31). In direct contrast to Iago, she makes no attempt to inflame his imagination and therefore his ambition; but she tries to persuade him, first, that he should do the murder

---

[28] *Shakespeare's Philosophical Patterns*, pp. 86-92.

because it befits his manhood—that is, that it is good—and, second, that he can carry it off. "The Will," says Hooker, "notwithstanding doth not incline to have or do that which the Reason teacheth to be good, unless the same do also teach it to be possible,"[29] and the scene follows this formula too closely for coincidence. Lady Macbeth's arguments that the murder is "good" are highly sophistic (and feminine): were you wrong when you first decided upon it? are you afraid? don't you love me enough? To which he replies:

> I dare do all that may become a man;
> Who dares do more is none.
>
> (I, vii, 46-47)

His remark is profoundly right both in recognizing the basis of her argument and in exposing its utter fallacy. But he is apparently overcome by her clever, though quite irrelevant, retort. At no point in the play is he represented as intellectually acute. His soliloquies describe frightful images; Hamlet's meditate logically. And the contrast is nicely adjusted to the strong warnings of Macbeth's conscience and the weak resistance of his intellect. So he tacitly accepts the argument that he should do the murder and shifts his ground to whether he can do it: "If we should fail?" (I, vii, 59). That the murder is possible Lady Macbeth has no trouble in demonstrating. Completely won, he expresses his admiration for her and even elaborates her scheme. But in his last words in the scene he evaluates the deed objectively, obviously speaking for Shakespeare, and perhaps for his own conscience:

> Away, and mock the time with fairest show;
> False face must hide what the false heart doth know.
>
> (I, vii, 81-82)

Two comments on this scene are perhaps in order. It is intended, as I remarked, to suggest that Macbeth has previously given a good deal of reflection to the problem. Like Brutus in

[29]*Laws of Ecclesiastical Polity*, I, vii, 5; *Works*, I, 222. My attention was first called to this parallel between Hooker and *Macbeth* by Professor J. V. Cunningham. See his unpublished Stanford dissertation "Tragic Effect and Tragic Process in Some Plays of Shakespeare," p. 345. Cf. his *Woe or Wonder*, pp. 125-26, for a briefer treatment. For Curry's analysis of Macbeth's choice, which is worked out in terms of Thomistic teaching, see *Shakespeare's Philosophical Patterns*, pp. 103-19.

the parallel scene, he has already advanced to one conclusion, that he will "jump the life to come." This becomes the basis of the present internal debate. Previous consideration of the murder is also indicated by his words to Lady Macbeth: "We will proceed no further in this business" (I, vii, 31). The same impression is carried on by her reply. Perhaps the same motive led Shakespeare to write the famous lines:

> What beast was't, then
> That made you break this enterprise to me? (I, vii, 47-48)

These may indicate, not that a scene or scenes have been cut as critics have sometimes argued, but that we are to imagine many such discussions as having occurred. When they had time to occur, I grant, it is hard to conjecture. But where would the scenes have fitted in?

The scene is also based upon suggestion in a more important respect. Lady Macbeth's arguments, one must admit, are very feeble. But no argument for murder can possibly be logically sound, and Shakespeare tries to show that her dialogue, like Brutus' soliloquy, involves a transparent fallacy: she begs the question. Her words, furthermore, are intended by their very femininity to make us imagine a considerable stretch of wifely nagging by which Macbeth's resistance has been worn down. Shakespeare makes no attempt at realistic presentation. He merely gives us enough to stimulate our imagination.

The next scene introduces the theme that the crime is a violation both of Macbeth's human nature and of the universal order of which he is a part:

> Merciful powers,
> Restrain in me the cursed thoughts that nature
> Gives way to in repose! (II, i, 7-9)

His deed involves, as he visualizes it, a complete suspension of the order of nature:

> Now o'er the one half-world
> Nature seems dead, and wicked dreams abuse
> The curtain'd sleep. Witchcraft celebrates
> Pale Hecate's offerings, and wither'd Murder,
> Alarum'd by his sentinel, the wolf,
> Whose howl's his watch, thus with his stealthy pace,
> With Tarquin's ravishing strides, towards his design
> Moves like a ghost. (II, i, 49-56)

Macbeth's premonitions are confirmed by events, as we learn from Lennox (II, iii, 59-66) and from Ross and the Old Man (II, iv, 1-19), all of whom describe the dreadful and unnatural happenings of the night.

The scene of the murder itself introduces two ideas that become increasingly important as Macbeth's degeneration proceeds. Blood becomes a symbol of the fact that crime leads to crime and that each sin makes easier and more inevitable the next, as a habit of subordinating reason to will is established. As usual, Macbeth feels what is happening, but Lady Macbeth is insensitive: "Will all great Neptune's ocean wash this blood clean from my hands?" he asks, and she replies: "A little water clears us of this deed" (II, ii, 60, 67). How dreadfully wrong she is her sleep-walking scene is intended to show. But the motive power for his descent is furnished by appetite, now manifested not as ambition but as fear. Miss Campbell has pointed out that, in organizing his play, Shakespeare made use of the traditional concept derived from Aristotle's *Nicomachean Ethics* which regarded virtues as rational norms between irrational but opposed vices of excess and defect, bravery being the mean between fear and rashness.[30] In *Antony and Cleopatra* Enobarbus explicitly describes rashness as a false and irrational courage growing out of fear:

> To be furious,
> Is to be frighted out of fear; and in that mood
> The dove will peck the estridge; and I see still
> A diminution in our captain's brain
> Restores his heart. (III, xiii, 195-99)

Macbeth has been a brave man; as reason ceases to control his conduct, he gives way increasingly to fear. Every noise appalls him (II, ii, 58); "Our fears in Banquo stick deep" (III, i, 49-50);

> But let the frame of things disjoint, both the worlds suffer,
> Ere we will eat our meal in fear and sleep
> In the affliction of these terrible dreams
> That shake us nightly. (III, ii, 16-19)

Finally, after the promises of the witches, he develops a false and irrational courage:

[30]*Shakespeare's Tragic Heroes*, pp. 208-39. Cf. also Spurgeon, *Shakespeare's Imagery*, p. 156; G. Wilson Knight, *The Wheel of Fire*, pp. 146-47.

Some say he's mad, others that lesser hate him
Do call it valiant fury.   (V, ii, 13-14)

I have almost forgot the taste of fears.
The time has been, my senses would have cool'd
To hear a night-shriek, and my fell of hair
Would at a dismal treatise rouse and stir
As life were in 't. I have supp'd full with horrors;
Direness, familiar to my slaughterous thoughts,
Cannot once start me.   (V, v, 9-15)

But his state of mind is irrational, a point which those who talk
of the bravery of his death have overlooked. Shakespeare was
careful to show that his false courage disappeared with his false
security. When Macduff explains that he was ripped from his
mother's womb, Macbeth cowers:

Accursed be that tongue that tells me so,
For it hath cow'd my better part of man
. . . .   I'll not fight with thee.
                         (V, viii, 17-22)

"Then yield thee, coward," says Macduff, calling him by his
right name, and he fights only as a last resort like a trapped
animal. Shakespeare was too stern a moralist even to let him
die with dignity.

But we have anticipated events. Too late Macbeth realizes:

For Banquo's issue have I fil'd my mind; . . .
                    and mine eternal jewel
Given to the common enemy of man.   (III, i, 65-69)

In his misery he and Lady Macbeth drift apart (III, ii, 8-11),
somewhat as did Brutus and Cassius. The end of the banquet
scene shows Macbeth on his way to becoming a tyrant ruling
a disordered kingdom, dependent upon the powers of hell, and
embarking upon a career of crime:

There's not a one of them but in his house
I keep a servant fee'd. I will to-morrow,
And betimes I will, to the weird sisters.
More shall they speak; for now I am bent to know,
By the worst means, the worst. For mine own good
All causes shall give way. I am in blood
Stepp'd in so far that, should I wade no more,
Returning were as tedious as go o'er.
. . . .
We are yet but young in deed.   (III, iv, 131-38, 44)

297

Lady Macbeth, blind to the end, thinks that he needs sleep!

Bradley remarks that there is a falling off of interest in the fourth act of *Macbeth*, and he is undoubtedly right. But, according to Shakespeare's thinking, those scenes have two very important functions. In the first place, they show that Macbeth's crimes have led to a breaking down of the entire social order.[31] Such is the purpose of the conversation between Lennox and "another Lord" (III, vi), and it is one of the functions of the scene between Macduff and Malcolm (IV, iii). Ross (recalling the line from Lucretius that Friar Lawrence used) describes Scotland as not "our mother, but our grave," where the good die speedily and their burial has ceased to arouse interest (IV, iii, 164-72). Macbeth's own dreadful conjuration of the witches (IV, i, 50-60) extends the disorder to "nature's germens,"[32] the very source of natural order itself.

But these scenes have a political significance as well. Macbeth is king of Scotland, and if rebellion is to be justified, he must be established as a tyrant. Malcolm begins calling him a tyrant as he talks to Macduff (IV, iii, 12), after events have amply justified his use of the term, and from then on Macbeth is regularly so described by those opposing him (V, iv, 8; vii, 14). Paul believes their actions adjusted to the teachings of King James himself. In his *Basilicon Doron* James had written: " . . . a Tyrannes miserable and infamous life, armeth in the end his own subjects to become his burreaux [hangmen]."[33] But he was also strongly opposed to the doctrine of legitimate tyrannicide and insisted that "subjects may never rebel against a bad king 'in respect they had once received and acknowledged him for their king.' "[34] Duncan's sons flee. Macduff never gives allegiance to Macbeth. He suspects foul play and leaves immediately after the murder, and he refuses to attend the coronation. The progress of the play is thus brought into line with the thinking of Shakespeare's chronicle plays and of *Julius Caesar*, and with royal political doctrine as well.

[31]Bradley, *Shakespearean Tragedy*, p. 57. Cf. Tillyard, *Shakespeare's History Plays*, pp. 315-16.

[32]This is the subject of an essay in Curry's *Shakespeare's Philosophical Patterns*. Cf. pp. 36, 60-61.

[33]Paul, *The Royal Play of Macbeth*, p. 136.

[34]Ibid., p. 195.

But through it all Macbeth feels and partly understands what has happened to him. Or at least Shakespeare feels and understands and puts the words into his mouth, words that form an ultimate revelation of the consequences of a life of crime. And we are quite prepared to believe that a man who could anticipate the horror of murder as does Macbeth could describe, with equal poetic power, the consequences to which that murder led:

> I have liv'd long enough. My way of life
> Is fallen into the sear, the yellow leaf;
> And that which should accompany old age,
> As honour, love, obedience, troops of friends,
> I must not look to have; but, in their stead,
> Curses, not loud but deep, mouth-honour, breath,
> Which the poor heart would fain deny, and dare not.
>
> (V, iii, 22-28)

Partly because it is artistically satisfying in a way that *Lear* somehow fails to be, partly, perhaps, because it concentrates upon one individual as *Lear* fails to do, *Macbeth* seems to me Shakespeare's greatest monument to the ethical system that his age inherited from Western Christianity and the classical world, and to which it gave a new and vital expression. For that tradition *Macbeth* is what the *Oedipus Rex* was for the Greek—an almost perfect dramatic embodiment. Into the play went a large body of learning that Shakespeare had been accumulating during his career: a theory of kingship, Aristotelian ethics and the accepted psychology, demonology, and finally the Christian world order and the Christian view of virtue and sin. All this he used with a perfect clarity and an adequacy of expression that he never again equalled. In fact, one finds irresistible the temptation to quote his own incomparable statement of each point rather than to write a weak paraphrase. Nor does this exact analysis make Macbeth or even Lady Macbeth less convincing as a person; rather it seems an important element in establishing their characters, so convincingly has the impossible been made probable by Shakespeare's art. If ever the "pale cast of thought" was justified in drama and literature, it was in *Macbeth*.

Macbeth is therefore the climax of a dramatic effort that extended from the morality plays through *Faustus*, in that it is concerned with the whole process of sin as developed by Christian thinkers from classical learning. It depicts temptation, choice, deed, and then the terrible wages. Shakespeare achieves as universal a treatment of this theme as the morality plays, even though his hero is Macbeth rather than Mankind and the moral choice is internal. This he accomplishes partly through the great soliloquies and the formula that he had developed. But he does it primarily by the superb imagery, which combines all the traditions that met in his mind and is itself a revelation of his learning and his thought. The play is more than action. It is blood and light and darkness, and nature that seems dead. It is also classical poetry, Hebrew scriptures, and Christian liturgy.[35] The blood recalls Seneca: "The safest way through crime is still more crime." But it has "the primal eldest curse upon it" and it "smells to heaven" like Lady Macbeth's hands. The use of light and darkness has as many levels of meaning as the simplest and most poetic of the collects in the Book of Common Prayer: "Lighten our darkness, we beseech thee, O Lord; and by thy great mercy defend us from all perils and dangers of this night." To Macbeth's night belong the owl and the wolf, Hecate and Tarquin—and he himself. "Let not light see my black and deep desires," he says. But the light which he fears is more than the stars; it shone in the darkness, and the darkness could not contain it. It returns with Malcolm at the end, and so does nature, almost in Ulysses' terms—"degree, priority, and place":

> This, and what needful else
> That calls upon us, by the grace of Grace
> We will perform in measure, time, and place.
>   (V, viii, 71-73)

Lear, as we have noted, deals with the same group of ideas as *Macbeth*, but it differs profoundly from the latter play in that it is concerned primarily rather than incidentally with the "moral laws of nature and of nations" and therefore opens with an act of moral choice, the consequences of which it develops. In beginning with Lear's preposterous contest of affection among his daughters, Shakespeare departed sharply from his main source, *The*

[35]Cf. Cormican, "Medieval Idiom in Shakespeare: (I) Shakespeare and the Liturgy." The last half of this essay is extremely stimulating.

True Chronicle Historie of King Leir, and his three daughters.[36]
The old play roughly paralleled Shakespeare's main plot, except
for the scenes on the heath and Edmund's role, although it gave
Leir and his faithful follower an interview with two murderers,
sent Leir to France, and ended happily. But it motivated the
contest of affection as a scheme to trap Cordella into marriage,
which Leir worked out with his counselors, two of whom remained behind to say:

> *Skalliger*: Ile to them before, and bewray your secrecy.
>
> *Perillus*: Thus fathers think their children to beguile,
> And oftentimes themselves do first repent,
> When heavenly powers do frustrate their intent.[37]

We see Skalliger enlightening Gonorill and Ragan, and after he
leaves, they decide to fall in with the scheme, since the men
whom they know their father to have in mind are quite acceptable. Apparently we are to assume that Skalliger has also warned
Cordella, although he does not do so in the play. At any rate,
her silence saves her from falling into a trap. All this Shakespeare
eliminated, just as he omitted the preliminary motivation in so
many of his sources, most notably in *The Merchant of Venice*;
instead he simply presented the decision to divide the kingdom
(which is in the source) and the contest of affection as postulates
of the drama, and he motivated what happens solely in terms
of the characters of the participants. To show the irrationality
of Lear's actions, he used Kent and the French King, but he
perhaps failed to clarify Cordelia's character as he should have
done. At least, it is not quite clear whether we are to regard her
as perfectly virtuous throughout the play or as sharing, by her
stubbornness, in the faults of this most irrational and passion-
driven group of characters.

From the ever-widening effects of Lear's original act of folly
results the kind of chaos which Ulysses described and which
Gloucester portrays almost as vividly:

[36]Chambers, *William Shakespeare*, I, 469-70. The old play is reprinted in
Hazlitt, *Shakespeare's Library*, II (Part 2), 307-87. Shakespeare also used Holin-
shed, *The Mirror for Magistrates*, the *Faerie Queene*, the *Arcadia*, and Samuel
Harsnett's *Declaration of Popish Impostures*.

[37]Hazlitt, op. cit., II (Part 2), 309-10.

Love cools, friendship falls off, brothers divide: in cities, mutinies; in countries, discord; in palaces, treason; and the bond crack'd 'twixt son and father. This villain of mine comes under the prediction; there's son against father: the King falls from bias of nature; there's father against child. We have seen the best of our time; machinations, hollowness, treachery, and all ruinous disorders, follow us disquietly to our graves.   (I, ii, 116-24)

The play seems almost to assume that nature is order and man is disorder, and it traces the complete destruction of the order of nature both in the kingdom and in the universe.[38] As Craig has shown, the manifestations of natural law in the political realm were very nearly equivalent to the principles of distributive justice, as they were accepted in the Renaissance, and all relationships among men recognized by writers on justice are violated during the play.[39] The cause of this disintegration Shakespeare sees in man's irrationality and his appetites, and the play is extraordinarily specific in its statement of philosophic principles—more careful of them, in fact, than of plot structure, for the number of minor inconsistencies and loose ends has been notorious since Bradley's essay, if not before.[40]

The laws of nature which may be apprehended by human reason are, in the absence of Divine revelation, the only basis of right conduct, and they should be a sufficient guide.[41] It is possible, as Bethell thinks,[42] that Shakespeare deliberately intended to study a world prior to Christian revelation; but that seems unlikely, for Christian principles do intrude and Shakespeare also avoids specifically Christian references in *Troilus and Cressida* and in *Cymbeline*, which comes from the same legendary British history and even contains a morning prayer to the heavens (III, iii, 1-9). *Lear* is concerned, furthermore, not with what man

[38]But Prior, for whose treatment of *Lear* I have great respect, regards the storm as an analogue rather than as a result of human passions (*The Language of Tragedy*, pp. 84-85).

[39]"The Ethics of King Lear," pp. 97-109. Craig might well have remarked that Wilson's *Arte of Rhetorique* also discusses nature in the context upon which this article is based. The best accounts of *Lear*, from the point of view of this study, are to be found in this article and in Spencer, *Shakespeare and the Nature of Man*, pp. 135-52.

[40]*Shakespearean Tragedy*, pp. 256-60.

[41]Cf. Hooker, *Laws of Ecclesiastical Polity*, I, viii, 9; *Works*, I, 233.

[42]*Shakespeare & the Popular Dramatic Tradition*, p. 54.

can or cannot achieve by the guidance of nature, but with the chaos that he causes by failing to obey nature's laws because of ignorance or passion. Three characters explicitly state an attitude toward nature, and each of them so misunderstands it that his downfall follows logically from his attitude. They are Lear, Edmund, and Gloucester in that order, which is probably not fortuitous.[43]

Lear first uses the order of nature to curse Cordelia:

> For, by the sacred radiance of the sun,
> The mysteries of Hecate and the night;
> By all the operation of the orbs
> From whom we do exist and cease to be;
> Here I disclaim all my paternal care,
> Propinquity and property of blood,
> And as a stranger to my heart and me
> Hold thee from this for ever. The barbarous Scythian
> Or he that makes his generation messes
> To gorge his appetite, shall to my bosom
> Be as well neighbour'd, piti'd, and reliev'd,
> As thou my sometime daughter.   (I, i, 111-22)

As his own words show, he is calling upon nature to witness his own violation of one of its fundamental relationships, that between parent and child. Later he calls Cordelia a wretch "whom Nature is asham'd almost t' acknowledge hers" (I, i, 215-16), obviously having in mind what he considers her unnatural lack of affection. How wrong he is and how contrary to reason he is acting, the King of France makes clear, alluding probably to the notion that monstrous births were the result of an unnatural union between man and beast or man and devil:

> Sure her offence
> Must be of such unnatural degree
> That monsters it, or your fore-vouch'd affection
> Fallen into taint; which to believe of her,
> Must be a faith that reason without miracle
> Should never plant in me.   (I, i, 221-26)

But Lear is also violating the natural obligations of a king to govern and of an old man to be wise. Kent reproves him roundly for his folly in giving up his authority (I, i, 150-53), and the

---

[43]Cf. the treatment of nature in Prior, *The Language of Tragedy*, pp. 80-84.

sisters comment that he has never shown wisdom (I, i, 297) and
that his age is "infirm and choleric" (I, i, 303). The Fool uses all
three ideas repeatedly as material for his comments: "Thou hadst
little wit in thy bald crown when thou gav'st thy golden one
away" (I, iv, 177-78). " . . . thou mad'st thy daughters thy
mothers; for when thou gav'st them the rod, and puttest down
thine own breeches .." (I, iv, 187-90). "Thou shouldst not have
been old till thou hadst been wise" (I, v, 48-49).

⟨Lear calls nature "dear goddess" (I, iv, 297); actually he has
regarded her as a maidservant, and therein lies his error. He has
enjoyed the authority which accrued to him as king, father, and
old man; but he has refused to accept the responsibilities belonging to these positions, just as he wishes to keep the trappings
and even the authority of royalty while he divests himself of his
responsibilities, as Goneril quite rightly remarks (I, iii, 16-18).
It is therefore only an example of the poetic justice in which the
play abounds when the sisters show themselves equally unnatural
in refusing to perform their duties as children. In his wrath Lear
curses their conduct in language which is even more frightful
than his denunciation of Cordelia and embodies the same demand
that nature be unnatural for his convenience:

> Hear, Nature! hear, dear goddess, hear!
> Suspend thy purpose, if thou didst intend
> To make this creature fruitful! . . .
> Turn all her mother's pains and benefits
> To laughter and contempt, that she may feel
> How sharper than a serpent's tooth it is
> To have a thankless child!
>
> (I, iv, 297-311)

Lear's relationship to nature Shakespeare illustrates powerfully
in his madness. He tries to outscorn the storm (III, i, 10) and
then to use it for his ends against "ingrateful man" (III, ii, 8-9);
then he accuses it of joining with his daughters against him
(III, ii, 19-25); and finally he bids it strike all guilty men since he is
"more sinn'd against than sinning" (III, ii, 49-60). The one common element in these passages is his colossal egotism that sees nature only in its relation to himself, whether it seems to conspire
against him or to inflict his will upon the whole world. Of nature
as order—as rights but also obligations, as reward but also punish-

ment—he has no notion, and his unstable mind is but an outward manifestation of the fundamental lack of sanity that he has always shown. Only the implied concession that he has sinned, a new note in his raging, shows that there is hope for him. The coming of spiritual sanity is therefore reflected by his dawning awareness that he has failed in his duty as king to "poor naked wretches." "O, I have ta'en too little care of this!" he cries (III, iv, 32-33), and then he realizes that he is responsible even for his daughters: " 'Twas this flesh begot those pelican daughters" (III, iv, 75-76). His tearing off his clothes is a final dramatization of the contrast between human fundamentals and the "lendings" upon which he has depended as king. He is on his way to recognizing, as he finally does, that men and their justice are both imperfect. The divinity that hedges a king is superimposed upon fallible humanity; the robes of the great hide, but do not correct, the imperfection that shows through rags so hideously. Here Shakespeare works out, with final tragic intensity, the implications of an idea that fascinated him in *Richard II* and *Henry V*. It is part of the superb irony of this play that Lear's first act of outright madness is also his first clear demonstration of moral sanity.

In contrast to Lear's rejection of the implications of degree stands Kent's acceptance of it. As so often, Shakespeare makes his point by choosing an extreme position. Even after Kent has seen the uttermost exhibition of Lear's incapacity, he says: " . . . you have that in your countenance which I would fain call master. . . . Authority" (I, iv, 29-32). If Lear will not recognize his obligation to use such service, Kent will still offer it, for Shakespeare assumes, anachronistically, that Lear is an "anointed" king by divine right (III, vii, 58).

Edmund, the second to reveal his attitude toward nature, makes a different kind of error. He recognizes that he should follow nature, but mistakes its character:

> Thou, Nature, art my goddess; to thy law
> My services are bound. Wherefore should I
> Stand in the plague of custom, and permit
> The curiosity of nations to deprive me,
> For that I am some twelve or fourteen moonshines
> Lag of a brother?   (I, ii, 1-6)

"The general and perpetual voice of men," says Hooker, "is as the sentence of God himself. For that which all men have at all times learned, Nature herself must needs have taught; and God being the author of Nature, her voice is but his instrument."[44] Hooker, of course, is only stating a view that underlies many Renaissance phenomena—including the endless parading of historical precedents in controversial works. Edmund, in rejecting custom, is also rejecting that nature which is the instrument of God. For it he is substituting man's own fallen nature deprived of grace. This nature should indeed "stand up for bastards," for it creates them; it is man's corrupted will. Edmund is intelligent. His judgment of his father's "evasion," "to lay his goatish disposition on the charge of a star" (I, ii, 138-39), is absolutely sound; and his craft is too much for the "foolish honesty" of Edgar and the more foolish sensuality of his father. When he falls, he does so because he has followed his will, and a combination of ambition and lust have played him false. He has overlooked nature's "moral laws" because he has mistaken its identity. It is certainly likely that Shakespeare intended Edmund to reflect the new naturalism of the Renaissance with its emphasis upon will and its rejection of traditional principles of restraint.[45] Edmund is a Machiavel in his adherence to Machiavelli's ethics as well as in his dramatic origin. But his references to custom and the "lusty stealth of nature" show, just as does Iago's praise of self-love, that Shakespeare was working him out in the habitual terms. He follows Richard III and Iago as one of a series who are slaves of nature and sons of hell (cf. *Richard III*, I, iii, 230).

Of the three Gloucester is blindest of all. He knows that men talk of nature (I assume that by "wisdom of nature" he means men who make a wisdom out of knowing nature), but he refuses to believe that it controls events—in other words, he doubts that there are laws of nature: "These late eclipses in the sun and moon portend no good to us. Though the wisdom of nature can reason it thus and thus, yet nature finds itself scourg'd by the sequent effects" (I, ii, 112-15). He is therefore perfectly consistent in seeing the evils that crowd upon him as evidence of a cruel

[44]*Laws of Ecclesiastical Polity*, I, viii, 3; *Works*, I, 227.
[45]Cf. Bethell, *Shakespeare & the Popular Dramatic Tradition*, pp. 58-59; Haydn, *The Counter-Renaissance*, pp. 638-40.

caprice in the fate of men and of a fundamental lack of design:

> As flies to wanton boys, are we to th' gods,
> They kill us for their sport.
>
> (IV, i, 38-39)

> 'Tis the time's plague, when madmen lead the blind.
>
> (IV, i, 48)

His own life has apparently been marked by irresponsible sensuality rather than by deliberate wilfulness, and his attitude toward Edmund at the beginning of the play is heartless rather than vicious. But it was once my duty to help a high-school student straighten out his affairs before induction into the army and to watch him nerve himself to face the implications of his own illegitimacy. Though I hardly knew the boy, I have never since been able to read the opening lines of *Lear* without finding Gloucester detestable beyond any villain in Shakespeare. I cannot believe that Edmund is to be thought of as out of earshot until line 25, as has been suggested. The repeated use of *this* almost suggests that Gloucester has laid his hand on Edmund's shoulder. Kent and Gloucester, returning from the council, must encounter him at line 8. As a well-bred young man, he stands quietly by until he is spoken to, and the dialogue was intended by Shakespeare to characterize Gloucester.

Edgar passes upon his father a judgment in harsh contrast to Cordelia's tenderness to Lear, a judgment both upon his conduct and upon his failure to acknowledge nature's laws:

> The gods are just, and of our pleasant vices,
> Make instruments to plague us.
> The dark and vicious place where thee he got
> Cost him his eyes.
>
> (V, iii, 170-73)

And even Gloucester has been given a remarkable flash of insight to point the justice of his fate: "I stumbled when I saw" (IV, i, 21).

Other characters are less explicit, because less important, but Goneril and Regan, at least, are false to their duties as queens, as wives, and as children. And one sin follows from another, as Albany tells Goneril:

307

That nature which contemns its origin
Cannot be bordered certain in itself.
She that herself will sliver and disbranch
From her material sap, perforce must wither
And come to deadly use.

(IV, ii, 32-36)

The ultimate horror of Goneril's conduct lies in its unnaturalness:

Proper deformity seems not in the fiend
So horrid as in woman.

(IV, ii, 60-61)

It would be easy to demonstrate that every character in the play except possibly Edgar falls short of complete, rational obedience to nature's laws, and even Edgar is, as Edmund points out, a little stupid.

Granted, then, that *King Lear* portrays a kingdom in chaos because of repeated violations of the laws of nature, the problem arises of explaining those violations. Shakespeare offers the two explanations that we should expect—ignorance (or rather reason's failure to recognize the laws) and appetite, always blended but blended in varying proportions. To separate them is impossible, but an attempt will be made for purposes of discussion.

⟨ The fundamental rôle of irrationality in the play has already appeared in the various attitudes toward nature. If rational conduct be defined, as Shakespeare clearly defines it throughout his last plays, as conformity to the laws of nature and therefore of God, then all the characters in this play are endowed with a combination of irrationality in themselves and ability to detect irrationality in others that is as remarkable as it is convenient for the dramatist in interpreting his action. It is, of course, this specific labeling of acts as unnatural that justifies us in giving the play a philosophic interpretation, just as the long discussions of nature prove that the adjectives "natural" and "unnatural" are used with a full understanding of their implications. Plenty of Shakespeare's characters do immoral or ill-considered acts; what is unique in this play is the regularity with which judgment is passed upon those acts in terms of a philosophic system.

Lear is, I believe, the only character in the play whose acts are repeatedly branded as foolish as well as unnatural. The French

King, Kent, the Fool, and the two sisters all stigmatize him as unwise, all but the first repeatedly. Other characters diagnose each other's failures primarily in terms of nature or degree, except that sisterly regard, which seems a little priggish but was obviously not intended to be so, restricts Cordelia to vagueness:

> I know you what you are;
> And like a sister am most loath to call
> Your faults as they are nam'd.   (I, i, 272-74)

Lear, as we have seen, makes nature the theme of his most horrible curses both of Cordelia and of Goneril and Regan, reaching a horrible climax in his madness:

> Crack nature's moulds, all germens spill at once
> That makes ingrateful man!   (III, ii, 8-9)

Kent lectures Oswald on violating propriety and degree (II, ii, 78-90) while he himself breaches good manners if not the peace. Even Gloucester, who does not believe in laws of nature, follows the fashion of rating conduct as natural or unnatural, although he is wrong in his facts. He calls Edgar "Unnatural, detested, brutish villain" (I, ii, 81-82) and Edmund "Loyal and natural boy" (II, i, 86). It is as though Shakespeare had set out to show every man beholding the mote in his brother's eye but perceiving not the beam in his own.

This emphasis upon unnatural conduct is carried over from specific statement into the imagery. The sisters, especially, are constantly compared to wolves, tigers, boars, serpents, and so on, as if to imply that they lack the reason which alone distinguishes man from the other animals. In a parallel way, the words "monster" and "monstrous" are also used repeatedly (although less frequently, I believe, than in *Othello*) to indicate unnatural, as distinguished from irrational, conduct. For a monster was, as we have noticed, contrary to nature.[46]

The Fool is the ultimate example of this element in the play. His images are constantly based upon "things that are upside-down or backside foremost, or out of the natural order, as things

---

[46]Cf. Prior, *The Language of Tragedy*, pp. 86-88.

are in Lear's erstwhile kingdom."[47] And among men gone mad or playing mad or merely mad but unrecognized as such, he manages consistently to call things what they are with a penetrating rationality that eludes those who are not professedly fools. And when the play needs pity rather than pungent exposure of folly he drops from sight.⟩

In the system of thought that Shakespeare was following reason was supposed to formulate its own plans and to pass judgment upon the desires of the appetites. Its function was often judicial, and appetite was the "Will's solicitor."[48] So it is in this play. Because reason fails to recognize the laws of nature and to direct action accordingly, the characters leave undone what they ought to have done, such as ruling kingdoms or caring for fathers; because appetite solicits the will, they do what they ought not to have done, such as exiling virtuous daughters, taking a lover, planning murders, and so on. By tradition going back to Plato the passions were divided into the irascible, which were connected with wrath and included grief, and the concupiscible, which sprang from desire.[49] Spenser, for example, used this scheme in arranging the temptations that beset Sir Guyon in Book II of *The Faerie Queene*. It was therefore no accident that Shakespeare selected the passions most representative of the two groups, wrath and lust, for detailed illustration in his play and principally to motivate the destruction of natural order, although other manifestations of appetite such as greed and envy are abundantly present. Lear and Kent (who in his liability to anger parallels Lear as so many plot elements in the play are doubled)[50] are driven by wrath. Goneril pairs poor judgment and choler as Lear's faults (I, i, 295-303), and his own actions certainly justify her words. At the slightest check on vexation he flies into a rage that borders upon madness, as even he recognizes:

> O, let me not be mad, not mad, sweet heaven!
> Keep me in temper; I would not be mad!
> (I, v, 50-51)

47Spencer, *Shakespeare and the Nature of Man*, p. 143.

48Hooker, *Laws of Ecclesiastical Polity*, I, vii, 3; *Works*, I, 221.

49Cf. St. Thomas Aquinas, *Summa Theologica*, Ia, Q. 81, A. 2; *Basic Writings*, I, 772-73. Robert Burton, *Anatomy of Melancholy*, I, ii, 3.3; Bohn, I, 297.

50Cf. Spencer, *Shakespeare and the Nature of Man*, pp. 136-38.

Kent's wrath at Oswald is almost as violent (cf. II, ii, 15-26). In fact, on the basis of the evidence at hand Cornwall and Regan are quite justified in putting him in the stocks.

Lust is much harder to present dramatically in a few lines than is wrath, and it is likely to attract less attention as one reads *Lear*; but it is an equally important element in the play in that the rivalry of the two sisters for Edmund leads to their final discomfiture and death and to Albany's aligning himself with Edgar. It makes Goneril and Regan false to their husbands as they have been false to father and sister, and it leads to the final chaotic self-destruction by which evil purges itself and order returns to a suffering world. But it is also generalized by Lear into a symbol of sin itself, of the human imperfection which smells in the mortality of Gloucester's hand (IV, vi, 136) and which invalidates all social order. It makes the beadle as lustful as the whore that he lashes, "the usurer hangs the cozener," and justice yields to gold (IV, vi, 164-71). The generalization of lust into all "appetite" implied by the sequence of Lear's ideas is again no accident, and the point is worth some attention, since Shakespeare has been regarded as showing a morbid interest in lust in the plays from *Hamlet* to *Lear*.[51] In concentrating upon lust, Shakespeare was following a Christian tradition which had a sound empirical basis, as well as a popular view which finally resulted in the present popular use of affection and passion to mean simply love or lust respectively.

The source of all sin, both in angels and in men, was, of course, inordinate self-love or pride. The actual sin of Adam and Eve was simply disobedience: they ate what they had been told not to eat. But as a result of their sin their will was turned from God, and their appetites became involuntary, in that the will could refuse to permit what appetite desired but could not prevent the appetite from arising.[52] Now the obvious proof that the appetites were independent of control lay in certain responses to erotic stimuli, and lust therefore became the accepted proof of the nature of appetite and the obvious example of its effects. St. Augustine so discusses it at length in Book XIV of *The City of God*, and Shakespeare therefore followed ancient tradition

[51]Cf. Spencer, *Shakespeare and the Nature of Man*, pp. 192-93.
[52]Cf. Hooker, *Laws of Ecclesiastical Polity*, I, vii, 3; *Works*, I, 221.

in using it in *Lear* to typify the revolt of man's sinful flesh against God's ordered nature. Speaking of original sin, the ninth of the Thirty-nine articles declares: "And this infection of nature doth remain, yea in them that are regenerated; whereby the lust of the flesh . . . is not subject to the Law of God." Spenser had made Sir Guyon, the knight of temperance, find Acrasia, who personified the "unruled" appetite which he must vanquish, dallying with a fair young man, and he describes her bower as a place of amorous indulgence; and in *Paradise Lost* Milton uses the appearance of lust in Adam and Eve to show the effects of the fall upon their moral nature.[53] The same identification of lust with man's rebellious nature underlies a labored joke in *The Merchant of Venice* (III, i, 37-38). Lear's realization of this radical fault in human nature is his final descent into the depths of reality from which he emerges a better and a wiser, even if a "foolish fond old man" (IV, vii, 60). What Lear learned slowly and said at length, the Fool summarized in a sentence, as he contrasted the wisdom which is possible only through God's grace with man's unregenerate nature: "Marry, here's grace and a cod-piece; that's a wise man and a fool" (III, iii, 41). His remark is indecent, but profound.

In *Lear*, therefore, Shakespeare attempted to study the effect upon the order of nature, especially in society, of human sin as it resulted from the failure of reason and the control of appetite. Nature emerged triumphant, as it must, but at a terrible cost in disorder and human suffering. In working out his play as he did, he had come a long way from the early chronicles of *Romeo and Juliet*, where Romeo cried, "I am Fortune's fool." Lear almost, but not quite, echoes him: "I am even the natural fool of fortune" (IV, vi, 194-95). In the light of the play he can only mean: Because of the operation of nature in me and upon me, I am the fool of fortune. Fortune has become almost destitute of implications as to causation, much as it is today. But Edmund uses another old figure in a way that is even more significant of the development of Shakespeare's thought. We have already noticed Edgar's judgment that "the gods are just" and that his father has paid the penalty for his own vices. To this assertion of cause and effect Edmund replies, thinking of his own downfall:

[53]Cf. C. S. Lewis, *A Preface to Paradise Lost*, pp. 68-69.

> Thou'st spoken right, 'tis true.
> The wheel is come full circle; I am here.
>
> (V, iii, 173-74)

The wheel is no longer Fortune's. It almost belongs to the world machine of a coming age. It reminds us that, while Hooker was writing of laws of nature to be apprehended by reason, Bacon was meditating his grandiose scheme to discover these same laws by induction. But Shakespeare's are still the "moral laws of nature and of nations."

CHAPTER XIII

The Last Plays, an Epilogue

I T SEEMS STRANGE to begin an epilogue when eight of Shakespeare's plays, over a fifth of his total dramatic output, are as yet uncovered. But I set out, after all, to study the development of his learning, not its maturity or its decline; and the changes to be observed in the plays after *Macbeth* are matters of dramatic technique rather than of intellectual growth. Only *The Tempest* breaks new ground; but, since it has no definite source, the methodology that I have been using is hard to apply, and I shall have relatively little to say.

There is, furthermore, an actual falling off in the last plays. In the four tragedies, *Hamlet, Othello, Lear,* and *Macbeth,* Shakespeare probably achieved his greatest heights as a dramatic artist. In them he embodied his most intense philosophic thinking as well, for the remaining plays, except perhaps *The Tempest,* are much simpler in their underlying ideas as well as less powerful in their dramatic impact. Only a few need be discussed, and those briefly.

Antony and Cleopatra and *Coriolanus* apply the now familiar tragic formula to Plutarch. But perhaps because Plutarch's material was already well interpreted, or more likely because Shakespeare was attracted to it by the slighter effort that he would have to expend upon it, both plays show much less concern to work out the dramatic action and to explain it in terms that are fundamentally philosophic. They seem also to reflect a slight failure of creative energy. *Antony and Cleopatra* has some superb poetry, although little that the reader recalls as he does passages from *Hamlet* and *Macbeth*; but Cleopatra herself is not made wholly consistent, and in much of the play Shakespeare merely dramatized successive episodes in his source as he did in the early chronicles. Despite its undoubtedly powerful scenes, the play has never completely succeeded on the modern stage. *Coriolanus*, on the other hand, is one of Shakespeare's most carefully constructed plays. There is perhaps no better way of acquiring an insight into his dramatic technique than to compare it with Plutarch's life scene by scene and line by line, inquiring why each episode has been selected or why incidents and scenes not in the source have been introduced. But somehow Coriolanus himself fails to move us emotionally, and that is a weakness for which no formal perfection of artistry can atone.

Shakespeare's interpretation of Antony is presented quite clearly in Philo's speech which opens the play:

> Nay, but this dotage of our general's
> O'erflows the measure. . . .
>   his captain's heart,
> Which in the scuffles of great fights hath burst
> The buckles on his breast, reneges all temper,
> And is become the bellows and the fan
> To cool a gipsy's lust.   (I, i, 1-10)

As this introduction shows, the tragic action of the play is centered upon Antony, who has so yielded himself to the passion of love that it has possessed his will and dethroned his reason. Cleopatra, although she is developed almost as fully as he is, remains the seductress, and only at the end does she become a participant in a tragedy of her own. In developing this interpretation, Shakespeare again built to a crucial choice. But he varied his formula in that the choice turns not upon a clear-cut moral issue as in the preceding plays but upon the wisdom of a course of action. The difference is slight, however, since it is obviously immoral for Antony to fail in his duties as ruler and to throw away the lives of his followers. Elizabethan drama from *Gorboduc* to *Lear* is clear on that point. For his failure, which came about because love destroyed his military judgment, Shakespeare prepared both in the opening speech quoted above and in Philo's final lines in the same scene:

> Sir, sometimes, when he is not Antony,
> He comes too short of that great property
> Which still should go with Antony.
>   (I, i, 57-59)

315

Antony "is not Antony," of course, when he is dominated by passion rather than by reason. To explain his crucial error, Shakespeare inserted a scene between Cleopatra and Enobarbus which shows that the latter, who serves throughout the play as the voice of reason, has forbidden Cleopatra to accompany Antony to fight Octavius (III, vii, 3-4). To her demand for an explanation, he replies:

> Your presence needs must puzzle Antony;
> Take from his heart, take from his brain, from 's time
> What should not then be spar'd.   (III, vii, 11-13)

But Cleopatra ominously concludes: "I will not stay behind" (III, vii, 20). It then becomes clear that she is determined upon a sea battle (III, vii, 29). Canidius and Enobarbus point out to Antony a number of convincing reasons why he should fight by land; these Antony peremptorily refuses to consider, merely repeating "By sea, by sea.... I'll fight at sea" (III, vii, 41-49) like a man dazed, as indeed he is. Because Shakespeare could not very well stage a sea battle, he made Enobarbus, Scarus, and finally Canidius, commander of Antony's army, watch Cleopatra's flight and then Antony's. They also interpret what is happening:

> The greater cantle of the world is lost
> With very ignorance.   (III, x, 6-7)

By ignorance Scarus must mean the absence of reason. Later he calls Antony "the noble ruin of her magic" (III, x, 19). The fullest explanation is given by Enobarbus, however, in what is perhaps the most straightforward psychological analysis in Shakespeare's plays. The same passage also establishes the relative positions of Antony and Cleopatra in the action of the play. It should be noted that *will*, as often in the other plays, means the will dominated by passion as opposed to reason:

> *Cleo.* Is Antony or we in fault for this?
>
> *Eno.* Antony only, that would make his will
> Lord of his reason. What though you fled
> From that great face of war, whose several ranges
> Frighted each other? Why should he follow?
> The itch of his affection should not then
> Have nick'd his captainship, at such a point,
> When half to half the world oppos'd, he being
> The mered question.   (III, xiii, 2-10)

True to his function as the voice of reason, Enobarbus observes that Antony, driven by despair, is falling into a fury, a false and irrational bravery in which "valour preys on reason" (III, xiii, 195-200). Maecenas confirms his diagnosis:

> Caesar must think
> When one so great begins to rage, he's hunted
> Even to falling.
>
> (IV, i, 6-8)

But Enobarbus' clarity of vision involves him in a personal tragedy that Shakespeare sketched in but did not develop, a conflict between his reason and his loyalty. He first states his dilemma with his usual perspicacity immediately after Actium:

> I'll yet follow
> The wounded chance of Antony, though my reason
> Sits in the wind against me.
>
> (III, x, 35-37)

But Shakespeare does not show him reversing this decision, and we merely hear a soldier tell Antony that he has gone to Caesar's camp. Even before Antony sends his belongings after him, he concludes:

> I have done ill;
> Of which I do accuse myself so sorely
> That I will joy no more.
>
> (IV, vi, 18-20)

And he kills himself calling upon Antony.

Coriolanus involves several interesting developments in the tragic formula. Menenius Agrippa now serves as the voice of reason, counseling Coriolanus and pointing out the excesses of his pride. He also treats the plebians to Shakespeare's wittiest exposition of the horrors of civil war, using for material the fable telling how the other members revolted against the stomach, which Shakespeare had encountered first in grammar school. But Coriolanus' pride is also exhibited by the contrast between him and his mother Volumnia, the best-drawn character in the play. She has trained Coriolanus and made him what he is; when she disapproves of him we know that he has gone too far, and so does he:

> I muse my mother
> Does not approve me further, who was wont
> To call them woollen vassals, things created
> To buy and sell with groats, to show bare heads
> In congregations, to yawn, be still and wonder
> When one but of my ordinance stood up
> To speak of peace or war.—I talk of you. [*To Volumnia.*]
> Why did you wish me milder? Would you have me
> False to my nature? Rather say I play
> The man I am.
>
> (III, ii, 7-16)

She persuades him to alter his conduct, and he agrees, resolving to follow a course of prudence and reason. The play therefore embodies a new and interesting variation of the crucial choice in that Coriolanus chooses rightly; but, under the well-calculated taunts of the Tribunes, he is unable to follow the rational course that he has chosen and succumbs to the passion of pride. The Tribunes, incidentally, are parallel studies of pride that leads to envy, and they are superb portraits of cheap demagogues in all ages. The choice again, as in *Antony and Cleopatra*, turns upon the wisdom of a course of action, but it now is divided into two scenes: right choice in preparation (III, ii); wrong choice in practice (III, iii). Coriolanus' yielding to his pride makes inevitable another and still more difficult choice between his mother and not only his pride but his very life, as he recognizes clearly:

> *Cor.*   O mother, mother!
> What have you done? Behold, the heavens do ope,
> The gods look down, and this unnatural scene
> They laugh at. O my mother, mother! O!
> You have won a happy victory to Rome;
> But, for your son,—believe it, O believe it—,
> Most dangerously you have with him prevail'd,
> If not most mortal to him. But, let it come.
>
> (V, iii, 182-89)

Shakespeare made no attempt to analyse the second choice psychologically as he did the first, grounding it simply upon natural affection, a more satisfying motivation than pride. The play loses effectiveness because the first choice, which determines the course of the plot and makes the action follow from Coriolanus' charac-

318

ter, is unconvincing emotionally, whereas the subordinate choice at the end is one of the most powerful scenes that Shakespeare ever wrote. Perhaps this is just another way of saying that a hero motivated by pride has a hard time arousing our sympathy, but a mother pleading for her country, even at the sacrifice of her son's life, moves us profoundly.

Timon of Athens recalls *Lear*, but at a vast distance, by its savage invectives against human failings and especially by the scene between Timon, Alcibiades, and Timandra (IV, iii), which reminds us of Lear's discourse upon lust and the hollowness of greatness. It is closer to *Lear*, however, in its use of nature. Timon's curse upon Athens involves an inversion of natural processes like those invoked by Lear against Cordelia and Goneril. But, like the play itself, this speech is carried to such an extreme that it becomes grotesque rather than horrible. The constant play in *Lear* upon the word *nature* itself is also suggested by one of the best passages in *Timon*:

> Twinn'd brothers of one womb,
> Whose procreation, residence, and birth
> Scarce is dividant, touch them with several fortunes,
> The greater scorns the lesser; not nature,
> To whom all sores lay siege, can bear great fortune
> But by contempt of nature.
>
> (IV, iii, 3-8)

But, if any sustained intellectual concept can be detected in *Timon*, I have been unable to find it. The play seems to rest upon the commonplaces of human ingratitude, and Shakespeare (or whoever wrote the relevant scenes) never faced honestly the fact that Timon is responsible for his own fall into poverty and that his foolish prodigality might well excite scorn rather than admiration and gratitude, even granted that the Elizabethans placed less emphasis upon thrift than was customary a century ago.

The Tempest is much more significant than any of the plays so far mentioned in that it reveals several interests of Shakespeare's that we might suspect from other plays but could hardly prove. No source has been found for the plot of *The Tempest*, and it is even possible that Shakespeare took the unusual course of devising one of his own, just as he certainly adopted the innovation, for him quite unprecedented, of observing the pseudo-Aristotelian

319

unities of action, time, and place as they were arbitrarily defined by Renaissance critics. But he drew a number of details in the play from pamphlets of 1610 narrating the wreck of Sir Thomas Gates and Sir George Somers in the Bermudas. In a storm they were separated from their fleet, which was carrying colonists to Jamestown, and their ship was driven between two rocks. All aboard escaped safely, and they finally reached Virginia in 1610. Luce, who has investigated the problem, concludes that Shakespeare may have used three pamphlets giving an account of these events: Silvester Jourdan's *A Discovery of the Barmudas, otherwise called the Ile of Divels: by Sir Thomas Gates, Sir George Sommers, and Captayne Newport, with divers others;* an official account, *A True Declaration of the Estate of the Colonie in Virginia, with a confutation of such scandalous reports as have tended to the disgrace of so worthy an enterprise. Published by advice and direction of the Councell of Virginia,* and a letter by William Strachy which Shakespeare must have seen in manuscript and which Purchas called "A true reportory of the wracke and redemption of Sir Thomas Gates, Knight, upon and from the Islands of the Bermudas; his comming to Virginia, and the estate of the Colonie there, and after, under the government of the Lord La Warre."[1] From these accounts Shakespeare took not only circumstances of the wreck but also many of the characteristics of Prospero's island, the Bermudas being notoriously enchanted but found by the shipwrecked Englishmen to be pleasant and fertile. Setebos, Caliban's devil-father, apparently derived his name from Richard Eden's *History of Travayle* (1577), where Setebos is a god of the Patagonians.[2] The play as a whole must have derived a good share of its popular appeal, as well as its atmosphere, from the interest in strange new islands beyond the seas shared by Shakespeare and his audience.

Shakespeare's debt to Montaigne has been much debated by scholars. A multitude of parallel passages have been produced; but none of them is completely convincing, at least to one who believes, as I do, that a convincing parallel must involve a group of ideas not easily derived elsewhere, rather than mere verbal simi-

[1]Arden *Tempest*, pp. xii-xiv, 149-69.
[2]Chambers, *William Shakespeare*, I, 494.

larity.[3] But there can be no doubt that Gonzalo's utopia derives in part (II, i, 159-64) from Montaigne's "Of the Caniballes,"[4] and other parallels between the play and this essay seem convincing enough in the light of that passage.

A reader feels instantly that the supernatural atmosphere of *The Tempest* is altogether different from that of *Hamlet* or *Macbeth*, and the explanation is to be found in Shakespeare's notion of Prospero's magic. One unfortunate effect of Renaissance neo-Platonism was that it interacted with other influences to produce a tremendous emphasis upon magic. Not only the spheres but the very elements were thought of as governed by daemons whom it was possible for man to control by proper understanding of their nature. These daemons were part of the neo-Platonic system of emanations, and their origin was good rather than evil. The white magic or theurgy by which they might be controlled therefore rested upon a complex of ideas altogether distinct from the traditional black magic of the Middle Ages, although the latter was derived, along with the demonology upon which it was based, partly from the same ancestry. The medieval Christian theory of angels and devils and their activities had been formed by combining the good and fallen angels of Hebrew tradition with fourth-century neo-Platonism as represented in *The Celestial Hierarchy* of the pseudo-Dionysius, who had himself combined Hebrew and Greek elements. The two related streams of thought inevitably merged again when neo-Platonism was revived during the Renaissance. Very roughly, writers generally confused the neo-Platonic daemons with the traditional demons, so that the former became evil and the latter acquired a more intimate association with natural forces and with the elements; believers in white magic were hesitant and apologetic, if not actually secretive.[5] And no satisfactory theoretical basis for a beneficent magic ever became a part of general learning, so that, while such magic was continuously talked about, its status was at best uncertain. Robert Burton perhaps reflects the prevailing attitude. The basis of white magic he

[3]Cf., for example, John M. Robertson, *Montaigne and Shakespeare*, pp. 1-118; George Coffin Taylor, *Shakespeare's Debt to Montaigne*.

[4]Arden *Tempest*, pp. 172-73.

[5]Cf. Curry, *Shakespeare's Philosophical Patterns*, pp. 168-69. It seems to me very unlikely that Shakespeare would know the more learned works mentioned, except possibly by report.

rejects firmly: "As for those orders of good & bad Devils, which the Platonists hold, [it] is altogether erroneous, & those Ethnicks' *boni & mali Genii* [good and bad Genii] are to be exploded."[6] But he then devotes most of his subsection to material that is ultimately neo-Platonic, and he has paragraphs on "Fiery Spirits or Devils," aerial, water, terrestrial, and subterranean devils. "Thus," he explains, "the Devil reigns, and in a thousand several shapes, *as a roaring lion still seeks whom he may devour*, 1 Pet. 5 [8], by earth, sea, land, air as yet unconfined."[7]

Shakespeare seems to have reflected this Renaissance confusion rather than the pure form of theurgy or white magic. Prospero is clearly a beneficent magician, who controls spirits through his books and who uses them to set matters to right. He bids his magic farewell when he returns to Milan. Ariel, his chief minister, who seems to direct the other spirits and who enjoys the broadest latitude of action in executing Prospero's general instructions, is of more ambiguous status. He is clearly an elemental spirit or daemon. His name implies that he is associated with air, and he has the rationality appropriate to a daemon of that rank; but he is perhaps symptomatic of Shakespeare's vague use of this system in that he seems to belong about equally to all elements:

> All hail, great master! grave sir, hail! I come
> To answer thy best pleasure, be't to fly,
> To swim, to dive into the fire, to ride
> On the curl'd clouds.   (I, ii, 189-92)

> *Prospero.* Thou dost, and think'st it much to tread the ooze
> Of the salt deep,
> To run upon the sharp wind of the north,
> To do me business in the veins o' th' earth
> When it is baked with frost.   (I, ii, 252-55)

Prospero finally dismisses him with the words: "Then to the elements be free, and fare thee well" (V, i, 317-18). So delicate and benign is Ariel that it comes as a shock when Prospero calls him "malignant thing" (I, ii, 257). Yet, despite Curry's objections to

---

[6]*Anatomy of Melancholy*, I, ii, 1.2; Bohn, I, 213.

[7]Ibid., p. 224. For a similar identification of devils with elements cf. Hooker, *Laws of Ecclesiastical Polity*, I, iv, 3; *Works*, I, 214-15.

the view,[8] "malignant" must reflect confusion of the neo-Platonic system with the traditional demonology, of elemental daemons with demons operating in the elements. As the latter, Ariel is a devil and therefore malignant.

Caliban is even more completely of the traditional system. Although Curry believes that his father must have been an aquatic daemon because of his fishy appearance and odor,[9] of which Trinculo makes fun (II, ii, 25-37), Shakespeare nowhere else uses language that would support such a theory. Caliban is said by Prospero to have been "got by the devil himself upon thy wicked dam" (I, ii, 319-20), as monsters were believed to result from such unnatural and unholy unions. Caliban himself describes Setebos as "my dam's god" (I, ii, 374), implying the witches' worship of Satan as part of their sabbat.

In contrast to his considerable knowledge of conventional demonology, Shakespeare's acquaintance with white magic and with the system of ideas that it postulated was therefore very slight. His failure to resolve the conflict between his view of Prospero and his account of Ariel—that is, to explain how a good character could control demons—is in striking contrast to the care with which he worked out the implications of the ghost in *Hamlet* or of the witches in *Macbeth*. It means, probably, that we are not justified in taking the supernaturalism of this play too seriously. Like the ghosts in *Richard III*, Ariel, Caliban, and the other spirits are a mechanism in the plot of the play and a means of making its meaning clear, but not a part of that meaning. As Curry remarks in his discussion of *The Tempest*, to which I am deeply indebted even though I differ from some of its conclusions, Shakespeare "seems to have had an astonishing capacity for absorbing traditional materials without the exercise of any great scholarly efforts,"[10] and these offshoots of the neo-Platonic tradition were a prime example of his skill in making a great deal out of relatively little.

The preceding remark might almost be taken as the conclusion of this investigation of the development of Shakespeare's learning

---

[8]*Shakespeare's Philosophical Patterns*, pp. 165-66.
[9]Ibid., p. 184.
[10]Ibid., p. 158.

and thought. We have watched him begin with the knowledge of rhetoric and Latin authors that he had acquired in grammar school and superimpose that limited store upon his sources to produce the early plays. By the time of *Love's Labour's Lost* he had acquired an easy, although apparently not an extensive, familiarity with contemporary literature and some knowledge of the current sciences. This acquaintance he broadened into considerable knowledge of contemporary psychology, theology, and demonology. But it is doubtful that he ever read widely. As we noted earlier, he hardly had time to become a scholar, and there is no positive evidence of wide reading in his plays. One bit of evidence to the contrary becomes increasingly apparent in his later plays. That is a habit of repeating the same bits of information not only in similar situations but to produce quite different effects. Macbeth's

> I am in blood
> Stepp'd in so far that, should I wade no more,
> Returning were as tedious as go o'er.
>
> (III, iv, 136-38)

is merely Shakespeare's finest elaboration of a famous *sententia* from Seneca's *Agamemnon* which he (and his contemporaries) used repeatedly. Unlike his reader, he seems never to tire of the rivalry between nature and art, which he first mentioned in *Venus and Adonis*. The painter and the poet in *Timon* try to outvary each other:

> *Painter.* It is a pretty mocking of the life.
> Here is a touch, is't good?
>
> *Poet.*　　　　　　　　　I will say of it,
> It tutors nature. Artificial strife
> Lives in these touches, livelier than life.
>
> (I, i, 35-38)

Polixenes lectures Perdita on the same theme, applying it to selective breeding of plants (*Winter's Tale*, IV, iv, 86-97). And Lear remembers the contrast between nature and art even in his madness (IV, vi, 86). The seeds of nature, which Shakespeare first used in *2 Henry IV*, reappear not only in *Macbeth* and *Lear*, where they are obviously appropriate, but even in *The Winter's Tale*, where Florizel says of his devotion to Perdita, with true adolescent violence:

It cannot fail but by
The violation of my faith; and then
Let Nature crush the sides o' th' earth together
And mar the seeds within!

$$\text{(IV, iv, 486-89)}$$

These repetitions are rare amid the infinite variety that has always been associated with Shakespeare. But they do illustrate his habit of using to the full what learning he had.

The same generalization can be applied to Shakespeare's sources. Many of the plays are based upon a few important collections of material—Halle and Holinshed, North's Plutarch, Painter's *Palace of Pleasure* and other collections of Italian tales. All of these, furthermore, had been in print for eight or ten years before Shakespeare used them. But during his career as a playwright he also came to use a variety of secondary sources. Minor chroniclers furnished picturesque details for the later history plays; accounts of the witchcraft trials involving King James, as well as the King's own writings, contributed to *Macbeth*; and Spenser and Sidney provided material for *Lear*. A number of plays also indicate his interest in current writing. *Love's Labour's Lost* reflects the Harvey-Nashe controversy, *Lear* draws upon Harsnet's *Declaration of Popish Impostures*, and *The Tempest* involves pamphlets only a year old describing the wreck of Sir George Somers in the Bermudas. But one gets the general impression that Shakespeare was a busy playwright with a curious mind and an interest in contemporary affairs, not a student or an omnivorous reader. His mind assimilated striking details and used them for maximum effect, but, except for the Homilies and Hooker, he did not absorb whole bodies of material.

The relatively limited extent of Shakespeare's reading made the sources that he used for his plays doubly important. They not only provided plots but also stimulated and directed his thinking. They furnished his mind as well as his stage. From Halle and, to a lesser extent from Holinshed, he derived an interpretation of history and the beginnings of a philosophic view of life. *The Troublesome Raigne* aroused his interest in the Tudor concept of monarchy and in the consequences of civil strife both for society and for the individual. As early as *Henry VI*, it probably gave point to the teachings of the Elizabethan Homilies, and it led directly to the elaborate treatment of themes from the Homilies in *Richard II*. It is very likely that the preoccupation with sensual love in *Hamlet* and *Troilus and Cressida*, as well as in other plays of the period, may have been stimulated by the portrayal of Gertrude's character which filled the closet scene of the old *Hamlet*, as it did the parallel section of Belleforest's narrative.

There can be no question that Shakespeare needed to acquire a great deal from his reading and from his sources, for the learning that he brought from Stratford was severely limited. As we have seen, it included the rhetoric and mythology of grammar-school Latin authors, a thorough religious training, and quite literally nothing else except for a knowledge of rural sights and sounds, of farming and the care of domestic animals. A slow but steady broadening of his learning is indicated by details of contemporary science that occur in his plays with increasing frequency.

No characteristic of Shakespeare's thinking is more significant than this slow germination of concepts after he encountered them. He probably knew the Homilies even before he came to London, and traces of their teaching on the kingship appear in his earliest plays. But their full impact upon his mind took almost five years to develop and reached ultimate expression in *Richard II*. Similarly, if we assume that he read Hooker shortly after *Of the Laws of Ecclesiastical Polity* appeared in 1594, he mulled it over for three or four years before showing its influence in his plays, and the elaborate exposition of its ideas in *Troilus and Cressida* came after six or seven years. This lag agrees remarkably well with the interval between his major sources and the plays based upon them. He may never have blotted a line, but he apparently did a good deal of thinking before committing the line to paper. That point deserves stressing.

It is also interesting that the impact of the Homilies and probably of Hooker appears first in details and then in the form of systematic exposition. When Shakespeare finally thought through the entire system, it gave meaning, in turn, to details, so that subsequent allusions became much fuller and more meaningful. This was particularly true of Hooker, who expounded what was, in effect, the central tradition of Western Christian thought and who furnished a framework into which Shakespeare could fit religious doctrine and psychological concepts.

More significant by far than the slow growth of Shakespeare's learning, if I am right in my interpretation, was the final development of this philosophic insight, which provided him with a notion of causation that transformed his character drawing and with a theory of tragedy that shaped his greatest plays. It is surely no accident that his first clear allusions to laws of nature, which imply a sequence of cause and effect, coincided roughly with his attempt to show the growth of Hal from boy to man. Almost immediately thereafter, the last romantic comedies and the tragedies began to motivate action in terms of mental processes that they revealed by soliloquies and asides as well as by less artificial devices, so that, as we watch or read them, we become more interested in what is happening to the souls of the characters than in the progress of events. In a way, we know Hamlet as we can never know our closest friends.

While Shakespeare was applying this concept of causation to the actions of individuals, he was also working out its implications on a universal scale. For a God who intervened actively, an incalculable Fortune, and an erratic human character, he was substituting, as the moving force in events, the regular operation of laws of nature. To this view of life he first gave adequate logical statement in *Troilus and Cressida*, which described a universal order of which the "moral laws of nature and of nations" were an expression. To these laws man was obedient if he was rational. If reason lost control and he violated them, he insured his own destruction and a violent disruption of the entire order of nature. The need for reason to control man's life and the fatal consequences of its failure to do so became the theme of the great tragedies, a theme worked out both in a personal and in a cosmic setting. By developing a tragic formula centered in moral choice, Shakespeare managed to give to his philosophy of life an almost perfect dramatic embodiment.

One may not believe that there are laws of nature; one may grant that there are principles of cause and effect which can be called laws without too much violence to metaphor and still doubt that they are moral, even in the cosmic sense in which they are moral in *Lear*. But one cannot deny that Shakespeare's vision of life invested his characters with meaning and with emotional conviction. What is even more important, it enabled him to face issues squarely and with a clarity that our own sentimental and fuzzy-headed age sometimes finds appalling. The wages of sin is death—of one kind or another—and Shakespeare confronted that fact honestly. Failure to use one's brains, both to chart a course of action and to follow it once it has been determined, may lead to disaster not only for one's self but for innocent bystanders as well, and Shakespeare presents the full consequences of ignorance and irrationality. Like the fundamental ideas of any period, those of the Renaissance had been tested by experience and found adequate; in using them, Shakespeare applied to his own observations the best thought of the ages, and the deeper his insight probed, the higher his dramatic achievement soared.

The Source of *Hamlet*

CONVINCING reconstruction of the lost Hamlet play often ascribed to Kyd is possible only if some reliance can be placed upon *Der bestrafte Brudermord*. We should perhaps note, therefore, that Frederick S. Boas, after working on the "Ur-Hamlet" in connection with his edition of Kyd, concluded that, "if traces of the old play survive at all, it is in the First quarto only that they are to be found."[1] And L. L. Schücking is almost equally doubtful of the value of the German play.[2] So we proceed at our peril despite their warning. But one thing is certain: the *Brudermord* contains parallels to Belleforest as against either of the quarto versions or the folio, to the first quarto as against the second quarto and folio, and to the second quarto and folio as against the first quarto. In other words, it has points in common with each of the extant versions as against all the others. It also has peculiarities of its own. In his careful discussion of its relationship to the Shakespearean play Duthie presents, in general, three hypotheses, although he distinguishes more elaborately among minor variants than is practicable in the present study. All three theories assume that some modifications of the text were made on the Continent. (1) The *Brudermord* was derived in some fashion from the second quarto text. (2) It was based upon the old play or "Ur-Hamlet," from which come its parallels to Belleforest as against Shakespeare; all parallels to Q1 and Q2-F1 it owes to survivals of the old play in two successive Shakespearean versions; those peculiar to Q1 reflect details in a first Shakespearean version subsequently modified; and those peculiar

---

[1] *The Works of Thomas Kyd*, p. xlix.
[2] *The Meaning of Hamlet*, p. 174.

to Q2-F1 come from details in the old play that were retained in Shakespeare's final version but were missed by the person or persons responsible for the theft of Q1. (3) Duthie himself proposes a theory involving a memorial reconstruction, chiefly from Q2 but also from Q1 and the pre-Shakespearean *Hamlet*.[3]

Of these hypotheses the first is obviously untenable because of parallels peculiar to the German play and Belleforest. As Duthie concludes: "Indebtedness to the old plays is a fact, but the extent of the indebtedness is not determinable."[4] His rejection of the second hypothesis in favor of his own, which postulates a far more complicated origin for the play and is therefore intrinsically less probable, seems to result from his conviction that the parallels of detail between the *Brudermord* and Q2-F1 are so numerous that they cannot be accounted for by assuming that traces of the language of the old play remained in Shakespeare. "If in the main the *Brudermord* represents the old Hamlet, then the latter resembled Shakespeare's full play very much more than I should be prepared to suppose was the case."[5] And he cites a list of thirty-six close parallels, although many of them amount to no more than a phrase or an idea. But what of the evidence presented by Shakespeare's *King John*? It would be no trick at all to construct a list of a hundred instances in which Shakespeare reflects the language or the thought of *The Troublesome Raigne*,[6] and echoes of the sources are equally numerous in plays founded upon Holinshed or Plutarch or in *Romeo and Juliet*. The survival in Shakespeare of frequent traces of the source play is exactly what we should expect, and those common to the *Brudermord* and Q2-F1 are not surprising even assuming that half or two-thirds of the original parallels disappeared in the process of translation and adaptation. The details that Shakespeare would retain, furthermore, are precisely the striking turns of thought in the original that would be most likely to survive translation and adaptation. The simpler hypothesis— that the *Brudermord* is a version of the old Hamlet play which has

[3] *The 'Bad' Quarto of Hamlet*, pp. 239-40, 269.

[4] Ibid., p. 268.

[5] Ibid., p. 253.

[6] Dover Wilson actually gives a list of 18 verbal parallels, in addition to a large number of parallel details already discussed, and concludes: "Many more parallels will be found in my notes, and so frequently do they occur that I have probably overlooked not a few" (New Cambridge *King John*, p. xxvii).

undergone some change during its life on the Continent—is also supported by Shakespeare's own habits of using his sources; for we are sure that the play was put together for a company traveling on the Continent, and another busy actor would also be likely to consult the minimum number of texts necessary to produce an actable play.

Since it will be necessary to consider the differences between Q1 and Q2-F1 in trying to see what they indicate as to Shakespeare's intentions, I shall not discuss the controversy over its relationship to Q2 at this point, except to remark that I find unconvincing the evidence adduced by Greg and Wilson to support their theory that the text of Q1 derives from some stage in the textual history of F1 after it became distinct from Q2. Obviously, if Q1 and F1 shared a number of readings in which they were clearly wrong whereas Q2 was clearly right in the equivalent passages, any theory that Q1 represented an earlier version of the play would have to be abandoned immediately. But, after careful examination, I do not see that such examples exist,[7] and I shall

[7]Consider, for example, Greg's list in his *Principles of Emendation in Shakespeare* (pp. 55-59). Of his four groups of readings in which Q1 and F1 agree against Q2, (a) and (b) are irrelevant, the former exhibiting errors in Q2 and the latter instances in which the Q1-F1 readings are preferable; Greg regards the Q2 readings as "manifestly inferior" but probably from Shakespeare's autograph. They have no standing as evidence, since many of a compositor's errors would make good sense and Greg's conjectures would be permissible if his theory were established but would have no standing as evidence. The discussion therefore hinges on groups (c) and (d), which he regards as erroneous readings shared by Q1 and F1. In group (c), according to his own account, editors are divided or the majority have accepted F1 readings in examples (I number them) 1, 2, 3, 4, 5, 6, 7, 9, 10, 12, 13, 14, 15, 16, 17, 18, 19. His list is constructed, in fact, on the assumption that any Q2 reading which can be defended should stand, a theory which assumes the point at issue. Witness his comments: (No. 6) "Apparently Elze alone has followed Q2, but there is no reason why it should not be what Shakespeare wrote;" (No. 12) "Few editors have followed Capell in adhering to Q2; yet it gives very good sense." (No. 15) "A few editors have followed Capell and Q2, but most, especially recent ones, have been biased in favor of F1 by the second half of the line" (and why, in the name of all sound editorial practice, should they not be!). This leaves only examples 8 and 11, which would not be too numerous for pure coincidence even if undoubted. But the shift from "desires" to "desire" in F1 (I, v, 129-30), plus the following phrase "Such as it is" and Hamlet's remark that he will "go pray," suggests to my perhaps depraved mind one of those indecent quibbles of which Hamlet is so fond; and the use of a singular verb with a plural noun can be paralleled in Shakespeare. In (d) No. 1 is a matter of punctuation where, as Greg remarks, the manuscript probably gave little guidance and Q2 perhaps inserted a colon correctly; in No. 2 Q1 actually supports Q2, as Greg remarks; No. 3 rests on Wilson's taste against the majority of editors. In short, granted that Q2 is surely the best text, Greg produces no examples in which following Q1 and F1 against

therefore proceed on the commonly accepted view that Q1 represents an earlier Shakespearean version.

Let us therefore assume the following relationship among the various versions of the play. The pre-Shakespearean *Hamlet* was based upon Belleforest, and *Der bestrafte Brudermord* was derived from it with some adaptation to production in Germany. Upon it Shakespeare also based his first version of *Hamlet*, of which Q1 was a stolen adaptation and condensation, in which the thief (or a reviser or editor of the reported draft) made good the gaps by levying upon contemporary drama or by outright composition. Q2 and F1 are substantially Shakespeare's final version, with some differences due to cutting for stage presentation in the folio text and to minor alterations for various reasons in both texts. Despite minor revisions Q2 may well be printed from the autograph, as Wilson argues. The result may be presented graphically as follows, hypothetical plays being bracketed:

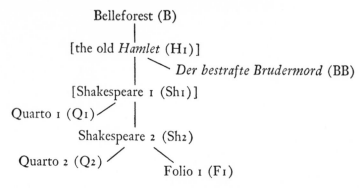

Let us now return to our main problem of ascertaining what changes have been made in these versions and what they show about Shakespeare's interests and intentions. If the *stemma* just

Q2 produces an impossible reading, as he must do if Q1 derived from F1 and therefore inherited its errors. In other words, he shows no common divergent errors such as are required to prove the dependence of one text upon another. Cf. also Wilson, *The Manuscript of Shakespeare's Hamlet*, II, 336-40. W. J. Lawrence (*Shakespeare's Workshop*, p. 111) proposes an altogether different theory of the origin of Q1: "My belief is that, late in 1601, some manager of a country company who happened to possess a copy of the *Ur-Hamlet* conceived the idea of presenting it on his rounds as the new Globe success, and strove to give colour to the deception by making sundry Shakespearean infiltrations, fuller and truer at the beginning than at the end." If so, the reconstruction of H1 would stand, but Sh1 would disappear.

constructed is correct, the following relationships among the different versions logically follow (barring pure coincidence):

1. Anything common to B and BB must have been in H1.

2. Anything common to B and Q1 or Q2-F1 (Sh2) must have been in H1 and Sh1.

3. Anything common to BB and Q1 or Q2-F1 must have been in H1 and Sh1.

4. Anything common to Q1 and Q2-F1 must have been in Sh1.[8]

On this hypothesis—recognizing fully that, at least from the reader's point of view, it is still only a hypothesis for which no proof has been advanced—we shall try to trace the evolution of the Hamlet story from Belleforest to Shakespeare's final version. I hope that the results will themselves serve to demonstrate the probability of the hypothesis, in that they will show our *Hamlet* to be a logical outgrowth of habits of work and of interests that we have watched developing throughout Shakespeare's plays.

Belleforest's story contains roughly the following elements.[9] Horvendile and Fengon were joint governors of the province of Ditmarsse in Denmark. Horvendile and Collere, King of Norway, engaged in single combat with the understanding that whoever won should gain the other's wealth. When Horvendile killed Collere and raided Norway itself, the King of Denmark was so impressed that he married his daughter Geruth to Horvendile. Sometime thereafter Fengon "incestuously abused"[10] Geruth, and finally he slew Horvendile at a banquet with the aid of a band of followers. He then married Geruth, committing "two-fold impietie, as incestuous adulterie and parricide murther."[11] Hamblet,

---

[8]Lewis (*The Genesis of Hamlet*, p. 69) gives a summary which is perhaps simpler, although it leaves out of account differences between Q1 and Q2-F1: "...whatever we find in both Belleforest and the German adapter, or in both Belleforest and Shakespeare, must have been in Kyd [the old play]; for how else could the later dramatist have stumbled upon it? And whatever we find common to the German dramatist and Shakespeare must also have been in Kyd, unless we are willing to accord large privilege to chance coincidence."

[9]Hazlitt, *Shakespeare's Library*, II (Part 1), 224-67; *The Sources of Hamlet* (The Shakespeare Classics), pp. 178-263. The latter is to be preferred, since it gives the original French text.

[10]French "incestueusement souillé" (*The Sources of Hamlet*, pp. 186-87).

[11]Ibid., pp. 188-89.

son of Horvendile and Geruth, pretended madness so that Fengon would think it unnecessary to kill him to eliminate a possible avenger of Horvendile; but, by the "sharp and pregnant spirit" underneath his supposed madness, he aroused the suspicion of the wiser sort, and they counselled Fengon to test him. To this end, they brought Hamblet together with a woman in the woods, but he was warned by a courtier to have nothing to do with the lady. "Which much abashed the prince, as then wholy beeing in affection to the lady, but by her he was likewise informed of the treason, as being one that from her infancy loved and favoured him, and would have been exceeding sorrowfull for his misfortune, and much more to leave his companie without injoying the pleasure of his body, whome she loved more than herselfe."[12] Hamblet therefore rejected the lady and survived the test. But one of Fengon's friends, still doubting Hamblet, proposed that Fengon go on a trip and Hamblet be shut up with his mother, while the friend hid behind a hanging. Hamblet, being suspicious, beat his arms like a cock against the hangings and, feeling something stir, thrust his sword through and killed the man,[13] whose body he cut up, had boiled, and cast down a privy. Hamblet then upbraided his mother for living in sensuality like a brute beast. She pleaded compulsion and promised to aid him in securing vengeance, which, Hamblet carefully explained, would "neither be fellonie nor treason . . . but I shall justly punish him as my subject."[14] Fengon, still suspicious, did not dare kill Hamblet outright, since he feared the king, Geruth's father, and was afraid to offend her. So he sent Hamblet to England with two of his faithful ministers. In the meantime, Hamblet gave Geruth instructions to prepare means for his vengeance when he returned. While his companions slept, he read their letter instructing the King of England to put him to death. This he altered so that it commanded that the companions be put to death and the King's daughter given to him in marriage. From there on Belleforest's story is no longer pertinent, except that, when Hamblet returns, he finds a funeral in progress (his own,

[12]". . . car elle l'aymoit des son enfance, et eust esté bien marie de son desastre et fortune, et plus de sortir de ses mains, sans jouyr de celuy qu'elle aimoit plus que soymesme" (ibid., pp. 202-203).

[13]The parallel "A rat, a rat!" in the English version is not in the French and must be derived from the play (ibid., pp. 206-207).

[14]So also the French (ibid., pp. 224-27).

however). The revenge itself was completely unsuitable for the stage, since Hamblet made the courtiers very drunk, bound them by nailing wall hangings to the floor, and burned them in their liquor somewhat like human *crêpes suzette*. It should be noted, however, that he killed Fengon by changing swords with him after he had nailed his own to its scabbard so that Fengon could not draw it.

Certain characteristics of this story are also relevant to the final play. The character of the female decoy was, at best, ambiguous, and perhaps it was never quite straightened out even after she was endowed with a family and a pathetic life (and death) of her own. A strong moralizing vein is apparent both in Hamblet's language to his mother, which is surprisingly close to what Shakespeare makes him say in the closet scene, and in the comments upon the evils of strong drink which are also reflected in Shakespeare.[15] Finally, the story has many traces of the clever hero of primitive folklore. Hamblet cannot tell a lie, even about the King's dead friend (although the point is forgotten when he alters the letter), and he resorts to an equivocation for which he has prepared with extraordinary foresight. He promises his mother to return in just a year and does so. He both speaks and solves riddles, and the latter part of the story after his revenge becomes increasingly like a fairy tale. The riddling element survives into Shakespeare, where Hamlet's bright but enigmatic remarks are calculated to unmask his pretense of madness just as they do in the source, where he also threatens his uncle publicly.

The adaptation of this story in *Der bestrafte Brudermord* involved, in general, the changes that we should expect in a revenge play on the model of *The Spanish Tragedy*. The play opens with a classical prologue, interesting only because it may imply that Erico and Sigrie (Claudius and Gertrude) had not committed adultery before the murder, whereas the play itself says clearly that they had. The ghost is then introduced exactly as in Shakespeare, while healths are drunk within to the sound of the trumpet. But Hamlet appears immediately, hears the ghost's revelations, and swears to revenge him. The ghost is, however, a very different figure from Shakespeare's. It clownishly gives the sentry a box

[15]This also is in the French, although one might suspect it of being an English addition (ibid., pp. 252-55).

on the ear, and it has neither dignity nor personality. Hamlet remarks, on hearing of its resemblance to the dead King: "I hope not; for the souls of the pious rest quietly till the time of their resurrection."[16] But it has none of the Christian atmosphere of Shakespeare's ghost. Horatio doubts it, and so does Hamlet later; but the doubt is never explained in Christian terms. In short, the ghost is still of the standard revenge type, although it is an integral part of the action. Hamlet explains that the ghost has revealed a matter of vengeance, and Horatio and Francisco swear to aid him in the unspecified revenge, spurred on by the ghost.

As soon as Francisco leaves, Hamlet takes Horatio completely into his confidence, revealing what the ghost has said and explaining: ". . . but from this moment I will begin a feigned madness, and, thus feigning, so cunningly will I play my part that I shall find an opportunity to avenge my father's death."[17] Since making the murder a secret and introducing the ghost eliminated the reason for feigning madness given in Belleforest, the madness now becomes a scheme to make the King and his guards less watchful and to gain an opportunity to kill him. The equivalent of Shakespeare's second scene now follows, but the King first requests Hamlet not to return to Wittenberg and then asks Corambus about his son Leonhardus, who has already returned to France with his father's permission. There is, however, no mention of Norway. The carousing turns out to be an attempt on the King's part to make his new wife forget her melancholy. This detail, which motivates the heavy drinking in the play (and may have prepared for Hamlet's understanding with his mother in the closet scene in the source play), is typical of the careful attention to motivation of action apparent throughout most of the play.

In the second act Corambus reports that Hamlet is mad (he indulges in the same logic-chopping and long-windedness as Polonius). Ophelia then appears to complain that Hamlet is giving her no peace, Corambus concludes on the spot that Hamlet is mad for love, the King asks to see Hamlet's madness on exhibition, and Corambus proposes that they hide while Ophelia shows him a jewel that he gave her. All this happens in a few lines, and the equivalent of Shakespeare's nunnery scene then follows immediately instead of after the arrival of the players.

[16] I, iv. Variorum *Hamlet*, II, 124.   [17] I, vi. Ibid., p. 126.

Hamlet appears for no apparent reason and insults Ophelia much as in Shakespeare. The references to a nunnery are made explicit: "No, go to a nunnery, but not to a nunnery where two pairs of slippers lie at the bedside."[18] And a story of a bridegroom's horror at encountering his bride without her artificial beauty perhaps corresponds to Shakespeare's "God hath given you one face and you make yourself another" (III, i, 149-50). After watching Hamlet, the King concludes that his madness is not genuine and that he must be "removed from here if not from life."

In a short scene Hamlet explains to Horatio: ". . . through this assumed madness I hope to get the opportunity of revenging my father's death. You know, however, that my father is always surrounded by many guards; wherefore it may miscarry. Should you chance to find my dead body, let it be honorably buried." These words are interesting as a restatement of the motivation of Hamlet's assumed madness and as a possible clue to the origin of the soliloquy "To be or not to be," which is, of course, a meditation not upon suicide but upon the death that may come from taking "arms against a sea of troubles."[19] Horatio then warns Hamlet again that the ghost has perhaps deceived him.

Corambus appears to announce the players. Hamlet comments: "When Marus Russig was a comedian in Rome, what a fine time that was" (cf. *Hamlet*, II, ii, 410) alludes to Jephthah's daughter, whereupon Corambus replies: "Your Highness always will be bringing in my daughter."[20] Though much shortened, this is very close to the parallel scene in Shakespeare. But, as Latham pointed out, Marus Russig suggests a learned playwright who confused Roscius the actor with Sextus Roscius Amerinus, whom Cicero also defended.[21] I would add that the kind of elaborate classical reference which must lie back of the blunder was characteristic of English drama in the late 1580's, as we have noticed in *Henry VI* and *The Troublesome Raigne*.

Hamlet then lectures the actors on proper dress and proper manners. He chooses a piece called King Pyrro which has the same plot as Shakespeare's play but suggests some connection with the

[18]II, iv. Ibid., p. 128.

[19]On this point I take my stand with Dr. Johnson against all comers. Cf. Variorum *Hamlet*, I, 204-206; New Cambridge *Hamlet*, p. 190.

[20]II, vi. Variorum *Hamlet*, II, 128-29.   [21]Ibid., II, 119.

declamation about Pyrrhus (*Hamlet*, II, ii, 472-519), and he warns
Horatio to watch the King as in Shakespeare (III, ii, 80-92). But
note that here Hamlet's request is natural enough, since Horatio
has known from the first what the ghost revealed. In Shakespeare
Hamlet also asks Horatio to corroborate his observations and says
that he has acquainted Horatio with the ghost's revelation (III, ii,
82), whereas we have seen him refuse to tell Horatio anything
(cf. I, v, 117-26). The court assembles for the play, and Hamlet
assures the King that it has no offensive matter. The dumb show
proceeds while Hamlet explains its meaning. The King rises immediately, and Hamlet and Horatio agree that the ghost's veracity
is proved. This arrangement, it will be noted, removes the major
problem present in Shakespeare's play of explaining why Claudius
did not take offence at the dumb show.[22]

Hamlet leaves Horatio to look for the King and finds him at
prayer before an altar in a temple. Again motives are more clearly
stated than in Shakespeare, although less intelligible, for Hamlet
starts to stab the King twice and then says: "But hold, Hamlet!
why wouldst thou take his sins upon thyself?"[23]

Corambus is discussing Hamlet's madness with the Queen when
Horatio appears to ask a private audience for Hamlet. She tells
Corambus to hide. This arrangement looks like an attempt to introduce strict court etiquette; as such, it parallels one of the themes
of Hamlet's lecture to the players. As soon as Hamlet arrives, he
begins to upbraid his mother, comparing pictures of the dead King
and the present one, and then he becomes suspicious. "But hush!
are all the doors shut fast?"[24] Corambus coughs and Hamlet stabs
him. This sequence of suspicion and cough is much inferior to
Shakespeare's management of events but also much closer to Belleforest. The ghost then appears and Hamlet leaves immediately.
The Queen has a peculiar soliloquy half blaming herself for causing Hamlet's madness and concluding: "If the pope had not allowed the marriage, it would never have taken place. I will go
hence, and try my best to restore my son to his former sense and
health."[25] She does not arrive at any understanding with Hamlet
as in Belleforest or the first quarto.

---

[22]Cf. Wilson's elaborate, but not wholly convincing, attack upon this problem
in *What Happens in Hamlet*, pp. 174-97.   [23]III, ii. Variorum *Hamlet*, II, 132.
[24]III, v. Ibid., II, 133.   [25]III, vi. Ibid., II, 133.

From here on the *Brudermord* deviates more widely from Shakespeare's play, although in some details it may be closer to the original version. Phantasmo, who corresponds to Osric, has a series of scenes with Ophelia, who is now mad. The entry of an elaborate character like Osric at the end of the play is a little peculiar, and behind the matter-of-fact statements of the *Brudermord* one can detect some outrageous but very funny comedy. Imagine Osric, trailing laces, ribbons, and especially perfume, being pursued by a mad woman who thinks him her sweetheart. She first discusses their going to bed and then, as she comes to windward, adds: "I will wash thee quite clean."[26]

The King sends Hamlet to England but makes double provision for his death. He instructs the attendants to kill him with daggers or pistols but gives them a letter, as in the source, to use if their first attempt should miscarry. They land on an island to eat, and there they plan to murder Hamlet, who escapes by getting the two attendants to shoot at him from opposite directions and kill each other when he falls forward. He then searches them and finds the letter. His clever little stratagem is obviously the subsequent inspiration of an inferior mind.

Leonhardus arrives demanding satisfaction for his father. Hamlet is reported back, and the King and Leonhardus devise a fencing match in which Leonhardus is to drop his rapier and pick up a sharp sword smeared with poison. If this fails, the King will give him a diamond pounded up with sugar in a beaker of wine. Ophelia enters and distributes wild flowers.

Hamlet appears regretting in a soliloquy that he cannot get at the King because he is surrounded by so many people. He then gives Horatio an account of his adventures. Phantasmo comes to report the King's wager on Hamlet's fencing, and Hamlet gets him to admit that he is hot, medium, and cold, the episode being derived from Juvenal and perhaps a little closer to the source here than in Shakespeare.

Just as the fencing commences, the Queen announces that Ophelia has thrown herself off a high hill and killed herself. After the King offers a perfunctory condolence to Leonhardis, the fight goes on. The exchange of swords is carefully explained. Leonhardus drops his rapier, seizes the poisoned sword, and wounds

[26]III, ix. Ibid., II, 134.

Hamlet in the arm. Hamlet parries so that they both drop their weapons. Hamlet gets the poisoned sword and wounds Leonhardus mortally. The King prepares to give them both the drink as he sees Leonhardus confessing to Hamlet, but the Queen drinks first. Hamlet stabs the King. Phantasmo confesses that he brought the poisoned cup, and Hamlet kills him. Feeling himself dying, he instructs Horatio to carry the crown to Norway to his cousin the Duke Fortembras, who has not previously been mentioned.

Der bestrafte Brudermord is peculiar. It makes its points in the fewest possible words and without any enrichment of language. Much of it reads like a full summary of a play that a very industrious but utterly unimaginative student might write. And that is perhaps its value to us. It is a principle of textual criticism that no scribe was so dangerous to the original text as one with learning and imagination and none so reliable as a careful plodder. The German play reveals that kind of transmission. Much of it, furthermore, reflects a very tidy source. The plot is developed with as few scenes as possible and with careful motivation of the action until the last act, where something is badly wrong. Ophelia gets all mixed up, and it is unthinkable that her death was originally reported during the fencing match. Her suicide, however, is probably closer to the old play than Shakespeare's account, which involves an obvious inconsistency between the Queen's report that she has drowned accidentally (IV, vii, 167-84) and the priest's statement that her death was doubtful (that is, suicide) and that she would not even have been buried in consecrated ground if pressure had not been brought to bear (V, i, 250-53). Her death must reflect the source, since it has no point in either play except to harrow Laertes' feelings even further.

We are finally ready to attempt a reconstruction of the old *Hamlet*.[27] It obviously involved a secret murder, a ghost who was doubted, and an immediate understanding between Hamlet and Horatio. As a revenge play, it had to keep the feigned madness, which it motivated as an attempt by Hamlet to penetrate the King's guards by seeming a harmless lunatic.[28] It cleverly joined into one family Belleforest's slain counselor and the decoy whom

---

[27]For other reconstructions of the old play cf. Lewis, *The Genesis of Hamlet,* pp. 66-91; Stoll, *Hamlet,* p. 4.
[28]Cf. Schücking, *Character Problems in Shakespeare's Plays,* p. 149.

Hamlet had loved and added a son to kill Hamlet in revenge, thereby achieving a masterly parallel of the main plot in the action of the subplot, and a contrast between Ophelia's authentic madness and Hamlet's feigning. Apparently it did not straighten out Hamlet's relationship to Ophelia, and perhaps it did not show Corambus' family together, since the *Brudermord's* statement that Leonhardus had already returned to France may be the original version changed by Shakespeare to keep him in Denmark for the scene with Polonius and Ophelia. The redactor of the *Brudermord* would not have felt bound to mention him if he cut a family scene in the old play, if we may judge by his handling of Ophelia's death; whereas, if the old *Hamlet* was as careful of plot structure as seems likely, it would have mentioned Laertes to prepare for his subsequent appearance.

There was probably but one ghost scene, and the nunnery scene came as it does in the *Brudermord* and in the first quarto, although that problem will be discussed later. By another stroke of genius the play was changed from a means of revenge, as in *The Spanish Tragedy*, to a test of the ghost's veracity. It was probably confined to a dumb show, and "The Murder of Gonzago" is Shakespeare's addition. The scene with the King at prayer followed, but probably Hamlet sought out the King and eluded his guards. He must have decided not to kill the King to make sure of his eternal damnation, since the motive which Hamlet states reflects both the injunction given him by the ghost in Shakespeare and the insistence by the ghost in *The Spanish Tragedy* upon revenge for all eternity. In the closet scene Gertrude promised aid to Hamlet, as in Belleforest and in the first quarto. This outcome would be motivated by her melancholy, of which such a point is made in the *Brudermord*, and it is, as we shall see, required to explain even the Q2-F1 text.

From then on reconstruction becomes difficult. The old play obviously retained the attendants and the letter from the source, but how Hamlet escaped we cannot tell. The fight with the pirates looks like one of those desperate expedients to which Shakespeare was sometimes driven in an effort to shorten a more probable series of events in his source. Ophelia went mad and committed suicide, and Laertes killed Hamlet much as in the present play. It is possible that Ophelia's funeral figured in the old play, since

Hamblet returned in Belleforest to find a funeral in progress and the fight in the grave could have been used to lead up to the fencing match. But all this is pure conjecture, and we have been confining our reconstruction of the old play to what can reasonably be inferred from the extant versions.

We are perhaps justified, however, in making a few inferences as to the character of the old play. Its action seems to have been simpler and more direct than Shakespeare's and to have avoided doubling the ghost scene and interweaving events leading up to the nunnery scene and the play. Such doubling and complicating of the action, especially in the early part of a play, is characteristic of Shakespeare. There is enough of Corambus in the *Brudermord* to show that Shakespeare took him over intact, just as he borrowed the nurse in *Romeo and Juliet* and the Bastard in *King John*. The moral emphasis of Belleforest and some of his learning carried right through into Shakespeare; so it must have been present in the old play. The old *Hamlet* must have raised the problem of incest created by Gertrude's marriage to her brother-in-law, which was forbidden by the Church of England as well as by Rome. One is tempted to see in the *Brudermord's* reference to the Pope's responsibility for the Queen's action a reflection of anti-Catholic propaganda in the old play, but it is more likely an independent addition by the redactor, since Shakespeare parallels Belleforest. References to Gertrude's adultery before the murder must have been unemphatic, if one may judge by the contradiction in the *Brudermord* and by Shakespeare's failure to stress the point, although I take him to be explicit enough. The single soliloquy in the German suggests that Hamlet must have lamented his inability to achieve revenge rather than his failure to do so.[29]

Finally, the old play was extremely well constructed. The handling of the ghost and of the dumb show was a stroke of genius, and so was the convergence of the subplot upon the main plot in such a way that Laertes' revenging of his father coincided with Hamlet's vengeance and destroyed them both. The only

[29]Shücking goes farther: "Shakespeare found in the figure of the *Urhamlet*, which is proved by the cognate principal character of *The Spanish Tragedy* to have possessed a far more diversified and fascinating physiognomy than is commonly assumed, a splendid model for his art of character refinement" (*Character Problems in Shakespeare's Plays*, p. 171).

loose end that can be detected was Hamlet's pat arrival for the nunnery scene, and Shakespeare failed to solve that difficulty. If the old play resembled the *Brudermord* in that Ophelia used a jewel instead of remembrances to open the conversation, it avoided a difficulty, since she might normally be wearing a jewel (Q1 makes her offer to return "a small remembrance, such tokens which I have received of you").

Comparison of Q1 with Q2-F1 reveals four main differences. These seem to prove that Q1 is derived from Shakespeare's first adaptation of the old play, and that Q2-F1 represent a further revision. The first divergence lies in the use of Corambus as the name of the chief counselor. The sharing of this name by the *Brudermord* and Q1 merely proves that the two must stand together as both derived from earlier versions of the play or from one adaptation of the folio text. We need not discuss this point further except to remark that any independent evidence that the *Brudermord* was derived wholly or in part from the old play must also establish Q1 as representing a draft prior to Q2 and further invalidates the theory advanced by Greg and Wilson. The second main difference is the placing of the nunnery scene, which in Q1 immediately follows its planning and precedes Hamlet's dialogue with Corambus (the present II, ii, 170-223). The textual evidence as to the original position of the nunnery scene is perhaps inconclusive. Against the Q1 order might be noted the awkwardness of Hamlet's entry, book in hand, to encounter Ophelia also reading[30] and Ophelia's being provided with Hamlet's "remembrances" when Corambus proposes the stratagem. But if the remembrances were jewelry, as in the *Brudermord*, that difficulty vanishes. On the other hand, Q2-F1 makes Polonius say to Ophelia: "Come, go we to the King" (II, i, 117). Yet he appears alone. Q1 prepares for her presence in the nunnery scene by making her enter with Polonius at a point equivalent to II, ii, 40. Previous discussions have generally turned on the few points mentioned, and the bearing of Hamlet's dialogue with Polonius (II, ii, 170-223) has not been sufficiently

[30]Craig cites parallels to show that the soliloquy is largely derived from Cardan's *Comforte* and remarks: "...one may point out that belief in the therapeutic power of books was characteristic of Renaissance students. If a hero found himself stricken with grief, as Hamlet did, it was natural that he should resort to a work on consolation." ("Hamlet's Book," p. 18.)

considered. In his *What Happens in Hamlet* Dover Wilson argues at some length that, in this same scene at is appears in Q2, Hamlet should appear on the inner stage some ten lines before the entry indicated at II, ii, 168, and should overhear Polonius say: "At such a time I'll loose my daughter to him." As evidence he cites Hamlet's calling Polonius a fishmonger (that is, a bawd) and his references to the danger of conception. These, he thinks, follow from Polonius' unfortunate choice of the word "loose."[31] He is certainly right in remarking that Shakespeare is accustomed to sustain the same imagery throughout a scene. But his arguments are equally pertinent, and involve no assumed stage direction, if used to prove that Ophelia has just been "loosed" to Hamlet and has just experienced the insults of the nunnery scene, which also turn on breeding sinners. Hamlet's words to Polonius then become an extension of his gibes at Ophelia and are his comment on the little scene which, according to dramatic tradition, he has recognized part way through as staged for the benefit of his enemies.

It seems to me absolutely clear that the Q1 version of the closet scene, which constitutes a third divergence, was the earlier. As the play now stands, Hamlet kills someone behind the arras, the Queen rebukes him for his "rash and bloody deed," and he retorts:

> A bloody deed! Almost as bad, good mother,
> As kill a king and marry with his brother.
>
> (III, iv, 28-29)

"As kill a king!" exclaims Gertrude, and, as Bradley comments,[32] her astonishment is evidently genuine. As he also points out, "The queen was not a bad-hearted woman, not at all the woman to think little of murder."[33] He is establishing the fact that she was ignorant of the murder, as is perfectly clear from the language of the play. But, like other critics, he overlooks the fact that, as the play stands, Shakespeare shows her being told that her late husband was murdered, being distracted by the discovery of Polonius' body, and then not investigating the alleged murder either as a revelation of the truth or as an illusion that would explain Hamlet's melancholy. Apparently she overlooked the

[31]Pp. 103-108.   [32]*Shakespearean Tragedy*, p. 166.
[33]Ibid., p. 167.

remark completely, nor was it recalled to her when Hamlet called Claudius "a murderer and a villain" who had stolen the kingdom. She must have been ten times as insensible as Hamlet accused her of being!

Now examine the sequence of Q1, and see how much better sense everything makes. Gertrude still, in effect, calls the ghost "the very coinage of your brain" (III, iv, 137), but she accepts the murder as a fact:

> Alas, it is the weaknesse of thy braine,
> Which makes thy tongue to blazen thy hearts grief:
> But as I have a soule, I sweare by heaven,
> I never knew of this most horride murder:
> But Hamlet, this is onely fantasie,
> And for my love forget these idle fits.

Later Hamlet says:

> Forbeare the adulterous bed to night,
> And win your selfe by little as you may,
> In time it may be you wil lothe him quite:
> And mother, but assist me in revenge,
> And in his death your infamy shall die.

To which she replies:

> *Hamlet*, I vow by that majesty,
> That knowes our thoughts, and lookes into our hearts,
> I will conceale, consent, and doe my best,
> What stratagem soe're thou shalt devise.

That her last lines involve a recollection of *The Spanish Tragedy* seems to indicate that the creator of this version recognized a parallel situation and recalled the earlier play, as he did repeatedly.[34] Hamlet has said nothing more about the murder than is in the accepted text, and yet all makes sense: she protests her innocence, he asks her to aid him, she promises to conceal his plan and to do her best, and he tells her, as in Q2, that he will trust Rosencrantz and Guildenstern like "adders fang'd":

> They bear the mandate. They must sweep my way,
> And marshall me to knavery.   (III, iv, 204-205)

Unless he has reached an understanding with Gertrude, this remark from Q2 is most imprudent. But the most convincing

---

[34]Cf. Duthie, *The 'Bad' Quarto of Hamlet*, p. 196.

evidence that Q1 represents an earlier version closer to the old play lies in the relation of the scene to the play as a whole. In Q2-F1 it is fundamental to our understanding of Hamlet, but from the death of Polonius on it has absolutely nothing to do with the plot of the play. In Q1 it characterizes Hamlet, but it also is part of the alignment of forces for the revenge. The inference is inescapable that, as so often, Shakespeare eliminated the key lines when he changed his design but left a good many loose ends. It may be replied that Gertrude does nothing much to aid him either in Q1 or in Q2-F1, and that is true. But she is fundamentally passive in all her relationships, and her first and only words after drinking the poisoned cup are a warning to Hamlet.

Of the scene in Q1 in which Horatio describes Hamlet's journey to the Queen and she tells him to warn Hamlet to be careful, Chambers writes: "Here the original version must be that of Q2 and F, since v. 2. 1-74 is represented in *B. B.*"[35] But he overlooks the obvious fact that the scene in Q1 is a conflation of two scenes, both of which are apparent in it. The first half mentions a letter and must represent whatever in Shakespeare's first version was equivalent to the present IV, vi; the second half corresponds to V, ii, in the *Brudermord* or Shakespeare's V, ii, 1-74.[36] The principle of economy also supports Q1 as the earlier version, which otherwise has nothing positive in its favor except its dependence upon the closet scene. If the earlier draft showed an understanding between Hamlet and Gertrude, Shakespeare had to bring the first of the two scenes which lay back of Q1 into conformity with Hamlet's new distrust of Gertrude. If Q1 was derived from Q2 and whoever was responsible for Q1 inserted the understanding, then he went to the trouble of composing a quite unnecessary scene, for the present IV, vi, and V, ii, 1-74, would do perfectly well with either arrangement of the closet scene.

The evidence therefore supports the arrangement of the versions of *Hamlet* assumed at the beginning of this discussion.

[35]*William Shakespeare*, I, 417.
[36]Note, however, that BB V, ii, precedes the report of Ophelia's death as does Q2-F1 IV, vi. Both the old *Hamlet* and Sh1 must have had two scenes which were combined independently in both BB and Q1.

BIBLIOGRAPHY

Separate plays in the New Variorum Shakespeare (ed. H. H. Furness, etc.), the Arden Shakespeare (ed. W. J. Craig and R. H. Case), and the New Cambridge Shakespeare (ed. Sir Arthur Quiller-Couch and John Dover Wilson) are not included in the following list. In the notes they are cited simply as Variorum *Hamlet*, Arden *Hamlet*, and New Cambridge *Hamlet* respectively. In the interest of uniformity all editions are listed under author rather than editor, even though prefatory matter has been used. Contributions to *Festschriften* and all other complete essays are listed under individual writers.

Adams, John Cranford. *The Globe Playhouse: Its Design and Equipment.* Cambridge: Harvard University Press, 1942.

Adams, Joseph Quincy. *Shakespearean Playhouses: A History of English Theaters from the Beginnings to the Restoration.* Boston: Houghton Mifflin, 1917.

Alexander, Peter. *Shakespeare's Henry VI and Richard III* (Shakespeare Problems, III). Cambridge: University Press, 1929.
—— *Shakespeare's Life and Art.* London: James Nisbet, 1939.

Allen, John W. *A History of Political Thought in the Sixteenth Century.* 2d ed. London: Methuen, 1941.

Allen, Mozelle Scaff. "Broke's *Romeus and Juliet* as a Source for the Valentine-Sylvia Plot in *The Two Gentlemen of Verona*," *University of Texas Studies in English,* XVIII (1938), 25-46.

Allen, Percy S. *The Age of Erasmus: Lectures Delivered in the Universities of Oxford and London.* Oxford: Clarendon Press, 1914.

Allott, Robert. *Wits Theater of the little World.* [London:] J. R[oberts] for N. L[ing], 1599.

Anders, H. R. D. *Shakespeare's Books: A Dissertation on Shakespeare's Reading and the Immediate Sources of his Works* (Schriften der Deutschen Shakespeare-Gesellschaft, Band I). Berlin: George Reimer, 1904.

Anderson, Ruth L. *Elizabethan Psychology and Shakespeare's Plays* (University of Iowa Humanistic Studies, Vol. III). Iowa City: University of Iowa Press, 1927.

Aphthonius. *Aphthonii Sophistae Progymnasmata, Partim à Rodolpho Agricola, partim à Ioanne Maria Catanaeo latinitate donata: Cum luculentis & utilibus in eadem Scholijs Reinhardi Lorichij Hadamarij.* Franc[ofurti]: Apud Chr. Egenolphum. Colophon 1553.

Aquinas, St. Thomas. *Basic Writings,* ed. Anton G. Pegis. 2 vols. New York: Random House, 1945.

Bacon, Francis. *The Works,* ed. James Spedding, Robert Leslie Ellis, and Douglas Denon Heath. 14 vols. London: Longman, 1857-74.

Baker, Howard. *Induction to Tragedy: A Study in a Development of Form in Gorboduc, The Spanish Tragedy and Titus Andronicus.* University: Louisiana State University Press, 1939.

Baldwin, Thomas W. *On the Literary Genetics of Shakspere's Poems & Sonnets.* Urbana: University of Illinois Press, 1950.
—— *The Organization and Personnel of the Shakespearean Company.* Princeton: Princeton University Press, 1927.
—— *William Shakspere's Petty School.* Urbana: University of Illinois Press, 1943.
—— *William Shakspere's Small Latine & Lesse Greeke.* 2 vols. Urbana: University of Illinois Press, 1944.

Bandello, Matteo. *The Novels of Matteo Bandello Bishop of Agen now first done into English prose and verse by John Payne.* 6 vols. London: Printed for the Villon Society, 1890.

Batman, Stephen. *Batman uppon Bartholome: His Booke De Proprietatibus Rerum.* London: Thomas East, 1582.

Battenhouse, Roy W. "*Measure for Measure* and the Christian Doctrine of Atonement," *PMLA,* LXI (1946), 1029-59.

Begg, Edleen. "Shakespeare's Debt to Hall and to Holinshed in *Richard III,*" *Studies in Philology,* XXXII (1935), 189-96.

Belleforest, François de. *The Sources of Hamlet: With Essay on the Legend by Sir Israel Gollancz.* London: Oxford University Press, 1926.

Bethell, Samuel L. *Shakespeare & the Popular Dramatic Tradition.* Westminster: P. S. King and Staples, 1944.

Boas, Frederick S. *University Drama in the Tudor Age.* Oxford: Clarendon Press, 1914.

Boecker, Alexander. *A Probable Italian Source of Shakespeare's "Julius Caesar"* (Ph. D. Dissertation). New York: New York University, 1913.

Boswell-Stone, Walter G. *Shakspere's Holinshed: The Chronicle and the Historical Plays Compared.* London: Lawrence and Bullen, 1896.

Boyer, Clarence Valentine. *The Villain as Hero in Elizabethan Tragedy.* London: George Routledge, 1914.

Bradbrook, Muriel C. *The School of Night: A Study in the Literary Relationships of Sir Walter Ralegh*. Cambridge: University Press, 1936.

Bradley, Andrew C. *Oxford Lectures on Poetry*. 2d ed. London: Macmillan, 1934.
—— *Shakespearean Tragedy: Lectures on Hamlet, Othello, King Lear, Macbeth*, 2d ed. London: Macmillan, 1922.

Bright, Timothy. *A Treatise of Melancholie*. New York: Columbia University Press for Facsimile Text Society, 1940.

Brooke, Arthur. *Brooke's 'Romeus and Juliet' being the Original of Shakespeare's 'Romeo and Juliet'*, ed. J. J. Munro. (The Shakespeare Classics, Vol. III). London: Chatto and Windus, 1908.

Burton, Robert. *The Anatomy of Melancholy*, ed. A. R. Shilleto. (Bohn's Popular Library). 3 vols. London: G. Bell, 1926.

Bush, Douglas. *Mythology and the Renaissance Tradition in English Poetry*. Minneapolis: University of Minnesota Press, 1932.

Cain, Henry Edward. "Crabbed Age and Youth in 'Romeo and Juliet,'" *Shakespeare Association Bulletin*, IX (1934), 186-91.

Calvin, John. *Institutes of the Christian Religion*, trans. John Allen. 7th American ed., 2 vols. Philadelphia: Presbyterian Board of Christian Education, 1936.

Campbell, Lily B. *Shakespeare's "Histories": Mirrors of Elizabethan Policy*. San Marino, California: The Huntington Library, 1947.
—— *Shakespeare's Tragic Heroes: Slaves of Passion*. Cambridge: University Press, 1930.

Campbell, Oscar James. *Shakespeare's Satire*. London: Oxford University Press, 1943.

Cato, Dionysius. *Catonis Disticha moralia ex castigatione D. Erasmi Roterodami vnà cum annotationibus & scholijs Richardi Tauerneri Anglico idiomate conscriptis in vsum Anglicae iuuentutis*. Londoni: Roberti Caly. 1555.

Certain Sermons or Homilies Appointed to be Read in Churches in the Time of Queen Elizabeth of Famous Memory. London: Society for Promoting Christian Knowledge, 1914.

Chambers, Edmund K. *The Elizabethan Stage*. 4 vols. Oxford: Clarendon Press, 1923.
—— *William Shakespeare, A Study of Facts and Problems*. 2 vols. Oxford: Clarendon Press, 1930.

Chambers, Raymond W. *The Jacobean Shakespeare and Measure for Measure* (Annual Shakespeare Lecture of the British Academy, 1937). London: Humphrey Milford, [1938].

Chapman, George. *The Poems of George Chapman*, ed. Phyllis Brooks Bartlett. New York: Modern Language Association of America, 1941.

Charlton, Henry B. "Notes on 'Love's Labour's Lost,'" *Modern Language Review*, XII (1917), 76-78.
—— *Shakespearian Tragedy*. Cambridge: University Press, 1948.

Cicero, M. Tullius. *M. T. Ciceronis quae exstant omnia opera: Pars Prima sive opera Rhetorica et oratoria*, ed. J. W. Rinn. Vol. I. Parisiis: A. Firminus Didot, 1831.

Cormican, L. A. "Medieval Idiom in Shakespeare: (I) Shakespeare and the Liturgy," *Scrutiny*, XVII (1950), 186-202.

Courthope, William J. *A History of English Poetry*. 6 vols. London: Macmillan, 1895-1910.

Craig, Hardin. *The Enchanted Glass: The Elizabethan Mind in Literature*. New York: Oxford University Press, 1936.
—— "The Ethics of King Lear," *Philological Quarterly*, IV (1925), 97-109.
—— "Hamlet's Book," *Huntington Library Bulletin*, VI (1934), 17-37.
—— "Shakespeare and Formal Logic," *Studies in English Philology: A Miscellany in Honor of Frederick Klaeber*, ed. Kemp Malone and Martin B. Ruud. Minneapolis: University of Minnesota Press, 1929. Pp. 380-96.
——, ed. *Machiavelli's The Prince. An Elizabethan Translation*. Chapel Hill: University of North Carolina Press, 1944.

Crundell, H. W. "Shakespeare, Lyly, and 'Aesop,'" *Notes and Queries*, CLXVIII (1935), 312.

Culmann, Leonard. *Sententiae Pueriles, Anglo-Latinae*. Boston: N. Buttolph, B. Eliot, D. Henchman, and G. Philips, 1723.

Cunliffe, John W. *The Influence of Seneca on Elizabethan Tragedy*. New York: G. E. Stechert, 1925.

Cunningham, James V. "Tragic Effect and Tragic Process in Some Plays of Shakespeare, and their Background in the Literary and Ethical Theory of Classical Antiquity and the Middle Ages." Stanford University unpublished dissertation, 1945.
—— *Woe or Wonder*. Denver: University of Denver Press, 1951.

Curry, Walter Clyde. *Shakespeare's Philosophical Patterns*. Baton Rouge: Louisiana State University Press, 1937.

Delius, Nicholaus. "Brooke's episches und Shakespeare's dramatisches Gedicht von Romeo und Juliet," *Shakespeare Jahrbuch*, XVI (1881), 213-27.

Deutschberger, Paul. "Shakspere on Degree: A Study in Backgrounds," *Shakespeare Association Bulletin*, XVII (1942), 200-207.

Duthie, George Ian. *The 'Bad' Quarto of Hamlet: A Critical Study*. Cambridge: University Press, 1941.

Elton, William. "Timothy Bright and Shakespeare's Seeds of Nature," *Modern Language Notes*, LXV (1950), 196-97.

Elyot, Sir Thomas. *The Boke Named the Gouernour*, ed. Henry Hubert Stephen Croft. 2 vols. London: Kegan Paul, Trench, 1883.

Erasmus, Desiderius. *Opera Omnia*. 10 vols. in 11. Lugduni Batavorum: Peter Vander Aa, 1703-1706.

Erskine, John. "Romeo and Juliet," *Shaksperian Studies by Members of the Department of English and Comparative Literature in Columbia University*, ed. Brander Matthews and Ashley Horace Thorndike. New York: Columbia University Press, 1916, Pp. 215-34.

"The Famous Victories of Henry the Fifth," *Chief Pre-Shakespearean Dramas*, ed. Joseph Quincy Adams. Boston: Houghton Mifflin, 1924. Pp. 667-90.

Fergusson, Francis. *The Idea of a Theater*. Princeton: Princeton University Press, 1949.

Foster, Joseph. *Alumni Oxonienses: The Members of the University of Oxford, 1500-1714*, etc. 4 vols. Oxford: Parker, 1891-1892.

Froissart, Jean. *The Chronicle of Froissart Translated out of French by Sir John Bourchier Lord Berners Annis 1523-25 With an Introduction by William Paton Kerr* (The Tudor Translations XXVII-XXXII). 6 vols. London: David Nutt, 1901-1903.

Granville-Barker, Harley. *Prefaces to Shakespeare*. 2 vols. Princeton: Princeton University Press, 1946-47.

Greg, Walter W. *The Editorial Problem in Shakespeare: A Survey of the Foundations of the Text*. Oxford: Clarendon Press, 1942.

—— *Principles of Emendation in Shakespeare*. (Annual Shakespeare Lecture of the British Academy, 1928). London: Humphrey Milford, [1928].

[Hall, Edward] *The union of the two noble and illustre famelies of Lancastre & Yorke.* London: Rychard Grafton, 1548 [title page], 1550 [colophon].

Harbage, Alfred. *As They Liked It; An Essay on Shakespeare and Morality.* New York: Macmillan, 1947.

Harrison, George B. "An Essay on Elizabethan Melancholy," in Nicholas Breton, *Melancholike Humours.* (An Elizabethan Gallery, No. 2) London: Scholartis Press, 1929. Pp. 49-89.

Hart, Alfred. *Shakespeare and the Homilies: And Other Pieces of Research into the Elizabethan Drama.* Melbourne: Melbourne University Press, 1934.

Harvey, Gabriel. *The Works of Gabriel Harvey, D.C.L.,* ed. Alexander B. Grosart. (The Huth Library) 3 vols. [London] Printed for Private Circulation Only, 1884-85.

Haydn, Hiram. *The Counter-Renaissance.* New York: Charles Scribner's Sons, 1950.

Hazlitt, William Carew. *Shakespeare's Library: A Collection of the Plays Romances Novels Poems and Histories employed by Shakespeare in the Composition of His Works.* 2d ed. 6 vols. London: Reeves and Turner, 1875.

Herbert, George. *The Works of George Herbert,* ed. F. E. Hutchinson. Oxford: Clarendon Press, 1941.

Holinshed, Raphael. *Chronicles.* 3 vols. London: John Harrison, George Bishop, Rafe Newberie, Henrie Denham, and Thomas Woodcocke, 1587.

Hooker, Richard. *The Works, ed.* John Keble. 7th ed. rev. R. Church and F. Paget. 3 vols. Oxford: Clarendon Press, 1888.

Horatius Flaccus, Quintus. *Satires, Epistles and Ars Poetica,* tr. H. Rushton Fairclough. (Loeb Library). London: William Heinemann, 1926.

Huarte de San Juan, Juan. *Examen de Ingenios. The Examination of mens Wits,* tr. R. C. Esquire. London: Adam Islip, for Thomas Man, 1594.

Hudson, Henry Norman. *Shakespeare: His Life, Art, and Characters.* 4th ed. 2 vols. Boston: Ginn, 1891.

Hunter, Sir Mark. "Politics and Character in Shakespeare's 'Julius Caesar,'" *Essays by Divers Hands, Trans. of the Royal Soc. of Lit.,* X (1931), 109-40.

James I. *Daemonologie* (*1597*); *Newes from Scotland* (*1591*). (The Bodley Head Quartos, ed. G. B. Harrison). London: John Lane, The Bodley Head, 1924.

Johnson, Francis R. "Shakespearian Imagery and Senecan Imitation," *Joseph Quincy Adams Memorial Studies.* Washington: Folger Shakespeare Library, 1948. Pp 33-53.

Jonson, Ben. *Ben Jonson,* ed. C. H. Herford and Percy Simpson. 11 vols. Oxford: Clarendon Press, 1925-52.

Knight, George Wilson. *The Wheel of Fire: Interpretations of Shakespearian Tragedy with Three New Essays.* London: Methuen, 1949.

Koeppel, Emil. "Shakespeares 'Richard III' und Senecas 'Troades', " *Shakespeare Jahrbuch,* XLVII (1911), 188-90.

Krappe, Alexander H. "Shakespeare Notes: The Source of 'King Richard III', Act I, sc. 11, ll. 1-4?" *Anglia,* LII (1928), 174-83.

Kyd, Thomas. *Works,* ed. Frederick S. Boas. Oxford: Clarendon Press, 1901.

La Primaudaye, Pierre de. *The French Academie,* tr. T. B. London: Edmund Bollifant for G. Bishop and Ralph Newbery, 1586.

Lavater, Ludwig. *Of Ghostes and Spirites Walking by Nyght,* 1572, ed. J. Dover Wilson and May Yardley. Oxford: University Press, 1929.

Law, Robert A. "On Shakespeare's Changes of his Source Material in *Romeo and Juliet*," *University of Texas Studies in English,* IX (1929), 86-102.

Lawrence, William John. *The Physical Conditions of the Elizabethan Public Playhouse.* Cambridge: Harvard University Press, 1927.
——— *Shakespeare's Workshop.* Oxford: Basil Blackwell, 1928.

Lawrence, William Witherle. *Shakespeare's Problem Comedies.* New York: Macmillan, 1931.

Lemnius, Levinus. *The Touchstone of Complexions,* tr. Thomas Newton. London: Thomas March, 1581.

Lever, Katherine. "Proverbs and *Sententiae* in the Plays of Shakspere," *Shakespeare Assoc. Bull.,* XIII (1938), 173-83, 224-39.

Lewis, Charlton M. *The Genesis of Hamlet.* New York: Henry Holt, 1907.

Lewis, Clive Staples. *The Allegory of Love: A Study in Medieval Tradition.* Oxford: Clarendon Press, 1936.
—— *Hamlet: The Prince or the Poem?* (Annual Shakespeare Lecture of the British Academy, 1942). London: Humphrey Milford, [1942].
—— *A Preface to Paradise Lost.* Oxford: University Press, 1942.

Liebermann, Felix. "Shakespeare als Bearbeiter des *King John*," *Archiv für das Studium der neueren Sprachen und Literaturen,* CXLII (1921), 177-202; CXLIII (1922), 17-46.

Lily, William. *A Shorte Introduction of Grammar,* ed Vincent J. Flynn. New York: Scholars' Facsimiles & Reprints, 1945.

Lipsius, Justus. *Two Bookes of Constancie,* tr. Sir John Stradling, ed. Rudolph Kirk. New Brunswick, New Jersey: Rutgers University Press, 1939.

Lovejoy, Arthur O. *The Great Chain of Being: A Study of the History of an Idea.* Cambridge: Harvard University Press, 1936.

Lucas, Frank L. *Seneca and Elizabethan Tragedy.* Cambridge: University Press, 1922.

Lucretius Carus, Titus. *De Rerum Natura Libri Sex,* ed. H. A. J. Munro. 4th ed. 3 vols. London: George Bell, 1905.
—— *Lucretius De Rerum Natura,* tr. W. H. D. Rouse. (Loeb Classical Library). London: William Heinemann, 1924.

Lyly, John. *The Complete Works of John Lyly,* ed. R. Warwick Bond. 3 vols. Oxford: Clarendon Press, 1902.

MacCallum, Mungo W. *Shakespeare's Roman Plays and their Background.* London: Macmillan, 1910.

Machiavelli, Niccolo. *The Prince,* tr. Edward Dacres, ed. W. E. C. Baynes. London: Alexander Moring, 1929.

McKerrow, Ronald B. *Prolegomena for the Oxford Shakespeare: A Study in Editorial Method.* Oxford: Clarendon Press, 1939.

The Macro Plays, ed. F. J. Furnivall and Alfred W. Pollard (E.E.T.S., Extra Series, XCI). London: Oxford Press, 1924.

Mahood, M. M. *Poetry and Humanism.* New Haven: Yale University Press, 1950.

Marlowe, Christopher. *Marlowe's Edward II,* ed. William Dinsmore Briggs. London: David Nutt, 1914.
—— *The Works,* ed. C. F. Tucker Brooke. Oxford: Clarendon Press, 1910.

Matthews, Brander. *Shakspere as a Playwright*. New York: Charles Scribner's Sons, 1913.

Mexia, Pedro. *The Foreste; or, Collection of Histories*, tr. Thomas Fortescue. London: Jhon Kyngston, for Willyam Iones, 1571.

Meyer, Edward. *Machiavelli and the Elizabethan Drama* (Litterarhistorische Forschungen, I). Weimar: Emil Felber, 1897.

Miriam Joseph, Sister. *Shakespeare's Use of the Arts of Language*. New York: Columbia University Press, 1947.

Montemayor, Jorge. *Diana of George of Montemayor*, tr. Bartholomew Yong. London: Edm. Bollifant, Impensis G. B., 1598.

Moore, Olin H. "Shakespeare's Deviations from *Romeus and Juliet*," *PMLA*, LII (1937), 68-74.

Morgan, Arthur E. *Some Problems of Shakespeare's 'Henry the Fourth:' A Paper Read before the Shakespeare Association on Friday, November 23, 1922*. London: Oxford University Press, 1924.

Mueschke, Paul, and Jeanette Fleisher. "Jonsonian Elements in the Comic Underplot of *Twelfth Night*," *PMLA*, XLVIII (1933), 722-40.

Noble, Richmond. *Shakespeare's Biblical Knowledge and Use of the Book of Common Prayer as Exemplified in the Plays of the First Folio*. London: Society for Promoting Christian Knowledge, 1935.

Norton, Thomas, and Thomas Sackville. "Gorboduc," in *Chief Pre-Shakespearean Dramas*, ed. Joseph Quincy Adams. Boston: Houghton Mifflin, 1924. Pp. 503-35.

Ovidus Naso, Publius. *Heroides and Amores*, tr. Grant Showerman (Loeb Classical Library). London: William Heinemann, 1914.
—— *Metamorphoses*, tr. Frank Justus Miller. (Loeb Classical Library). 2 vols. London: William Heinemann, 1916, 1926.

Painter, William. *The Palace of Pleasure*, ed. Joseph Jacobs. 3 vols. London: David Nutt, 1890.

Palingenius, Marcellus. *Marcelli Palingenii Stellati Poetae doctissimi Zodiacus vitae: hoc est. De hominis vita, studio, ac moribus optime instituendis*, Libri. XII. In aedibus Henrici Bynneman, 1572.
—— *The Zodiake of Life*, tr. Barnabe Googe, ed. Rosemond Tuve. New York: Scholars' Facsimiles and Reprints, 1947.

Parks, George B. "The Development of *The Two Gentlemen of Verona*," Huntington Library Bulletin, XI (1937), 1-11.

Paul, Henry N. *The Royal Play of "Macbeth."* New York: Macmillan, 1950.

Pearson, Lu Emily. *Elizabethan Love Conventions.* Berkeley: University of California Press, 1933.

Pettet, E. C. *Shakespeare and the Romance Tradition.* London: Staples Press, 1949.

Phillips, James Emerson. *The State in Shakespeare's Greek and Roman Plays.* New York: Columbia University Press, 1940.

Plutarch. *Four Lives from North's Plutarch* (Plutarch's Lives of Coriolanus, Caesar, Brutus, and Antonius in North's Translation), ed. R. H. Carr. Oxford: Clarendon Press, 1906.
—— *The Lives of the Noble Grecians and Romanes,* tr. Thomas North. Stratford-upon-Avon: Shakespeare Head Press, 1928.

Pollard, Alfred W. *Shakespeare's Fight with the Pirates and the Problems of the Transmission of his Text.* 2d ed. Cambridge: University Press, 1920.

Prior, Moody. *The Language of Tragedy.* New York: Columbia University Press, 1947.

Private Prayers Put Forth by Authority during the Reign of Queen Elizabeth, ed. Rev. William Keatinge Clay. (Parker Society, Vol. XXXVII). Cambridge: University Press, 1851.

Quiller-Couch, Sir Arthur. *Shakespeare's Workmanship.* Cambridge: University Press, 1931.

Quintilianus, Marcus Fabius. *The Institutio Oratoria,* tr. H. E. Butler (Loeb Classical Library). 4 vols. London: William Heinemann, 1921-22.

Rainolde, Richard. *The Foundacion of Rhetorike,* ed. Francis R. Johnson. New York: Scholars' Facsimiles & Reprints, 1945.

Reid, J. S. "Shakespeare's 'Living Art,'" *Philological Quarterly,* I (1922), 226-27.

Robertson, John M. *Montaigne and Shakespeare: and Other Essays on Cognate Questions.* 2d ed. London: Adam and Charles Black, 1909.

Root, Robert Kilburn. *Classical Mythology in Shakespeare* (Yale Studies in English, XIX). New York: Henry Holt, 1903.

Rose, Edward. "Shakespeare as an Adapter," *The Troublesome Raigne of John, King of England: The First Quarto, 1591, which Shakspere rewrote (about 1595) as his "Life and Death of King John."* Part I. London: C. Praetorius, 1888.

Saviolo, Vincentio. *Vincentio Saviolo his Practise. In two Bookes. The first intreating of the use of the Rapier and Dagger. The Second, of Honor and honorable Quarrels.* London: Iohn Wolfe, 1595.

Schücking, Levin L. *Character Problems in Shakespeare's Plays: A Guide to the Better Understanding of the Dramatist.* London: G. G. Harrap, 1922.

—— *The Meaning of Hamlet,* tr. Graham Rawson. London: Oxford University Press, 1937.

Seneca, Lucius Annaeus. *Seneca's Tragedies,* tr. Frank Justus Miller. (Loeb Classical Library) 2 vols. London: William Heinemann, 1916-17.

Shackford, Martha Hale. "*Julius Caesar* and Ovid," *Modern Language Notes,* XLI (1926), 172-74.

Simpson, Percy. *Shakespearian Punctuation.* Oxford: Clarendon Press, 1911.

Sisson, Charles J. *The Mythical Sorrows of Shakespeare* (Annual Shakespeare Lecture of the British Academy, 1934). London: Humphrey Milford, [1934].

Small, Samuel Asa. *Shakespearean Character Interpretation: The Merchant of Venice.* Göttingen: Vandenhoeck & Ruprecht, 1927.

Smart, John Semple. *Shakespeare: Truth and Tradition.* London: Edward Arnold, 1928.

Smith, George C. Moore. "Shakespeare's *King John* and *The Troublesome Raigne*," *An English Miscellany Presented to Dr. Furnivall in Honor of his Seventy-Fifth Birthday.* Oxford: Clarendon Press, 1901. Pp. 335-37.

Sonnenschein, E. A. "Shakespeare and Seneca," letter to *Times Literary Supplement,* September 16, 1904; p. 280.

Spalding, Thomas Alfred. *Elizabethan Demonology.* London: Chatto and Windus, 1880.

Spencer, Theodore, *Shakespeare and the Nature of Man* (Lowell Lectures, 1942). New York: Macmillan, 1942.

Spurgeon, Caroline F. E. *Shakespeare's Imagery and What It Tells Us.* Cambridge: University Press, 1935.

Stauffer, Donald A. *Shakespeare's World of Images: The Development of his Moral Ideas.* New York: W. W. Norton, 1949.

Stewart, John I. M. *Character and Motive in Shakespeare: Some Recent Appraisals Examined.* London: Longmans, Green, 1949.

Stoll, Elmer E. *Art and Artifice in Shakespeare.* Cambridge: University Press, 1933.
—— *Hamlet: An Historical and Comparative Study* (University of Minnesota Studies in Language and Literature, No. 7). Minneapolis: University of Minnesota, 1919.
—— *Othello: An Historical and Comparative Study* (University of Minnesota Studies in Language and Literature, No. 2). Minneapolis: University of Minnesota, 1915.
—— "Othello the Man," *Shakespeare Association Bulletin*, IX (1934), 111-24.
—— *Shakespeare Studies, Historical and Comparative in Method.* New York: Macmillan, 1927.
—— *Shakespeare's Young Lovers* (The Alexander Lectures at the University of Toronto, 1935). London: Oxford University Press, 1937.

Stopes, Charlotte C. *Shakespeare's Industry.* London: G. Bell and Sons, 1916.

Strathmann, Ernest A. *Sir Walter Raleigh: A Study in Elizabethan Scepticism.* New York: Columbia University Press, 1951.

Susenbrotus, Joannes. *Epitome Troporum ac Schematum et Grammaticorum et Rhetoricorum.* Londini: Ex typographia Societatis Stationariorum, 1621.

Tassin, Algernon de Vivier. "Julius Caesar," *Shakespearian Studies by Members of the Department of English and Comparative Literature in Columbia University.* New York: Columbia University Press, 1916. Pp. 255-87.

Taylor, George Coffin. *Shakespeare's Debt to Montaigne.* Cambridge: Harvard University Press, 1925.

Taylor, Rupert. *The Date of Love's Labour's Lost.* New York: Columbia University Press, 1932.

Thorndike, Ashley H. *Shakespeare's Theater.* New York: Macmillan, 1928.
—— "Shakspere as a Debtor," *Shaksperian Studies by Members of the Department of English and Comparative Literature in Columbia University.* New York: Columbia University Press, 1916. Pp. 165-84.

Tillyard, Eustace M. W. *The Elizabethan World Picture*. London: Chatto and Windus, 1943.
—— *Shakespeare's History Plays*. New York: Macmillan, 1946.

Tolman, Albert H. "Shakespeare's Manipulation of his Sources in *As You Like It*," *Modern Language Notes*, XXXVII (1922), 65-76.

Trevelyan, George Macauley. *England Under the Stuarts*. 12th ed. New York: G. P. Putnam's Sons, 1925.

Vatke, Theodor. "Shakespeare und Euripides. Eine Parallele," *Shakespeare Jahrbuch*, IV (1869), 62-93.

Vaughan, William. *Naturall and Artificial Directions for Health*. London: Richard Bradocke, 1600.

Walley, Harold R. "Shakespeare's Debt to Marlowe in *Romeo and Juliet*," *Philological Quarterly*, XXI (1942), 257-67.
—— "Shakespeare's Portrayal of Shylock," *The Parrott Presentation Volume*. Princeton: University Press, 1935. Pp. 213-42.

Watson, Foster. *The Zodiacus Vitae of Marcellus Palingenius Stellatus: An Old School Book*. London: Philip Wellby, 1908.

Whitaker, Virgil K. "Shakespeare's Use of his Sources," *Philological Quarterly*, XX (1941), 377-89.

Whitford, Richard, trans. *A boke newely translated out of Laten into Englysshe, called The folowynge of Cryste*. London: Robert Wyer, ca. 1535.

Wieler, John William. *George Chapman—The Effect of Stoicism upon his Tragedies*. New York: King's Crown Press, 1949.

Wilhelm, Friedrich. "Zu Seneca und Shakespeare ('Richard III')," *Archiv für das Studium der neueren Sprachen und Literaturen*, CXXIX (1912), 69-73.

Wilson, John Dover. *The Essential Shakespeare: A Biographical Adventure*. Cambridge: University Press, 1932.
—— *The Fortunes of Falstaff*. Cambridge: University Press, 1944.
—— *The Manuscript of Shakespeare's Hamlet and the Problems of its Transmission: An Essay in Critical Bibliography*. 2 vols. Cambridge: University Press, 1934.
—— "The Origins and Development of Shakespeare's *Henry IV*," *The Library*, XXVI (1945), 2-16.
—— *What Happens in Hamlet*. Cambridge: University Press, 1935.

Yates, Francis A. *The French Academies of the Sixteenth Century*. London: Warburg Institute, University of London, 1947.
—— *A Study of Love's Labour's Lost* (Shakespeare Problems, V). Cambridge: University Press, 1936.

Young, Karl. "The Shakespeare Skeptics," *North American Review*, CCXV (March, 1922), 382-393.

Zeeveld, William Gordon. "The Influence of Hall on Shakespeare's English Historical Plays," *English Literary History*, III (1936), 317-53.

INDEX